COMMODITY SPREADS
*YEAR-ROUND TRADING STRATEGIES TO
BEAT INFLATION AND BUILD CAPITAL*

COMMODITY SPREADS
YEAR-ROUND TRADING STRATEGIES TO BEAT INFLATION AND BUILD CAPITAL

by T. KALLARD

Editor

MILTON WALLER

optosonic press

This book is not to be construed, under any circumstances, by implication or otherwise, as an offer to sell or a solicitation to trade in the commodities herein named.

While the information set forth in this book has been compiled from sources believed to be both reliable and correct, neither the Author nor the Publisher can assume responsibility for its completeness and accuracy. Charts are prepared by the Author unless otherwise indicated.

The Author and Publisher specifically disclaim any liability, loss, or risk, personal or otherwise, which is incurred as a consequence, directly, or indirectly, of the use and application of any of the contents of this work.

COMMODITY SPREADS:
Year-Round Trading Strategies to
Beat Inflation and Build Capital.
Copyright © 1982 by Thomas Kallard.
All rights reserved. No part of this book may be reproduced in any manner, including photocopying, without written approval of the publisher.

Published by OPTOSONIC PRESS
Scientific, Technical and Business Books
Box 883, Ansonia Post Office
New York, N.Y. 10023 (U.S.A.)

Additional copies may be obtained by addressing the publisher. Quantity discount schedule available upon request.

First Edition
First Printing
ISBN 0-87739-010-X
Library of Congress Catalog Card Number: 80-82181

Printed in the United States of America

"This time, like all times,
is a very good one
if we but know what
to do with it."
— RALPH WALDO EMERSON

"A feast is made for laughter,
and wine maketh merry; but money
answereth all things."
— (Eccl. 10:19)

PREFACE

Since 1974, when the first printing of *MAKE MONEY IN COMMODITY SPREADS!* came off the presses, the need for an updated version of that book has been a recurring one. Feedback from our readers confirmed the need and initiated the writing of this book. At least that is the way it began.

As the work progressed, however, the conviction grew that merely updating was not going to do the job. There was too much new information that had to be included and to leave out any part of it would have lessened the book's value to that extent.

It is not that the basic techniques of futures trading have changed; they remain the same now as before. It is rather that the commodity market itself has changed. New commodities -- new in the sense that until recently they have not been listed on the Exchanges -- are now traded daily. Among these are:

- Long and short term obligations of the U.S. Treasury. (Bonds, notes and T-bills)

- Government agency obligations. (Ginnie Maes)

- Foreign Exchange. (The currencies of as many as five different countries are traded every market day)

- Cocoa. (An old staple dressed up in a new contract)

These are only some of the changes that have taken place in the market over the last few years and an updated book could not have given adequate space or attention to them. A new book is the best way to deal with a new market and the best way to serve our readers, both old and new.

The new trader, considering an investment in commodity futures, often turns away from it because he is not really sure of how it works. Also, he still harbors the belief that in futures trading the risks are too high. We shall endeavor here to overcome the first by simple explanation and rebut the second with actual transaction examples.

It goes without saying that every investment involves a certain amount of risk. If money is to be used to make more money, the risk is inherent. The size of the risk is usually commensurate with the percentage of return on the investment; as one increases so does the other. The fact is, however, and this book will establish it, that commodity *spreads* tend to minimize the risk while maximizing the percentage of return.

The text is divided as follows:

Part 1 -- For those who have never before participated in futures trading. It reviews and defines the basic techniques and underlying theory of the futures market.

Part 2 -- A detailed introduction to spread trading.

Part 3 -- Deals with individual and specific commodities. Many spread trading opportunities are pointed out and illustrated with charts.

Part 4 -- A year-round program is outlined for systematic spread trading.

As to understanding the principles and techniques of spread trading, the problem is still what it has always been: primarily one of language. There are new words, and some old words that are used in new ways. Futures traders and their brokers have evolved a kind of spoken shorthand, a language well suited to the nature of their transactions. This book will define that language and analyze the transactions. To expedite the task, a glossary of terms is included; use it as you would a dictionary. New words and odd sounding phrases are listed alphabetically and defined without recourse to jargon.

An extensive bibliography is also included and, following that, a Catchword Title Index, this last for those readers interested only in special trading areas. An appendix contains charts, graphs and trading facts and figures in addition to those incorporated in the text. There is blank chart paper as well, for those who want to construct their own charts. The blank chart grids taken from this book and put into any office copier will turn out a few or a few dozen extra sheets if they are needed - at a considerable saving.

And now, a final word about updating. Because it changes, however slightly, from one day to the next, today's commodity market must be watched more carefully than ever. It is the author's and the publisher's intention to keep pace with and be aware of these changes and to keep our readers informed. This book will be kept current, and if we know who you are and where to reach you we will be glad to let you know when the updatings we plan will become available. Fill out the printed form at the end of the book and send it to us at Optosonic Press. Your name in our files is all the insurance you need to keep yourself abreast of changing markets and new opportunities for profit.

It is the author's belief that a proper attention to the principles laid down in this book must lead to a better risk/return ratio than will be found in any other type of investment. But, a careful reading of the text is necessary, and possibly a re-reading. The time thus spent will be well spent. It will pay off with enhanced profits.

Our thanks to the many brokerages and institutions whose expert suggestions and advice are incorporated into this publication. Special thanks to our editor, Milton Waller, for his invaluable assistance and his painstaking edit of the entire manuscript.

May, 1982
New York, New York

T. KALLARD

CONTENTS

PREFACE VII

COMMODITY FUTURES - AN OVERVIEW 3

    The futures contract - Trading units - Delivery months - The Commodity Exchange - Hedgers and Speculators - Price movements - How to read price quotations - Price forecasting - Charts - Technical analysis - Volume and Open Interest - Sources of information - Statistics - Where the action is - The trading account - Selecting a broker - Margins and leverage - Commissions - Types of orders - Calculating profits and losses - The trading plan - Risk and reward.

SPREAD TRADING IN COMMODITY MARKETS 33

    What is a spread - How can spreads produce profits - Why trade spreads - Leverage on spreads - Carrying charges - Limited risk spreads - Interest rates - Risk calculation - Some trading hints - Inverted markets - Types of spreads - Interdelivery spreads - Intermarket spreads - Intercommodity spreads - Money spreads - Raw materials versus product spreads - The soybean crush spread - Analysis of spreads - How to read a spread chart - How to place spread orders - Protective stops - Tracking a spread position - Liquidating a spread position - The two-unit trading method - Dynamic spreads - Commissions.

MARKETS AND SPREAD TRADING OPPORTUNITIES 64

    GRAINS 64

        Corn - Oats - Wheat

SOYBEAN COMPLEX 84
    Soybeans - Soybean meal - soybean oil

LIVESTOCK & MEATS 104
    Live cattle - Feeders - Hogs - Pork bellies

FOODSTUFFS 122
    Cocoa - Coffee - Orange Juice - Sugar

FIBER & FOREST PRODUCTS 134
    Cotton - Lumber - Plywood

METALS & PETROLEUM 152
    Copper - Gold - Silver - Heating Oil

CURRENCIES 170
    British pound - Canadian dollar - Deutsche mark - Japanese yen - Swiss franc

FINANCIAL INSTRUMENTS 188
    Treasury bills - Treasury bonds - GNMAs

YEAR-ROUND PROGRAM FOR SPREAD TRADERS 213

BIBLIOGRAPHY 219
    Books & Catchword Index

GLOSSARY OF TERMS 241

APPENDICES 263
    Simplified spread calculations: Examples - Telephone information sources - Commodity exchanges - Sources of relevant books - Periodicals - Newspapers - Newsletters - Chart services - Periodic reports - Statistical sources - Miscellaneous data - Sample chart grids for the chartist.

* * *

COMMODITY FUTURES— AN OVERVIEW

WHAT IS A COMMODITY

In the context of this book, a commodity is anything transportable that can be bought and sold. Examples of the most frequently traded commodities are: grains, oil, meal, livestock, metals, foodstuffs and, of course, what has been called the ultimate commodity, money itself. Whatever the product, it needs only be transportable and easily divided into standard units.

COMMODITY TRADING

Commodities are traded either on a cash-and-carry basis or on organized commodity exchanges. When traded on an Exchange, contracts for future delivery are made between buyers and sellers.

WHAT IS A COMMODITY FUTURES CONTRACT

The commodity futures contract is a standard agreement to buy and receive, or to sell and deliver at a stated future date, a specific quantity and designated quality of a commodity at an agreed upon price. Note the key words: future date. The contract is designed by an organized commodity exchange. The price is determined by open auction on the Exchange's floor.

FUTURES TRADING

On the early commodity exchanges business was conducted on a cash basis. The Exchange's primary function was to find a buyer and seller to take and make delivery of the actual commodity. Today, fewer than 1% of all futures contracts are settled by delivery. Commercial and speculative traders, both, usually find it advantageous to terminate their contractual obligations by initiating equal but opposite offsetting transactions. A trader who is *long* in wheat, for example, will liquidate his position before the delivery date by selling his contract in the open market. A trader who is *short*, conversely, must buy contracts for the commodity to cover the sales of it he has already made.

Modern commodity exchanges have thus become financial markets where commercial traders buy and sell futures contracts as a means of protection, a *hedge* against the volatility of commodity prices. Speculators on the other hand are attracted by the possibility of profit from this same volatility against which

3

the commercial traders need protection. The speculator profits from price fluctuations when he forecasts them correctly. His profit or loss is determined by the difference in the prices from the time of initiation to the liquidation of his transaction. Brokerage costs must be included; they are an addition to loss and a subtraction from profit.

Speculators are the market's life blood. They provide the liquidity needed to absorb the commercial hedging activity. When a commercial trader sets up a hedge to protect his financial interests, the speculator is on the other side of the transaction where he trusts he has called the right turn on the market's movement. The point, however, is, that both the trader and the speculator have achieved their purpose. The mechanics of their transactions are specific and will be gone into later, with dollars and cents examples.

On any commodity exchange one can buy or sell a contract for delivery only in the designated delivery months set by that Exchange. Buying a contract is called taking a *long* position, selling a contract, a *short* position. On most Exchanges, trading is confined to a few calendar months each year. In wheat and corn, for example, the designated delivery months are March, May, July, September and December. Although the price is set in the market when the trade is made, the delivery month must be determined before the trade is made.

TRADING UNITS

Although there are approximately 50 different commodity futures contracts now traded on North American exchanges there is yet no such thing as a typical contract. Wheat, corn, soybeans, for example, are all traded on the Chicago Board of Trade, and each is for 5,000 bushels per contract. Sugar #11, however, on the Coffee, Sugar and Cocoa Exchange is for 112,000 pounds per contract. On the New York Mercantile Exchange No. 2 Heating Oil is for 42,000 gallons. Live Beef Cattle contracts on the Chicago Mercantile Exchange are for 40,000 pounds and U.S. Treasury Bills on the same Exchange, are sold in the amount of one million dollars per contract.

When a trader gives his broker an order, therefore, he does not have to say how many pounds, bushels or ounces he wants, only how many contracts and on which Exchange. If he says: "Buy one December gold on the COMEX (Commodity Exchange, Inc)," the broker understands it is for the Exchange's contract unit of 100 troy ounces. The trader must specify the Exchange, however, because sometimes different Exchanges will have different trading units. Specific data on different futures contracts will be found elsewhere in this book.

DELIVERY AND DELIVERY MONTH

Delivery is the fulfillment of a futures contract by delivering or by accepting delivery of the actual physical commodity. It is the obligation of the seller (short position) to deliver the commodity as soon as trading officially ceases for a given delivery month. The owner of a contract (long position) may be notified during the expiration month that delivery will be made. If such long position remains open after trading for the delivery month ceases, delivery of the physical commodity will be made.

The owner of a contract who does not want delivery can close out his long position by selling an equivalent contract at any time prior to the close of trading (final trading day) for the delivery month. The trader who is short, with delivery approaching, must buy an equivalent contract in order to offset his obligation.

WHAT IS A COMMODITY EXCHANGE

An Exchange provides the facilities for futures trading. It establishes and enforces trading rules, and collects and disseminates information about the commodities traded. The Exchange is, itself, not in the business of buying or selling commodity futures but is a financial institution licensed by a Federal agency, the Commodity Futures Trading Commission (CFTC). It is set up as a non-profit, membership organization.

Trading on an Exchange is conducted on the floor, around *rings* or *pits*, by open outcry and by corresponding hand signals. Each ring or pit serves a particular commodity. When an order is placed to buy or sell through one of the member brokers, he, or his agent executes the order on the Exchange's floor. Trades result from the meeting of bids with offers in a competitive auction.

Every transaction, as well as every bid or offer on which there is a price movement is fed via computer to price quotation boards on the trading floor. At the same time it is transmitted over wire services, ticker systems and telecommunications systems to offices and quotation boards in every part of the world.

All trades are guaranteed and verified by the Exchange's Clearing House, a service offered by each commodity exchange. The Exchange's clearing house operates much like a bank's clearing house by making it unnecessary for brokers to make daily cash settlements with each other. At the end of every trading day each broker's position, the record of all he has bought and sold is on file with the clearing house. The C.H. then matches all the day's transactions and acts the role of the opposite party to each of them. It plays seller to every buyer and buyer to every seller. It relieves the original parties to any trade of any obligation to each other, a system which makes for speed and ease of trading.

WHO TRADES FUTURES AND WHY

There are two kinds of traders in the futures markets:

1) <u>Hedgers</u>: Those who use the market as insurance against unforeseen price changes.

2) <u>Speculators</u>: Those who buy or sell for the purpose of making a profit.

Hedgers may be producers, processors, handlers, users or large scale marketers of agricultural or any other commodities. Money managers and exporters also are sometimes hedgers. Hedgers use the futures markets primarily to protect the prices at which they will sell or buy commodities for cash at some future time.

Speculators in the futures market find fertile ground for their activities. When the hedger places his orders, when he, in a manner of speaking, buys insurance, it is usually the speculator who sells him the insurance. Essentially, speculators in the futures market are not the gamblers their title suggests. They, in fact, assume a risk that is already there and their long range effect on the market is to stabilize it.

Hedgers and speculators are essential to each other because the market could not function without the interaction between them. The speculator assumes the hedger's risk by taking the opposite side of the hedging contract. With appropriate long or short positions in the futures market, speculators provide the liquidity necessary for the market to operate efficiently. The speculator, thus, plays a vital role in the conduct of his country's business. He assumes the risk, always present, when goods are marketed in a free economy.

Who are the speculators? In addition to the professional traders, they may be doctors, accountants, lawyers, brokers, engineers, professors, housewifes, farmers -- people of all kinds. Anyone can play, anyone who is willing to risk his money on his judgment.

HEDGING AS A MANAGEMENT TOOL

Futures exchanges provide a means for the risks inherent in any business to be minimized. By hedging, a business enterprise can take a position in the futures market opposite to the one it holds in the actual commodity. This technique is equally valuable for producers, for users and for middlemen -- people who have no wish to speculate. Their aim is to earn a good return on investment simply by merchandising their products or services. Professional managers, and especially financial managers, now feel that the truest form of speculation is in the failure to hedge.

SELLING HEDGE - FOR PRODUCERS

The purpose of the *selling hedge*, or *short hedge*, is to protect the value os existing inventory. The hedger owns or purchases the actual commodity on the cash market and sells an equivalent quantity of it on the futures market. In this way an adverse price movement in either market will be offset by a favorable one in the other. At worst, it will be only approximately offset because cash and futures prices, while they tend to move up or down together, do not always travel

the same distance or at the same speed. For example, a
potato grower might go short by selling contracts in the
futures market to protect his commodity against a price
decline. Also, visualize a bond dealer who is holding an
inventory of bonds for eventual resale to permanent investors. Since the dealer is worried about rising interest rates
and the falling bond prices that will result, he creates a
short hedge by selling an appropriate number of U.S. Treasury
bond futures contracts. If the interest rates go up, the
inventory bonds will be sold at a loss, but the gain on the
T-bond futures will offset this loss.

BUYING HEDGE - FOR USERS

The *buying hedge* is the purchase of futures to protect an
inventory not yet acquired. The buyer (the user of the
commodity) hedges against a possible price increase of the
physical (cash) commodity prior to its purchase. The buying
hedge, also called a *long hedge*, is used by all those in the
market who need a steady year-round supply of raw material
at a stable price. Grain elevator operators, cattle raisers,
manufacturers, and exporters are all long hedgers. Example:
a manufacturer of gold jewelry must prepare a catalogue and
price sheet months ahead of the selling season. He must know
the cost of the gold he will use in his products. Since he
knows only the current price of gold, he can protect himself
against price increases by purchasing gold futures contracts.
As another example: An oil dealer can protect himself against
a price increase from his own source of supply by buying fuel
oil futures contracts.

Multinational corporations, banks and export/import firms can
use both types of hedges when dealing with foreign currencies.
Buying and selling hedges could be set up in foreign currency
futures to hedge against adverse exchange-rate fluctuations.

THE SPECULATOR

Speculators will purchase futures contracts (go long) when
they believe that the price of a commodity will increase.
Conversely, they will sell contracts (go short) when they
think that prices will decline. This speculative activity
often involves taking the opposite side of trades offered by
those who are hedging. Speculators, thus, stand between the
producers, who want maximum price for their production, and
the users who want the best price for their products.

TYPES OF SPECULATORS

Most commodity speculators are *position traders*. They study
fundamental data as background information and then analyze
price history to predict price change. Technical analysis is
the position trader's tool, the one they use most to make trading decisions. These speculators take long-term risks because
their positions are held for several weeks or months.

The *short-term traders* attempt to profit from intermediate
price changes or sudden changes in market psychology. Their
positions are usually held for a few days or weeks.

The *day trader* completes all transactions within a single trading day.

The *scalper* trades in the pit where the supply/demand situation changes from moment-to-moment. The scalper makes a multitude of trades with profit margins as small as 1/4 of a cent per trade. His hyperactivity provides additional fluidity to pit trading.

Another type of speculator uses a technique called *spreading*. The spreader searches for special situations where there are distorted or perhaps abnormal price differences between related commodities... or, unusual price differentials between two delivery months of the same commodity... or, an unusual relationship between two different commodity markets. A spreader, accordingly, may buy oats and sell corn, or buy Kansas City wheat and sell Chicago wheat. Spread traders simultaneously buy and sell futures contracts of related commodities in the hope that the out-of-line price differentials (spreads) will move back to normal, as they usually do, and thus yield a profit.

To be a successful speculator one must be a successful money manager. Commodity speculation must be approached as a business venture and good business techniques and judgment must be used. Even the most successful speculators are more often wrong than right in their market judgments. When wrong, however, they have the discipline to limit their losses.

Successful speculators pick their spots carefully and concentrate on trends rather than short-term fluctuations. They take the attitude that the market is always right and try, therefore, to stay in tune with it and follow its direction. When right, they will let their profits run, and may add to them by increasing their positions. Because they stay with a sound trading plan, successful speculators need be right only 30 or 40 percent of the time in order to come out ahead in any twelve month period.

COMMODITY PRICE MOVEMENTS

Commodity exchanges do not set prices. They are free markets in which the forces that affect prices interact in open auction. On the Exchanges, all price-making factors of the moment are translated into a price which is recorded and instantaneously available.

The commodity trader is certain only of uncertainty. The more uncertain prices appear to be, the more the hedger needs the commodity futures markets. The more prices fluctuate, the more attractive the market is to the speculator. The system works.

Generally, the supply and demand for any commodity are the forces that will set its price of the moment. Things like the weather, government policies, acreage under cultivation, carryover stock from previous crops, domestic usage and others will, of course, influence both supply and demand, especially as they apply to agricultural products. Labor relations, national and international politics are additional supply/demand/price factors.

The price of any single commodity is influenced somewhat by the overall level of all commodity prices. An index published by the Commodity Research Bureau, Inc. records the prices of commodities traded on futures exchanges. The awareness of price trends in various commodity groups, such as grains, livestock, meat and metals is helpful in the study of specific commodities.

Some of the long range factors that affect prices are:

★ Varying costs of production which cause changes in the price of the final product.

★ Population growth which creates more worldwide demand for goods and this, in turn, bolsters prices.

★ The forces of nature and climate, plus the buying and selling habits of producers and users often create seasonal price patterns.

★ Another long range factor which causes the prices of commodities to change, is the value of money. As currency declines in value and loses its purchasing power as a result of inflation, commodity prices tend to increase since more money has to be used to make a purchase.

On August 15, 1971, President Nixon stopped the sale of gold by the U.S. This action made currency hedging more necessary than ever. For people in export-import, the move to floating currencies introduced yet another unpredictable in commodity prices. The world monetary situation, the energy crisis, even changing weather patterns induced important business people all over the world to get price insurance by hedging in the futures markets.

In their continuing efforts to maintain an orderly market, the Exchanges have established rules with regard to commodity price fluctuations. These rules apply to both extremes of the price's movement. They state the minimum amount a quoted price may change from one bid or offer to another and also the maximum amount a commodity's price may move -up or down- during any one trading day.

MINIMUM PRICE FLUCTUATIONS

The *minimum price fluctuation* in most commodities is in one-hundreths of a cent. In trading cotton on the New York Cotton Exchange the market fluctuates in points, each *point* being equal to one-hundredth of a cent per pound. Since each contract involves 50,000 lbs. of cotton, each point equals $5 and a price move of a full cent equals $500 per contract. Grains are quoted in quarters of a cent per bushel, with one quarter of a cent the minimum fluctuation in most markets. Since a grain contract calls for 5,000 bushels (Note: There are mini-contracts on the MidAmerica Commodity Exchange for 1,000 bushels), the fluctuation of a full cent in the price of wheat, corn, oats and soybeans equals $50 per contract, and each minimum fluctuation of a 1/4 cent is worth $12.50 per contract.

DAILY PRICE LIMITS

At intervals, news bulletins which tell of crop catastrophes, war scares, etc. appear and are so sensational that the market reacts to them with violent price movements. The *daily price limit* set by the Exchange for allowable maximum daily fluctuation serves to prevent what might otherwise become a runaway up or down price move. Most Exchanges have formulas for expanded and variable daily price limits for the commodities traded. The formulas are applied after two or three days of limit moves in the same direction for an affected commodity. When expanded limits are put into temporary use margins, too, are usually increased. When the market settles down, however, the Exchange reverts to its original daily price limitations.

PRICE QUOTATIONS AND HOW TO READ THEM

Most people cannot spend much, if any, time in brokerage offices watching the commodity price quotation boards. They have to obtain the information necessary for trading from other sources. Some of these sources are listed below...

- Some major city newspapers
- The Journal of Commerce (daily)
- The Wall Street Journal (daily)
- Barron's (weekly)

The listed publications also furnish the following price information along with relevant news items.

OPEN: the range of prices at which the first bids and offers were made, or the first transaction completed.

HIGH: the top bid or the top price at which a contract was sold during the day or week.

LOW: the lowest offer or the lowest price at which a contract was sold during the day or week.

CLOSE: the price, or range of prices, in the final moments of trading. Also quoted sometimes is the *settlement price* which is a figure computed by formula using the range of prices recorded during the final moments of trading.

COMMODITY FUTURES TRADING

December 31, 1981

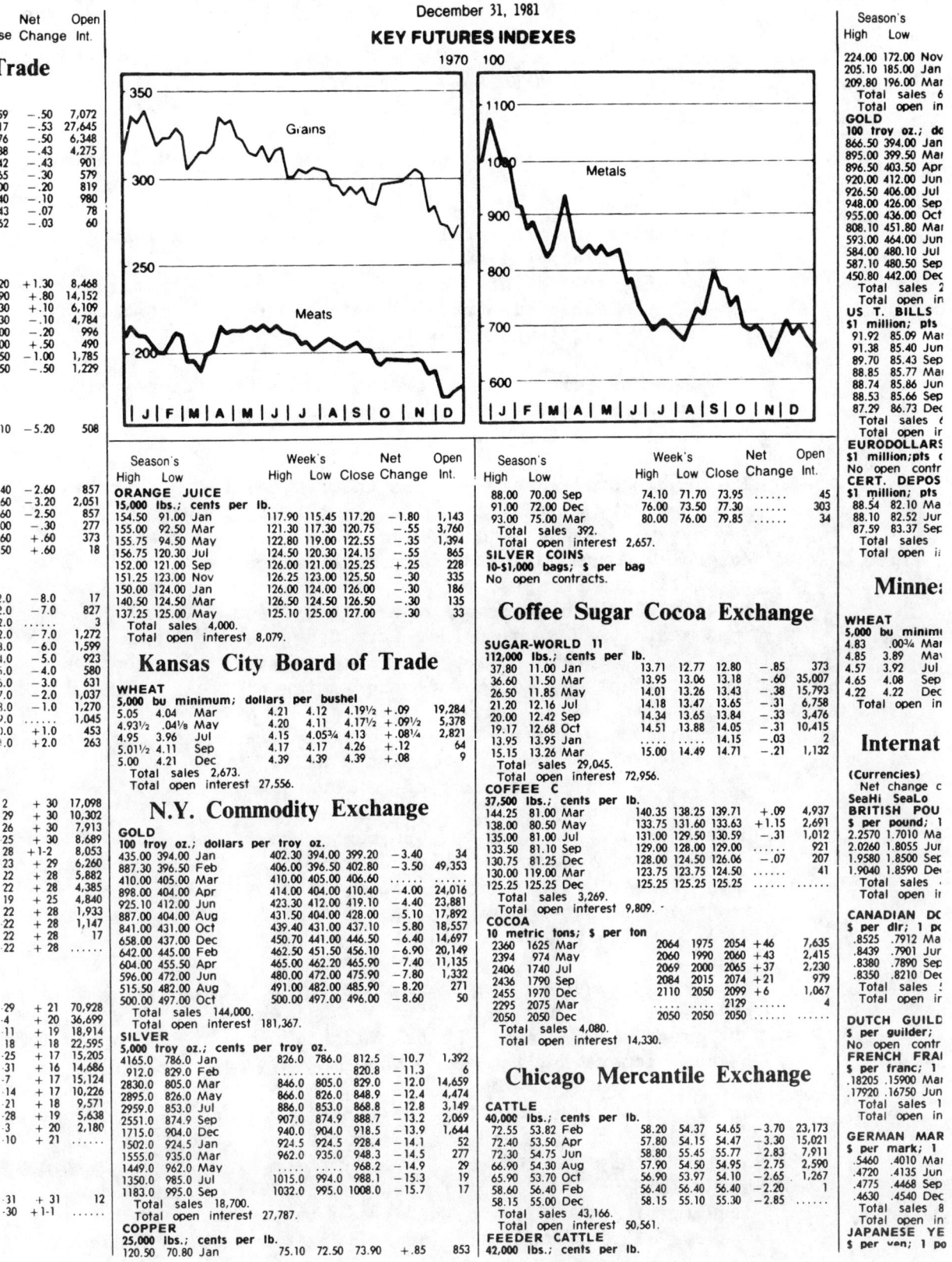

Source: BARRON'S National Business and Financial Weekly.

NET CHANGE: the amount of increase or decrease in price from the previous day's or week's close. Some papers show the *previous close* from which the reader can calculate the net change.

LIFE-OF-CONTRACT HIGH/LOW: the highest and lowest prices recorded from the first trading day to the present.

VOLUME: is the estimated number of contracts traded for each delivery month during the trading day or week.

OPEN INTEREST: the total number of outstanding long OR short positions (always equal) yet to be liquidated. This figure indicates only one side of each contract since the other side of each open contract is assumed by the Exchange's clearing house.

PRICE FORECASTING

There are systems used to forecast commodity futures prices. The two most popular are: 1) the fundamental and 2) the technical.

The *fundamental system* assumes that prices can be forecast for any commodity by analyzing the constantly changing forces of supply and demand. The *technical system* assumes that if current and past price patterns are analyzed with the help of carefully kept charts, future prices can be forecast. Many successful speculators combine both systems. They use fundamentals to predict long term trends and technical analysis to interpret short term movements. They hope, by this combination, to improve the timing of their transactions.

Speculators constantly study and analyze all the *political and economic information*, that affects price movements. In a given time period prices tend to move in cycles, but any beginning student in economics knows this. *Cyclical price movements* are the norm because many other things move in the same, repetitious way. There are cyclical movements in astronomy, biology, climate and geology, to name just a few. Studying the particular cycles that affect business activity will help the trader to plan his moves.

Business cycles, as they have come to be known, were first given serious study in 1883 by an Englishman, Dr. Hyde Clarke. But even before Clarke, Samuel Bennet, an American, noted that prices, generally, tended to move in rhythmic cycles.

Cyclic analysis shows that between delivery months commodities are subject to a repetitive accumulation/liquidation cycle of approximately 6-1/2 weeks. The duration of seasonal cycles is about 12 months and this is true not only for agricultural but industrial commodities as well. Short-term trading cycles are usually multiples of 6-1/2 weeks, while long-term cycles may last many years. For example, the cycle for hogs is 4 years,

10 years for sugar, 5.9 years for cotton and 9 years for cattle.

Seasonal factors exert an important effect on the price movements of many commodities. Grain prices, for example, often reach their bottoms in the summer when the marketing of wheat and oats reach their peaks. Non-agricultural commodities also show seasonal characteristics and the speculator should be as aware of them as he is that excessive supplies or shortages can offset seasonal influences.

It is unusual for commodity prices to rise during a recession but they tend to do so when inflation lifts the general price level. It is possible, therefore, that prices will move in a contra-seasonal direction but the seasonal factor is always there and must always be considered. To disregard it makes the odds against successful futures trading that much longer.

CHARTS AND TECHNICAL ANALYSIS

According to fundamental theory, the price of a commodity today reflects all the available information. Analysts, however, who use the technical method for forecasting, believe that markets have dynamic qualities of their own, qualities not dependent on supply and demand but arising from patterns of group behavior.

Technicians use chart analysis in their study of market action. Their working tool is a chart which depicts price movements over a period of time. The forecasting process consists of identifying and interpreting the various configurations of the chart. Technicians have their own jargon. They identify trend lines, support areas, resistance areas, tops and bottoms, head-and-shoulder formations, pennants, flags, triangles, gaps and other recognizable patterns. Many of these patterns appear and re-appear regularly. Once the speculator diagnoses the beginning formation of a pattern, the price objective is calculated on the assumption that future price fluctuations will complete the pattern.

The purpose of chart reading is to measure the relative strength of buying and selling pressures in the market. If, at a given time, buying pressure is more powerful than selling pressure, prices will rise. The reverse, of course, is equally true.

CHART TYPES

Charts used in price forecasting are of three basic types: the bar chart, the point-and-figure chart and the moving averages chart.

On a *bar chart*, the vertical axis represents price, the horizontal axis time (the trading day or week). The high and low price quotes for the day (week) are connected with a vertical line, - a short line is drawn across it at the closing price. This is done for every trading day (or week).

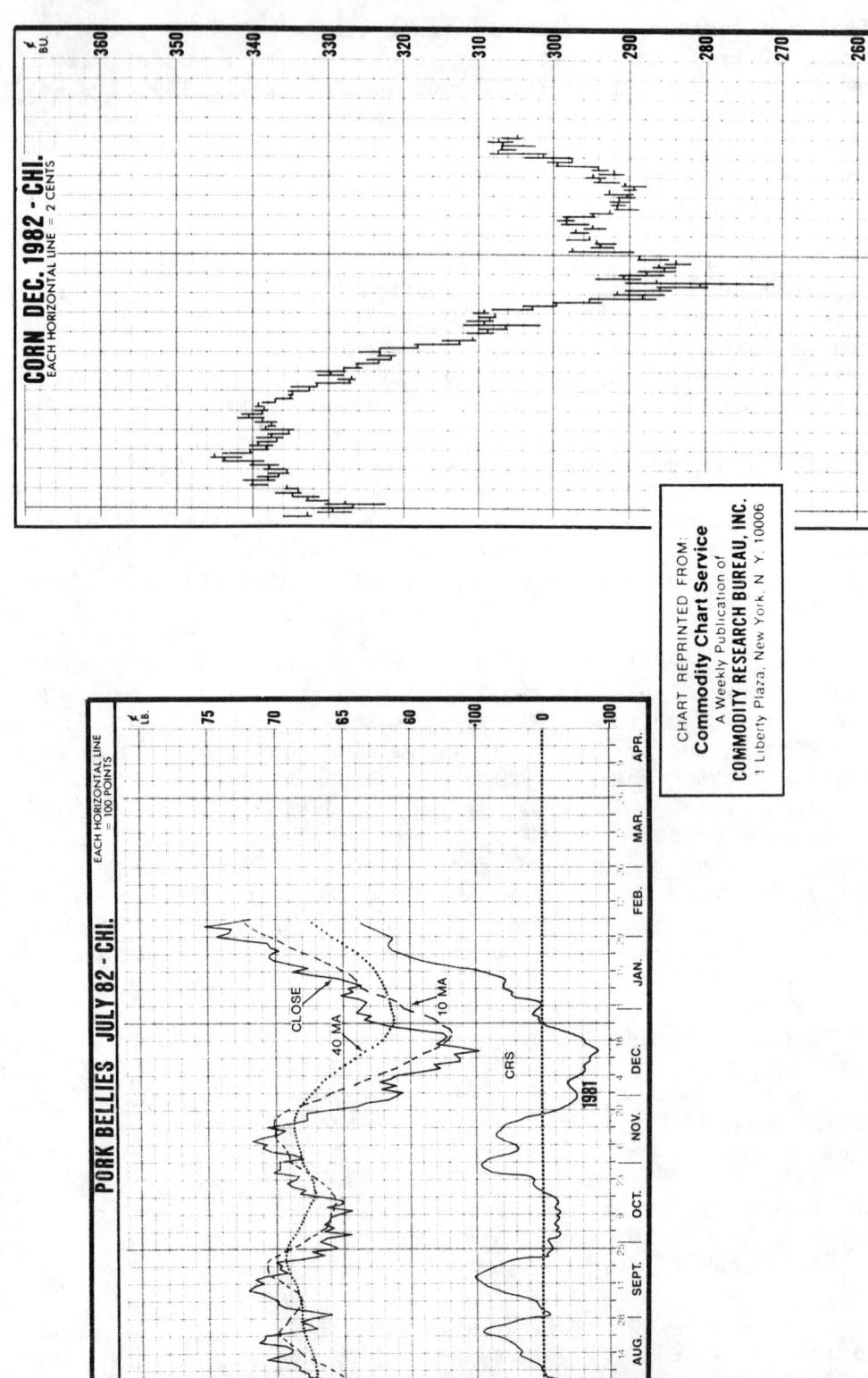

Above: Moving averages and oscillator chart

At right: Daily bar chart

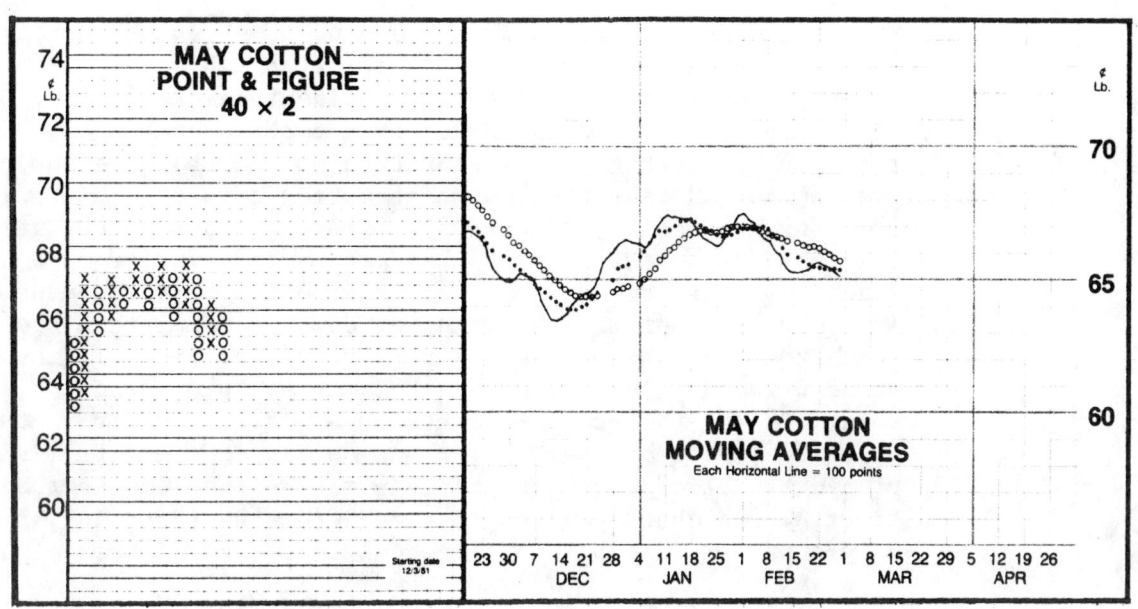

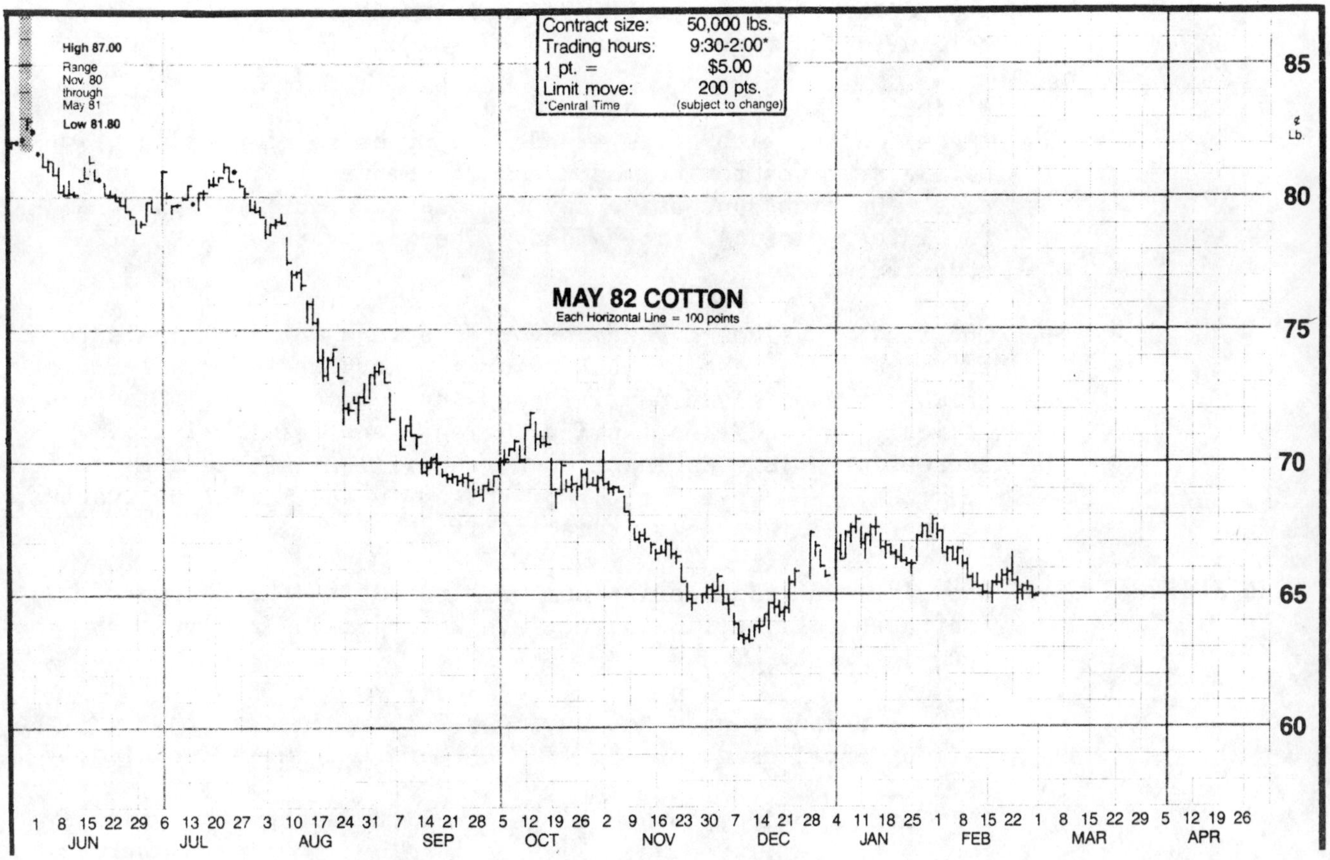

Upper left: Point-and-figure chart
Upper right: Moving averages chart
Above: Daily bar chart

Charts reprinted from COMMODITY PRICE CHARTS
219 Parkade
Cedar Falls, IA 50613

The *point-and-figure chart* is prepared on a cross-hatch type of chart paper. The chartist first establishes a vertical scale, that is, assigns a certain value to each box. For example, 1 or 2 or 3 cents, or a certain number of points for each box vertically. Preparation of the chart begins by placing an "x" into the box which corresponds to the closing price of the intial day. Let's assume, each box on the vertical scale represents 2 cents. If there is no price move of 2 cents or more on a given day, then no new entry is made. If a move of 2 or more cents up or down is made, then one or more "x" marks are placed in the vertical column. If the up or down trend persists, more "x" marks are placed in the same column. When the trend reverses by at least 2 cents in the opposite direction, an "x" (or, an "o" in some charts) is placed at the appropriate price in the next column to the right. These charts, as can be seen from the foregoing, have only a price scale but no time scale.

A variation of the point-and-figure (p & f) chart is the *reversal chart* in which the price trend must be reversed by a predetermined amount before an entry is made in the next column to the right.

Moving averages, a technique used by speculators to help them trade in line with price trends. By the use of closing prices, moving averages for commodities are computed for 3, 5, or 10 days. On each successive day the oldest price is dropped and the latest closing price added. The new average is then computed.

TRADING VOLUME

The trading volume figures reported by the exchanges indicate the number of trades in ALL futures contracts for a particular commodity on a given day. Increasing volume during an uptrend indicates an additional price increase and, similarly, increasing volume during a downtrend will reinforce the price decrease. When a major top or bottom in the market approaches, volume usually expands dramatically.

OPEN INTEREST

Open interest figures are numbers indicating the number of contracts not yet liquidated. Following is an analysis of open interest:

O.I. up & prices up = New buying = Technical strength.
O.I. up & prices down = Selling & short hedging = Technically weak.
O.I. down & prices down = Longs are liquidating = Technically strong.
O.I. down & prices up = Shorts are liquidating = Technically weak.

The above shows that the market is technically strong when volume and open interest are moving in the same direction as price.

CONTRARY OPINION

Contrary opinion traders establish positions opposite those prevailing. This system is based on the assumption that once the large traders have established their positions there won't be enough new money flowing into the market to keep the trend going and, therefore, a trend reversal may be expected.

Understand, that chart analysis is not an exact science. Weather developments, unexpected government actions, international developments and wars are only some of the things that can negate price forecasts made on the basis of chart patterns or any other system.

INFORMATION SOURCES

There is no quick or easy way to become and then remain informed about world events. Reading widely is perhaps the best way. It keeps the reader aware of the ever changing issues and their proponents. Listed below are some of the better known and most used sources of current financial news. The comments about them are the author's.

The New York Times: Indispensable for news. Its editorial page expresses established liberal opinion on current issues. Its viewpoint, however, is through the distorting lenses of its own liberal hopes.

The Wall Street Journal: The best editorial page for market traders. It represents a moderately conservative viewpoint, except on economic issues where it is strictly 'free market'.

International Herald Tribune: A general review of what is happening around the world.

Barron's: A must for anyone involved with any kind of investments.

U.S. News & World Report: More useful information than any other magazine.

The Financial Times and *The Economist:* Both from England, should be read as often as possible.

The New Republic: Excellent Washington coverage.

The New Yorker: The best magazine reporting in the country. Their analysis of the Washington political scene is comprehensive.

Time and *Newsweek:* Worth a quick look to see what is currently in the news.

TV News Broadcasts: Concentrate on visual reporting. TV newscasters often play up trivial matters and ignore the important issues. Thorough reporting is impossible because of time limitations. So called reporting must be taken with a grain of salt because it is often slanted toward the station's point of view. An important exception is the *MacNeil/Lehrer Report*, an objective program which gives good coverage of current events.

ECONOMIC STATISTICS

Gross National Product: (GNP) Represents the total value of the nation's production of goods and services; a guide to the strength of the economy. Two figures are issued by the Commerce Department every three months: the first is in terms of current dollars, the second is an appraisal of the annual rate of growth or decline of the true GNP. This second figure is arrived at by eliminating changes in prices so that what is being measured is the actual volume of production. It is estimated that real GNP must grow about 4% annually to provide additional openings for new workers entering the job market.

Consumer Price Index: (CPI) Issued monthly by the Labor Dept. It gives a rough guide to changes in the cost of living. It is calculated by following the prices of several hundred retail items in the market basket, things in daily use.

Industrial Production: Appraised by the Federal Reserve Board. An index that measures the output of factories, mines and utilities and is closely watched between reports on GNP.

Other examples of key economic statistics reported periodically by the U.S. Government are - *Retail Sales*, and *Leading Indicators* by the Commerce Department; the *Wholesale Price Index*, *Unemployment*, and *Housing Starts*, each reported monthly by the Labor Department.

All statistics gleaned from the sources listed above and many others are published in Barron's. They appear under the title "The Week in Charts" as the information becomes available.

Statistics are especially important to the trader/speculator in currency futures. He considers interest rates, balance of trade figures, unemployment, industrial production, inflation, reserve assets, and all relevant factors to help him evaluate the prices of foreign currencies in relation to the U.S. dollar.

The U.S. Goverment, through its Departments of Agriculture (USDA), Commerce, Labor and Bureau of Mines, is the most important information source of all. Reports from these government departments cover many commodities and have a noticeable effect on the market. Government reports are released at stated intervals and all precautions are taken to prevent leakage of information prior to the moment of release. The reports are issued after the close of a day's trading. This gives traders the opportunity to evaluate the reports before trading resumes the next day.

The Commodity Futures Trading Commission (CFTC) publishes weekly statistics on stocks of grain available for delivery in licensed warehouses in Chicago. Monthly reports cover the

The Week in Charts

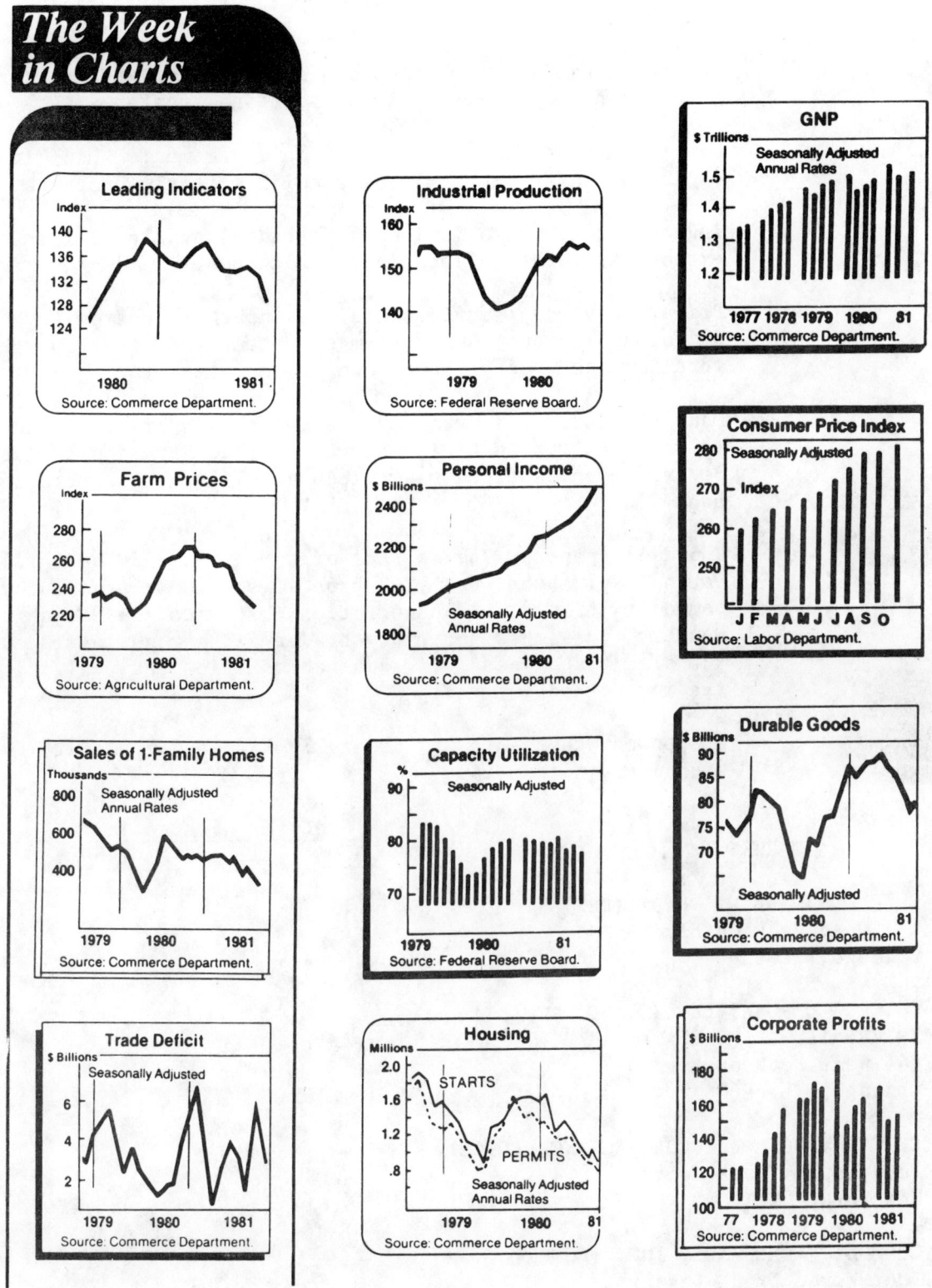

Source: BARRON'S National Business and Financial Weekly.

19

commitments of large traders in grain futures.

The Weather Bureau puts out a daily map of weather conditions for the entire country.

Several commodity exchanges publish daily or weekly market reports which are available at a nominal cost.

Many brokerage firms have research departments which issue their own market letters and special situation reports.

Industry trade associations and trade journals publish extensive amounts of statistics and news.

Private advisory services analyze information from government and other sources, among them competent private crop estimators, and then offer their own price forecasts.

Many sophisticated traders combine studies of both fundamentals and charts in their efforts to reach trading decisions. Several excellent chart services are listed elsewhere in this book.

Two daily papers, *The Journal of Commerce*, and *The Wall Street Journal*, plus the weekly, *Barron's*, should be studied by every commodity trader. A subscription to *Commodities Magazine*, a monthly, is a must for every trader. The magazine is educational; it analyzes individual commodities and evaluates trading methods.

WHERE THE ACTION IS...

At present there are ten federally licensed commodity futures exchanges in the U.S.A.:

MARKET:	Contracts traded in: 1970	1980
1. CHICAGO BOARD OF TRADE (CBT) 141 West Jackson Blvd. Chicago, IL 60604	7,940,661	45,281,295
2. CHICAGO MERCANTILE EXCHANGE (CME) & INTERNATIONAL MONETARY MARKET (IMM) 444 West Jackson Blvd. Chicago, IL 60606	3,316,065	22,261,295
3. COFFEE, SUGAR & COCOA EXCHANGE (CSCE) Four World Trade Center New York, NY 10048	666,614	4,886,416
4. COMMODITY EXCHANGE, INC. (COMEX) Four World Trade Center New York, NY 10048	872,430	11,009,389

	Contracts traded in:	
MARKET:	1970	1980

5. KANSAS CITY BOARD OF TRADE (KCBT)
   4800 Main Street, Suite 274
   Kansas City, Missouri 64112 — 179,954 — 1,298,047

6. MIDAMERICA COMMODITY EXCHANGE (MIDAM)
   175 West Jackson Blvd.
   Chicago, IL 60604 — 56,660 — 2,993,636

7. MINNEAPOLIS GRAIN EXCHANGE (MGE)
   150 Grain Exchange Building
   Minneapolis, Minnesota 55415 — 49,744 — 360,978

8. NEW YORK COTTON EXCHANGE (NYCE)
   Four World Trade Center
   New York, NY 10048 — 110,811 — 2,653,294

9. NEW YORK FUTURES EXCHANGE (NYFE)
   20 Broad Street
   New York, NY 10005 — (Approved May 28, 1980) — 183,993

10. NEW YORK MERCANTILE EXCHANGE (NYME)
    Four World Trade Center
    New York, NY 10048 — 417,760 — 1,154,095

Below are listed the commodities currently traded for which there are approved futures contracts. The numbers in parenthesis refer to the numbers above, next to each of the CFTC approved Exchanges and show on which specific Exchanges each of the commodities is traded.

British pound (2)
Canadian dollar (2)
Cattle, live (2) (6)
Cattle, feeder (2)
Cocoa (3)
Coffee (3)
Copper (4)
Corn (1) (6)
Cotton (8)
Deutsche mark (2)
Eggs (2)
Frozen orange juice (8)
GNMA certificates (1)
Gold (2) (4) (6)
Heating oil No. 2 (10)
Hogs, live (2) (6)

Iced broilers (2)
Japanese yen (2)
Lumber (2)
Oats (1) (6)
Platinum (10)
Plywood (1)
Potatoes (10)
Silver (1) (4) (6)
Soybean meal (1)
Soybean oil (1)
Soybeans (1) (6)
Sugar (3)
Swiss franc (2)
U.S. Treasury bills (2)
U.S. Treasury bonds (1) (9)
Wheat (1) (5) (6) (7)

THE COMMODITY TRADING ACCOUNT

Trading is done only between member firms of an exchange. The first step then for the novice trader is to open an account with a broker. It may be either with a large, diversified brokerage house or with a firm dealing exclusively in commodities.

If the would-be commodity trader already has a stockbroker who also handles commodity orders, it will not be necessary to open a new account. The broker will require that the customer sign forms having to do with the internal segregation of funds and also a standard margin agreement. This last binds the customer to make good any losses suffered in the course of trading. Once the forms are signed and the necessary margin funds deposited, the account is ready to go.

The margin deposit is money left in the account to protect the broker against sudden and large price changes in the customer's position. These funds do not earn interest and are used when additional margin is needed for the account. They are also evidence of the customer's good faith.

The cost of trading in commodities is low compared to similar costs in securities trading. On the stock and bond markets brokerage fees depend on the dollar value of each transaction. In commodities, the fees are lower to begin with and only one commission is paid, the *round turn* one, due when the position is liquidated.

HOW TO SELECT A BROKER...

The commodity representative is the person in the brokerage house responsible for handling the customer's account. He accepts the customer's orders and, at the customer's request, provides information and guidance.

When selecting a broker, look for one who:

▲ Specializes in commodity trading or is at least knowledgeable about it.

▲ Promises prompt and reliable execution of trades and prompt call-backs on completed trades.

▲ Has a good commodity research organization behind him, or her.

▲ Is willing and interested to send you free daily and/or weekly fundamental and technical market letters and special situation reports.

▲ Is at least conversant with and interested in commodity spread trading - which will be your major area of interest.

▲ Is willing to discuss the firm's margin requirements for outright as well as spread positions.

▲ Will quote the brokerage fees for outright and spread positions (Note: there are large differences in the fees charged by full-service brokerage houses as well as among discount brokers.).

MARGINS AND LEVERAGE

When buying or selling a contract, or when setting up a spread, which involves simultaneous buying and selling, a margin deposit must be made. Margin money is required by the Exchanges to bind the broker to the transaction. Margin rates for each commodity are set by the Exchanges on which they are traded. The Exchanges establish the minimum *initial margins*, but individual brokerage houses usually require higher ones. Unlike those on security accounts, which represent an ownership interest for the buyer of the security, margins in commodities do not mean actual ownership. They are instead more like a security deposit, a token of good faith, so called *earnest money*. Commodity margins are amounts deposited by both buyer and seller of futures contracts as an assurance that their contractual commitments will be met.

After the initial margin is deposited and a trade is made, margin equity must be maintained to cover an adverse price change. Besides the initial minimum margins, therefore, the Exchanges also specify *minimum maintenance* schedules. Let's say the minimum initial margin required by the Exchange is $1,500 for a given contract. The brokerage house may ask for a $2,000 margin deposit with a maintenance margin of $1,500. A price move in excess of $500 against the trader means that the trader must bring the margin deposit back up to $2,000 by depositing the additional funds required. On the other hand, any gain resulting from a favorable price move is credited every day to the trader's account. The profit may be withdrawn from the account at any time or re-invested elsewhere like in a *money market fund* where it will earn interest daily. Many brokerage houses have tie-ins with money market funds and automatically transfer idle funds into them.

Margin requirements are usually 5-15 percent of contract value, but when markets become volatile, margins may be raised substantially. (Note: In low-risk spread positions, the margin required may be less than 5%).

While low margins provide the opportunity to establish large positions on small margin capital, a relatively small adverse price fluctuation can create large losses relative to the capital involved. A $40 stock would require $2,000 to $3,600 margin (50-90% margin) per hundred shares. A move to $50 would result in $1,000 profit to the speculator who is long the stock. The commodity trader who is long one contract of copper at 80¢ per pound may be required to deposit $2,000 in initial margin. If the price of copper moves up by 20¢ to $1.00/lb., the trader would have a profit of $5,000. This large profit (or loss) potential gives the commodity markets the reputation of extreme price volatility.

Let us look at another example: A trader may decide to buy a contract for 5,000 bushels of wheat for $5 per bushel. Initial margin of $1,500 is deposited with the broker and a purchase is made for the trader's account. A 5% increase in the price of wheat to $5.25 ($1,250 gain in contract value) will mean a profit of 80% on the margin deposit after a commission of $50 is paid. The same profit would have been realized by a trader who sold short if the price of wheat decreased by 5%.

5,000 bushels of wheat X $5/bushel = $25,000 contract value.

$25,000 X 0.05 = $1,250 (profit on a 5% increase in price)

Profit minus commission: $1,250 - $50 = $1,200 net profit.

$1,200 (net profit) ÷ $1,500 (margin) = 80% profit on margin.

If the price moves adversely, the leverage will work against the trader. If this happens, and the trader's maintenance margin level is reached, he will get a call from his broker for additional margin money.

The trader now has two choices:

    (1) Put up more margin money,

    (2) Liquidate the position.

Note this, however: If the trader chooses to liquidate, it may happen that the broker cannot execute the order immediately because of a limit price move by the commodity on that particular day, or a string of limit moves over a period of time. This is unfortunate but, understand, the trader is responsible for the ensuing losses until his position finally is liquidated.

During the last ten years is has not been unusual for many commodity futures contracts to make four or more consecutive daily limit moves. This may help explain why margin requirements have been climbing. Increased margins not only protect the brokerage house which must settle every day with the Exchange's clearing house, but serve as well to discourage speculators who lack sufficient funds (risk capital). Higher margins also reflect the increased dollar value of the contracts traded.

COMMISSIONS

The single commission charged by the brokerage firm for a futures contract is for the round turn. This includes both the initial and the offsetting trades. Commissions are paid by the trader at the time the contract is closed out.

Commissions vary with the different commodities traded but, in general, they are modest when compared with those charged for transactions in the securities markets. On March 4, 1978, brokerage house commissions on futures contracts became negotiable, but unless the customer has a very large account or is a professional money manager, the broker will be reluctant to discuss a lower fee than the one his firm has already established. Shop around then, explore the qualifications of several firms before making a final decision about a brokerage house. All else being equal, it will pay to select the one with the lowest fee.

If neither a broker's advice nor his firm's research department is needed, then certainly a discount broker should be chosen. In any event, look for competence in handling orders, availability during market hours, open telephone lines so that orders can be placed any time during the trading day and coverage during lunch hours or any other times the broker may be away from his desk.

Read immediately and check all confirmations, statements, and other communications from the broker. Get brokerage errors corrected as quickly as possible. Correct erroneous margin calls, missed markets, equity figures, errors in reports and commission rates, etc. Check everything! Take nothing for granted. People still make mistakes, even with all the sophisticated machinery used in brokerage houses.

TYPES OF ORDERS

Following are types of commodity orders most often used.

Market order. The broker receives an order from the trader to buy or sell *at the market*, without specific instructions regarding price. This type of order should be executed for the customer at the best possible price and as soon as possible after receiving the order.

Limit order. The customer wants to buy or sell *within a specific time period,* or at *a specific price.* Such a limit order can be executed only within the given time limits, or at the specified price, or better. Limit orders may be marked G.T.C (good-till-cancelled). G.T.C. is also known as an *open order.*

Day order. Unless specific instructions to the contrary are given by the customer all orders are considered day orders by the broker. Day orders not executed during the trading day are automatically cancelled.

Stop order. This type of order is used to (1) liquidate a position to limit losses, (2) protect profits gained on a position, and (3) initiate new positions. The stop order registered with the broker becomes a market order to sell if prices drop or to buy if prices rise to a specified point. Your broker cannot be held precisely to a stop order because in fast moving markets the price may jump right over the stop price or drop right through it before the floor broker has a chance to act. Since the stop order becomes a market order only when the stop price has been reached, the eventual purchase may be made at a somewhat higher price, - or, the sale at a lower price - than the order specified.

The trader should study these various types of orders. They are important money management tools.

An existing open contract is *closed out (liquidated, offset)* when a buyer sells, or a seller buys back the contract. When the transaction is completed, the broker first sends a confirmation and then a P & S memorandum (Purchase & Sale). The latter is a statement of account showing the purchase and selling prices (or selling and purchase prices in case of a short position), the commission charge, and the resulting profit or loss.

HOW TO FIGURE PROFITS AND LOSSES

Let's assume that in May 1980 a speculator purchased one contract (100 troy ounces) of December 1980 gold at a price of $550 per troy ounce. In July 1980 the speculator decided to take profits at $675. A fluctuation of $1 in the market price of gold is equivalent to $100 ($1 x 100 troy ounces). Since the price of gold advanced by $125, the speculator's gross profit came to $12,500 on the transaction. Assuming a commission of $80, the speculator gained $12,420 net profit in the successful trade. Needless to say, if the market had declined by $125, the speculator would have suffered a cash loss of $12.580 including commissions.

To sum up, a speculator's profit or loss is realized in the difference between the price at which the position was initiated and the price at which it was liquidated. In addition to the price differential the transaction costs must be considered. The transaction's costs are the broker's commissions and the *opportunity costs*, these last being the loss of the interest the speculator's money would have earned had it not been used to provide the margin deposit required for each contract.

Most people with only stock market experience would use margin money as the basis for figuring profits or losses. In commodity trading this is poor technique. Margin requirements are not actually relevant to profit or loss calculations. Margin money is a surety deposit. It is not a cost, or a measure of value, an investment or a purchase price. Commissions on the other hand, are a real cost and their effect on the profitability of a trade can be substantial.

The success of a trade can be measured by the percentage of profit realized on the amount of funds invested: *the rate of return.*

The rate of return is calculated as follows:

Net Profit divided by *Cost* equals *Rate of Return* (in %).

To determine the *Net Profit*, calculate the gross profit from a trade, then deduct the commission payable, and the interest income lost on the margin deposit while the trade was open. Let us say the sum for margin deposit was withdrawn from a money market fund for the duration of the trade. To determine the *Cost*, we add the interest lost and the commission.

In order for the rate of return figure to be meaningful, it must be calculated on an annual basis. This is done as follows: Once the rate of return has been calculated, multiply this by 52 (weeks). Then, divide this amount by the number of weeks it took to complete the transaction, from the time the position was established until it was liquidated. The figure obtained will show the *annualized rate of return*. This then is the formula:

Percentage Rate   Weeks elapsed   Annualized Rate
   of Return   X 52 ÷ during transaction = of Return (%)

As an example, take a second look at the gold transaction described at the beginning of this section. The speculator's gross profit was $12.500 and the trade was open for five weeks. Eighty dollars were paid for commission, and margin deposit was set at a very high $15,000 a result of the volatile fluctuations and high price of gold. The margin money was withdrawn for five weeks from a money market fund which at the time yielded 9% annually.

<u>Cost</u>:   Commission + Loss of Interest
         $80   + $130   = $210

<u>Gross Profit</u>: $12,500
<u>Minus Costs</u>:   210
                    Net Profit: $12,290

<u>Rate of Return</u>: Net Profit ÷ Cost
              $12,290 ÷ $210 = 5,852%

Rate of Return X 52 ÷ Weeks Elapsed = <u>Annualized Rate of Return</u>
    5,852   X 52 ÷   5   =   60,865%

Thus, the true, annualized rate of return on this trade is a fantastic sixty thousand percent. But, the trader who put up $15,000 margin to initiate the trade and in five weeks made a net profit of $12,290 will tend to calculate the profit to be 82% ($12,290 ÷ $15,000), and the annualized rate of return as a still hefty 853% (82 x 52 ÷ 5). But from the loser's viewpoint, the $125 upside move against a short position would have created a loss of $12,500 plus commission ($80), plus loss of interest ($130), to add up to a total loss of $12,710, meaning that about 85% of the initial margin would have been wiped out.

ON TRADING

- People read reports on the specifics of supply and demand. They look at charts, consider trendlines and other technical factors. Then, according to their interpretation of the market situation, place a buy or sell order. Their combined actions make prices move. But, even though all the information is available to anyone who wants it, the fact is that very few people can act on it in a rational and realistic way. The majority of traders lack emotional control and make their decisions on the basis of mob psychology. They are plagued equally by stubbornness and fear, by greed and embarrassment. These are the losers.

- The novice trader should begin by practice-trading on paper. Actual trading might start in small lots of 1,000 bushels of grain, the so-called mini contracts on the MidAmerica Commodity Exchange.

- Before a trading decision is made, the speculator should always question whether the investment is likely to provide sufficient return to justify the risk. The potential profit should be large, at least 2:1 or 3:1, in relation to risk.

- The speculator should find and then follow the market trend, trade with the market, not against it.

- Attempts to forecast the reversal points of trends is too risky. One should not try to pick market tops or bottoms.

- In commodity trading, short and long positions should have equal priority. The trader must be prepared to think bearish, - and be ready and willing to change direction quickly.

- Never add to a losing position. Preservation of capital is a key goal in speculation and protective stops should be set at the initiation of the trade.

- The speculator must be prepared to accept several small, successive losses.

- One must use discipline and exercise patience by letting profits run. The possibly smaller number of successful trades will offset the losses, pay the commissions, and on balance, by the end of a 12-month period, leave the speculator with a fair profit.

TRADING PLAN

The speculator must have a trading plan and stay with it. Some things to consider...

(1) Carefully select a trade.
(2) Analyze risk/reward potential.
(3) Set loss point and minimum profit objective.
(4) Enter the order but limit the amount of capital invested in any single trade to a small portion of available risk capital.
(5) If order is filled, make sure the broker has the stop loss order on file. Obtain written confirmation.
(6) If stop-loss point is reached, make sure the position is liquidated.
(7) If minimum profit objective is reached either liquidate the position or cancel old stop-loss order and enter so called *trailing stops*. In this way one can keep riding profits until stopped out by a market reversal.
(8) In case of a multi-contract position, consider partial profit taking when the minimum profit objective is reached.
(9) Additions to an initial position should be made only after profits have already been accumulated.
(10) Additional commitments should be in amounts smaller than the initial position. This is called *pyramiding*.

RISK & REWARD

During the past decade the commodity markets have been unusually volatile. Crop failures, accelerating inflation, ever increasing international demand for commodities combined with changing weather patterns, price controls, devaluations, and skyrocketing energy prices have all contributed to the wide price swings. Some traders undoubtedly made large amounts of money by correctly forecasting and trading the alternating bull and bear markets. Others made some money for a while, only to lose it by sudden trend reversals.

Many investors in securities are aware of the high leverage in commodity futures trading. They understand how this leverage magnifies the already wide price fluctuations and how this, in turn, produces generous profits or heavy losses. Very few conservative investors, however, are prepared to take on the risks associated with the substantial reward potential.

Yet, today's investor also knows that he will lose money if funds are allowed to remain in a bank, or in money market funds; that he will probably lose as well with stocks, bonds, and other traditional, and conservative investments. The middle class investor faces a frightening dilemma: he needs at least a 20% to 30% return on his money, just to break even after taxes and inflation.

One way to resolve the dilemma is to take an open minded look at the *spread trading method* of commodity speculation. This type of operation offers many profitable trading opportunities and is suitable to today's often frenzied markets.

For the beginning trader/speculator, spread trading in limited risk situations is an ideal way to learn about the market without being subject to an excess of either financial or emotional stress. For the sophisticated speculator, advanced spread trading strategies offer a most satisfying intellectual challenge.

The balance of this book will describe spread trading techniques, opportunities in various markets and, finally, an outline for a year-round trading plan.

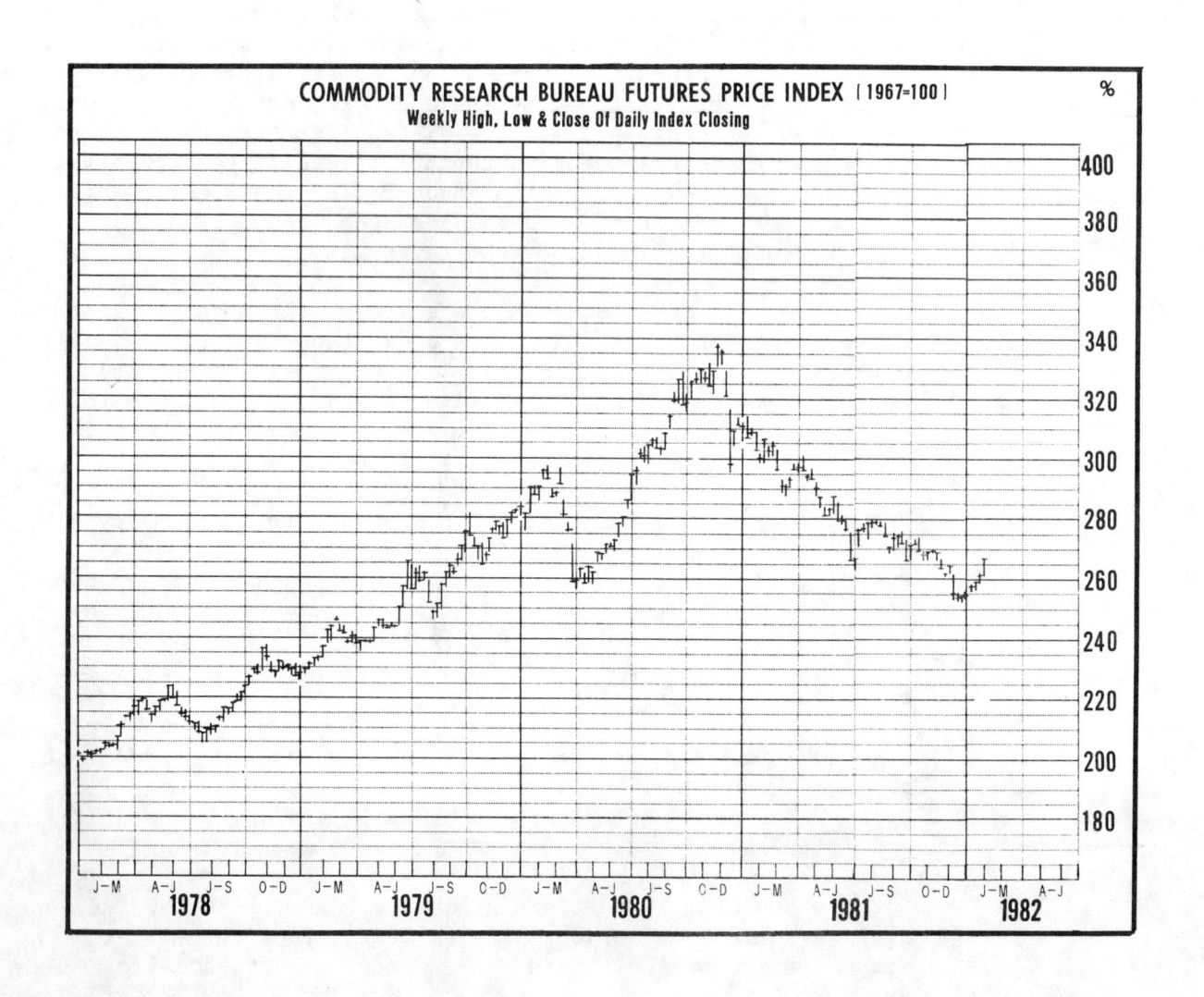

* * *

SPREAD TRADING IN COMMODITY MARKETS

WHAT IS A FUTURES SPREAD?

When a commodity trader puts on a spread he simultaneously takes a long position in one futures contract against a short position in another. When he buys July wheat, for example, against the sale of September wheat or when he buys May corn against the sale of July corn.

The term *straddle* is sometimes used to refer to simultaneous trades in two different markets, like the purchase of July wheat in Chicago against the sale of July wheat in Kansas City; or the purchase of August pork bellies against the sale of August hogs. At times, the Chicago versus Kansas City wheat transaction will be called an *arbitrage*. At other times, especially among those who trade cotton, it will be called a *straddle*. Note: In this text the term is *spread* and spread is synonymous with arbitrage and straddle. When a trader buys May corn and, at the same time, sells July corn, he has a spread position. Although two contracts are involved, one long and one short, the trader is said to have one spread, one May versus July corn spread.

A trader will put on a spread when in his opinion the price difference between the two futures contracts is abnormal. He will establish the spread position in the expectation that the spread difference will eventually widen or narrow and return to normal. When this happens he will liquidate the spread at a profit. Thus, spread traders in futures markets are not necessarily concerned with the up or down price movement in either contract. The profitability of a spread position is determined by changes in the difference (the spread) between the prices of the two futures contracts. The educated trader notes this difference between two related prices and attempts to forecast whether the spread will become wider or narrower. Naturally, the two futures contracts in a spread position must have some economic relationship to each other. If they do not, the trader will have merely a net long position in one contract and a net short position in another. You cannot, for example, spread cattle against copper.

Successful forecasting of spreads requires an analysis of supply and demand along with the many other factors that affect the spread. The U.S. government publishes much material to aid forecasting: situation reports, crop forecasts, foreign agriculture bulletins and others. Additonal sources of information include trade journals, financial publications, The Wall Street Journal, The Journal of Commerce and Barron's. Brokerage firms and subscription advisory services are also sources for information. The bibliography section of this book lists many more.

Fundamental analysis will reveal profit opportunities on spread positions. Technical and historical analysis of the spread will help to choose entry points, thus limiting risk and at the same time setting realistic profit objectives.

HOW CAN SPREADS PRODUCE PROFITS?

In the stock and commodities markets a trader profits only if he is right in forecasting the market's direction. If long, for example, the trader profits only if the market goes up; if short, he profits only if it goes down.

In spread trading a trader attempts to position himself so that he will profit within a wide latitude of a price movement in either direction. His profits are produced by having the difference (spread) between the prices of his original positions move in the direction he predicted.

After a spread position is established it, with time, will narrow, widen, or stay the same in line with the fluctuations in the price of the underlying commodity or commodities. This narrowing or widening, or failure to do either will determine the profit or loss of the spread.

Let's look at an example:

During a recent bull market in sugar a trader expected the price of May sugar to rise faster than October sugar. Accordingly, he established the following bull spread:

    Bought: One May sugar contract at 12.00¢
    Sold: One October sugar contract at 12.50¢

Two months later the spread position was liquidated:

    Sold: One May sugar contract at 16.00¢
    Bought: One October sugar contract at 15.75¢

This trader was long in May sugar. He bought it at 12¢ and sold it at 16¢ for a 4¢ profit. At the same time, the trader was short October sugar at 12.50¢. Later when he liquidated it (bought it back), the price was 15.75¢ and he suffered a loss of 3-1/4¢ per pound. Thus, the net profit on the spread was 3/4¢ per pound. In two months the trader made an $840 profit. The spread margin deposit required by his broker was

$600. With the spread technique described relatively small changes in price will produce attractive profits and this is only one example of how a spread trade can work to produce a profit. Actually, the long May versus short October sugar spread could have become profitable in any of five different ways:

1. The long side (May) rises, the short side (October) rises by less.
2. The long side rises, the short side remains unchanged.
3. The long side remains unchanged, the short side falls.
4. The long side falls but the short side falls further.
5. The long side rises, the short side falls.

These five are examples of bull spreads. As the name implies, they are used in bull markets. More about them later... Right now the important thing to remember is that, in the example given, the trader profits if the spread narrows, that is, if the difference in price between the contract bought and the contract sold decreases.

WHY TRADE SPREADS?

One reason to consider spreads as a trading method is that margin requirements are usually much smaller for spreads than for outright long or short positions. Recently, a large brokerage house required $2,500 in margin for an outright position in copper and $4,000 in margin for cotton. The spread margins for these same two commodities, however, came to only $500 and $1,500. In another example, margin for an outright Swiss franc contract may be between $3,000 and $5,000, depending on the brokerage house, while a Swiss franc spread would require only $500 to $750. An extreme example was the great silver bull market in 1980 when $50,000 was required for an outright long or short position but only $1,500 for a spread. In some commodities the margin requirements are prohibitive. Spreads, however, offer an affordable, alternative approach.

A further advantage of spreads is the protection they offer against sudden and sometimes heavy losses from unforeseen economic or political happenings. Since the prices for delivery in different months, or the prices of related commodities, tend to move up or down together, spreading offers protection against extreme price volatility. If a spread trader's long position suffers a sudden, unpredictable loss, his short position in the spread will produce a profit of equal magnitude. Matter of fact, when the market is in a panic and trading is frenzied, the value of the spread is usually unchanged because both the long and short components, the *legs* of the spread, each moves the daily permissible limit.

It must be noted that profit opportunities may exist for spreads although the commodity itself is inactive and trendless. Also, with experience the trader will find there will be times when spreads offer better risk/reward ratios than outright positions.

Experience in spread trading gives insights into market direction and thus is a valuable aid in trading outright positions. The spread trader has the additional advantage of knowingly picking the strongest delivery month for a proposed long position, or the weakest for a short position and in this way significantly increasing his profit.

LEVERAGE ON SPREADS

At no time should it be inferred that spread trading is altogether risk free, only that the risk in spreads is usually much smaller than in outright positions.

Remember too, that the reduced risk in spreads is the reason for the much lower margin requirements than those needed for outright positions. As a result of the smaller margin spreading offers magnified leverage. The successful spreader will realize a greater return on his investment than the net long or short trader provided the same dollar amount is invested. And he will do so with less risk.

CARRYING CHARGES

Adequate supplies of a storable commodity usually cause futures for more distant delivery to be at a premium to the nearby futures. This is a normal market in that the price differential or spread between the futures months reflects the actual costs of owning the commodity for the specified time. These costs include interest, storage, and insurance, of which storage and insurance are known as fixed costs. The interest costs vary considerably, depending on the price level of the commodity and the interest rate at the time. The following table shows how much it costs to own, store and insure a bushel of grain or soybeans per month. The carrying charges shown in the table include an arbitrary five cents per bushel per month for storage and insurance.

GRAIN CARRYING CHARGES/MONTH

Price of grain or soybeans/bushel:	------Interest rate (prime rate + 1%)--------						
	10%	12%	14%	16%	18%	20%	22%
$2	6.67¢	7¢	7.33¢	7.67¢	8¢	8.33¢	8.67¢
3	7.50	8	8.50	9.00	9.5	10.00	10.50
4	8.33	9	9.67	10.33	11.0	11.67	12.33
5	9.17	10	10.83	11.67	12.5	13.33	14.16
6	10.00	11	12.00	13.00	14.0	15.00	16.00
7	10.83	12	13.17	14.33	15.5	16.67	17.83
8	11.67	13	14.33	15.67	17.0	18.33	19.67
9	12.50	14	15.50	17.00	18.5	20.00	21.50
10	13.33	15	16.67	18.33	20.0	21.67	23.33

The above table reflects full monthly carrying charges. Payment of full charges is a rare occurrence in the futures markets because the price difference between delivery months seldom reflects the full costs of interest, storage and insurance.

TYPICAL CARRYING CHARGES

(Per month; date: Sept. 25, 1980; prime rate + 1% = 13.25%)

Wheat	10¢
Corn	8¢
Oats	6¢
Soybeans	14¢
Bean oil	40 points
Bean meal	490 "
Copper	130 "
Cotton	120 "
Gold	840 "
Orange Juice	140 "
Plywood	285 "
Silver	2,530 "

The above carrying charges were calculated using the closing prices of the nearest contract month at the given date. The following fixed costs for storage and insurance were added and the totals rounded off on the high side: 4.2¢ per bushel per month for wheat, corn, oats and soybeans; 9 points per contract per month for bean oil; 210 points per contract per month for bean meal; 25 points per contract per month for cotton; 2 points for gold, 15 points for silver and 65 points for plywood per contract per month. Many calculations were and will be made in point values rather than dollars and/or cents. A method for converting points to money values will be given later.

CALCULATING CARRYING CHARGES

Following is the formula for the calculation of carrying charges:

The current prime interest rate + 1% is multiplied by the market price of the commodity using the price quoted for the nearest delivery month on the board. The result is divided by 12 and then the monthly costs of storage and insurance are added. For example, the nearest futures contract for wheat is quoted at $4.40 (440¢). Consider the prime rate at 17%: (440 x .18) ÷ 12 = 6.6¢ plus 4.2¢ for storage & insurance comes to about 11¢ per bushel per month as full carrying charges.

Full carrying charges, - as has been noted - are rarely paid in practice, not even in an extremely bearish market. If the trader is looking at a spread and calculates the maximum price differential between the two contracts will be 15 cents, and then initiates the spread at a 9 cents differential, the total risk is limited to 6 cents because the spread cannot widen to more than the full carry, which is 15 cents. Thus, the risk is limited to 6 cents but the profit potential is not limited. In a bullish market the spread can continue to narrow, the two contracts can go to even money and the carrying charges then disappear.

INVERTED MARKET

Severe scarcity may cause the nearby futures to be priced at a premium over the deferred, more distant futures. This price relationship is referred to as inverse or inverted markets.

In an inverted market, the maximum extent of the spread cannot be defined or calculated because the premium of the nearby contract over the deferred, theoretically, is unlimited. Scarcity causes high prices in both the nearby futures and the cash markets because eager buyers are pressuring reluctant sellers.

THE LIMITED RISK SPREAD

Some spreads are more risky than others. The least risky are those that involve completely storable, seasonally-produced commodities, like the grains, pork bellies and others.

To qualify as a limited risk spread, the transaction must fulfill the following requirements:

(1) A long position taken in a nearby contract against the short sale of a more distant one of the same commodity. The word *nearby* does not refer to the nearest delivery month on the quotation board. It only means that the long position must mature before the contract month in which a short position was taken. Example: A long January versus a short May soybean spread.

(2) The commodity must be one which will be accepted on delivery when the nearby long contract matures and be eligible for delivery without re-inspection when the deferred contract, which was sold short, matures. Because the cost of carrying the commodity is the basis for calculating the risk involved in a limited risk spread, it is not suggested that the trader accept delivery and carry the actual physical commodity until the more distant delivery month.

(3) The commodity must be physically available for delivery without dependence on transportation.

(4) The short sale in the deferred month should be made at a premium over the price of the nearby long month. This premium should cover a portion of the carrying costs. Since the carrying costs usually limit the amount by which the deferred contract may trade over the nearby contract, the risk exposure is limited and can be calculated.

The cost factors involved in carrying the commodity in storage from one time period to the next include: storage for the entire period, handling, insurance, shrinkage, commission to buy and accept delivery, commission to sell and make delivery and interest on investment.

INTEREST RATES

As shown below, the largest cost is the interest on the money needed to carry the physical commodity from the time it is delivered until it is re-delivered against the deferred month. This cost varies with both the price of the commodity and with the short-term interest rates.

Let's assume that the prime interest rate is 10% per annum, and the price of soybeans is $5 per bushel. The value of a standard 5,000 bushel soybean futures contract is then $25,000. In case of a January versus May soybean spread, interest on the money for four months amounts to $833.33 or about 16-1/2¢ per bushel. This is a simplified calculation because we would have to pay for the borrowed money over and above the prime lending rate and we would have to add the costs of storage and insurance.

If the trader initiates the spread by selling the May contract at a premium of 10¢ over the cost of the January contract, and buys January beans at $5 and sells short May beans at $5.10, he would have an interest expense of 16-1/2¢ from which he must deduct the 10¢ premium built into the spread when it was initiated. His risk exposure would be about 6-1/2¢ in case the spread widened out to the carrying charges which we calculated as 16-1/2¢ per bushel for the four months.

If, however, at a later date the interest rate climbs to 18%, and the price of soybeans goes up to $8 per bushel, the carrying charges will reach 12¢ per month per bushel, or 48¢ for the Jan/May spread (12¢ x 4 months). Thus, we see that the so-called 'limited risk' spreads do not limit the trader's risk for the whole duration of a spread trade. As interest rates rise and fall so do carrying charges. While falling interest rates benefit limited risk spreaders, a sudden rise in interest rates can destroy the risk limitation expectation that was in effect when the trade was initiated.

The profit potential, on the other hand, is in no way limited. There is no limit to the higher price a nearer month can demand over that of a more distant month. As mentioned before, in a severe shortage situation, theoretically, the possible gain is unlimited.

Commodities that lend themselves to limited risk spread trading provided the two contract months are in the same crop year are: wheat, corn, oats, soybeans, soybean oil, soybean meal. Frozen orange juice, cotton, coffee, cocoa, currencies, T-bonds, T-bills and Ginnie Maes. Pork bellies must involve two contract months of the same calendar year.

Commodities which cannot be carried from one delivery month to another cannot be traded as limited risk spreads. Because of perishability and transportation problems limited risk spreads in the following commodities cannot be established: eggs, broilers, cattle, hogs and pork bellies when spreading different calendar years (for example, August vs. next year's February bellies). Sugar must be delivered at country of origin, and potatoes, also cannot be traded as limited risk spreads.

CALCULATED RISK

As another example of risk calculation, assume, a speculating trader places the following order with his broker:

"Buy March and sell May bellies at 100 points premium for May," The order is filled, March bought at 54.40¢ and May sold at 55.40¢.

The pork belly contract is written for 38,000 pounds. Current price, near month: 54.40¢ per pound.

    Contract value: ($.5440 x 38,000) = $20,672.-
    Interest at 18% per annum = $3,721.-
    Interest per month: ($3,721 ÷ 12) = $310.-
    Interest from March to May = two months = $620.-
    $620 is the equivalent of 163 points (1 point = $3.80)
    163 points = carrying charges excluding storage & insurance.

When a commercial trader can sell the more distant month at a premium equal to interest on the money required to carry the physical commodity, he will probably be willing to support the price difference (spread) at that point. Thus, the speculating spread trader is taking a calculated risk of 63 points if he establishes a position at a 100 point differential, May over March.

There are conditions under which limited risk spreads may go wrong. All stored commodities must be kept in good condition while in storage. In case of pork bellies, for example, a power blackout could render the bellies in the storage freezer non-deliverable even after conditions are restored to normal. Another circumstance that could hurt the limited risk spread trader is a sudden change by a commodity exchange of the rules regulating trading. The exchange, for example, may decide not to permit the re-tendering of the commodity once a delivery notice is issued. Such action by an exchange, in an effort to cool speculative involvements, would weaken the nearbys while the distant delivery months could go to unusual premiums. Another unusual circumstance is the federal government's imposition of price ceilings on nearby deliveries. While the nearbys would be limited by the ceiling, the distant delivery months could go to very high premiums in anticipation of much higher prices once the price controls are abolished. We live in uncertain times. The limited risk trader must remain ever alert to liquidate the spread once the calculated maximum price difference is -for whatever reason- conclusively violated.

As has been noted, the interest rate and the price of the commodity under consideration are two factors of major importance to the commodity spread trader. Another is the supply/demand situation. If, for example, reduced supplies of hogs and pigs were coupled with strong demand for bellies, the trader might not get a *fill* on his order to buy March and sell May bellies at May 100 points over the price of the March bellies. The trader must adjust to existing conditions and reconsider the price differential (spread) he is willing to accept when entering the trade. He might have to take a larger risk to obtain the spread he wants but the trade would still be a limited risk spread with a larger loss exposure.

AVERAGING DOWN

A trader dealing in limited risk spreads can average down against a known maximum price difference which is not expected to change or change to the advantage of the trader. There are three such possibilities: 1) Interest rates are holding steady, 2) interest rates appear to be topping out, or 3) interest rates are coming down. Embarking on a trading plan which involves averaging down, the trader will place several *open orders* with his broker.

For example:

1. Buy March & sell May bellies,   75 pts. May over (1 unit)
2. "   "   " "   "   "   100 "   "   "   (1 unit)
3. "   "   " "   "   "   125 "   "   "   (2 units)
4. "   "   " "   "   "   150 "   "   "   (2 units)

Since the trader moves with the ebb-and-flow of the spread, he places a liquidation order with his broker immediately upon a fill. If on trade 1, above, he receives such a fill his next instruction to the broker would be an open order, good-till-cancelled (GTC): "Sell March and buy May bellies, 25 points May over," thus aiming at a 50-point profit. If and when this target is reached, he will take his profits and immediately reinstate his No. 1 open order with the broker. This same method would be followed with trades 2, 3, and 4 if notice of a fill was received from the broker. In trade No. 3, the liquidation order would read: "Sell 2 March and buy 2 May bellies at 75 points May over." This 50-point profit objective was chosen arbitrarily but it is considered a reasonable goal in view of long-term, historical spread charts. Each spread No. 1 through No. 4 should be treated separately. It is a rule never to break a spread by lifting one *leg* of it. Orders No. 1 through No. 4 must be placed as spreads and liquidated as spreads.

The trading program above may not be active enough for some traders. It is the greedy, outright position trader, however, who pours huge sums of risk capital into the market in the hope of making quick profits. The well diversified spread trader who has a good trading plan, and realistic profit objectives as part of that plan, stands a good chance of capturing some of the risk capital. The true professionals are those spread traders who stay in business year after year and those with the most capital who control the market by using strategically placed spreads. The small trader can benefit from the big power plays by coat-tailing the ebb-and-flow of this market.

During recent years many spreads have shown frequent changes of substantial size. In the March/May pork belly spread detailed above, the trader took a calculated risk and arbitrarily limited his profits to 50 points per trade. The educated trader, however, can take advantage of a possibly big move by trading an even number of spread positions for each trade.

TWO-UNIT TRADING

In our example, in trades No. 1 and No. 2 he buys two, four, six, or more March contracts (always even numbers) and sells the same number of May belly contracts. In trades No. 3 and No. 4 he doubles the amount. Half the spread positions in each trade are liquidated at the predetermined profit objective of 50 points. The remaining spreads are held for the longer term. If the big move materializes, these contracts are closed out when a protective stop signalling a change in the market is touched.

Often limited risk spreads fluctuate in a very narrow range until the first delivery day approaches. At that time the nearby contracts gain relative to the more distant ones. If this situation develops, the trader, hoping for more profits, will stay with the spread as long as possible. By doing so he may overstay his position and receive delivery on the nearby long position. Should this occur, the trader would instruct his broker to sell, re-tender the commodity and liquidate the short leg of the spread at the same time. The trader, of course, would pay an extra commission, and probably one day's interest and storage would be assessed. While many traders will panic and liquidate before the first delivery day, often large and profitable moves occur between the first delivery and the last trading day. Close contact with one's broker is advisable during this period since deliveries for every day are posted and the broker receives this information each delivery day. If deliveries are small, the spread should be liquidated before trading ceases in the nearby, long contract.

INVERTED MARKETS

Thus far we have looked at normal, so-called carrying charge markets. In periods when a commodity is in short supply the premium will narrow for the deferred contract months. If a true scarcity develops, the carrying charges will disappear and the nearby futures will be priced higher than the deferred futures. This type of price relationship is known as an inverse or inverted market, and involves *negative carrying charges.*

When traders correctly anticipate acute shortages of a commodity, bull-spreads (long nearby vs. short deferred contracts) are very profitable. As an example, during November 1973, the December '73 wheat contract reached a premium of more than 65¢ over the deferred May '74 contract.

TYPES OF SPREADS

There are four major types of spreads:

(1) *INTERDELIVERY SPREADS*, also called intra-market or intra-commodity spreads. These long and short positions involve two different delivery months of the same commodity on the same exchange. For example, July wheat is spread against December wheat, or May corn against July corn. This is the most common type of spread and includes the limited risk spreads, often referred to as carrying-charge spreads.

(2) *INTERMARKET SPREADS.* The long and short positions involve the same delivery month of the same commodity traded on two different commodity exchanges. For example, Chicago wheat versus Kansas City wheat, or New York silver versus Chicago silver.

(3) *INTERCOMMODITY SPREADS.* Long and short positions between two different but related commodities, usually, but not necessarily for the same delivery months, or on the same exchange. Examples: cattle vs. hogs; corn vs. oats; plywood vs. lumber; gold vs. silver; GNMA vs. T-bonds.

(4) *COMMODITY VERSUS PRODUCTS SPREADS.* Long and short positions spread between a commodity and the product(s) derived from it. Best known of this type spread is the one between soybeans and its products, soybean oil and soybean meal. Spreads between hogs and pork bellies also are in this category. The spread is for the same or different delivery months on the same exchange.

INTERDELIVERY SPREADS

For seasonally-produced, completely storable commodities, grains, for example, there are three spreading possibilities:

(a) Old crop delivery months spread.
Example: December '81 against March '82 wheat,

(b) Old crop futures against new crop futures.
Example: May '82 against July '82 wheat,

(c) New crop delivery months spread.
Example: September '82 against December '82 wheat.

SPREAD SCOPE
Commodity Spread Charts

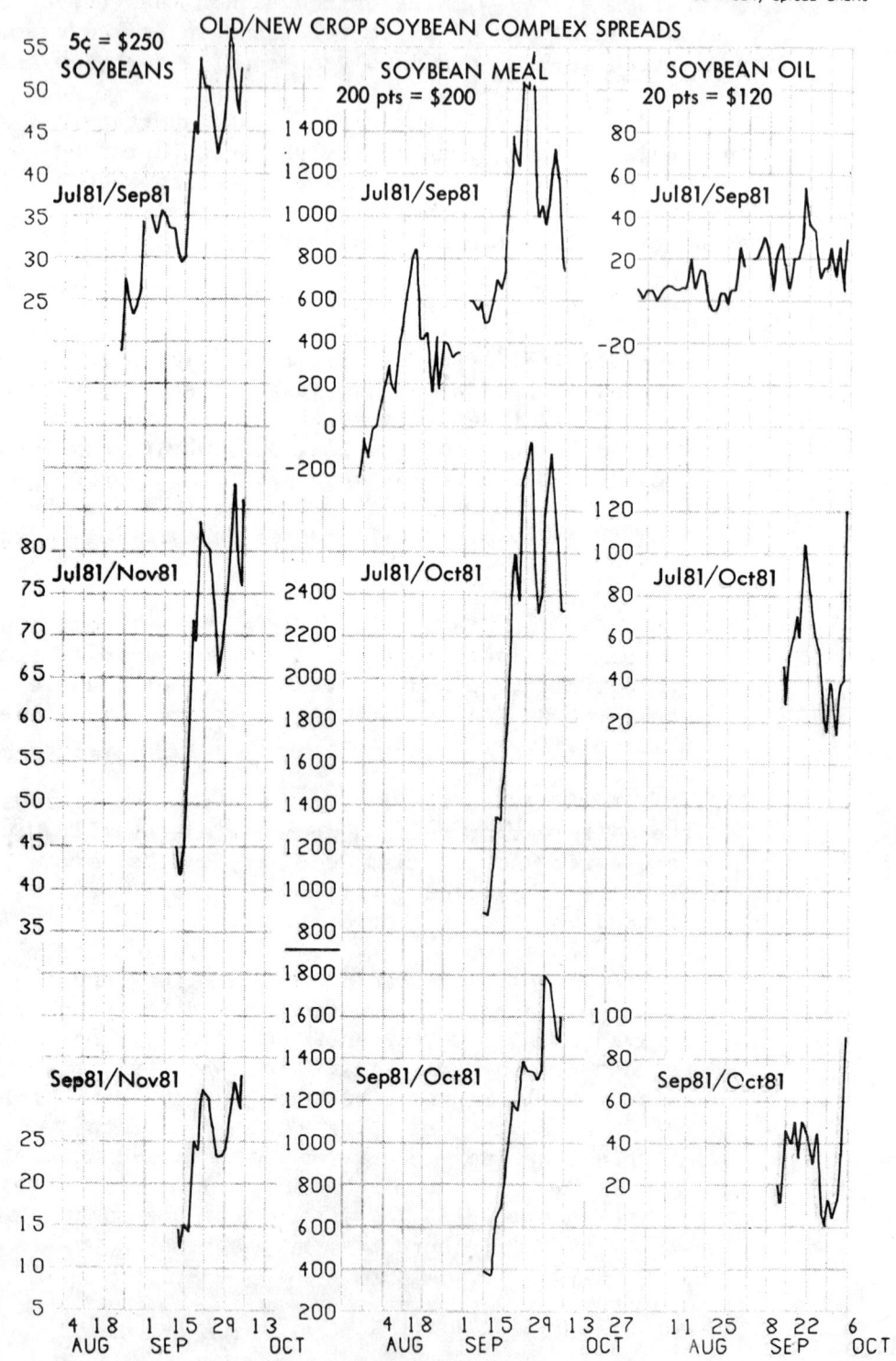

OLD/NEW CROP SOYBEAN COMPLEX SPREADS

SOYBEANS 5¢ = $250
- Jul81/Sep81
- Jul81/Nov81
- Sep81/Nov81

SOYBEAN MEAL 200 pts = $200
- Jul81/Sep81
- Jul81/Oct81
- Sep81/Oct81

SOYBEAN OIL 20 pts = $120
- Jul81/Sep81
- Jul81/Oct81
- Sep81/Oct81

Old crop/New crop spread charts reprinted from SPREAD SCOPE, INC.
P.O. Box 5841
Mission Hills, CA 91345

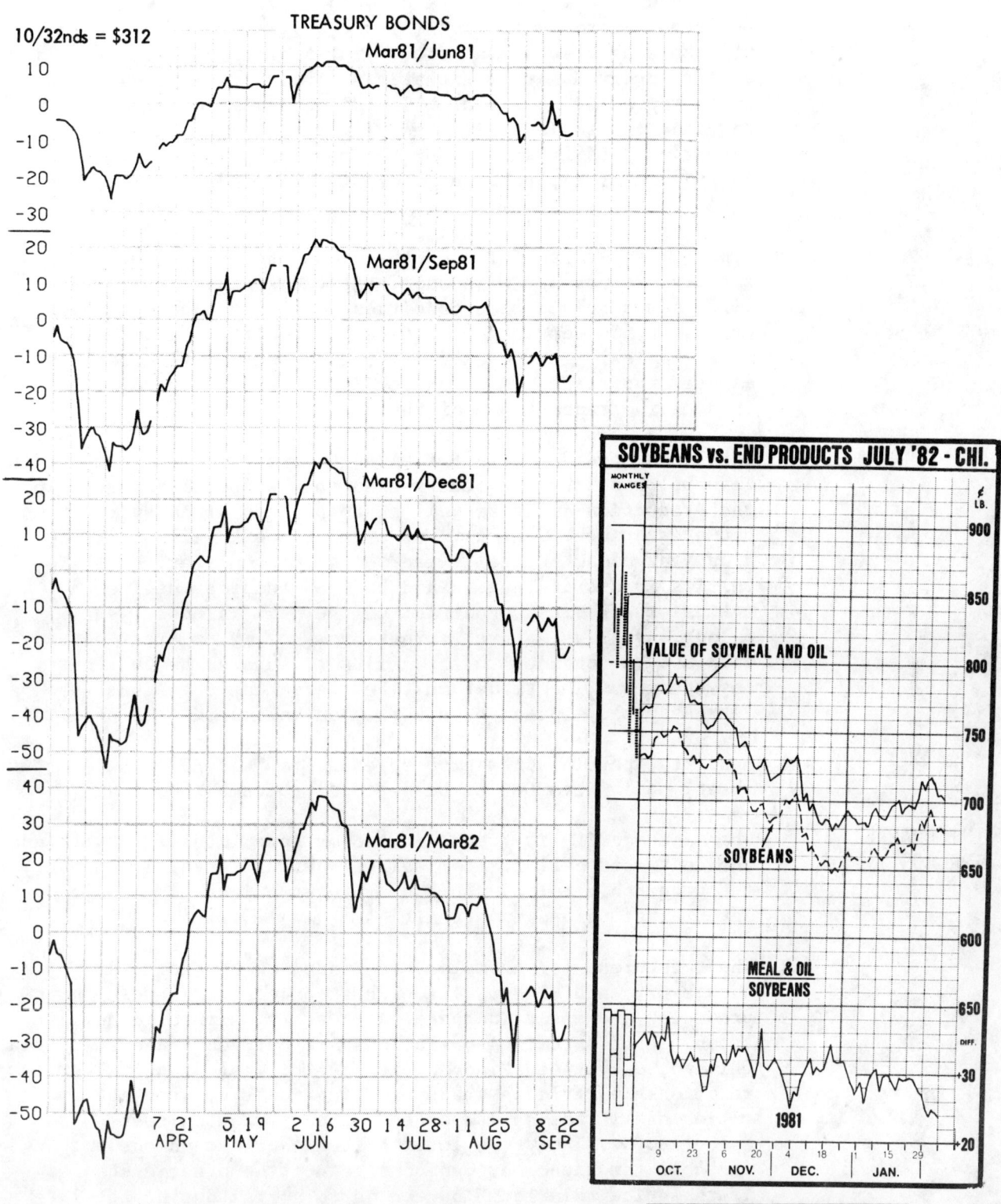

SPREAD SCOPE
Commodity Spread Charts

Above: Inter-delivery spread charts

Charts reprinted from SPREAD SCOPE, INC.
P.O. Box 5841
Mission Hills, CA 91345

CHART REPRINTED FROM:
Commodity Chart Service
A Weekly Publication of
COMMODITY RESEARCH BUREAU, INC.
1 Liberty Plaza, New York, N.Y. 10006

45

Spreads (a) and (c) are also called intra-season spreads. Spreads of the (b) type are also known as inter-season or *intercrop* spreads. Types (a) and (c) include the limited-risk spreads also known as carrying-charge spreads, as well as the inverted market situations already described. It is worth repeating here that while discounts rarely reach full carrying charge level in these limited risk situations, the potential clearly exists for the discount to exceed today's carrying charges, because interest rates and/or prices can rise.

Type (b) spread positions between old-crop and new-crop futures are popular with sophisticated speculators. Since different supply-demand conditions apply to each season or crop year, forecasting of future price differentials is more complex. The possibility of wide market fluctuations exposes the trader to more risk in intercrop spreading than it does in transactions of the intra-crop type.

Intercrop spreads are not limited to crops grown in the soil. Plywood, broilers and others also show seasonal response to the production cycle as well as to periods of in-storage and out-of-storage movement. For example, pork bellies of one crop year cannot be delivered the next crop year. That is, bellies in storage August and before cannot be delivered against the February contract of the next calendar year. A long August vs. short February pork belly contract spread will not be confined to the limits calculated by full carrying charges. The trader must be aware that the August vs. February belly spread puts him in an unlimited risk position.

Among the popular intercrop spreads are March/July Kansas City wheat; July/November soybeans; July/December cotton.

INTERMARKET SPREADS

When a commodity is traded in two or more futures markets and the contracts call for *par delivery* at different locations, the geographic relationship of futures prices may create intermarket spread opportunities.

Wheat futures, for example, are traded on Exchanges in Chicago, Kansas City and Minneapolis. Wheat prices are lowest in the producing areas and increase as wheat is shipped to deficit areas. Most spreading operations are between Kansas City and Chicago, or between Minneapolis and Chicago. A normal price relationship reflects transportation costs between the two cities and if the spread exceeds transportation costs, the speculator will buy the lower priced contract on one exchange and sell the higher priced contract on the other exchange. If the price relationship returns to normal during the life of the spread, the speculator will obtain a profit equal to the price differential above transportation costs. In this situation the commercial trader has an advantage. He does not have to hope for a return to normal relationship in the spread because he has a locked in profit. All he needs do is take delivery on the lower priced market, transport the product to the delivery point of the higher priced market and fulfill his obligation by re-delivering against his short position. Thus, any time wheat quotations in Kansas City or Minneapolis are lower than in Chicago and in excess of transportation costs, there will be traders buying contracts in Kansas City and/or Minneapolis and selling short in Chicago.

Transportation costs are one factor in determining the price differences between these markets. Another is the intrinsic value of the class and grade of wheat deliverable at each market. Kansas City wheat futures usually reflect the price of No. 2 Hard Red Winter wheat. Minneapolis requires delivery of No. 1 Northern Spring wheat. Chicago wheat futures usually reflect the price of No. 2 Soft Red Winter wheat. Each market thus reflects the price of a different class of wheat. These classes of wheat have different uses which make it difficult to substitute one for the other. The soft wheats are used in quickbreads and cakes. The hard red winter wheat is used for making bread and rolls and is primarily an export commodity.

The third factor influencing intermarket price spreads between the three wheat futures contracts is the harvest time. Winter wheat, deliverable in Chicago and Kansas City, is harvested in June and July. Spring wheat, deliverable at Minneapolis, is harvested in August and September. Thus, trading in July means dealing in new-crop wheat futures at Chicago and Kansas City, while July will be still an old-crop futures contract in Minneapolis.

As mentioned before, the original Chicago Board of Trade wheat contract, in operation for about 130 years, is primarily a Soft Red Winter wheat future, which meets the domestic market requirements.

World demand for wheat, particularly of the high protein Hard Red Winter variety, has grown intensely over the past decade. Expanded trade agreements with the Soviet Union and Red China, have created a huge demand for grains. The Hard Red Winter wheat sold to the USSR in the summer of 1972 was the largest grain sale ever by any nation.

To sum up, if a trader believes that price differences are out-of-line between commodities trading in two different cities, he will sell the higher-priced contract and buy the lower-priced one. Popular positions of this type include Chicago versus Kansas City or Minneapolis wheat; New York versus Chicago silver; New York sugar or cocoa against London sugar or cocoa. Note: This type of spread trading does not offer margin advantage and there is no commission advantage either.

INTERCOMMODITY SPREADS

In intercommodity spread transactions, futures contracts on the same exchange for the same delivery month are spread

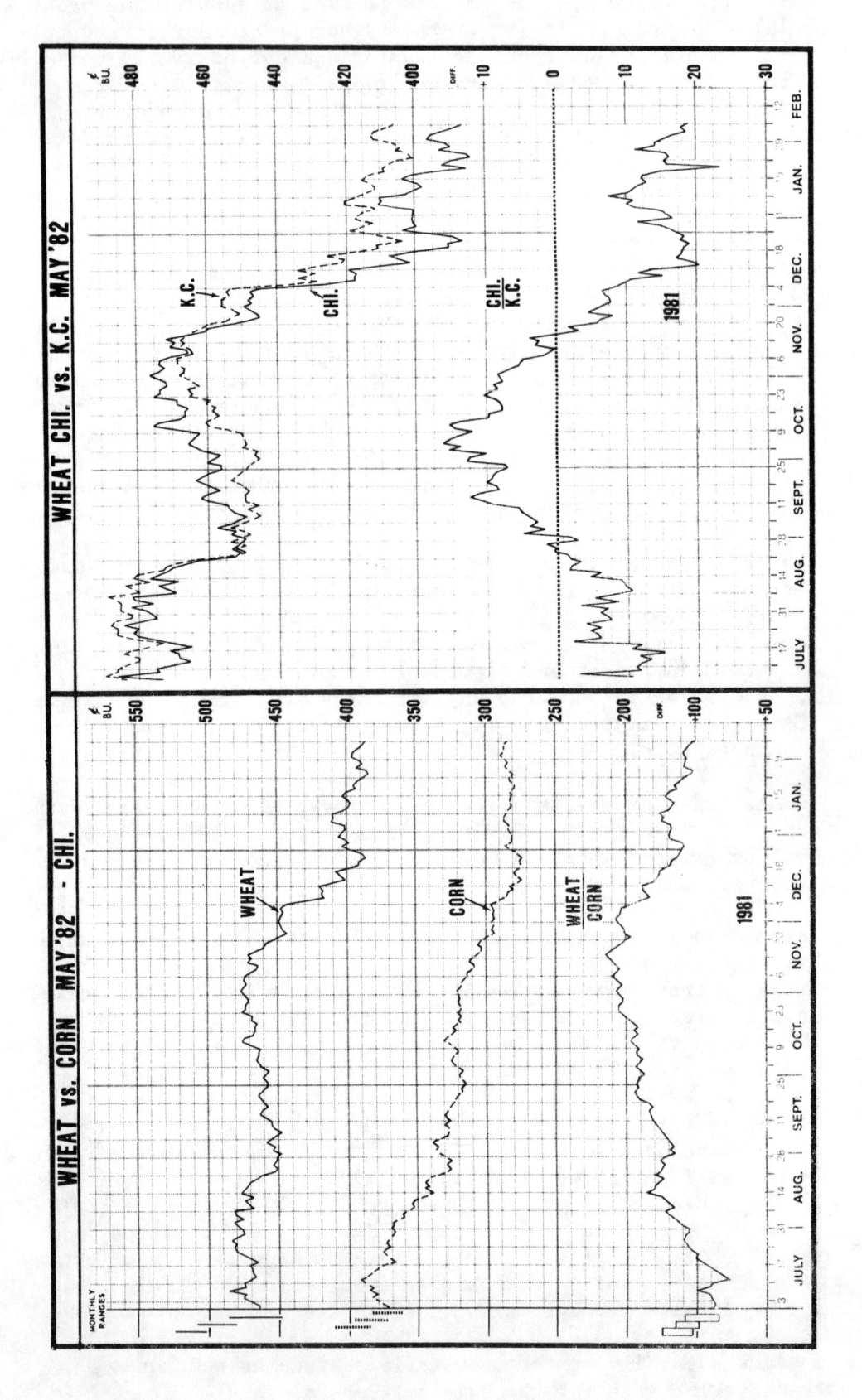

Inter-market spread

Inter-commodity spread

between two different commodities which substitute for each other in usage.

Example: Corn and oats are both feed grains used to feed livestock and poultry. Their prices are closely related because of their inherent physical and economic relationships. A price change in one of these commodities will directly affect the price of the other. As the price of corn rises relative to the price of oats, the use of oats as livestock feed will increase. Even though oats are usually lower in price than corn, this shift in usage will slow the price rise in corn and increase the price of oats. In order to establish that the price difference between futures contracts of such related commodities is out of line, the price analyst must consider the following: A bushel of oats weighs 32 pounds and corn weighs 56 pounds; a pound of oats has 95% as much feed value for milk cows as corn and 85% as much value for beef cattle and hogs. The trader, therefore, would spread two units of oats against one unit of corn. This compensates for the smaller weight of a bushel of oats and its generally narrower price swings relative to corn.

The price relationship between oats and corn tends to develop a seasonal pattern which must be considered. Seasonal price trends may account for out-of-line price spreads between substitute commodities and result in spreading opportunities for the speculator.

Oats are harvested in July and August; corn is harvested in October and November. Harvest pressure weighs on oats during July and August and may depress oats prices to 50% or less of the price of corn. In this situation the trader will purchase two December oats contracts and sell one December corn contract. While corn is under maximum harvest pressure in November, oats prices, with harvest pressure removed, may strengthen and the price spread between oats and corn probably return to the realistic level of 60%. The trader will then liquidate the spread and profit by the seasonal change in the price relationships. Since this spread would be initiated in August and held through November, the corn situation should be carefully checked before establishing the spread position. Anything that could hurt new-crop corn production, such as blight, or drought, could result in advancing corn prices. If the new crop situation became serious, the spread differential expected by the speculator would widen instead of narrowing, with, theoretically, no limit to where it would have to stop.

The most popular intercommodity spreads are in the corn and wheat markets. Wheat is used primarily as a food grain but, it can also be used as feed for livestock. A bushel of wheat weighs 7% more than a bushel of corn and, per-pound, wheat has about 5% higher feed value. On this basis, a bushel of wheat should be worth 12% to 13% more than a bushel of corn for livestock feeding. If the price differential is less than 12%, the spread trader will buy wheat and sell corn in anticipation of a widening spread.

Wheat is usually at its lowest price during harvest time. Relatively heavy harvest shipment of Chicago (Soft Red Winter) wheat often results in seasonally low prices in July. Since corn harvest occurs in the fall, July is often the seasonally strong month for corn futures and speculators establish their spreads in June, going long December wheat versus short December corn. They liquidate the spreads in November or December.

To take advantage of the low price in wheat during the harvest season, speculators take opposite positions: Long December corn against short December wheat, initiating the spread in March and liquidating in June.

The prices of some grains are more volatile than others. An analysis of the supply/demand situation in wheat, corn and soybeans may indicate profitable spread opportunities during seasonal weakness. If there are indications of a relatively small soybean crop, the beans usually show a larger seasonal price advance than wheat or corn. Thus, spreading long soybeans versus short wheat or corn futures could result in highly profitable spread trades.

The largest quantities of corn and soybeans are produced in the corn belt states of Nebraska, Iowa, Illinois, Indiana and Ohio. In these states corn planting starts early in May and is expected to be completed by May 25. Soybeans are planted in the same states during the second half of May. If prior to and during the planting period the ground is too wet to plant, each day of delay in planting is likely to result in a switch of more acreage from corn to soybeans. If a speculator expects soybean acreage to be increased at the expense of other crops (corn, grain sorghum and cotton), he will sell March of the next calendar year soybeans and expect that the spread premium for soybeans will decrease versus corn. Keep in mind, however, that each day corn planting is delayed beyond May 25 will reduce the yield by one bushel per acre.

MONEY SPREADS

In intercommodity spreading it is important to study the price dynamics of the commodities involved. For example, when pork belly futures make a 5¢ per pound move, hogs might move simultaneously but only 2¢ to 3¢ per pound. Due to the unequal size of the contracts traded, a one-cent move in bellies equals $380 per contract, while a one-cent move in hogs is equivalent to $300 per contract. Thus, such spreads cannot be charted in price differentials of so many points but must be charted on a contract-dollar difference basis.

The soybean meal/oil spread must also be judged in terms of money differences. The dollar value of one contract of 100 tons of meal must be compared with the dollar value of one contract of 60,000 pounds of oil.

In the meat market cattle and hogs keep a steady price relationship for a while but then move wide apart with prices based on changed supply/demand conditions. Here again, pound-for-pound differences in futures prices do not give a true picture to the trader who wants to keep track of equity fluctuations.

Let's assume a trader buys cattle at 70¢ per pound and sells hogs at 50¢ per pound. The spread differential based on price would be 2,000 points (1¢ = 100 points), cattle over. If both contracts moved up one penny (+100 points), the spread differential would still be 2,000 points but the spread trade would show a net $100 profit because 1¢ profit on cattle brings $400 and 1¢ loss on the short hogs nets $300, thus the $100 net profit. The correct arithmetic for calculating money spreads is based on the dollar value of each contract.

```
Buy 1 December cattle @68.95¢  ($.6895 x 40,000) = $27,580
Sell 1 December hogs   @48.25¢  ($.4825 x 30,000) =  14,475
              Dollar value differential:           $13,105
```

Two months later the trader decides to close out the spread:

```
SLD 1 December cattle @65.95¢  ($.6595 x 40,000) = $26,380
BOT 1 December hogs   @49.00¢  ($.4900 x 30,000) =  14,700
                                                   $11,680
```

In this example the trader's assessment of the livestock markets was poor. Both the long position in cattle and the short position in hogs showed a loss. The trade resulted in a loss of $1,425 ($13,105 minus $11,680) before commissions.

Unlike the interdelivery spread, there is seldom a commission reduction for spreads involving more than one commodity. The margin on wheat against corn is as it would be for wheat taken alone, the higher outright margin for either. This, of course, is much greater than in the interdelivery spread, where the margin on the spread is less than it would be on only one side. Some typical money spreads include the following commodities: cattle/hogs; feeder cattle/live cattle; lumber/plywood; gold/silver; bean oil/meal; pork bellies/hogs; bean meal/corn; foreign currencies; interest rate futures (for example, GNMAs/T-bonds).

RAW MATERIALS VERSUS PRODUCT SPREADS

This intercommodity spread involves the sale or purchase of futures contracts in a basic, raw commodity against the simultaneous opposite purchase or sale of futures contracts in finished products derived from the raw commodity. For example, hogs are spread against pork bellies. The most popular spread of this type involves soybeans and its products, soybean oil and soybean meal. The B.O.M. (_beans_, _oil_, _meal_) spread involves three different futures contracts in related

THE CONVERSION SPREAD

but separate markets. Soybeans also are spread against either product - oil or meal.

Soybeans are crushed to manufacture meal and soybean oil. The profit in soybean processing rests on the processor's ability to buy soybeans at less than the combined income from the end products, meal and oil. To minimize the risk of higher soybean prices and lower future product prices, the processor may establish a hedge called a *conversion spread* (also known as a *crush spread*) which involves buying soybean futures contracts in anticipation of future need for soybeans and simultaneously selling meal and oil futures contracts. All this is in anticipation of future sales of the manufactured products. The processor is fairly well protected against adverse price fluctuations due to the tendency of cash and futures prices to move in approximately parallel lines.

Regarding the above, all three contracts are traded on the Chicago Board of Trade. The size of the contracts is: Soybeans: 5,000 bushels, soybean oil: 60,000 pounds and soybean meal: 100 tons. The processor who buys 5,000 bushels of beans against the sale of one contract of oil and of meal can be reasonably sure he has a hedge that will insure a favorable processing margin on futures transactions. This hedge will offset possible losses resulting from unfavorable cash prices at a later date. A large operator will purchase 10 contracts of soybeans against the sale of 12 contracts of meal and 9 contracts of oil. A hedge of this volume and relationship is closely balanced to the actual production of a processing plant.

Soybean processors want to buy beans at a price that will allow a reasonable profit after selling the oil and meal. To determine the processor's margin, the product value over cost of raw commodity, consider that the processor recovers approximately 48 pounds of meal and 11 pounds of oil from each 60-pound bushel of soybeans processed.

Example: January '81 soybeans........ $8.47
          January '81 bean meal...... $250.00
          January '81 bean oil....... $.2650   (26½¢)

To find the value of 48 lb. of meal (per bushel of beans), the $250 (per ton) price is divided by 2,000 lb. which gives a price of 12½¢ per lb. The 48 lb. of meal obtained from the crush would have a value of $6.00. A short cut: apply a factor of .024 to the price of meal: $250 x .024 = $6.00.

To find the value of 11 lb. of oil (from one bushel of beans), multiply the price of oil by 11. In our example: .2650 x 11 = $2.92.

The processor's margin is calculated on the following page...

```
       Value of meal per bushel of beans.........  $6.00
       Value of oil per bushel of beans...........   2.92
                    Total value of products.......  $8.92
       Deduct price of soybeans per bushel........   8.47
                    PROCESSOR'S MARGIN:            $  .45
```

The calculation shows that the combined value of the products is 45 cents more than the price of beans per bushel but it does not include the cost of processing the beans.

There are times when the processing margin shrinks to where there is no profit in crushing soybeans. When the combined value of the products is below the price of beans (negative margin, or minus conversion) one might expect crushing operations to cease. This rarely happens. Instead, the processor initiates a *reverse conversion* or *reverse crush spread*.

THE REVERSE CONVERSION SPREAD

When the price of soybeans is higher than the combined value of oil and meal, the processor will sell soybeans, buy oil and meal futures, and at the same time, slow down his manufacturing operations. Speculators tend to join the processors in this type of operation. The heavy selling pressure on soybean futures combined with the purchase of oil and meal futures eventually will reverse the price relationship.

In the cash market, meanwhile, the slowdown in crushing operations will tend to reduce demand and weaken soybean prices. It must follow that the decline in manufacturing will lead to reduced oil and meal stocks and result in higher prices for these products. Thus, the cash markets and futures markets work together to create a price readjustment to the point where the processing margin is once again favorable.

SPREAD CLASSIFICATION

All spread positions are variations of the two basic ones: bull-market spreads and bear-market spreads. The two differ by whether the near month is a long or a short position.

BULL-MARKET SPREADS. In a bull, or upward moving market, nearby contract prices will rise more sharply than those of more distant months. The advantageous speculative tactic in a bull market, therefore, is to go long the nearby and short the distant month. The bull market spread is better put on in a carrying charge market, one with a normal price structure. As an example, take long March vs. short May soybeans, when March is selling 15 cents under May and the full carrying charge is calculated to be 35 cents. This spread would have a maximum risk of 20 cents or $1,000 per contract if the spread widened to full carry. On the other hand, the spread could narrow considerably... not merely to even money, but the nearby March could go to a premium over the distant May.

BEAR-MARKET SPREADS. During a bear market the knowledgeable trader will put on the opposite of a bull spread; he will go short the nearby and long the more distant contract month. The spread trader anticipates the nearby price will fall faster than the distant month's price and this will bring about a widening of the spread to yield a profit. Bear spreads must be handled with care. Their profit potential is limited by the carrying charges but the loss potential is unlimited and can skyrocket. If a trader makes a false appraisal of the market and the nearby short rises faster than the distant long position, the spread will continue to narrow. This trader must use a stop-loss order to protect himself in the event he has guessed wrong.

Note: As a general rule, nearby contracts of a given commodity will tend to gain on distants in a bull market and to lose against distants in a bear market. Commodities which tend to follow this rule include wheat, corn, oats, soybeans, bean oil, bean meal, frozen orange juice and pork bellies.

Other commodities: potatoes, precious metals and currencies have a reversed relationship to the above. In these others the spreads widen in bull markets and narrow in bear markets. For the commodities which do not follow the general rule a long deferred versus a short nearby spread is a good substitute for an outright long position.

ANALYSIS OF SPREADS

The spread trader must be aware of the five components of spread analysis:

1) **LONG-TERM PRICE RELATIONSHIPS:** Regardless of the price level of the commodity, there is a tendency for spreads to find support and resistance at certain price differentials. Historical (long-term) spread chart collections are available and listed in the bibliography.

2) **FUNDAMENTAL CONSIDERATIONS:** Supply/demand data, both historical and current, paint the broad picture.

3) **SEASONAL TENDENCIES:** Powerful trend factors in the market. Futures markets show seasonal price trends that have recurred 80% or more of the time. Knowledgeable traders have the odds for profit with them because they will not trade against the seasonals, not unless they know of influences equally powerful and contra-seasonal.

4) **CURRENT EVENTS:** Things will happen in the news which override well established seasonal trends. A trade embargo for example, or a large Soviet or Chinese grain purchase could well be the catalyst for contra-seasonal behavior. A trader must be in close touch with current events, and all the other factors which influence the market.

5) **TECHNICAL ANALYSIS:** The art of using past market activity to forecast future price action. Current charts for a given spread provide indications of support, resistance

and trend. These help the trader to pick entry and exit points, as well as to estimate the risk and profit potentials. The details of chart construction and analysis are beyond the scope of this book but numerous sources for information are listed in the bibliography.

HOW TO READ A SPREAD CHART

Spread charts depict the price relationship between one commodity futures contract and another. The vertical axis of the chart represents the spread value, the price differential in dollars, or cents, or points. The horizontal axis denotes the trading week and month charted. The first contract mentioned in the title of the spread chart is the nearer month. The price difference plotted is the price of the first contract minus the second. For example, December/March '82 in corn means December '81 corn versus March '82 corn. If the chart title referred to a March/December '82 spread, it would represent an entirely different situation: it would then mean a March '82 versus December '82 spread. Remember, when dealing with inter-delivery spreads, that the first contract mentioned informs it is for the nearer month. It says nothing about being the long or the short contract.

In a lumber/plywood inter-commodity spread the dollar value of the plywood contract is deducted from the dollar value of the lumber contract. There are other inter-commodity spreads in which the contracts are different in size and, consequently, the spread charts show the difference between the contract values in dollars. Some examples: soybean meal vs. oil; soybean meal vs. corn; cattle vs. hogs; gold vs. silver and some intercurrency spreads.

Spreads between different commodities, like those above, are known as *money spreads*. An inter-commodity spread, however, such as wheat vs. corn, is not calculated or charted as a money spread because both the wheat and the corn contracts are the same size, specified for 5,000 bushels. Thus, a one-cent move in either commodity is equal to $50 (5,000 x 1¢ = $50).

When the first contract in the chart title is trading at a discount, the price differential is plotted below the base line of the chart. The base line is zero, or even money. When the first contract given in the chart title is trading at a premium to the second one, the price differential is plotted above the base line. For example, in a July/November soybean spread, July is quoted on a given day at 90¢ over (+90¢) if it sells at a 90¢ premium to November, or 90¢ under (-90¢) if it is selling at a discount of that amount to November.
Equally: A February/August pork belly spread refers not only to the same crop year in bellies but the same calendar year, like February '82 versus August '82 bellies. Aug/Feb bellies, however, would refer to an intercrop spread, such as Aug. '82 versus Feb. '83.

To repeat: For the purpose of chart construction the value of

the second contract in the chart title is always deducted from
the value of the first. Which is long and which is short will
be indicated in the text which will inform also whether it is
a bull or bear spread under consideration and whether it is a
limited risk or high risk trade.

HOW TO PLACE SPREAD ORDERS

Market orders, whenever possible, should be avoided. The floor
broker, only human, is apt to give away too much in the price
negotiation rather than let the commission get away from him.
When this happens the fill price is usually more than the
trader hoped to spend, and the profit margin thereby less.

Price or *limit orders* are the most desirable types of spread
instructions because although they give the broker some discretion they, at the same time, protect the trader against
bad fills.

When using a spread limit order the limits are set but absolute
price levels are not quoted. The order must indicate the
delivery months to be purchased and sold, however, as well as
the spread between the two contracts.

Example for inter-delivery spread: Buy 2 July '81 soybeans
and sell 2 November '81 soybeans; July 90¢ over or less.

Example for inter-commodity spread: Buy 1 May '81 wheat and
sell 1 May '81 corn; wheat 170 cents or less over.

Example for inter-market spread: Buy 3 December '80 Kansas
City wheat and sell 3 December '80 Chicago wheat; K.C. 30¢
or more under (or, K.C. 30¢ or more discount).

STOP ORDERS FOR SPREADS

Spreads are calculated on a closing price basis and then charted.
The charts are used to establish support and resistance levels,
trendlines and set loss limiting stops on a 'close only' basis.
In this way the many intra-day fluctuations that would stop out
an otherwise good trade are ignored. Some Exchanges do not
accept 'close only' stops and for these Exchanges the trader's
broker should be instructed to place a regular stop-loss order
at the chosen level and enter the order a few minutes before
the close of trading. If the spread closes on a given trading
day at its stop-loss point or beyond and the broker is unable
to liquidate the spread during the last few minutes of the
trading day, the spread must be liquidated immediately after
the market opens next morning.

TRACKING A SPREAD POSITION

In order to follow a spread position from initiation to liquidation, the trader must set up a uniform and consistent method
for bookkeeping. The trader's concern in a spread is the change
in its price difference. This difference is given in points or
money and always expressed as a positive or negative number.

(a) *POINT SPREADS* involve futures contracts in which the trading units are identical in size, such as the grains which are

5,000 bushels per contract, or 1,000 bushels per mini-contract. A typical inter-delivery spread would be May/July soybeans. Let's say the price difference at initiation of May minus July is minus 9 cents. The fact that the differential is a negative number (-9¢) means that the July contract is 9 cents higher priced than the May contract. If the trader initiates a bull-spread (long May vs. short July) at -9¢ and a week later the spread narrows to -5¢, the trader has a 4¢ profit. At even money he would have 9¢ profit. If May went to +3¢ premium over July as it would in an inverted market, the profit would come to 12¢ (from -9¢ to +3¢). Another trader, one who misjudged the market, and initiated a bear spread (long the distant July versus short the nearby May) in the above example would show 4¢, 9¢ and 12¢ losses, respectively.

(b) A typical *MONEY SPREAD* involves live cattle versus live hogs. Let's say we buy December cattle at 68¢ and sell short December hogs at 48¢. Keep in mind that the cattle contract is written for 40,000 lbs. while the hogs contract involves only 30,000 lbs. We cannot say that the spread between the two commodities is 20¢ and watch whether it narrows to 19¢ or widens to 21¢. The point is that even if the spread of 20¢ remains unchanged money could be made or lost on the spread. A one penny move in the cattle contract is worth $400 while the same move in the hog contract is worth only $300. Assume now that the price of cattle and hogs moves parallel, each up by exactly the same amount. At liquidation the spread between the two contracts would still be 20¢. If liquidation were effected at a 10¢ higher price level, a pound of cattle would be worth 78¢ and a pound of hogs 58¢. But a ten-cent rise on the long December cattle means a $4,000 profit while the ten-cent loss on the December hogs means a $3,000 loss. A net profit of $1,000 will have been made on this spread trade.

The above example shows that the correct way to calculate money spreads is to take the dollar value of the cattle contract at current price level minus the dollar value of the hogs contract also at current level:

(40,000 lbs. x $.68) - (30,000 lbs. x $.48) = +$12,800

The plus sign indicates that at the time the spread was set up the cattle contract was worth $12,800 more than the hogs contract. Later, when the spread was liquidated, the numbers were:

(40,000 lbs. x $.78) - (30,000 lbs. x $.58) = +$13,800

The net result was a profit of $1,000, less commissions of course.

LIQUIDATING A SPREAD POSITION

Assume that the spread under consideration was moving favorably before the position was initiated. From the beginning the trader must set a strategy for liquidating the position should the spread turn against him. If this happens the trader must attempt to conserve capital and exit at a break-even price, the price at which there is enough profit on the spread to pay for commissions. If that is not possible then the spread should be abandoned at the price differential at which it was initiated, which means, of course, the loss of the roundturn commission. If, after entry, the spread closes against the trader for two consecutive days, it is a general rule to abandon it in order to conserve capital. If the entry point or the timing of the entry proves wrong, losses must be taken quickly, without hesitation.

Should the spread prove profitable -if it goes over the break-even point- it should then be permitted to fluctuate without a protective stop until it reaches 100% profit on margin or falls back to its breakeven price. Either way, the 2-day stop protection mentioned above should be reinstated so as to lock in a sizable profit or avoid an unnecessary loss.

With an inter-commodity spread the price action of the more volatile of the pair must be monitored. A stop-loss should be placed for that one more volatile contract with instructions to the broker, if the stop is hit, that the entire spread should be liquidated immediately.

THE TWO-UNIT TRADING METHOD

Spread trading, a method of minimizing speculative risks in commodity trading offers, also, a way to take advantage of extreme market swings and temporary market aberrations.

Trading the limited risk spread with the two-unit method is the most conservative way to participate in big market moves. One spread unit is always liquidated at a realistic, predetermined, profit level. As the spread fluctuates, this trading unit may be reinstated and several round turns made until final liquidation when the nearby future (the long position) approaches maturity. The second trading unit is held for a longer time, waiting for the big move which could occur as the result of crop diseases, weather damage, political decisions, wars, monetary problems, shortages - whatever. Once a major price change occurs, excitement takes over the market and no one can forecast exactly how high it will go. The second trading unit is closed out only when a protective stop is touched which would signal a change in the market's direction. At this point of profit-taking the trader may decide to stand aside, or reverse his spread position by going short the nearby contract and long the distant one. Example: Short March/long July pork belly contracts. But this is now a bear spread with unlimited risk and the trader must protect himself immediately against a crushing loss. He must place a protective stop which will liquidate the bear spread once the old high is surpassed. In a wild market it might be impossible to fill the stop-loss order at the specified price difference, which could be somewhat higher than the previous high. The loss then would be greater than expected.

DYNAMIC SPREADS

Between 1972 and 1974 inverted markets have been the rule; the nearer months selling at a premium to the more distant ones. As long as the strong uptrend is intact, bull-spreads may be established with the hope of profit from further widening of the spread. Trading on charts is the standard method of determining when to enter into and when to liquidate these bull spreads. If the spread is initiated on a news event and does not show a profit within a few days, it should be liquidated. Either the importance of the news item was overestimated, or it was anticipated and already discounted by the market. The change in price difference between delivery months is relatively slow compared to an outright (net long or net short) position, but once a spread trend develops, it is likely to continue. When the bull market ends and the inevitable market reversal occurs, the bull-spread should be liquidated. Perhaps a bear-spread could be initiated and held until a stop-loss order liquidates the position.

The only truly limited risk spread is an inter-delivery spread initiated not too far from the calculated carrying charges which are the loss-limiting factors. Once the spread moves in the trader's favor, the spread narrows. Eventually the two contracts may trade at even money. Then, if due to severe scarcity there develops a very bullish market the near month goes to a premium and the market is inverted. A bull-spread initiated in an inverted market is still a limited-risk situation because there is a theoretical loss limit set by carrying charges. When the trader enters an inverted market he faces a dynamic situation. Perhaps the market has a long way to go up and the bull-spread will be very profitable. On the other hand a market reversal can unwind the inverted market and the trader who initiated his bull-spread late in the game will suffer heavy losses. These high risk situations are referred to as dynamic spreads.

Raw materials versus products, two products which are related, competing commodities, different marketing timings, or subsequent crops of the same commodity can be analyzed in each leg of a spread and set up as dynamic spreads. Many examples can be found among the spread charts in this book.

Dynamic spreading, essentially, is very simple. Fundamental analysis is used to discover the potential for a strong price trend. Once the potential is acknowledged, the trade is set up, either as a bull-spread or a bear-spread, depending on the anticipated price trend. In this type of transaction the trader must develop the flexibility to reverse spread positions quickly upon a market reversal. He must beware of falling so much in love with his spreads that he is unable to reverse them when it becomes necessary. An unemotional decision and quick action are a trader's best protection.

COMMISSIONS

From the trader's point of view commodity trading is not a zero-sum game. If one trader decides to take profits at $400, naturally, on the other side of the transaction another trader must suffer an equivalent loss. Both traders, however, pay roundturn commissions... let's say $80 each and this is where commodity trading stops being a zero-sum game. After deducting commissions, the winner takes home only $320, while the loser is out $480.

With the advent of discount commodity brokers, those traders who plan their own moves, and especially spread traders, now have the option to choose between traditional, full-service brokerage houses and reliable discount firms. At this writing if a full-service broker's commission is $80, the discount broker will charge approximately half of that for the same transaction. On an annual basis the savings accrued by dealing with the discount broker can be considerable. Many commodity traders, however, are willing to pay the higher commission because:

- they receive in-depth fundamental and technical reports,

- they receive regularly the firm's market letters,

- they obtain fast, accurate fills and fast confirmations,

- their idle cash balances in the account are placed in high-interest bearing money market funds made available, sold and/or managed by the brokerage firm.

The basic function of any broker, -traditional, or discount- is to obtain fast, accurate fills. Discounters will never replace traditional brokerage firms but margin requirements and the commissions charged are items of concern to every commodity trader. To compare fee structures and quality of performance, open a second account at another brokerage.

* * *

MARKETS AND SPREAD TRADING OPPORTUNITIES

GRAINS

CORN

The U.S. produces more corn than the total amount from all other countries combined. About 90% of the corn grown in this country is used for fodder, fed by American farmers to hogs, beef and dairy cattle, poultry, and sheep. What remains goes to the corn-processing industry or is exported.

The corn crop year begins on October 1 and extends to the following September 30. The month of October is the principal month of harvest. On the supply side of the equation, weather is a major factor with July and August the critical weather months for corn. Since 90% of the corn is used as animal feed, strong demand for meat and meat-products especially cattle is essential to the demand for corn.

From January to March the price movement is usually flat. The planting period extends from beginning May to mid-June. The upward price move in April, May and June can be attributed to concerns about new crop planting and uncertainty about the size of the total supply. During the fall period as the size of the new crop becomes known and it is harvested, there is usually a strong downturn in the price of corn from the July highs. Active harvesting continues from mid-October to the end of November. The harvest lows in October and November create peak demand for corn. During the winter period prices strengthen from November to January with the post-harvest rally in December the result of heavy commercial buying.

While the strongest influence in grain markets is the growing season, the lack of Great Lakes shipping in winter and the opening of the Lakes in April also exert a strong influence on prices. When the Great Lakes shipping season opens, exports surge. This increased draw on lake terminal stocks during the month of April usually causes the May contract to gain on the July contract.

The above seasonal price movement suggests the following trade:

LONG MAY CORN VS. SHORT JULY CORN

Expected entry into the spread would be late February or beginning March. Suggested entry level: Even money or July carrying a premium to May. Expected exit: During the last week in April. This is a low risk - low profit trade but it is one of the most consistent seasonal spreads in the corn market.

Also popular with traders is the July versus December corn spread. Both contracts are of the same calendar year. This is an *old crop* versus *new crop* spread and July is the last important old crop futures delivery month. The intercrop spread trades during the new crop's planting and early growth period. It is quite reliable and usually the December contract gains on the July contract from the fall into the spring or summer. The spread is set up as

SHORT JULY CORN VS. LONG DECEMBER CORN.

It is entered about mid-November of the current year but only if December is trading at sharp discount to July. One expects to exit this spread late March or during April of the following year. By late March, December's discount is expected to be much less or perhaps December will trade at a premium over July and result in a profitable spread trade.

To avoid any misunderstanding here is an example of this spread: Sell July '83 and buy December '83 corn. Initiate this spread about November '82, shortly after the distant December starts trading and liquidate it late March or in April '83.

The above position can be reversed after liquidation of the previous spread:

LONG JULY CORN VS. SHORT DECEMBER CORN.

Enter: About mid-April (watch for bottom formation in the spread chart).
Exit: About mid-June.

Seasonal tendencies indicate that old crop July corn tends to gain on new crop December during the second quarter of the year. This tendency is reinforced by the opening of the Great Lakes in April.

Note: The July/December corn spread must be watched carefully during the critical month of December. If the spread is not in a downtrend during December, it is doubtful that a typical seasonal move will develop the following year.

***

The December versus July corn spread is a popular interdelivery spread. Both contracts are of the same crop year. For example December '82 versus July '83.

The price differential (spread) between these contracts reflects
1) the size of the existing supplies of corn,
2) the near-term demand for corn,
3) available stocks in Chicago and Toledo, and
4) the cost of holding the crop from month-to-month.

65

SHORT DECEMBER VS. LONG JULY CORN

This spread will be profitable if a large new corn crop is expected, if demand is moderate, and interest rates are high. Since these factors will force corn spreads toward full carrying charges, traders would go long July, shorting December, thus establishing a bear-spread. Corn spreads are seasonally weak going into harvest. July corn has gained on December corn in nine of the last ten years from mid-August until the end of October.

Full carrying costs between December and July (next year) must be calculated and the spread established only if the price differential between contract months traded is 50% or less of full carry. The spread's first objective is to reach 60 to 65% of full carry. The final objective is 70-80% of full carry.

High interest rates increase the cost of holding stocks and work in favor of the bear spread. An early frost scare, rising demand, low or declining interest rates should be considered negative factors when contemplating this spread.

***

OATS

Like corn, oats is a grain crop and used primarily for fodder. The crop year in the U.S. begins July 1, thus, the July contract represents new crop oats.

Unlike corn which is harvested in the fall, the oats crop is harvested in July. The largest movement of oats to market occurs during August, and seasonally low oats prices reflect this. Because corn is harvested later than oats, harvest pressure weighs on oats during July and August and may depress oats prices relative to corn. In such a situation the trader would buy oats and sell corn short. This trade is based on the premise that after harvest the oats prices will become firmer while the later corn harvest will weaken corn prices.

Since this spread would be initiated in August and held through November, the corn situation should be carefully checked before establishing the spread position. The following factors must be considered:

    a) the total supply of each commodity related to the rate of usage,
    b) the stocks at Chicago,
    c) anything that could lower new crop corn production,

such as corn blight, or a drought. These could cause strongly advancing corn prices.

The seasonal tendency of oats to gain on corn has been consistent: about four in every five seasons over the past 20 years.

The trader must remember that a bushel of oats weighs only 32 pounds against 56 pounds for a bushel of corn. Thus, it becomes necessary to spread two units of oats against one of corn, or for still better balance, seven oats contracts against four corn contracts to reflect the greater weight and value of a bushel of corn versus a bushel of oats. The value, as animal feed, is almost the same per pound for either commodity.

An example of this spread: Long two units December oats vs. short one unit December corn. The spread is initiated in mid-August and liquidated in November. A rule of thumb is to buy oats and sell corn when oats sell for less than half the price of one corn. Two units of oats seldom trade beyond 24% over or 15% under the value of one unit of corn.

The seasonal nature of the spread offers the trader two spreading opportunities each year:

1) When oats are approaching harvest in July/August and at the same time corn is entering its critical growing phase, the tendency is for corn to gain on oats prior to or during the oats harvest.

LONG 1 DECEMBER CORN VS. SHORT 2 DECEMBER OATS.

Entry: In April/June.
Exit: July/August

2) The spread is reversed when the seasonal low is near...

LONG 2 DECEMBER OATS VS. SHORT 1 DECEMBER CORN.

Entry: About mid-August.
Exit: During November.

***

WHEAT

Futures contracts are available on several types of wheat grown in the U.S.

Hard Red Winter wheat is the variety most grown. It is raised in the Southwestern and Western states and traded in Kansas City.

Another type, Soft Red Winter wheat is grown largely in the Midwest and traded in Chicago.

Spring wheat is grown in the Plains states and harvested late in the summer. Hard Red Spring wheat is traded in Minneapolis.

Nearly 80% of U.S. wheat is winter wheat; price-wise the strongest contract months in wheat are December and May, and the weakest is July. The March contract tends to be weak for all grains due to constrictions in shipping, the Lakes are closed, and seasonally heavy livestock marketings also tend to depress the grains in March.

The wheat harvest in May, June and July is responsible mainly for the seasonal lows in the cash market during these months. The futures market, however, often makes its low about a month before the cash market. The wheat futures market reaches its peak usually near the end of the calendar year and then, after some sideways movement, begins to drop again the following February.

May vs. July Chicago Wheat

A popular spread of the old crop/new crop type is May versus July Chicago wheat. Here, the speculator trades on the differences in fundamentals and goes long the old crop May and short the new crop July during the summer months. The spread is held until November or later, and reversed when the May contract begins to lose on July. If a tight supply/demand balance develops it will cause May to be in demand and close above July as the May contract approaches maturity.
Note that for the last 11 of 13 years July Chicago wheat gained on the May contract from mid-November to mid-March. To take advantage of this move, the trader goes short May Chicago wheat versus long July Chicago wheat. One would enter this spread in December and exit in late January or early February. If the spread chart confirms a strong bear trend, the position can be held until March or even April.

Another popular wheat spread is:

Short May vs. long December Chicago Wheat.

Early in the calendar year December wheat tends to be heavily discounted but it tends to gain on the May contract as the year progresses. Since this is a bear-spread, the trader must be alert to bullish news events. It is important to note that even when a bull market develops, the spread tends to collapse before the maturing May contract goes off the boards.

The short May vs. long December Chicago wheat spread is an intercrop spread. Both futures are of the same calendar year. Thus, if both futures mature in '83, the spread would be set up during

December '82 and liquidated before the end of April '83.

LONG DECEMBER VS. SHORT MARCH (OR MAY) CHICAGO WHEAT

Both contracts are of the same crop year and, this is, therefore, an interdelivery bull spread. The December contract is of the current year. March, or May, is the next calendar year. Entry should be planned for the end of August and the spread liquidated by mid-December.

Note: In times of booming interest rates, bull spreads tend to widen toward carrying charges. While this spread is, theoretically, a limited-risk spread, the risk is limited by the carrying charges. As a result of interest rate rises, however, carrying charges can increase to the point where farmers will not want to store their grains. This increase in carrying charges is significant for the spread trader; it means that the spread (price differential) can widen further than initially calculated. The December/March spread should be contemplated when:
1) The current spread is a high percentage of the current full carrying charge,
2) Interest rates are high but there are indications they will decline soon,
3) There is the chance of a bull move.

This spread should be protected with a stop-loss order on close-only basis. If the spread deteriorates and the stop is activated, the trader will be out of a small amount of cash and commissions. If a reasonable bull move develops while interest rates come down, the trader can reap large profits with this spread.

***

Wheat provides more opportunities for spread traders than most commodities. In addition to interdelivery and intercrop spreads, already sampled, there are *intermarket* spreads among Chicago, Kansas City and Minneapolis. These last offer trading opportunities when there is unusual variation in the supply and demand of the various types of wheat.

First let's look at Chicago versus Kansas City wheat spreads. Note that Chicago trades Soft Red Winter wheat while Kansas City trades Hard Red Winter wheat. Chicago wheat is used domestically; K.C. wheat is used primarily for export. This intermarket spread is volatile but it has a reliable seasonality. In a bull market Chicago will rise faster; in a bear market Chicago will decline faster. However, in extremely bullish or bearish situations, where a string of daily limit moves occur, K.C. may pull away from Chicago because the daily permissible limit price move is 25¢ for K.C. wheat compared to 20¢ for Chicago wheat.

March Chicago WHEAT vs March Kansas City WHEAT

Seasonally, the March Chicago contract tends to gain on K.C. from October through January. This price strength is a combination of seasonal factors plus export activity. The trader must watch soft red wheat (Chicago) exports and the buying patterns of the Russians and Chinese. Also to be considered is the huge amount of soft wheat available from the European Economic Community, a negative factor for Chicago's soft red wheat. Another negative factor is that navigation on the Great Lakes is closed down in late fall and, thus, Chicago is isolated for months from the export market. Note that if the Russians buy more wheat they will purchase hard red wheat used in making bread (traded in K.C.) and not the soft red wheat traded in Chicago and used for crackers and pastry.

July Chicago WHEAT vs July Kansas City WHEAT

The long July Chicago wheat, short July K.C. wheat spread worked well for several years. When it does not work, the losses are small. In a good year the trader should be able to pick up at least 15¢ in profit. Since two different markets are spread, the broker should be given a discretion of two cents. This will help in putting on and later unwinding (liquidating) the spread. Margin on this, or on any intermarket spread, will probably be charged on one side only (full margin) with full commissions payable on both sides of the spread.
Expected entry: Beginning March.
Projected exit: Second half of June.

Chicago vs Minneapolis WHEAT

Another intermarket spread popular with grain traders is between the Chicago and Minneapolis wheat contracts.

The hard red spring wheat that is traded in Minneapolis is harvested in the late summer and, therefore, tends to lose on Chicago and K.C. wheat futures in the summer. Then Minneapolis tends to gain on the other two from September through next June.

The trader must remember that Minneapolis is a thin market. It is often difficult to set up this spread.

***

WHEAT vs CORN SPREADS:

The most popular *intercommodity* spreads are in the corn and wheat markets. The successful spread trader will consider the demand for each commodity in attempting to determine their relative strengths. Although wheat is primarily a food grain, it can also be used as a livestock feed.

A bushel of wheat weighs 7% more than a bushel of corn, and on a per-pound basis wheat has about 5% higher feed value. On this basis alone a bushel of wheat should be worth 12% more than a bushel of corn for livestock feeding. If the price differential is less than 12%, therefore, the spread trader will buy wheat and sell corn in anticipation of a widening price spread. For example, if wheat sells for a premium of 6% over corn, chances are that feed-grain users will switch from corn to wheat in their feed mix. At this price relationship wheat exports can be expected to increase because foreigners can use our wheat either as animal feed or for the production of flour.

A favorite of long-term spread traders has been

December Chicago WHEAT vs. December CORN.

Because wheat is harvested in the fall, the trade takes advantage of the tendency for both wheat and corn prices to decline during their respective harvest periods.

The speculator would establish the spread in June, going long December wheat versus short December corn, and liquidate the spread during its anticipated peak in October-November-December.

This spread can be worked from a reverse angle. In the spring, with the summer wheat harvest approaching the speculator would take advantage of the harvest low price in wheat by taking opposite positions: Long December corn vs. short December wheat. This spread would be initiated in March and liquidated in June.

***

July wheat is the first new crop future of the coming marketing year and July corn is the last important old crop futures month for the current marketing year...

July CORN vs. July Chicago WHEAT

In early December a trader should look for an opportunity to buy July corn and sell July Chicago wheat expecting a price move in favor of corn until the end of May or early June.

For this spread the seasonal high occurs often between November and February while in the past the low has often come in May-June.

The long July corn, short July Chicago wheat spread is not as reliable as the previously described long December wheat versus short December corn spread. When the July/July spread fails to work the losses can be quite heavy.

COMMODITY:	CORN
EXCHANGE:	Chicago Board of Trade
TRADING HOURS:	9:30 to 1:15 Central Time
DELIVERY MONTHS:	Mch, May, July, Sep, and Dec.
TRADING UNIT:	5,000 bushels
PRICE QUOTED IN:	Cents per bushel
MINIMUM PRICE FLUCTUATION:	1/4¢ / bushel
VALUE OF MINIMUM FLUCTUATION:	$12.50 per contract unit
VALUE OF ONE CENT MOVE:	$50.00
DAILY LIMIT OF PRICE MOVE:	+-10¢
VALUE OF DAILY LIMIT:	$500
FIRST DELIVERY DAY NOTICE:	Last business day of month preceding delivery month
LAST TRADING DAY:	Eight business day prior to end of contract month
CROP YEAR:	October 1 to September 30

COMMODITY:	CORN
EXCHANGE:	MidAmerica Commodity Exchange
TRADING HOURS:	9:30 to 1:30 Central Time
DELIVERY MONTHS:	Mch, May, Jly, Sep. and Dec.
TRADING UNIT:	1,000 bushels
PRICE QUOTED IN:	Cents per bushel
MINIMUM PRICE FLUCTUATION:	1/8¢/bu.
VALUE OF ONE CENT MOVE:	$10.00
DAILY LIMIT OF PRICE MOVE:	+-10¢
VALUE OF DAILY LIMIT:	$100.00
LAST TRADING DAY:	7th last business day of contract month

COMMODITY:	OATS
EXCHANGE:	Chicago Board of Trade
TRADING HOURS:	9:30 to 1:15 Central Time
DELIVERY MONTHS:	Mch, May, Jly, Sep, and Dec.
TRADING UNIT:	5,000 bushels
PRICE QUOTED IN:	Cents per bushel
MINIMUM PRICE FLUCTUATION:	1/4¢/bu.
VALUE OF MINIMUM FLUCTUATION:	$12.50 per contract unit
VALUE OF ONE CENT MOVE:	$50.00
DAILY LIMIT OF PRICE MOVE:	+-6¢
VALUE OF DAILY LIMIT:	$300.00
FIRST DELIVERY DAY NOTICE:	Last business day of month preceding delivery month
LAST TRADING DAY:	8th last business day of contract month
CROP YEAR:	July 1 to June 30

COMMODITY:	OATS
EXCHANGE:	MidAmerica Commodity Exchange
TRADING HOURS:	9:30 to 1:30 Central Time

DELIVERY MONTHS:	Mch, May, Jly, Sep, and Dec.
TRADING UNIT:	5,000 bushels
PRICE QUOTED IN:	¢/bu.
MINIMUM PRICE FLUCTUATION:	1/4¢/bu.
VALUE OF MINIMUM FLUCTUATION:	$12.50/contract unit
VALUE OF ONE CENT MOVE:	$50.00
DAILY LIMIT OF PRICE MOVE:	+-6¢
VALUE OF DAILY LIMIT:	$300.00
LAST TRADING DAY:	7th last business day of contract month

COMMODITY:	WHEAT
EXCHANGE:	Chicago Board of Trade Kansas City Board of Trade Minneapolis Grain Exchange
TRADING HOURS:	9:30 to 1:15 Central Time
DELIVERY MONTHS:	Mch, May, Jly, Sep, and Dec.
TRADING UNITS:	5,000 bushels
PRICE QUOTED IN:	¢/bu.
MINIMUM PRICE FLUCTUATION:	1/4¢/bu.
VALUE OF MINIMUM FLUCTUATION:	$12.50 per contract unit
VALUE OF ONE CENT MOVE:	$50.00
DAILY LIMIT OF PRICE MOVE:	+-20¢ (+-25¢ in K.C.)
VALUE OF DAILY LIMIT:	$1,000 ($1,250 in K.C.)
FIRST DELIVERY DAY NOTICE:	Last business day of month preceding delivery month
LAST TRADING DAY:	8th last business day of contract month
CROP YEAR:	July 1 to June 30
NOTES:	Soft Red Winter wheat (CHI) Hard Red Winter wheat (K.C.) Spring wheat & Durum (MNPLS)

COMMODITY:	WHEAT
EXCHANGE:	MidAmerica Commodity Exchange
TRADING HOURS:	9:30 to 1:30 Central Time
DELIVERY MONTHS:	Mch, May, Jly, Sep, and Dec.
TRADING UNIT:	1,000 bushels
PRICE QUOTED IN:	¢/bu.
MINIMUM PRICE FLUCTUATION:	1/8¢/bu.
VALUE OF MINIMUM FLUCTUATION:	$1.25 per contract unit
VALUE OF ONE CENT MOVE:	$10.00
DAILY LIMIT OF PRICE MOVE:	+-20¢
VALUE OF DAILY LIMIT:	$200.00
FIRST DELIVERY DAY NOTICE:	Last business day of month preceding delivery month
LAST TRADING DAY:	8th last business day of contract month

***

CORN: JULY / DECEMBER

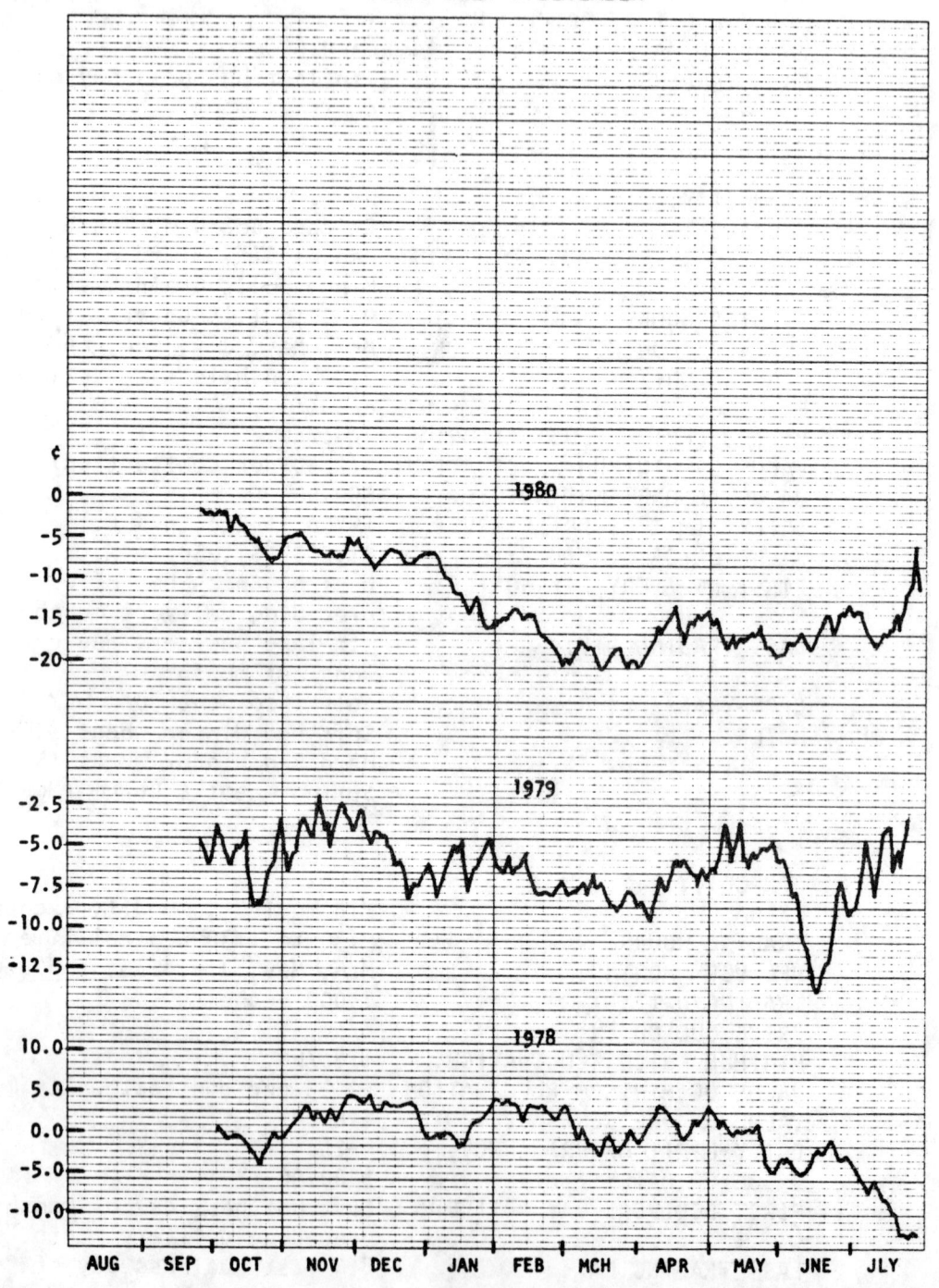

1 December '81 Corn / 2 December '81 Oats

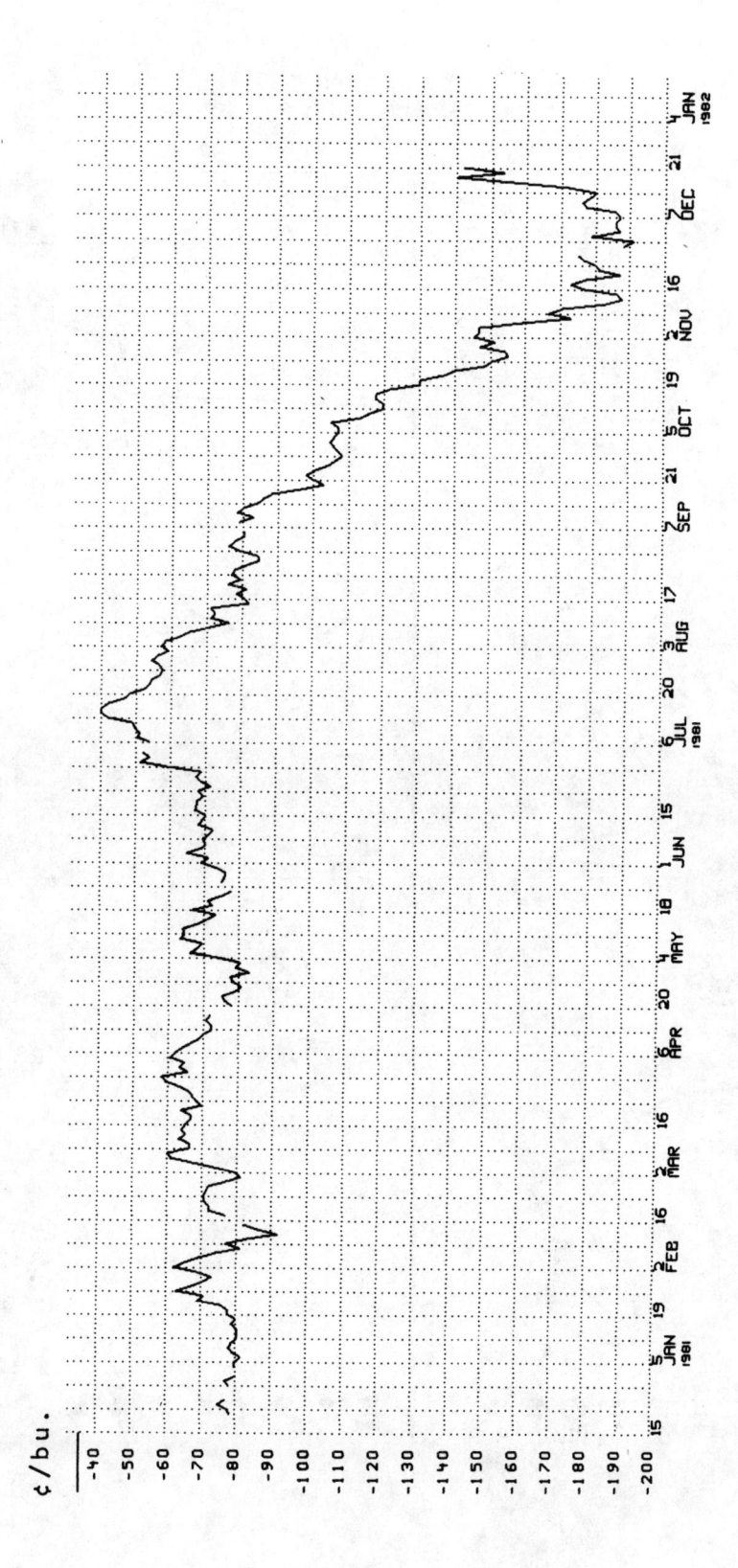

Spread chart courtesy of Spread Scope, Inc.

WHEAT (CBT): MAY 81 / JULY 81

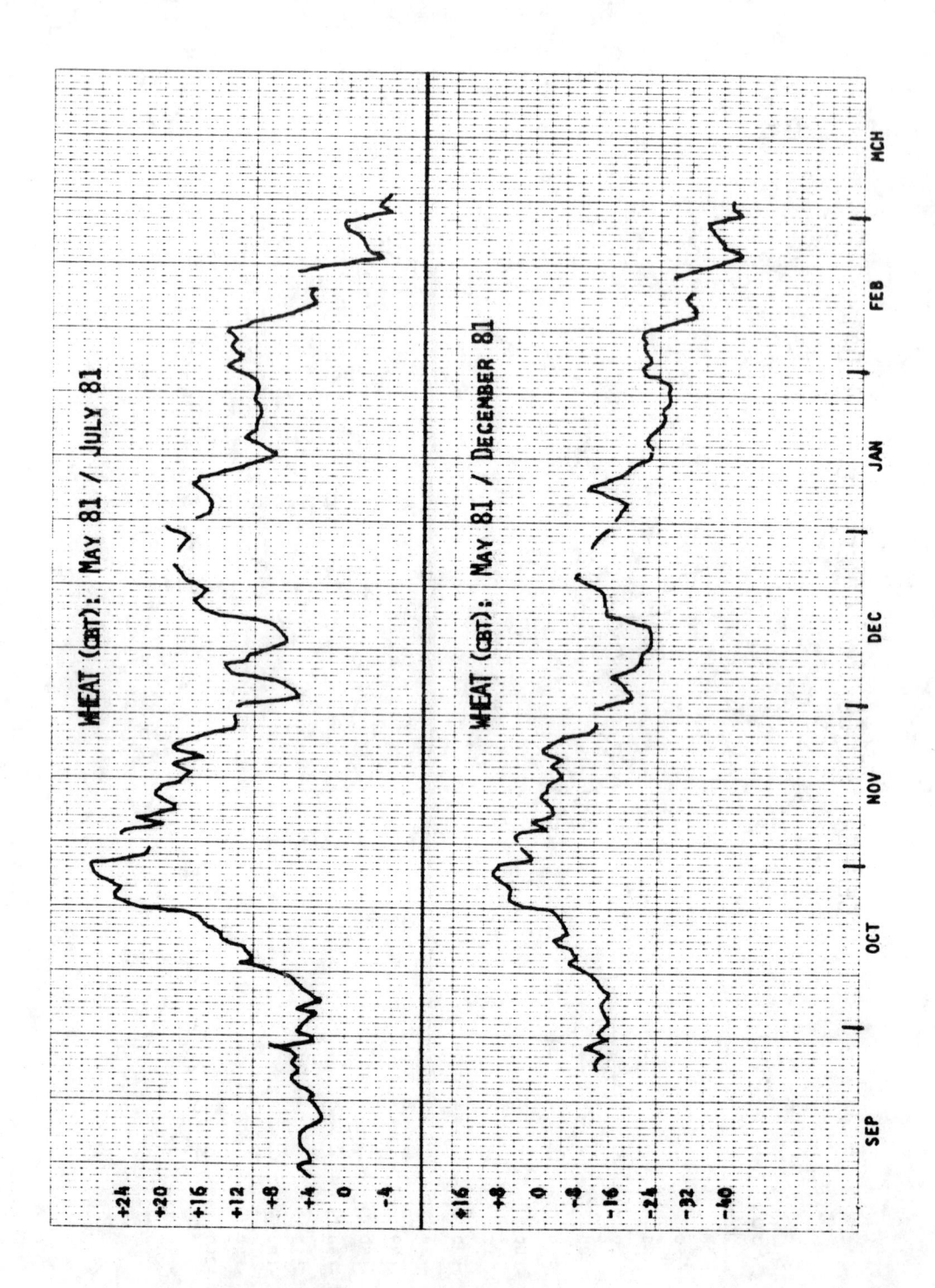

WHEAT (CBT): MAY 81 / DECEMBER 81

WHEAT: MAY / DECEMBER

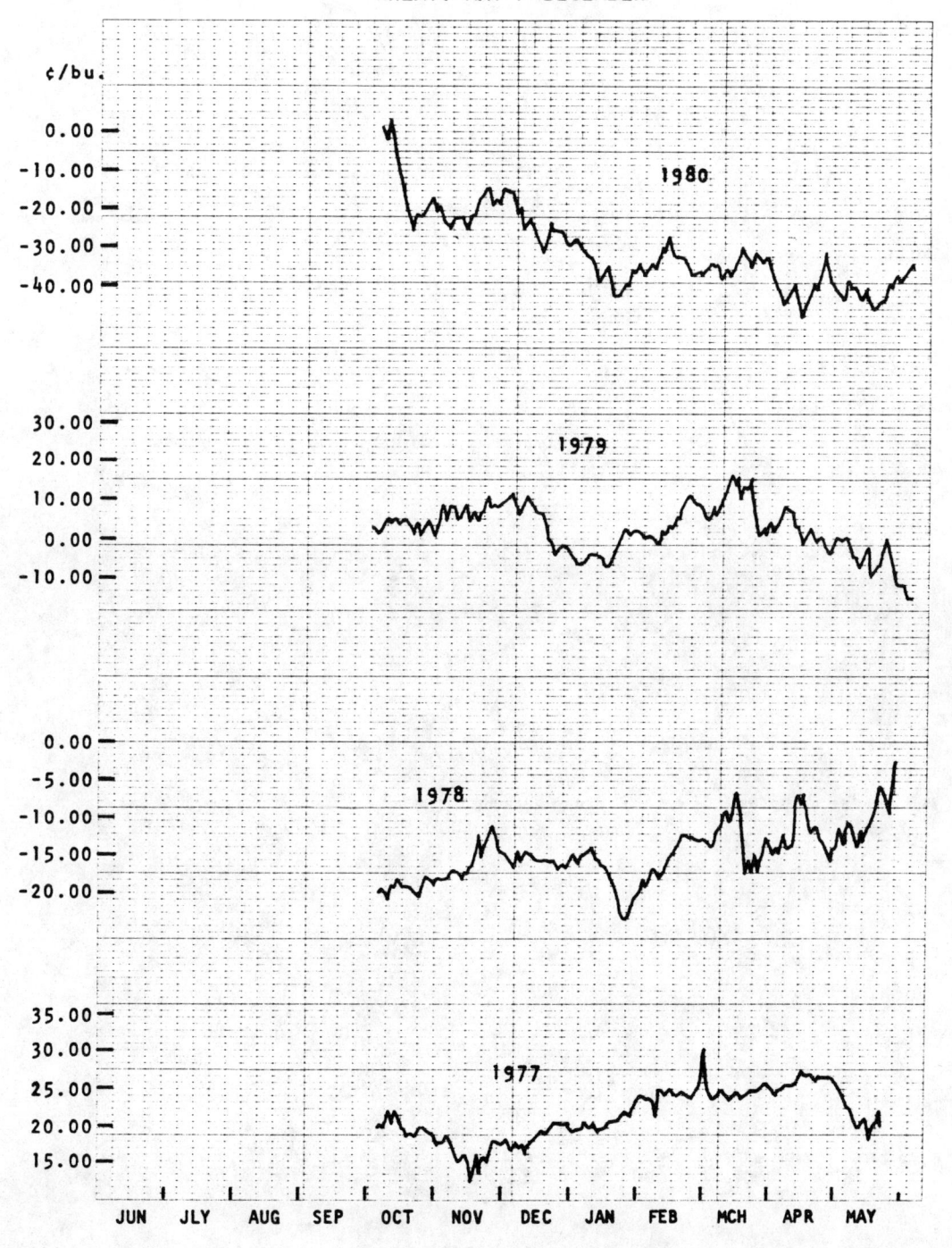

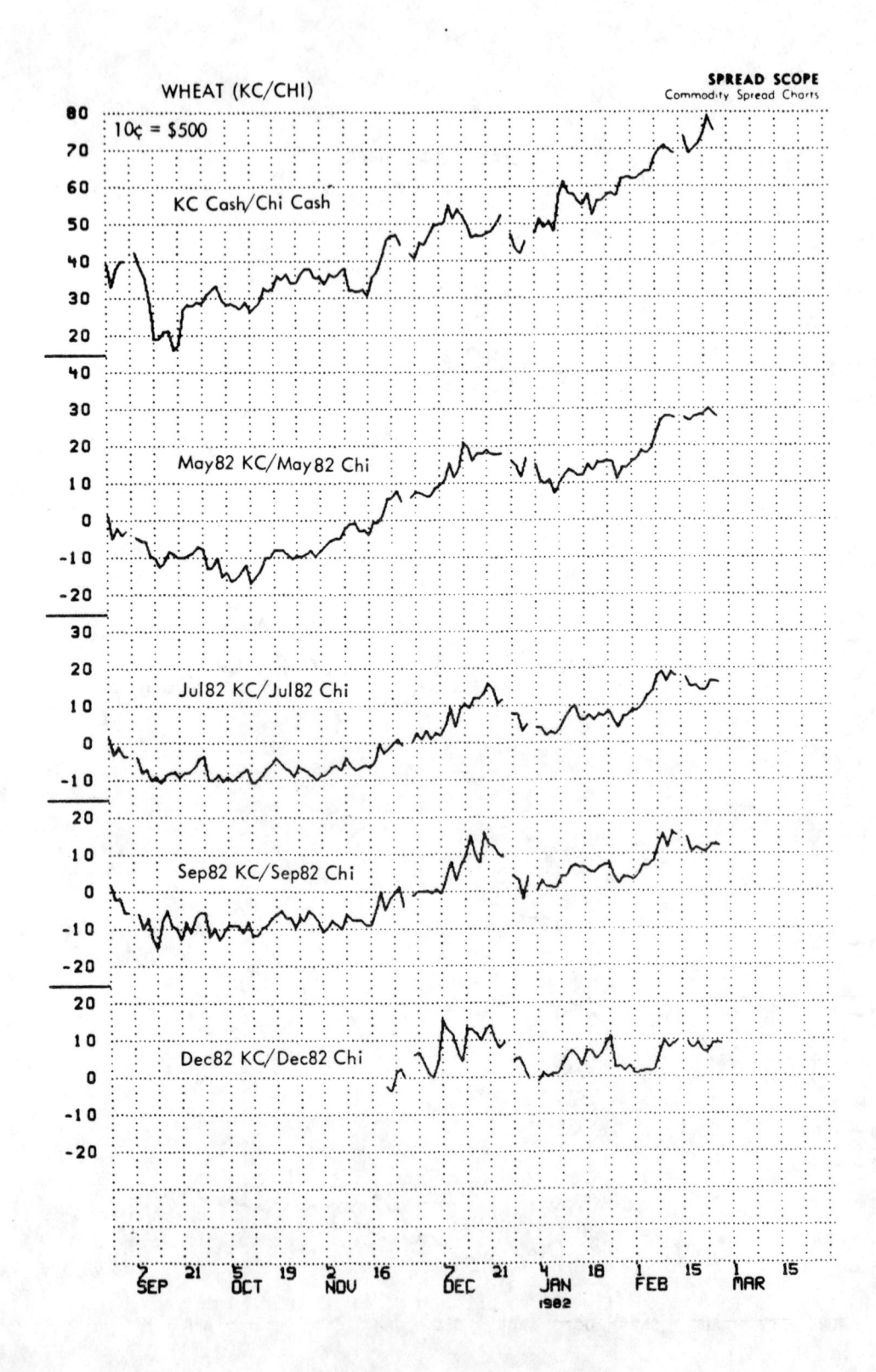

Spread chart courtesy of Spread Scope, Inc.

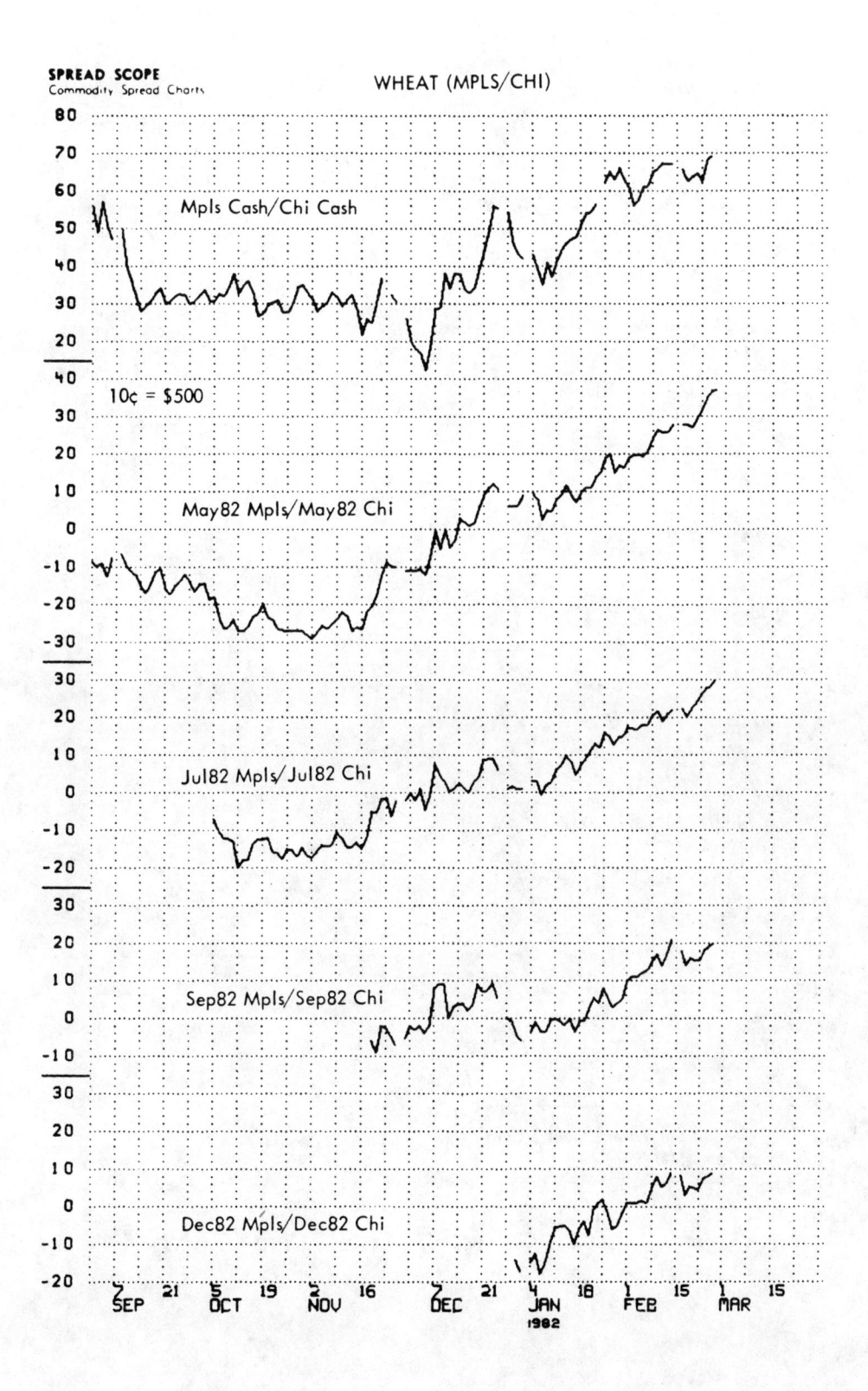

Spread chart courtesy of Spread Scope, Inc.

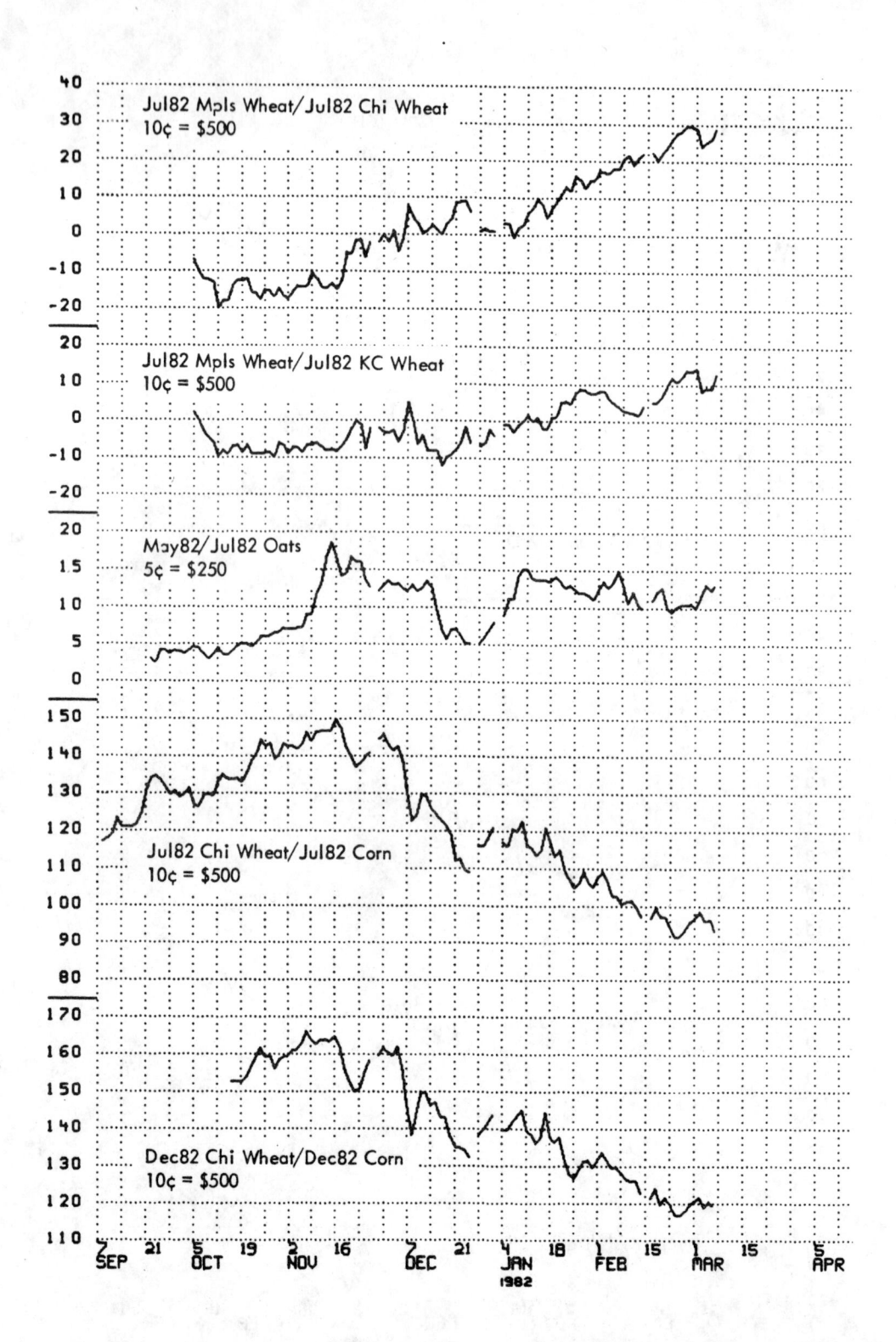

Spread chart courtesy of Spread Scope, Inc.

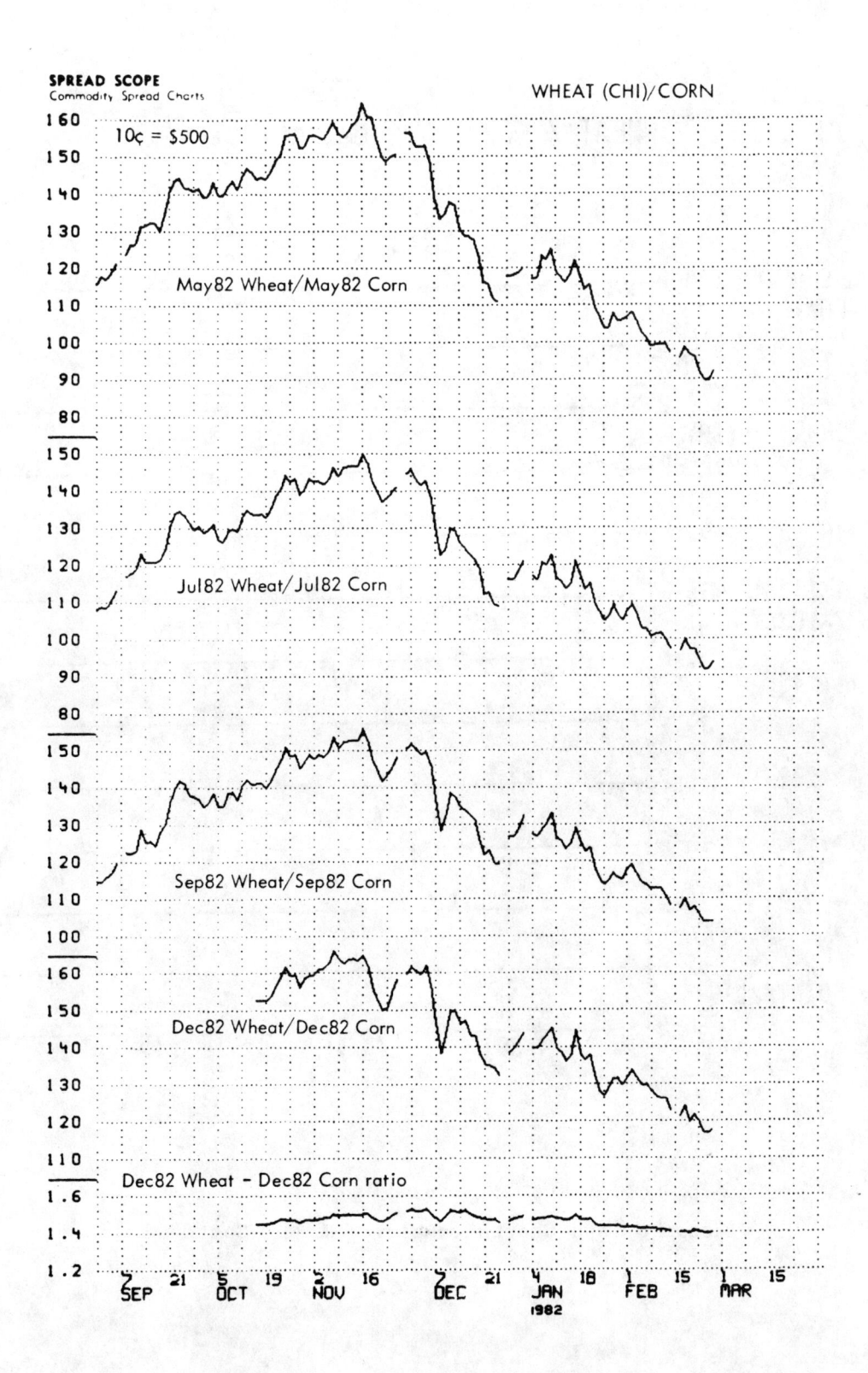

Spread chart courtesy of Spread Scope, Inc.

WHEAT / CORN: DECEMBER 1981

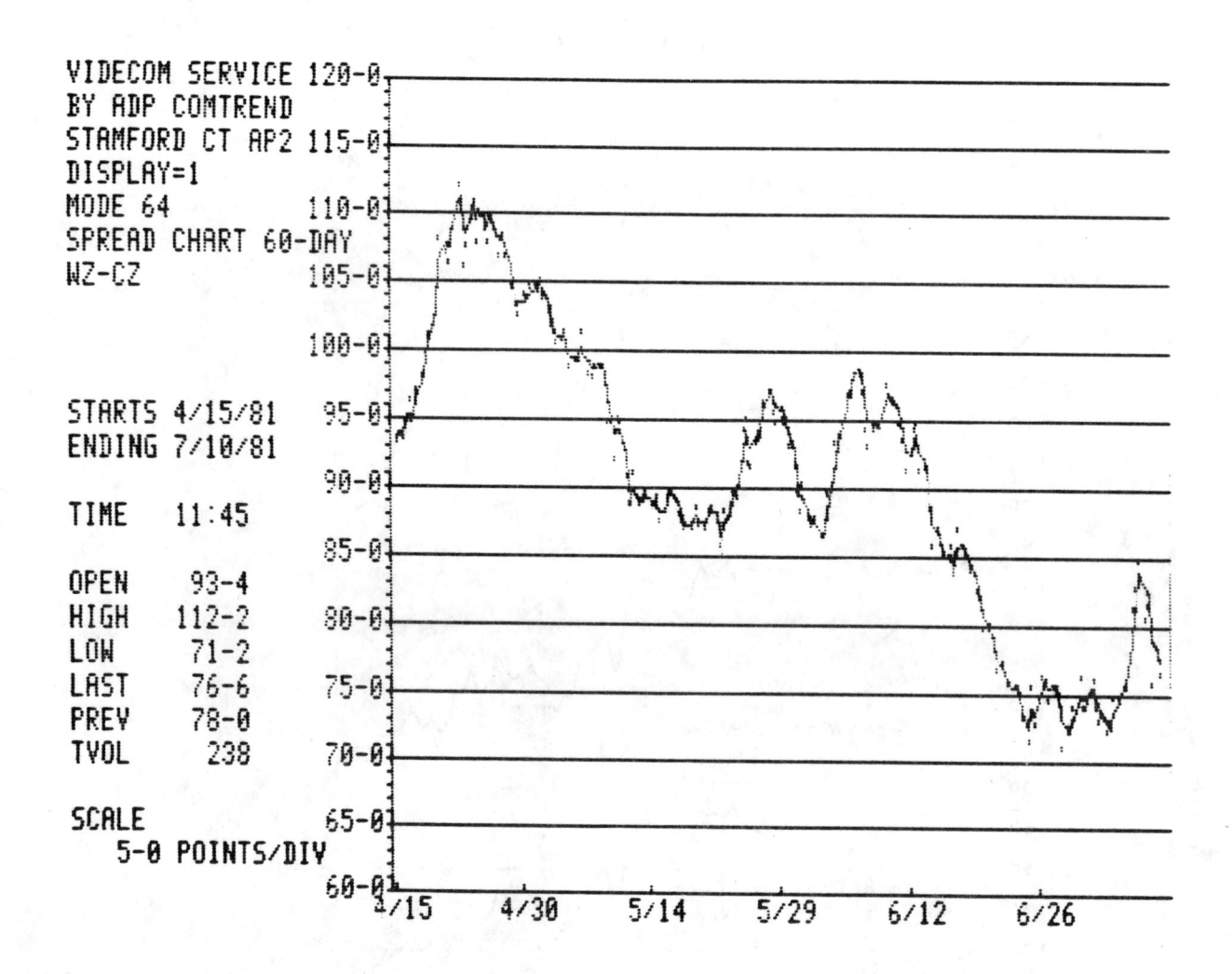

Videcom Spread Charts courtesy of ADP Comtrend.

THE SOYBEAN COMPLEX

SOYBEANS

The world's largest source of edible high-protein meal is the soybean and the United States produces about 80% of the world's output.

Whole soybeans have little utility of their own; they are processed (crushed) to obtain the primary products, soybean oil and soybean meal. Each bushel of beans yields 47 pounds of meal which is used as a high-protein animal feed and 11 pounds of oil, a low-cholesterol vegetable oil used in cooking and salad oils.

Illinois and Iowa are two largest soybean producing states, followed by Indiana, Missouri, Minnesota, and Arkansas. Planting takes place in May and June, and active harvesting occurs in late September or October.

Soybeans follow the classic price pattern of most annual crops, harvest time lows are followed by late season highs. From the harvest lows in September and October, prices tend to rise until April. Note: The bulk of Brazil's harvest is in April. In April and May increased supplies from South America may put pressure on the price of May and July beans. After May, prices tend to peak, the result of uncertainty about the size of the new crop. By July, however, the crop size is known. The three-month period of June, July, and August is an important turning point in the soybeans market. Prices can go in either direction. By August, however, in most years, a reliable bear-trend develops. Prices go down until the peak harvest period in late October. Soybeans, thus, offer excellent opportunities to the spread trader.

***

July vs. November SOYBEANS

This spread involves the July contract for the current marketing year which ends August 31, and the November contract for the next marketing year which starts September 1. This inter-crop spread, where July represents the last major old crop marketing month and November is the first major new crop marketing month, is dynamic and risky but, potentially, it is a highly rewarding trade.

In the event of a bullish crop year July usually rises to a sizable premium over November. In bearish crop years the July contract drops to a discount to November. When the carryover stocks are tight, as the marketing year ends on August 31 (bullish situation), July goes to a premium over November. When there is a large carryover (bearish situation), it drives

July down relative to November. High, or rising interest rates are bearish for this spread and would result in pressure on July prices relative to November.

When interest rates move in the opposite direction of bean prices, the combined effects on the spread may be offset somewhat. However, a violent swing in interest rates, like a 5% change coupled with a $1.00 per bushel price change of beans in the same direction, would result in a nearly 5¢ per bushel change in the carrying charges per month. For the July/November spread, 4 months in duration, this would mean a 20¢ widening or narrowing of the carrying charges. Thus, the influence of interest rates on these spread relationships makes it mandatory for the trader to practice strict money management discipline. He must do this regardless of supply/demand/carryover and other fundamental considerations in the market.

Since even in very bearish situations, the market rarely reflects more than 80% of full carrying charges, the spread trader can look for limited risk situations in soybeans if interest rates hold firm, especially when a near term drop in interest rates is anticipated.

The July vs. November soybean spread can be set up as a bull as well as a bear spread and be profitable in both instances. The spread is first initiated as:

Long July vs. Short November SOYBEANS.

This bull spread is best initiated during the fourth quarter of the year and liquidated in April or early May. Consideration of this spread should begin early in November. If there is a carrying charge there is then little likelihood of a strong bull market. The trader should try to initiate the spread at even money or July showing only a few cents premium over November. If July has a large premium, 30¢ or more over November so early in the season, it is a contra-seasonal indication and the spread should not be given further consideration. The spreader should then await such time as the bear spread can be initiated...

Short July vs. Long November SOYBEANS.

This spread is initiated about the end of May and liquidated on the last trading day in June. This spread is quite reliable.

To recapitulate: For July vs. November soybeans there are two key strategies...
1) In a normal year, when the seasonal pattern works, the bull spread is first set up. It is then liquidated and reversed to a bear spread.
2) In a contra-seasonal year the bull spread idea is abandoned and only the bear spread is used later in the year.

A somewhat less risky and very reliable trade is...

Short September vs. Long November Soybeans.

A low risk bear spread. It should be initiated late May or early June. If entered later it should be at a 25¢ - 30¢ premium September or better. It should be terminated mid-September in anticipation of a narrowing of the spread to even money or a premium November.

The September/November spread is a carrying charge spread within the new crop if set up as a bull spread. Let us say this spread stands at two-thirds full carry. In this case...

Long September vs. Short November Soybeans

could narrow from these levels during July, August and early September. The narrowing could result from:
    a) adverse growing conditions,
    b) a tightening of the basis, or
    c) an easing of interest rates.

Any one of the above factors could cause the September contract, the first new crop month, to gain on the November.

***

SOYBEAN OIL

In relative strengths and weaknesses, soybean oil seasonal prices closely parallel soybeans. Oil demand, however, tends to be fairly constant during the year and is fairly inelastic in price. The market responds, primarily, to changes in supply.

Short December vs. Long May Soybean Oil

A bear spread, initiated in early August by selling December (current year) contracts and buying May (next year) contracts. The seasonal highs are often made in August. The average liquidation period between mid-September and early October when the normal seasonal low period is expected.

Long September vs. Short December Soybean Oil

The September contract tends to gain over the December contract from the beginning of the year until mid-February. In May, however, a sharp reversal occurs. This is a bull spread. Almost every year there is a good runup of September over December oil. The difficulty here is timing.

***

Long March vs. Short September SOYBEAN OIL

In this bull spread March tends to gain on September from early November (current year) until the expiration of the March contract (next calendar year). This trade seems to work only if the October high for the spread is superseded soon after the end of the month. If the spread rises to new highs in November, normal seasonal pattern can be expected. If not, the spread should be liquidated. Often there is a sharp dip in January which can be used to add new spread positions, or to originate the spread if it was not established in late October or early November. Note: the long May vs. short August soybean oil spread has a similar pattern.

***

SOYBEAN MEAL

Because soybean meal consumption is highly seasonal it offers excellent trading opportunities every year. A number of trades have 80% to 90% reliability and, when bull moves occur in the soybean complex, meal moves right along with beans. Soybean meal is a lower risk alternative to trading soybeans.

Since the price of meal is largely determined by the price of beans, the two price charts are similar in shape or pattern. Soybean charts, however, can act as a leading indicator because soybeans may bottom out seasonally in September, while meal will reach its seasonal low in October. The reason for this time lag is that new crop beans, after being processed, will appear on the market as meal during October. Immediately after the October low in meal there is usually a runup in price because commercial interests (meat producers) buy heavily in the late fall, especially if a cold winter is expected. Here, one must remember that soybean meal is a major ingredient in pigfeed. Thus, fewer hogs means less need for meal. Meal, however, is not on important component of cattle feed and a change in the size of the U.S. cattle herd will not be a serious meal price determinant.

Long January vs. Short March (or May) SOYBEAN MEAL

This is a limited risk spread. In eight of the last eleven years January meal gained on the March or May contract from early October to late December. As mentioned before, strong feed demand late fall and early winter results in intensive buying and makes the nearer option gain over the deferred one. This spread is also helped by the prospects of the Brazilian crop harvested during our spring, thus possibly depressing the price of the March or May contract.

High and/or increasing interest rates and high bean prices will prevent this spread from working. Low bean prices and decreasing interest rates benefit this spread.

It is important that in September the nearby month, January, sells at a generous discount to the deferred month, March or May. During the month of October the spread usually turns in favor of the January contract. Then, during the months of November and December, there is usually a strong seasonal up-move in the spread. Meaning January meal gains over March or May meal. The spread is usually liquidated mid- or late-December.

Three important notes:

1) If the spread moves according to normal seasonal tendencies, additional spreads may be entered into once the seasonal turning point in October is confirmed,
2) If there is no upward trend change by the end of October, or if the October low has been violated, traditional seasonal relationship probably will not work during that particular year,
3) The November (!) futures contract must be carefully watched during August-September. If the November contract begins to gain on the deferred contracts it is an advance indication the January/March or January/May spread will work, and the seasonal upmove may begin in late September or early October. This motivates an early entry into the suggested spread trade.

Long September vs. Short December Soybean Meal

Another highly seasonal bull spread. The trader buys September and sells December soybean meal late in January. He anticipates that September will gain strongly over December until the month of May when the spread will be liquidated. This spread has shown a tendency during recent years to top out earlier and earlier. The spread chart, therefore, should be watched for topping action during the month of April.

September/December is considered a limited risk spread but it is still volatile and, thus, quite risky. Immediately after the topping action (usually in May) this spread goes into a sharp decline and this prompts high-risk traders to reverse positions. They will sell September meal and buy December meal and close out this bear spread immediately after Labor Day.

This second phase of the September/December spread is not recommended for three reasons:
1) The spread must be constantly monitored.
2) The original bull spread may reach its peak in May, or April, even in March. Thus, ill timed reversal of the position will

cause either sizable losses or sharply diminished profits.
3) If an unexpected bull move develops it can cause September to run up in price against December, causing heavy losses.

To sum up: The trader will try to find limited risk spread opportunities where the nearby meal contract is selling at a large discount to the deferred months. Bean and meal price levels will be considered together with the interest rate trends. Calculation of carrying charges will indicate how limited the risk is for any contemplated spread.

***

OIL vs. MEAL

Seasonal divergences create spreading opportunities within the soybean complex. For example, soybean meal tends to move up in price during the spring, while soybean oil prices remain fairly steady during the same time. This would indicate long meal versus short oil spreads during the early part of the year and liquidation when meal reaches its seasonal high for the year. Oil/meal spread charts indicate that during the last twelve years this spread hit its high during the month of July. Most of the lows came late in August, and during September and, once or twice even in early October.

Long December OIL vs. Short December MEAL

The trader should establish this spread in July at a premium for meal over oil, as high as possible. The premium of soybean meal is calculated by subtracting the money value of one contract of soybean oil from the money value of one contract of soybean meal. This is an example of a so-called *money spread*, one in which contract values are compared. In case of this spread, if a $1,000 profit on the trade is made we shall say that the meal contract dropped $1,000 relative to the oil contract, or, that the oil contract gained $1,000 in value relative to the meal contract.

For example: On Friday, July 2, 1981, the price of meal was given as $215.00 per ton while the price of oil was quoted at $.2346 per pound. The meal contract is for 100 tons, the oil contract is for 60,000 pounds.
The premium of soybean meal is calculated as follows:

($215.00 x 100 tons) - ($.2346 x 60,000 lbs.) = $7,424.00

On Friday, September 4, 1981, the spread narrowed to $6,008.00 and on Friday, October 9, 1981, it was calculated as $5,972.00.

The margin for this spread will be required, probably, on the meal side (consult your broker), but commissions will have to be paid on both sides of the trade.

***

MEAL vs. CORN

Both soybean meal and corn are fed to animals. Spreads between meal and corn are calculated on the dollar value of the contracts traded. This is another money spread. In studying these spread charts students of soybean meal versus soybean oil and meal vs. corn spreads found a harmonious recurrence of up and down trends. These cyclic price moves should be examined closely back over a period of 16-20 months and trading ranges established. At the bottom of the price range one would buy meal and sell corn; when the spread rallies to the top of the price range one would buy corn and sell meal.

***

THE REVERSE SOYBEAN CRUSH SPREAD

The reverse soybean crush spread has one of the most consistent and strongest seasonal relationships available to the commodities trader. In almost every year for the past twenty, this *raw material versus products* spread has peaked during the November-December period.

Soybeans are not used until they are processed. This involves crushing the beans and obtaining the by-products, oil and meal. A bushel of soybeans weighs 60 pounds, average. When processed, it will yield about 11 pounds of crude soybean oil and 48 lbs. of meal. The one pound remaining is waste, lost in processing.

The relatively constant yield relationship makes it possible to calculate cost versus income by using a formula called Gross Processing Margin (GPM). The formula is a measurement of the difference between the acquisition cost of the soybeans and the combined value of the processed soybean oil and meal.

For soybean processing to be profitable, the manufactured oil and meal must have a combined sales value higher than the cost of the soybeans plus manufacturing. The existence of futures markets in soybeans, oil and meal gives the soybean processor the opportunity to set up a three-way hedge. This kind of hedging is known as "putting on the crush," or B.O.M. (Bean, Oil, Meal) spreads. To hedge, the soybean processor will buy soybean futures and sell soybean oil and meal futures. Eventually, he will buy beans in the cash market and sell his processed meal and oil, also in the cash market.

At times, the GPM can deteriorate to where there is little or no profit in crushing soybeans. At this point the spread between beans and products is very narrow but is expected to widen, eventually. In such a situation the speculator would establish a REVERSE CRUSH spread: buy the products and sell the beans.

The reverse crush spread works reliably year after year because:
1) The farmer sells his old crop beans to meet his June and July bills,
2) During the fall newly harvested beans tend to depress soybean prices relative to the soybean products which remain fairly stable in price during the same time,
3) Brazilian soybean supplies decline during the November-February period,
4) Export demand for oil and meal increases prior to the closing of the Great Lakes,
5) Users of animal feed in the U.S. and Europe accumulate contracts for future delivery of feed and thus support the soybean meal futures prices during the Nov. - Feb. period.

The above listed factors usually cause the reverse crush spread to widen, often to widen substantially - in both bull and bear markets.

The reverse crush is quoted at the Chicago Board of Trade as the value of oil and meal converted to cents per bushel of soybeans minus the price of a bushel of soybeans.

As an example, let us calculate the Gross Processing Margin for August 28, 1981 prices, using the January '82 contracts:

Price of January '82 soybean futures: $6.88/bushel
Price of January '82 SB oil futures: $22.48/100 lb.
Price of January '82 SB meal futures: $198.00/ton

Oil value ($22.48 x .11) = $2.47 per bushel
Meal value ($198.00 x .024) = $4.75 per bushel

Combined sales value... = $7.22 per bushel
Less soybean cost... -$6.88 per bushel

Gross Processing Margin... = $0.34 per bushel

If a trader decided to take a January 1982 reverse crush position on August 28, 1981, the position would have been taken at 34¢ per bushel crush margin.

In the foregoing example the January futures contracts were used because January reverse crush spreads, historically, have made higher highs than March, May or other deliveries.

The reverse crush can be done on a one oil, and one meal, and one beans contract (1-1-1) basis:

One contract of 5,000 bushels (300,000 lbs.) of beans yields:

        55,000 lbs. of oil
      240,000 lbs. of meal
        <u>5,000</u> lbs. of waste
      300,000 lbs. of soybeans per contract.

Since one futures contract of oil involves 60,000 pounds, and a futures contract of meal involves 100 tons (200,000 lbs.), it is clear that a 1-1-1 spread will not give the correct proportions. For practical purposes, however, it is close enough. A better approximation of the correct proportions is obtained by selling ten contracts of beans and buying nine contracts of oil and 12 contracts of meal. Thus, this well balanced, full reverse crush spread involves a total of 31 futures contracts.

Since the reverse crush spread is considered a relatively low risk transaction, the Chicago Board of Trade has reduced margin requirement for it. While the exchange required margin for a full reverse crush spread may move between $2,500 and $3,500, most brokers will ask for deposits of $7,500 to $10,000, or more. A conservative trader would put up a deposit of $15,000, possibly in T-bills or money market funds, which would pay interest to the customer while on deposit with the broker. The round-turn commission could total from $700 to $1,500 on all 31 contracts; it will vary with the brokerage firm.

In the earlier example, on August 28, 1981, the reverse crush was calculated at 34¢ difference. Traders on the exchange floor probably will bid this situation at 33¢ and offer the spread at 35¢. To establish (enter) a position, one would have to pay the 35¢ offer. If we were to liquidate (exit) the spread, we would expect to sell at 33¢.

***

Long January MEAL & OIL vs. Short January BEANS

This spread should be entered at any time after the beginning of June at 30 cents or below, premium products. It would be ideal to enter it at 20¢ and below. If it is impossible to enter the spread at these levels, try to place the reverse crush with the products selling at less than 35¢ over the beans. This should be done, if possible, no later than the first week of September. Risk should be limited to 20¢ from the entry point. The spread should be liquidated late in November or early in December.

The suggested entry points were applicable in 1981. Remember, the crushers broke even at about 25¢ before the oil embargo in 1973. At this writing they break even between 45 and 55 cents because the processing of soybeans more than doubled since the early 70s. Note that crushers deal in CASH prices and, therefore, the crusher's break-even point is calculated on the basis of cash prices! In the reverse crush spread the the deal is in futures contracts and calculations based on futures prices may be below the crusher's break-even point. This does not guarantee that the spread will have to climb up to the break-even level, because cash quotes are often much higher than futures prices.

***

SOYBEANS vs. CORN or WHEAT

Some grains are more volatile in price action than others. Soybeans usually show a larger seasonal price advance than wheat and corn. Thus, spreading long soybeans against short wheat or corn futures can result in highly profitable spread trades during bullishness in grains. An analysis of the supply/demand situation of wheat, corn and beans may indicate profitable spread opportunities also during seasonal weakness.

The largest quantity of both corn and soybeans is produced in the Corn Belt states, Iowa, Illinois, Minnesota, Indiana, Nebraska, Ohio, Missouri and South Dakota. There, the corn planting starts early in May and is expected to be completed by May 25. Soybeans are planted during the second half of May in the same states. If prior to and during the planting period the ground is too wet to plant, each day of delay in planting is likely to result in a switch of more acreage from corn to soybeans. If the speculator expects soybean acreage to be increased at the expense of other crops such as corn, cotton, and grain sorghum, he will buy March corn and sell March soybeans (both of next calendar year) as an example, expecting the spread premium for soybeans to decrease. This spread would be initiated between June 1 and July 15 (current year). One additional factor to keep in mind is that each day corn planting is delayed beyond May 25, the yield will be reduced by one bushel per acre.

***

COMMODITY:	SOYBEANS
EXCHANGE:	Chicago Board of Trade
TRADING HOURS:	9:30 to 1:15 Central Time
DELIVERY MONTHS:	Jan, Mch, May, Jly, Aug, Sep, Nov.
TRADING UNIT:	5,000 bushels
PRICE QUOTED IN:	¢/bu.
MINIMUM PRICE FLUCTUATION:	1/4¢/bu.

VALUE OF MINIMUM FLUCTUATION:	$12.50 per contract unit
VALUE OF ONE CENT MOVE:	$50.00
DAILY LIMIT OF PRICE MOVE:	+-30¢/bu.
VALUE OF DAILY LIMIT:	$1,500.00
FIRST DELIVERY DAY NOTICE:	Last business day of month preceding delivery month
LAST TRADING DAY:	8th last business day of contract month
CROP YEAR:	September 1 to August 31

COMMODITY:	SOYBEANS
EXCHANGE:	MidAmerica Commodity Exchange
TRADING HOURS:	9:30 to 1:30 Central Time
DELIVERY MONTHS:	Jan, Mch, May, Jly, Aug, Sep, Nov.
TRADING UNIT:	1,000 bushels
PRICE QUOTED IN:	¢/bu.
MINIMUM PRICE FLUCTUATION:	1/4¢/bu.
VALUE OF MINIMUM FLUCTUATION:	$2.50 per contract unit
VALUE OF ONE CENT MOVE:	$10.00
DAILY LIMIT OF PRICE MOVE:	+-30¢/bu.
VALUE OF DAILY LIMIT:	$300.00
LAST TRADING DAY:	7th last business day of contract month

COMMODITY:	SOYBEAN MEAL
EXCHANGE:	Chicago Board of Trade
TRADING HOURS:	9:30 to 1:15 Central Time
DELIVERY MONTHS:	Jan, Mch, May, Jly, Aug, Sep, Oct, Dec.
TRADING UNIT:	100 short tons (2,000 lbs./ton)
PRICE QUOTED IN:	$/ton
MINIMUM PRICE FLUCTUATION:	10 cents/bu. (10 points)
VALUE OF MINIMUM FLUCTUATION:	$10.00 per contract unit
VALUE OF ONE DOLLAR MOVE:	$100.00
DAILY LIMIT OF PRICE MOVE:	+-$10.00/ton
VALUE OF DAILY LIMIT:	$1,000.00
FIRST DELIVERY DAY NOTICE:	Last business day of month preceding delivery month
LAST TRADING DAY:	8th last business day of contract month
CROP YEAR:	October 1 to September 30

COMMODITY:	SOYBEAN OIL
EXCHANGE:	Chicago Board of Trade
TRADING HOURS	9:30 to 1:15 Central Time
DELIVERY MONTHS:	Jan, Mch, May, Jly, Aug, Sep, Oct, Dec.
TRADING UNIT:	60,000 lbs.
PRICE QUOTED IN:	¢/lb.
MINIMUM PRICE FLUCTUATION:	1/100¢/lb. (1 point)

VALUE OF MINIMUM FLUCTUATION:	$6.00 per contract unit
VALUE OF ONE CENT MOVE:	$600.00
DAILY LIMIT OF PRICE MOVE:	+-One cent/lb. (100 points)
VALUE OF DAILY LIMIT:	$600.00
FIRST DELIVERY DAY NOTICE:	Last business day of month preceding delivery month
LAST TRADING DAY:	8th last business day of contract month
CROP YEAR:	October 1 to September 30

***

SOYBEANS: JULY / NOVEMBER

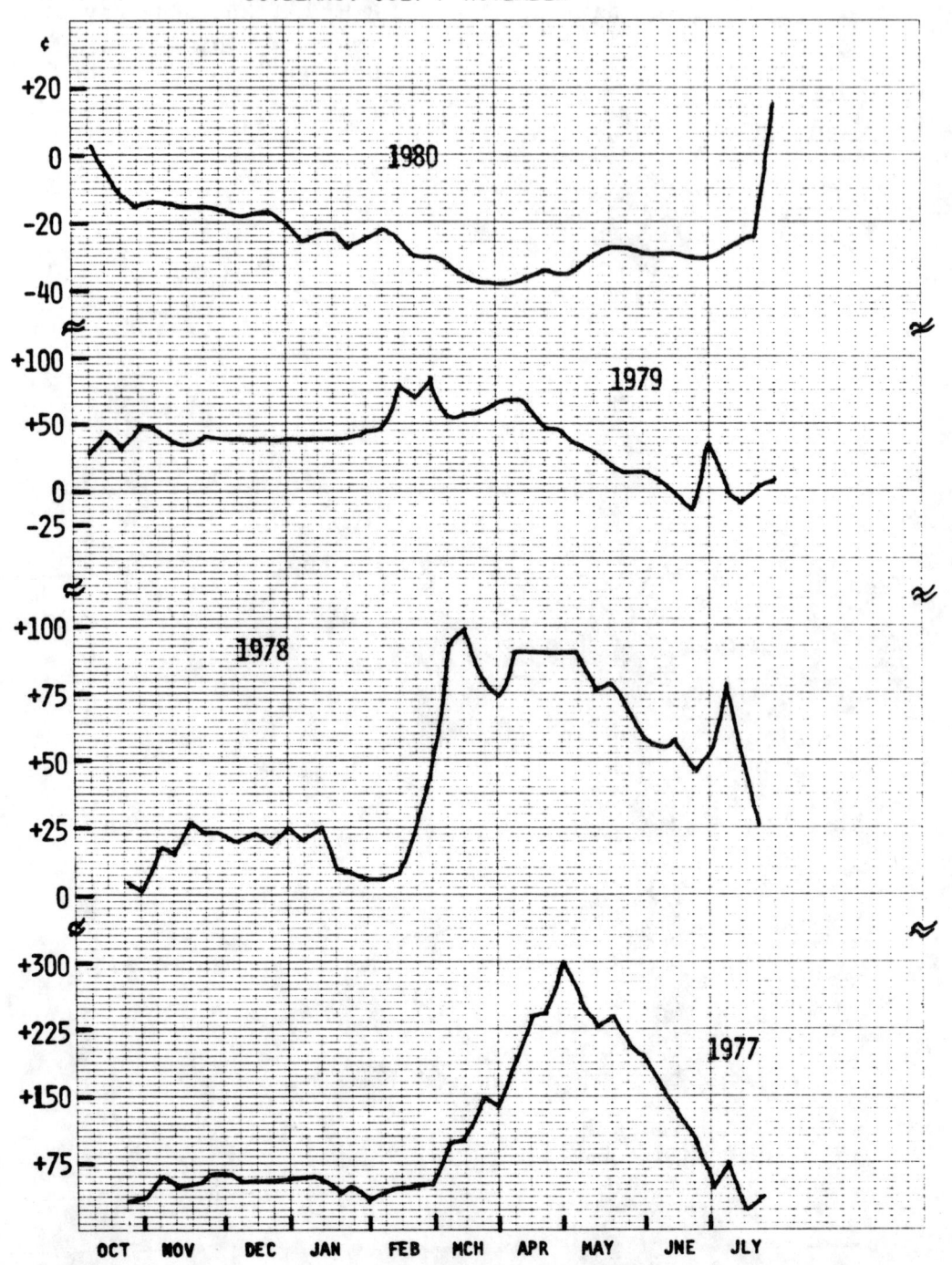

SOYBEANS: JULY / NOVEMBER 1981

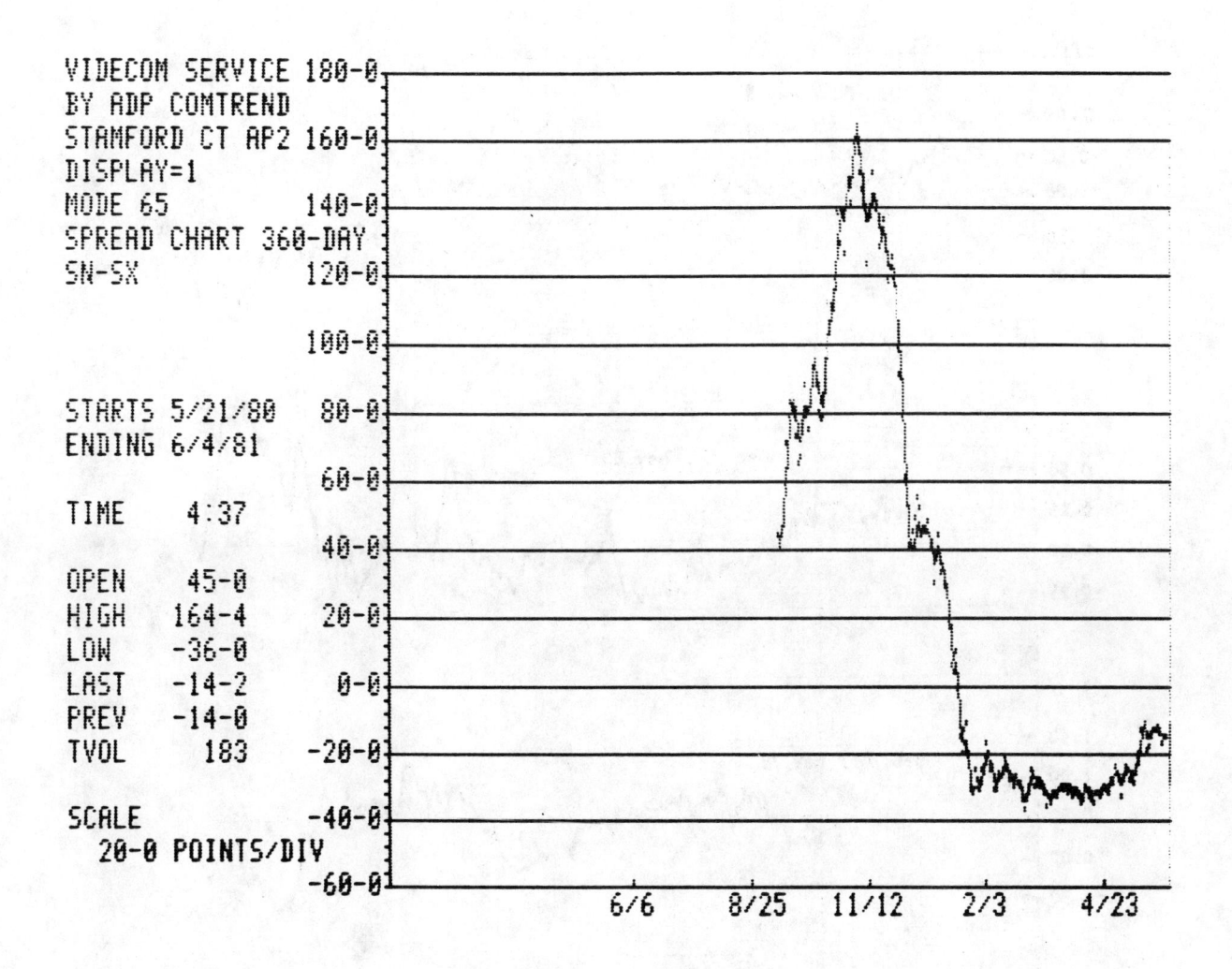

```
VIDECOM SERVICE
BY ADP COMTREND
STAMFORD CT AP2
DISPLAY=1
MODE 65
SPREAD CHART 360-DAY
SN-SX

STARTS 5/21/80
ENDING 6/4/81

TIME      4:37

OPEN       45-0
HIGH      164-4
LOW       -36-0
LAST      -14-2
PREV      -14-0
TVOL       183

SCALE
  20-0 POINTS/DIV
```

Videcom Spread Charts courtesy of ADP Comtrend.

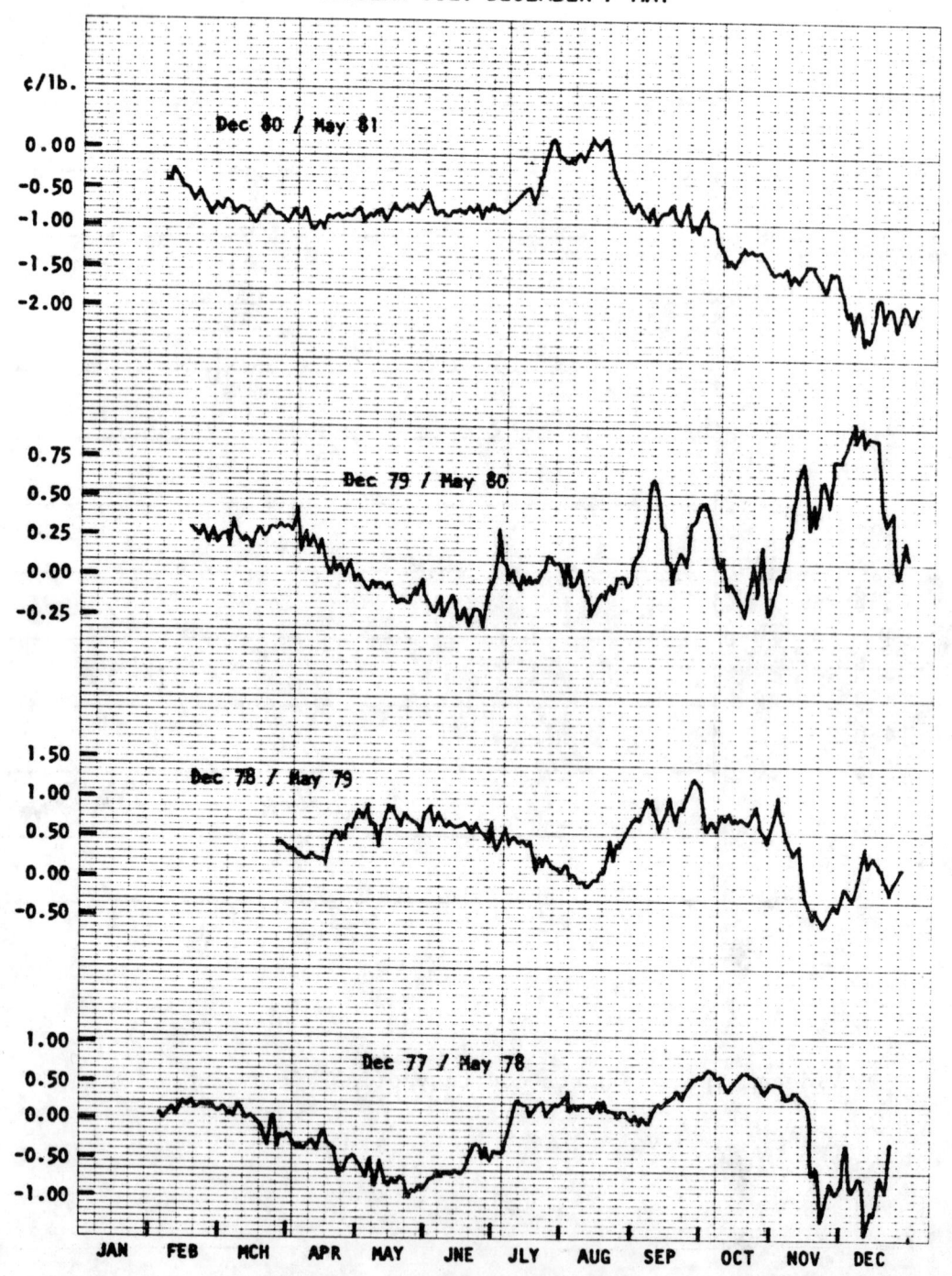

SOYBEAN OIL: DECEMBER / MAY

SOYBEAN MEAL: JANUARY / MARCH

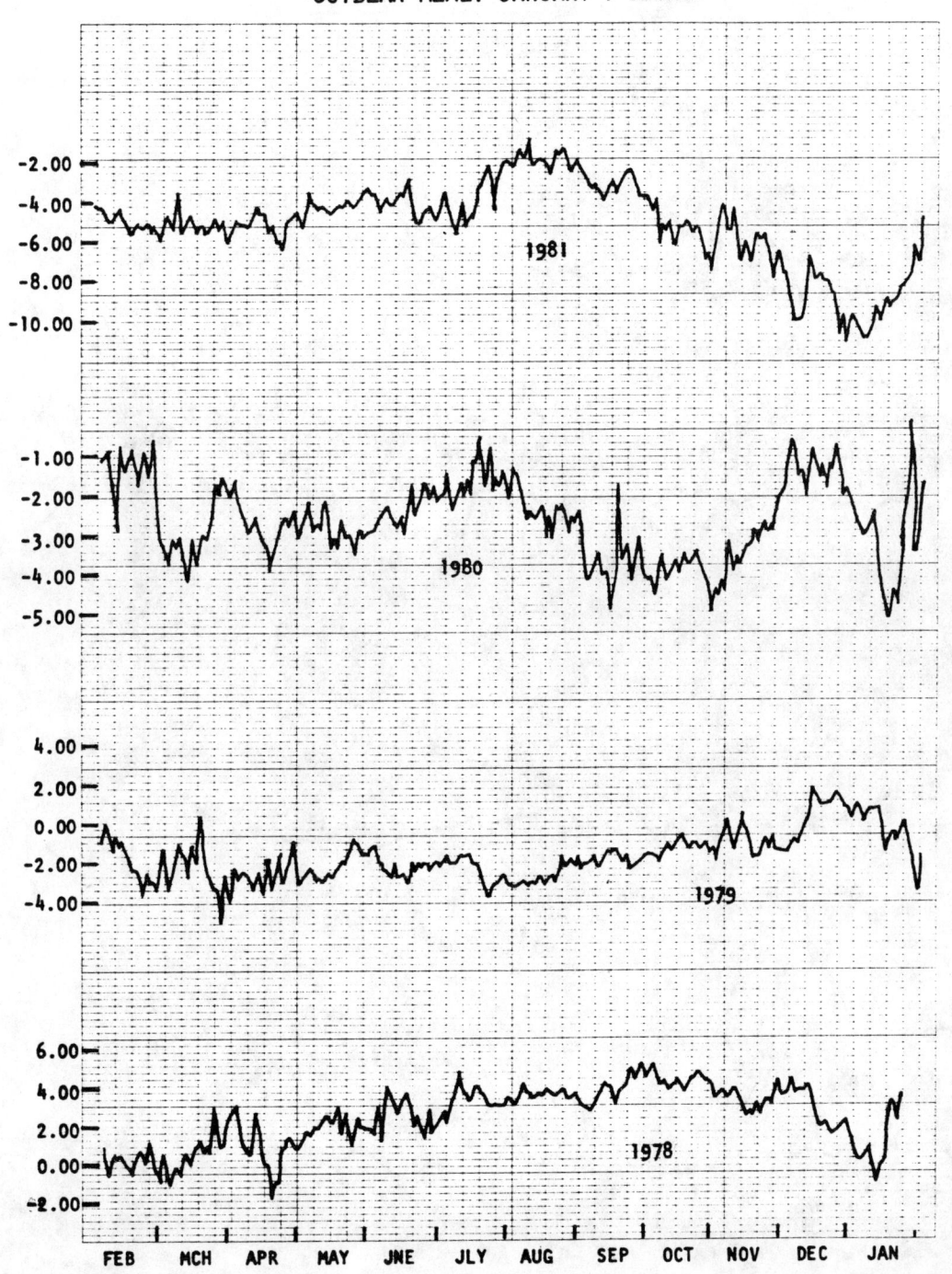

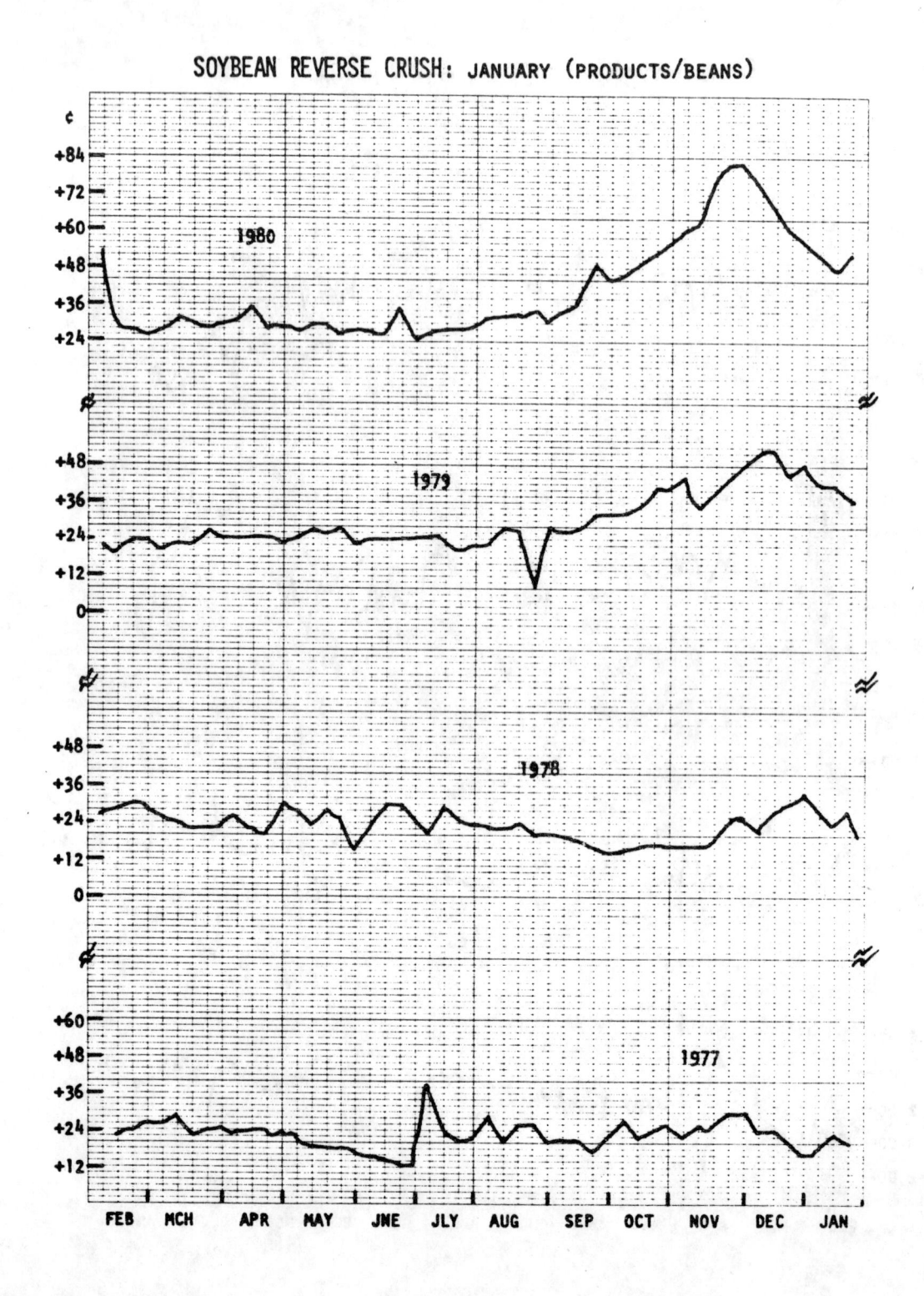

SOYBEAN REVERSE CRUSH: JANUARY (PRODUCTS/BEANS)

SOYBEAN REVERSE CRUSH: JULY 1981

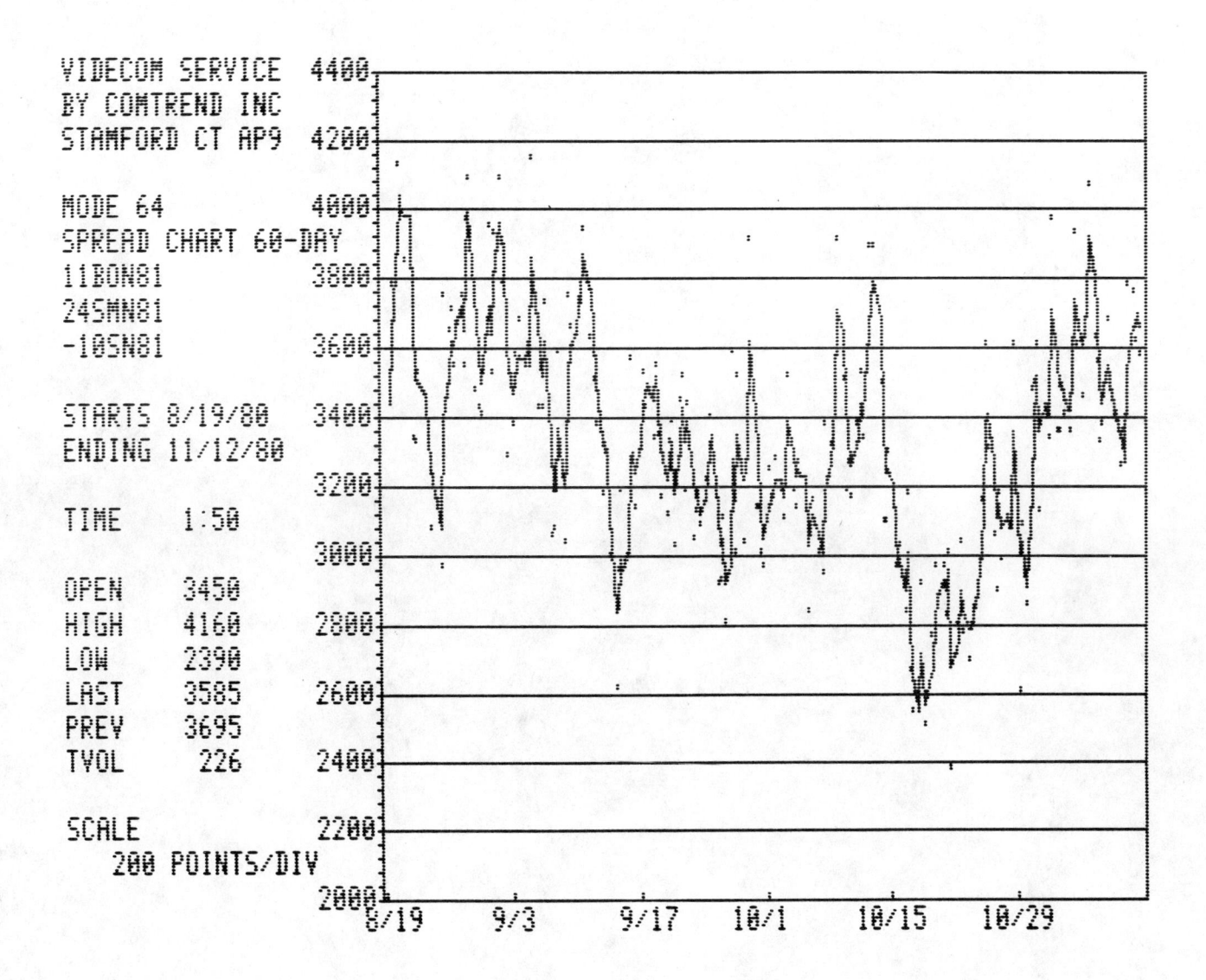

```
VIDECOM SERVICE
BY COMTREND INC
STAMFORD CT AP9

MODE 64
SPREAD CHART 60-DAY
11BON81
24SMN81
-10SN81

STARTS 8/19/80
ENDING 11/12/80

TIME      1:50

OPEN      3450
HIGH      4160
LOW       2390
LAST      3585
PREV      3695
TVOL       226

SCALE
    200 POINTS/DIV
```

11 soybean oil + 24 soybean meal − 10 soybeans.

Videcom Spread Charts courtesy of ADP Comtrend.

101

LIVESTOCK & MEATS

LIVE CATTLE

Live cattle is not a carrying charge market since, by definition, it is a nonstorable commodity. Cattle, ready for marketing in February, cannot be carried into April; the two, thus, are separate entities. Despite that cattle are marketed throughout the year, there are seasonal periods during which consistent profit opportunities offer themselves. Cattle slaughter and cattle prices vary inversely with each other. Slaughter tends to be greatest in the fall and early winter when prices are low, and least in mid-winter and late spring with higher prices. Before entering a seasonal trade, the trader should look for counter-seasonal indications. He must consider not only the yearly seasonals but the longer term factors of herd building, marketing and liquidation. These are known as the cattle cycle. The cycle lasts for about nine years and is independent of agricultural and economic cycles.

Because most calves are born within 45 days of April 1, and weaned within 45 days of October 1, there is good reason to assume that slaughter will have some tendency to peak in October and be at its lowest in February. All other factors being equal, February cattle tends to gain on deferred contracts from November through January. June and August cattle tend to lose on later options in March and April, but they reverse and gain into the summer.

Seasonally, July is the strongest of the cattle delivery months and February is the second strongest. The December contract is usually stronger than October but weaker than the February contract. The April Contract is also weaker than February but may show sudden strength near its expiration date.

Long June vs. Short October Cattle

This is one of the most reliable spreads in the cattle market. One seasonal pattern is for the June cattle contract to gain on October cattle from mid-January until mid-May. When the current cattle market is bullish and the nine-year cattle cycle is in its upward phase, this bull spread can be very profitable by June going to substantial premium versus the October contract, substantial meaning several hundred points. Even when the longer cycle is in its declining phase, June may achieve 100 to 200 points premium. If the spread can be initiated with October at a premium, the trader may look forward to a profitable trade provided supplies are not abnormally large. A milder-than-average winter may cause heavy marketings of cattle in January-February, and bring counter-seasonal lows at this time of the year. With all the caveats, the long June vs. short October cattle spread, when initiated during the first quarter of the year, has high reliability and should be a part of every spread trading program. Once the spread moves in the expected direction and June gains 150-200 moints, the prudent trader will use money management stops to lock in his profits. There has been only one year in the past eleven when after mid-March June cattle did not trade at least a 175-point premium to October. Due to seasonal, counter-seasonal and longer term cyclical cross currents in the market, traders often begin to put on this spread during January and add to the position on a scale down basis in anticipation of the seasonal low during the first quarter.

***

Short October vs. Long December CATTLE

The pattern while similar to the above June/October (or, June/December) spread this one is not as consistent. This bear spread should be put on early in August if October trades at 50 points or more premium over December. It should be liquidated during the second or third week of September, as the October contract approaches maturity. Several times, in recent years, December reached 200+ points premium but conservative traders should begin (at least partial) profit taking when December trades 100 points or more over October. The price collapse of the October cattle contract usually begins in mid-August.

***

Short December vs. Long February CATTLE

When the statistical situation is bearish, it will keep the December contract from gaining too much on the next year's February contract. This bear spread would be initiated in the fall with at least 25 points December premium and added to on a scale-up basis every 25 points. December cattle usually weakens sharply as it approaches expiration and a 150-200 point December discount is not unusual.

***

The December vs. April CATTLE Spreads

Traders sometimes play this relationship first as a bull and then as a bear spread. They carefully watch the spread chart between February and mid-July. If the April contract is between 100 and 300 (or more) points premium over December and a trend reversal is indicated by the chart, they will buy December and sell April. The trend change means that the spread broke out in favor of December. As prices move upward, December can peak at 200-300 points premium by the end of August. Then, if there is another trend reversal, the trader will buy April cattle or next year and sell December cattle of current year. This second spread, a bear spread, shows fairly good seasonal tendency. In three out of four years December cattle loses on an average 200 points between October and the end of November or beginning December.

***

FEEDER CATTLE

Feeder cattle prices reach their seasonal lows during the October-November period. By December, prices begin to rise and tend to rise through February and into April.

The feeder cattle inter-delivery spreads have a similar pattern to those of live cattle but traders prefer the more liquid, live cattle market for inter-delivery spreading. (Note: live cattle is often called finished cattle or fat cattle.)

Frequently, however, feeders are spread against fat cattle. It takes a little more than five months to mature a feeder steer from the feeder cattle delivery date until it is deliverable against the live cattle contract. The most popular inter-market feeder vs. fat cattle spreads are:
    (a) Long May feeder cattle vs. short October fat cattle,
    (b) Short October feeders vs. long February (next) fat cattle,
    (c) Long November feeders vs. short April (next) fat cattle.
Seasonal strength in the spring is used to initiate (b); (a) is initiated during the period of weakness of meats in the early winter.

***

HOGS

The cost of feeding is important in raising hogs for the marketplace. Since corn is the primary feed for hogs, the majority of hog production in the U.S. is centered in the Corn Belt states.

With pork, both supply and demand follow highly seasonal patterns. On the supply side, most of the farrowings (pig births) tend to occur during March, April and May. Since it takes about five to seven months to fatten the pigs for slaughter, the 'spring pigs' are brought to market between August through December. Then, there is a shortage of births during December, January and February and, because of this there is a shortage of production during the summer, when demand for pork tends to be at its highest for the year. From the above we can see that the lowest hog prices tend to occur between August and December. In the December to February period we may see transition of weakness to modest strength but then, in March, hog prices may drop as a result of marketing those hogs which farrowed the previous fall. The month of April is often weak due to pre-planting marketing: farmers dump their excess hogs into the market before they start field work. May, June and July are the strongest period for hog futures because supply is low and demand for processed luncheon meat and bacon is high. Prices may slip at the time of the June Pig Crop Report. The month of October is weak due to pre-harvest marketings. December is the month of transition from weakness to strength.

Many analysts rely on what is known as the hog/corn ratio to predict the direction in which hog production is heading. The hog/corn ratio is computed by dividing the price of 100 pounds of live hogs by the price of a bushel of corn. The ratio tells us how many bushels of corn at Omaha could be bought for 100 lbs. of hogs, but it does not represent the number of bushels of corn it takes to produce 100 lbs. of pork. When the hog/corn ratio is higher than usual, hog feeding is more profitable than usual and farmers respond by breeding and feeding more hogs. When the hog/corn ration is lower than usual, the opposite holds true. Low ratios (below 14) suggest narrow profit margins and low future production. High ratios indicate higher profits and greater future production. As an example, if the price of live hogs is $42 per hundredweight and the price of corn is $2.62 per bushel, the hog/corn ratio would be: 42 ÷ 2.62 = 16. In other words, if the ratio drops below 14, the break-even point, many farmers believe that it is to their advantage to sell their corn rather than to feed it to hogs. Thus, we see, how a high hog/corn ratio promotes herd expansion. Here it must be mentioned that non-feed costs, such as interest rates, have been at record highs recently. This fact increases the necessity of having a high hog/corn ratio as an incentive for hog producers to withhold breeding stock to expand farrowings.

As a rule, ten months is considered the lead time for production of hogs, since a pig's gestation period is approximately 112 days and it takes about six months on feed to bring hogs to slaughter weight. A monthly chart of the hog/corn ratio can be a useful tool for price forecasting. In view of the ten-month lead time, when the hog/corn ratio chart peaks, one expects hog prices to bottom ten months later. And when the ratio chart bottoms, one looks for hog prices to peak ten months in the future.

When the hog/corn ratio is high above the break-even figure of 14, most farmers will come to the conclusion there is money to be made in raising hogs. As a result, an expansion in hog production occurs. Increased pork production eventually depresses the price of hogs. But all this is many months away. Meanwhile, the spread trader must keep in mind that when the farmer decides to expand his herd, he will have to be holding back hogs from the market to retain them for breeding. Since market supplies will be reduced temporarily, the farmers' decision to expand hog numbers will actually turn out to be bullish for nearby futures contracts.

Short April vs. Long July Hogs

This is one of the most reliable hog spreads. It is a bear spread and is entered into before mid-February. Most likely exit is between late March and the first few days of April. The spread reflects the consistent tendency of summer hogs (July futures) to gain on spring hogs (April futures). It should be initiated at less than 150 points premium July, with the expectation of closing out with at least 200-300+ points premium July.

***

Long June vs. Short October Hogs

This bull spread is expected to benefit from rising prices due to high demand/lower marketings as June draws near. It should be initiated between mid-February and the end of March and liquidated during mid-May. June should have no more than 50 points premium at entry, preferably less, and if the spread is available with an October premium (meaning June dips below October) extra positions should be added to those already established. Expected profitability: 200-300 points premium June.

***

Long July vs. Short December Hogs

Similar to the previous spread. Seasonally, because of the low slaughter, July is one of the strongest months in both the cash and futures markets. Enter the spread after the March Hogs and Pig Report and liquidate this bull spread beginning July.

***

Long February vs. Short April Hogs

Hog supplies are reduced during the early winter months because of lower farrowings during the hottest part of the summer.

February hogs are expected to gain on April hogs into the new year. These spreads are established late in October and liquidated at the end of January.

***

LIVE CATTLE vs. LIVE HOGS

Notes:
1) A balanced 'money spread' consists here by trading four hog contracts against 3 cattle contracts.
2) Cattle versus hog spreads are volatile and must be watched carefully.
3) The price relationship between cattle and hogs is dependent on both meat production and current economic conditions. For example, in recessionary times when spendable income declines consumers purchase more pork than beef products.
4) An upward price trend in grains tends to strengthen hog prices relative to cattle prices. Seasonally, corn and soybeans begin price uptrends in February-March and continue until late spring or early summer.

***

The cattle/hogs inter-commodity spreads are popular on the Chicago Mercantile Exchange. The most popular combinations match up with seasonal cycles: Feb/Feb, June/June, and Oct/Oct.

For example, one expects June cattle to gain on June hogs during the first quarter of the year because of the larger cattle cycle. In turn this leads to expectations of strength in cattle relative to hogs in the spring. This type of seasonal consideration may be overshadowed by technical and fundamental factors and inflation.

***

PORK BELLIES

The term 'pork belly' refers to uncured bacon which comes from the underside of the hog. Because pork bellies are a by-product of hogs, the size of the pig crop and the pattern of the hog slaughter tend to dictate bellies prices, especially since the demand for bellies remains relatively unresponsive to price changes. Pork bellies are used primarily in the manufacture of bacon.

The pork bellies market is the sole carrying charge market in the meats futures complex. Unlike hogs, which are perishable and are brought to market soon after they reach slaughter weight, pork bellies are frozen and placed in storage. The "Monthly Cold Storage Reports" are important to traders because the amount of bellies stored and the changes in stored stocks are important indicators of price changes.

Storage stocks are determined by the rate of slaughter and by consumption. The peak period of fresh pork bellies production is late fall and early winter, from October to December. It falls to a minimum during June, July and August. This pattern of production is the result of the seasonal pattern of hog farrowing. Thus, storage stocks tend to increase during the winter and reach a peak early in May. From May through September the slaughter rate diminishes and stocks are drawn down during the summer. In general, bellies prices will peak between July and September as stocks are being drawn out of storage at an increasing rate. Storage figures thus become important to the trader late in the crop year.

As we know, carrying charges have three main components: the costs of storage, insurance and money. Since the contract is for frozen, not fresh, pork bellies, significant storage costs are involved, particularly in view of high energy costs. The trader must keep in mind, therefore, that when pork belly prices are increasing and/or interest rates are static or going higher, the carrying charge would expand, - and vice versa.

Pork bellies, like other meats, have strong and weak months. February and July are the strong months; March is the weakest.

Note: Be aware that, while frozen, bellies may remain in storage for as long as eight months; this applies only to a specific calendar year by contract definition.

Bellies placed in storage before November 1 cannot be delivered against the following year's futures contracts.

***

February vs. May Pork Bellies

The chart of this spread usually exhibits sideways movement or bottoming action until August-September. This is the time to establish long February vs. short May pork bellies bull spreads. The trader should calculate the full carrying charge and then, starting at better than 50% of full carry, initiate a position and add to the position on a scale-down basis. These units would all be limited risk spreads, the risk being limited by the full carrying charge. Limited risk opportunities are rare and of short duration and the trader looking for these opportunities must repeatedly re-calculate full carrying charges at the then current interest rates and futures prices. Let us say the trader was able to initiate the Feb/May spread at

50% full carry, and add to his position at 60% and 75% full carry. Chances are that in August or September the February contract begins to gain over the May. If the bull move develops it is usually of short duration and the trader will gain perhaps 75-150 points per spread.

By mid-October the February contract will probably show signs of weakening and this trend change is a signal to the trader to take the other side by back-spreading: go long May and short February bellies. This is now a bear spread and it has been found reliable over the years because the February contract has the tendency to go off the board weak relative to May or to the other deferred contract months. The trader must watch the spread in mid-November because the February contract tends to be strong for a week or two. If no contra-seasonal trend develops, the bear spreads are held until late January when they are finally liquidated. All bear spreads should carry stop loss protection because they are not limited risk situations.

***

March vs. July Pork Bellies

Similar to February/May bellies this spread can also be set up as a bull spread in August, held for a September-October runup and then reversed to a bear spread. Again, there is the possibility of a seasonal up move mid-November, followed by a gradual weakening of the March contract in terms of July until the spread is liquidated in February.

***

August vs. February Pork Bellies

The old crop/new crop spread between July or August of one year and the February contract of the following year represent an extremely high risk position. Even though the component parts of this spread are only six months apart, there is no direct relationship between the two crop years because by contract rules old crop (August) bellies are not eligible for delivery against the new crop (February) futures contract. In other words, each crop year must be treated and analyzed as a separate entity.

***

February Pork Bellies vs. February Hogs

For balance purposes these spreads should consist of three

bellies against four hogs. Reason: a one cent move in
bellies is worth $380 while the same one cent move in hogs
is worth only $300.

Over the years pork bellies often traded at premiums of more
than twice the price of hogs. About three years back the
picture changed. There were large storage stocks, high
interest rates and adverse publicity relative to bacon; its
cholesterol content and the preservatives used in its preparation were the reasons for the weakness of bellies relative
to hogs. The price ratio collapsed so sharply that for the
first time bellies dropped to several cents discount to hogs.

Therefore, it seems there is not any true correlation between
bellies and hogs. The trader may take two factors into
consideration:
1. Bellies are the 'leader' in this spread, that is, in a bull
   market belly prices will move up faster than hog prices and
   the spread will widen. In bear markets the spread will
   narrow since belly prices will decrease more relative
   to hogs.
2. A seasonal pattern seems to have evolved in recent years:
   February bellies tend to lose to February hogs from
   August-September until November-December, then reverse to
   strength in February bellies versus weakness in February
   hogs and this relationship seems to last till mid-January.

***

July PORK BELLIES vs. July HOGS

This is another popular inter-market spread with high risk and
high profit potential. The hogs contract has a seasonal tendency to gain on the July bellies contract during the April-
June quarter. In ten of the last eleven years there was an
average move of 5¢/lb. in favor of hogs and once a 2¢/lb. loss
when the spread was initiated in mid-April and liquidated in
mid-June. Whenever the price of July bellies approaches the
price of July hogs take advantage of this opportunity by
buying the July bellies and selling the July hogs.

Pork bellies versus hogs charts show wide amplitude in the up
and down fluctuations. Many who trade this inter-market
spread ignore trends and whatever seasonality there is but
keep an eye on the spread chart. When the bellies vs. hogs
spread trades near the historical lows they go long bellies
and sell hogs in anticipation that on rallies they can take
several 4-5¢ profits while limiting losses with 2¢ stops on
these trades.

***

COMMODITY:	LIVE BEEF CATTLE
EXCHANGE:	Chicago Mercantile Exchange
TRADING HOURS:	9:05 to 12:45 Central Time
DELIVERY MONTHS:	Jan, Feb, Apr, Jne, Aug, Oct, and Dec.
TRADING UNIT:	40,000 lbs.
PRICE QUOTED IN:	¢/lb.
MINIMUM PRICE FLUCTUATION:	2-1/2/100¢/lb. (1 point=$4)
VALUE OF MINIMUM FLUCTUATION:	$10.00 per contract unit
VALUE OF ONE CENT MOVE:	$400.00
DAILY LIMIT OF PRICE MOVE:	1-1/2 cents (+-)
VALUE OF DAILY LIMIT:	$600.00
FIRST DELIVERY DAY NOTICE:	The last business day (Mon-Thu) of the month preceding the contract month
LAST TRADING DAY:	20th calendar day of the contract month or business day preceding if 20th is not a business day.

COMMODITY:	LIVE BEEF CATTLE
EXCHANGE:	MidAmerica Commodity Exchange
TRADING HOURS:	9:05 to 1:00 Central Time
DELIVERY MONTHS:	Jan, Feb, Apr, Jne, Aug, Oct, Dec.
TRADING UNIT:	20,000 lbs.
PRICE QUOTED IN:	¢/lb.
MINIMUM PRICE FLUCTUATION:	.00025¢/lb.
VALUE OF MINIMUM FLUCTUATION:	1 point = $2 per contract unit
VALUE OF ONE CENT MOVE:	$200.00
DAILY LIMIT OF PRICE MOVE:	+-1½¢/lb.
VALUE OF DAILY LIMIT:	$300.00
FIRST DELIVERY DAY NOTICE:	see above
LAST TRADING DAY:	20th calendar day of delivery month or business day immediately preceding.

COMMODITY:	FEEDER CATTLE
EXCHANGE:	Chicago Mercantile Exchange
TRADING HOURS:	9:05 to 12:45 Central Time
DELIVERY MONTHS:	Jan, Mch, Apr, May, Aug, Sep, Oct, and Nov.
TRADING UNIT:	42,000 lbs.
PRICE QUOTED IN:	¢/lb.
MINIMUM PRICE FLUCTUATION:	2½/100¢/lb. (1 point = $4.20)
VALUE OF MINIMUM FLUCTUATION:	$10.50 per contract unit
VALUE OF ONE CENT MOVE:	$420.00
DAILY LIMIT OF PRICE MOVE:	1½¢
VALUE OF DAILY LIMIT:	$630.00
FIRST DELIVERY DAY NOTICE:	First business day of contract mo.
LAST TRADING DAY:	20th calendar day of contract month or business day preceding if 20th is not a business day.

COMMODITY: LIVE HOGS
EXCHANGE: Chicago Mercantile Exchange
TRADING HOURS: 9:10 to 1:00 Central Time
DELIVERY MONTHS: Feb, Apr, Jne, Jly, Aug, Oct, Dec.
TRADING UNIT: 30,000 lbs.
PRICE QUOTED IN: ¢/lb.
MINIMUM PRICE FLUCTUATION: 2½/100¢/lb. (1 point = $3)
VALUE OF MINIMUM FLUCTUATION: $7.50 per contract unit
VALUE OF ONE CENT MOVE: $300.00
DAILY LIMIT OF PRICE MOVE: +-1½¢
VALUE OF DAILY LIMIT: $450.00
FIRST DELIVERY DAY NOTICE: Delivery on Mon-Thu after sixth calendar day of month
LAST TRADING DAY: 20th calendar day of contract mo. or business day preceding if 20th is not a business day.
CROP YEAR: October 1 to September 30

COMMODITY: LIVE HOGS
EXCHANGE: MidAmerica Commodity Exchange
TRADING HOURS: 9:15 to 1:05 Central Time
DELIVERY MONTHS: Feb, Apr, Jne, Jly, Aug, Oct, Dec.
TRADING UNIT: 15,000 lbs.
PRICE QUOTED IN: ¢/lb.
MINIMUM PRICE FLUCTUATION: .025¢/lb. (1 point = $1.50)
VALUE OF ONE CENT MOVE: $150.00 per contract unit
VALUE OF MINIMUM FLUCTUATION: $3.75
DAILY LIMIT OF PRICE MOVE: +-1½¢/lb.
VALUE OF DAILY LIMIT: $225.00
LAST TRADING DAY: 20th calendar day of contract month or business day immediately preceding.

COMMODITY: PORK BELLIES
EXCHANGE: Chicago Mercantile Exchange
TRADING HOURS: 9:10 to 1:00 Central Time
DELIVERY MONTHS: Feb, Mch, May, Jly, Aug.
TRADING UNIT: 38,000 lbs.
PRICE QUOTED IN: ¢/lb.
MINIMUM PRICE FLUCTUATION: 2½/100¢/lb. (1 point = $3.80)
VALUE OF MINIMUM FLUCTUATION: $9.50 per contract unit
VALUE OF ONE CENT MOVE: $380.00
DAILY LIMIT OF PRICE MOVE: +-2¢
VALUE OF DAILY LIMIT: $760.00
FIRST DELIVERY DAY NOTICE: First business day of the contract month
LAST TRADING DAY: Business day immediately preceding the last 5 business days of contract month
CROP YEAR: October 1 to September 30

***

CATTLE: OCTOBER / DECEMBER

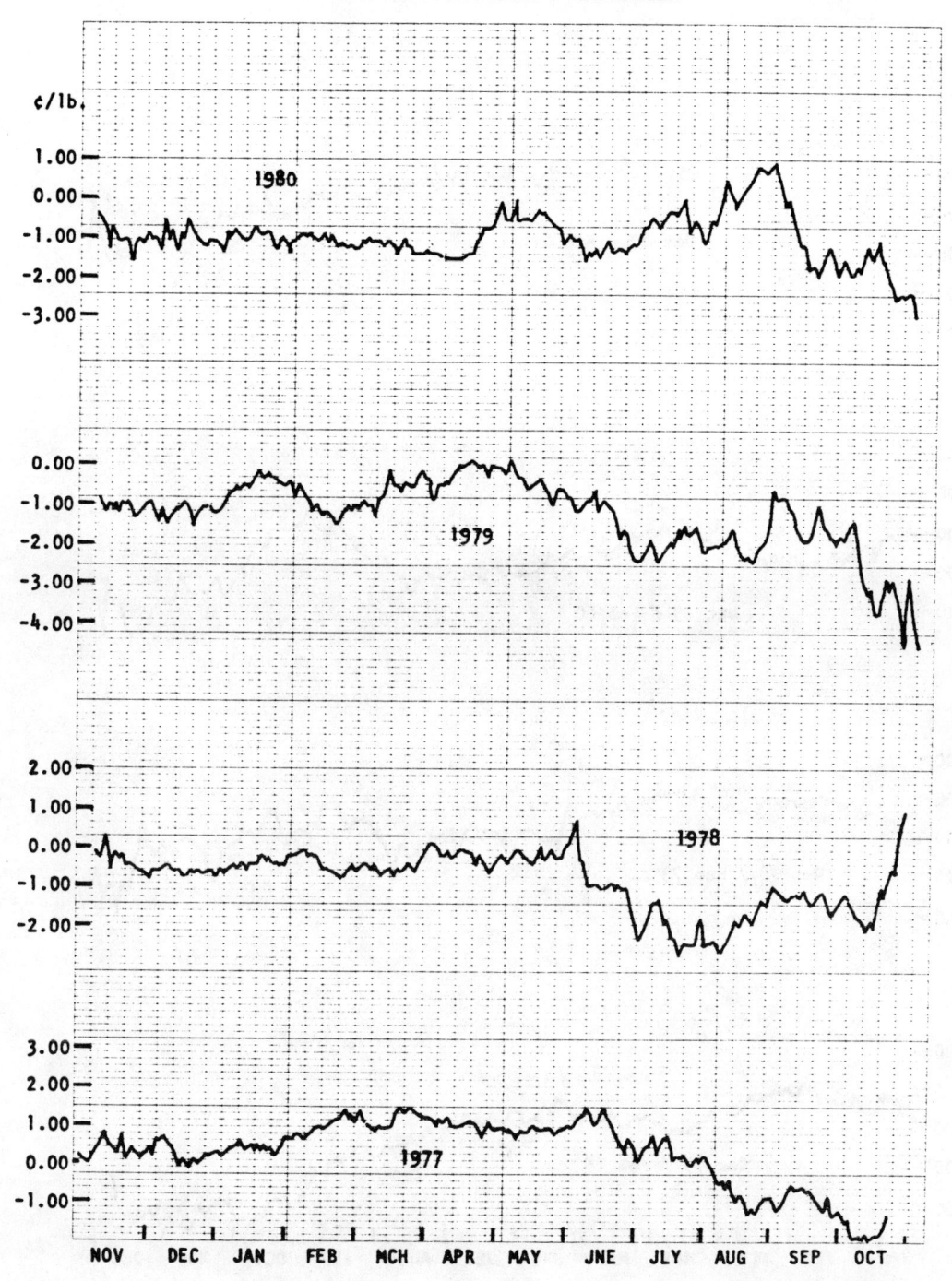

CATTLE: DECEMBER / FEBRUARY

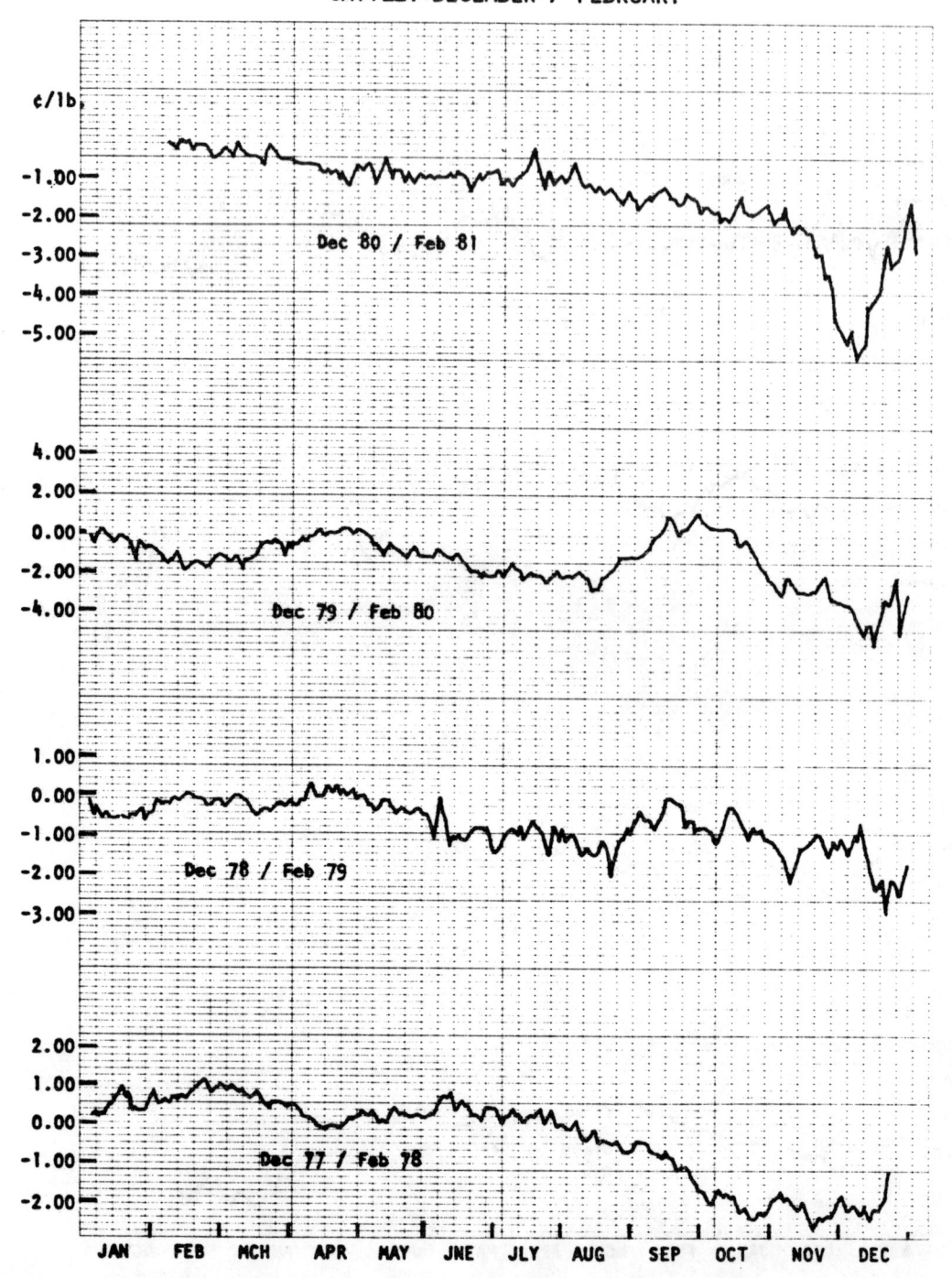

HOGS: FEBRUARY / APRIL

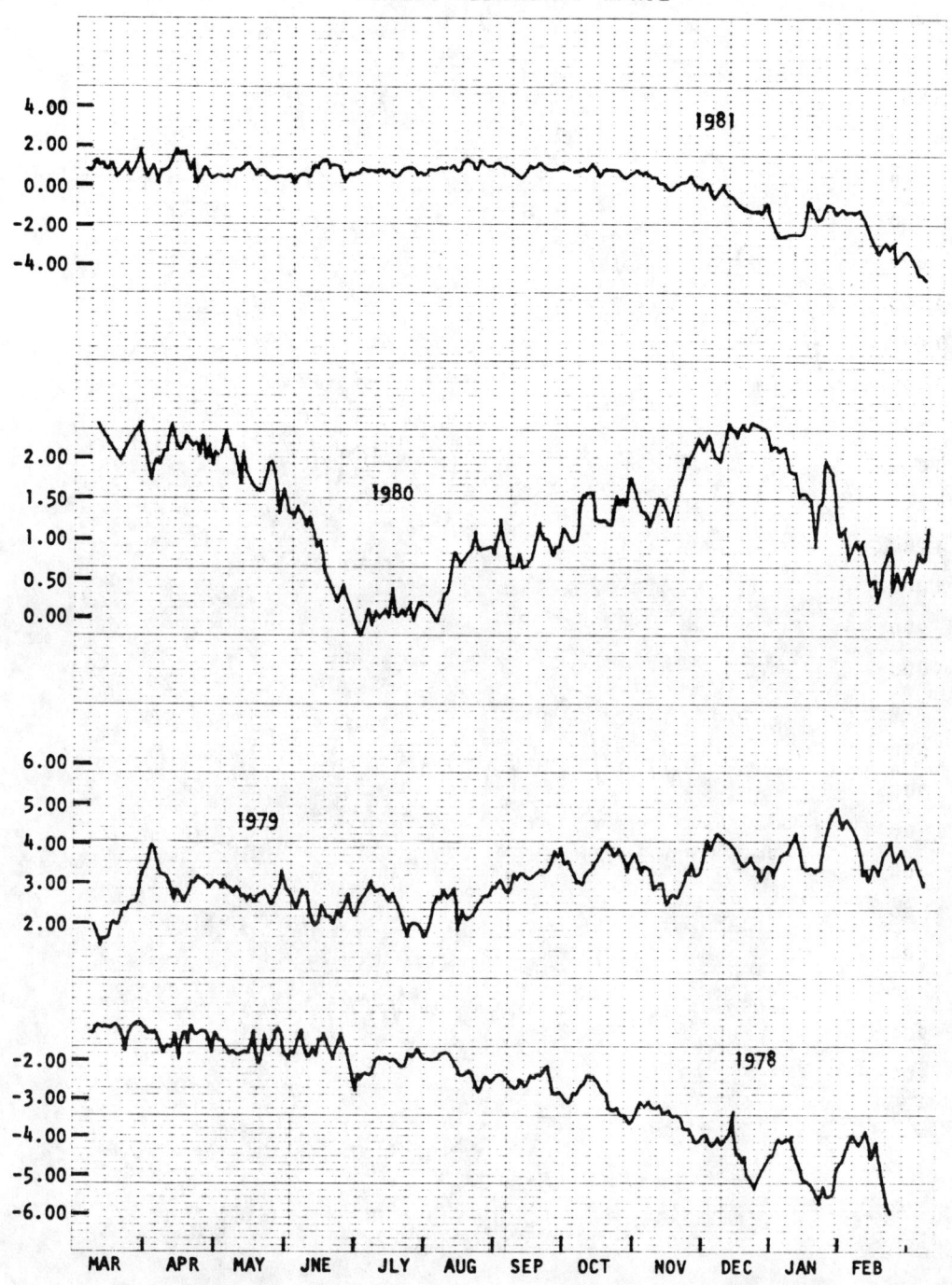

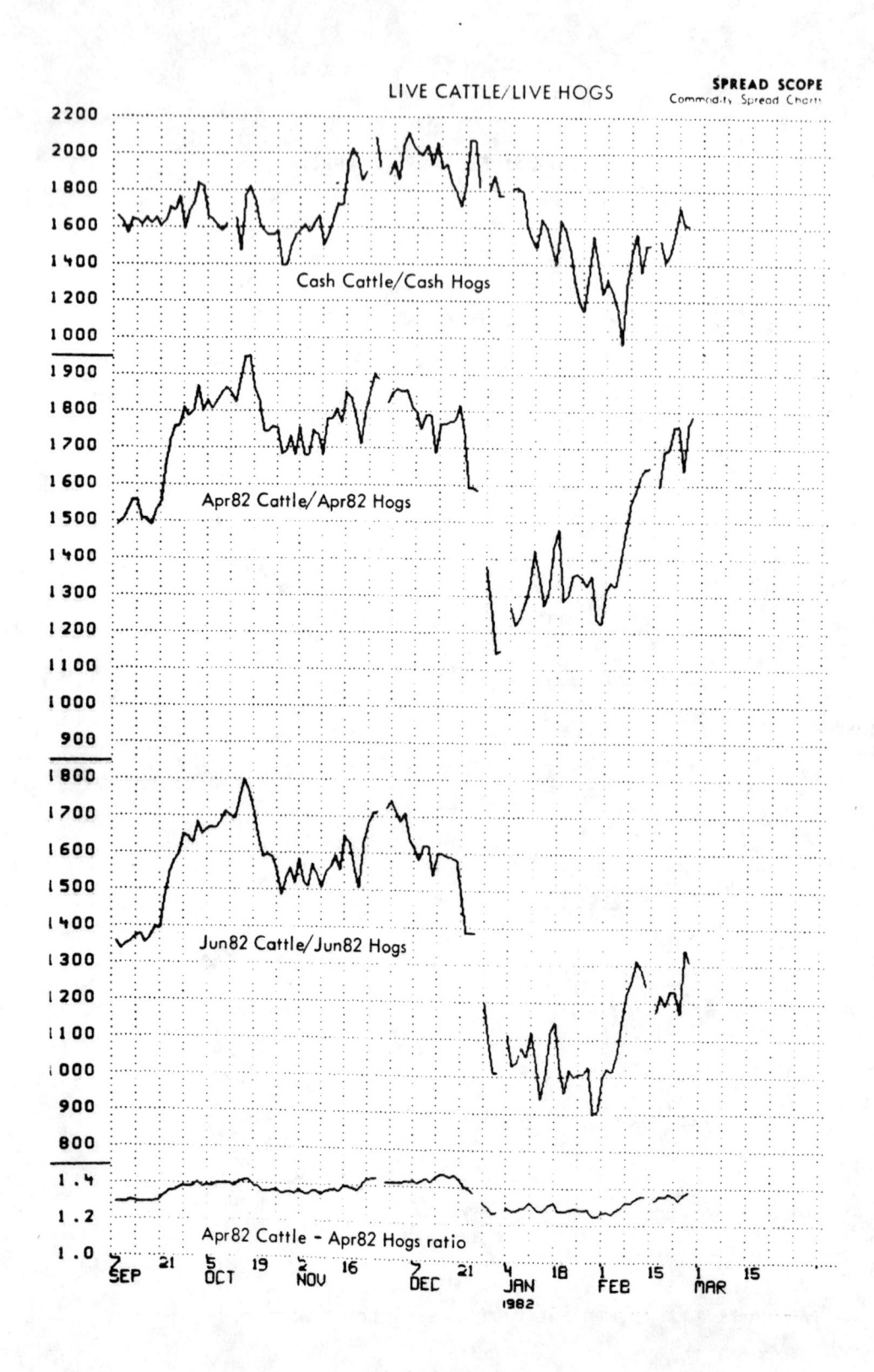

Spread chart courtesy of Spread Scope, Inc.

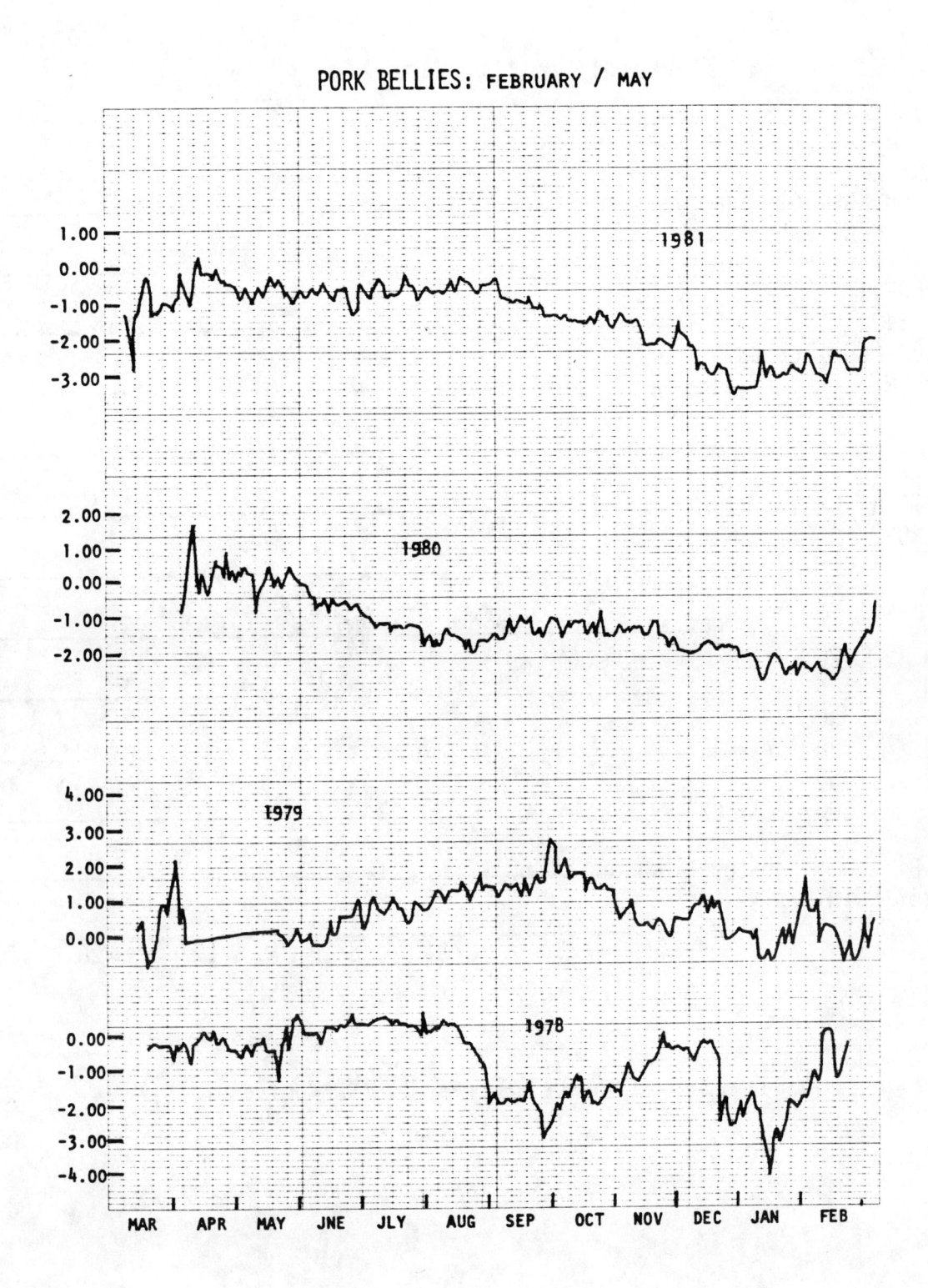

PORK BELLIES: FEBRUARY / MAY

PORK BELLIES / LIVE HOGS: JULY 1981

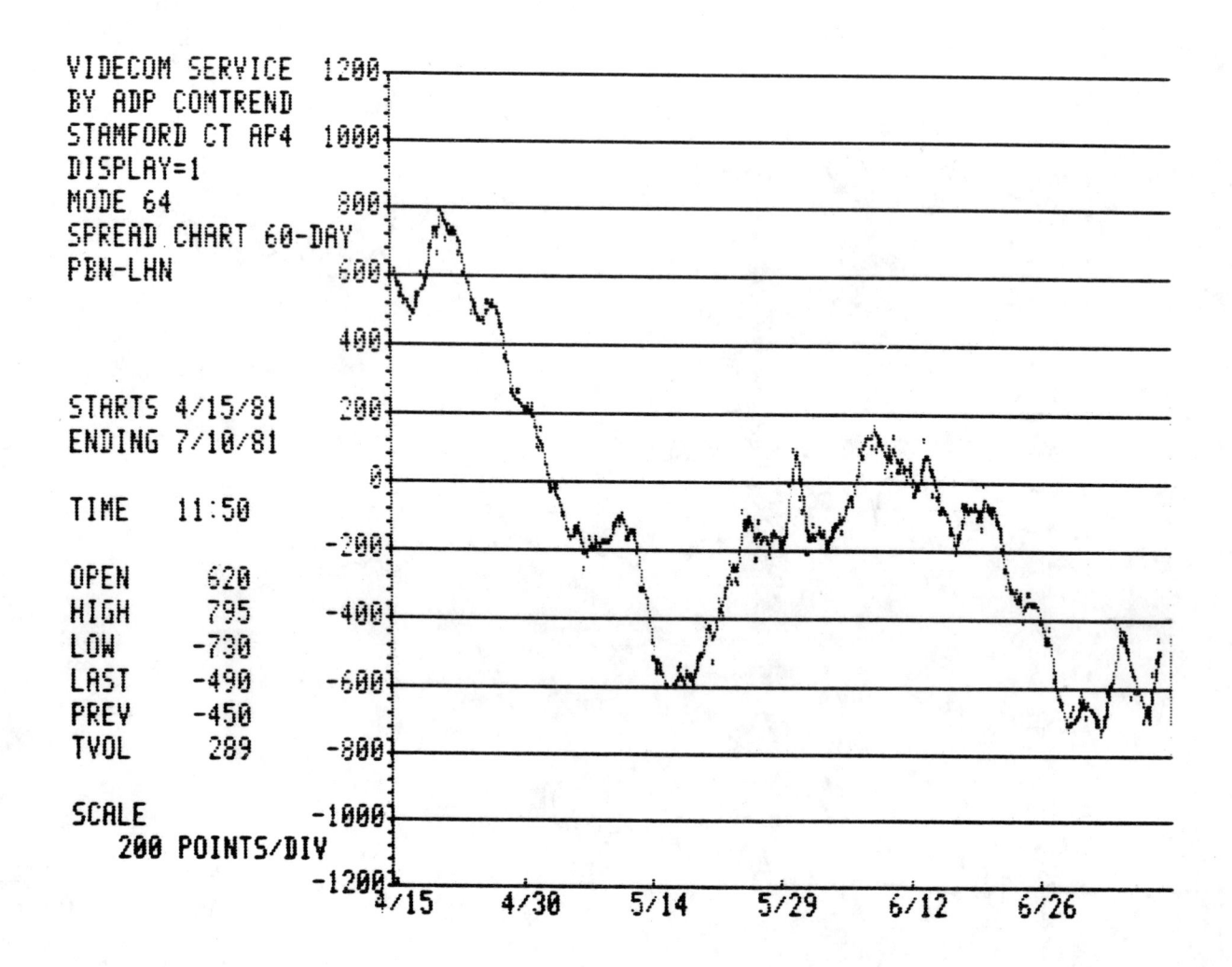

```
VIDECOM SERVICE
BY ADP COMTREND
STAMFORD CT AP4
DISPLAY=1
MODE 64
SPREAD CHART 60-DAY
PBN-LHN


STARTS 4/15/81
ENDING 7/10/81

TIME    11:50

OPEN     620
HIGH     795
LOW     -730
LAST    -490
PREV    -450
TVOL     289

SCALE
   200 POINTS/DIV
```

Videcom Spread Charts courtesy of ADP Comtrend.

FOODSTUFFS

COCOA

The crop year for cocoa extends from October through the following September. Cocoa is harvested in two main periods: The first, from October to March, is called the main crop and accounts for 80% of the world's output. The second, the mid-crop, is harvested later, usually in May and June. It is interesting that, in Brazil, the mid-crop is larger than the main crop. Another fact to be kept in mind is that it takes four years before a cocoa tree will bear fruit.
A single season of inclement weather, therefore, can affect the crop for a number of years.

Cocoa price moves, at one time, were characterized by long and sustained up-trends and down-trends. It was easy to trade this market with technical tools because, except when major price reversals occurred, trend lines were seldom violated. This predictable, seasonal pattern, however, has been badly distorted by the explosive price movements of several recent years.

As a result of heavy harvesting, cocoa prices tend to be depressed between November and March. This, also, is the period when manufacturers do the bulk of their buying. The first six months of the calendar year are influenced by predictions of crop conditions in West Africa. By September the crop facts are known. This knowledge and the fact that the harvest in Brazil is completed, combine to bring about lower prices in September.

Fall is the time when manufacturers process the cocoa beans. Since fall is also the time of heaviest grindings and the processors already have purchased the beans they need, autumn is a time of lower prices. There are two periods the trader must watch carefully:
1) During the summer months there often is a sharp runup in prices while the market discounts the fall grindings,
2) A sudden price increase during October-November due to lack of information about the main crop size.

November seems to be the swing month: cocoa either begins to make its up-side move or collapses.

Cocoa is traded on the Coffee, Sugar & Cocoa Exchange, Inc. The contract was revised recently. As of December 1980, prices are quoted in dollars per metric ton, and the contract is for delivery of ten metric tons. A price move of one dollar is equivalent to a profit or loss of $10 for the trader.

Cocoa prices, traditionally, have been quoted in cents per lb. To convert $/metric ton to ¢/lb., divide the metric figure by 22.05. For example, a price of $2,145/metric ton is equivalent to 2,145 divided by 22.05, or 97.28¢/pound. To convert ¢/lb. to dollars/metric ton, one has to multiply the figure in cents by 22.05. Note: Each drop of $100 per metric ton produces an equity dip of $1,000.

***

Long December vs. Short May Cocoa

This is a fairly reliable bull spread. It should be initiated early May (current year) by buying December (current year) cocoa and selling May (next year) cocoa. If seasonal factors work as expected, December cocoa will gain over May cocoa until 4-6 weeks before December expires.

***

Long July vs. Short December Cocoa

Cocoa highs are often made in June-July, while lows are made in December. The long July/short December cocoa bull spread is another reliable, though high risk, spread. It should be considered in April-May, and if initiated, it should be liquidated late in June.

***

COFFEE "C"

Coffee, like cocoa, is a commodity whose seasonal pattern has been distorted by the volatile price swings of the last few years. Because coffee is grown everywhere in the world and is always being harvested somewhere, there is not much of a seasonal variation in coffee prices. The trader should remember, however, that while it is easy to store green coffee beans, it is not a carrying charge commodity.

The seasonal decline (if any) during February-March can be atributed to increased supplies from the harvest in Latin America. The frost season in Brazil is May 30 to Sept. 15. The frosts mean little to actual coffee production, but almost every season there are several freeze scares which lead to firmer prices during this period. Once the worry over crop damage abates, the price decline continues from July through September with a possible upswing late in September, the result of pre-winter high consumption levels. From October through February prices are likely to move upward.

***

Long September vs. Short December COFFEE

If world stocks of coffee are low and consumption figures are bullish, these two factors should increase any upward price move resulting from weather scares. This bull spread should be initiated during the March-May lows and liquidated during the July-August highs.

***

Long December vs. Short March COFFEE

This bull spread, and the previous one, should be set up, if possible, whenever the deferred contract trades with a premium of at least 100 points over the nearby contract. When coffee prices move up sharply the spread will invert and the nearby contract often will trade for a substantial premium over the deferred contract. Several times in the past the nearby's premium has reached two thousand points.

***

ORANGE JUICE

Because frozen concentrated orange juice is available throughout the year, orange juice does not suffer harvest lows. Seasonal lows are seen from June through September and seasonal highs are expected from November through January. Orange juice becomes a weather market each fall and winter due to the freeze scare season which extends from December through early March.

Freeze scares in mid-January to mid-February have been particularly profitable for orange juice traders. In March, April, and May, the danger of severe frost in Florida recedes and prices reach their lows. The main harvest begins in April and the price soon begins to climb in response to summer demand. Demand remains high into the fall and prices remain firm or climb sharply if traders predict a decreased orange crop, or if an early freeze is anticipated. Under these circumstances orange juice prices may skyrocket by October.

The cold storage inventories tend to be lowest at the end of the crop year and this adds to price firmness during October, November, and December. If there is a decline in prices in December, it is the result of the beginning of the Florida harvest. Florida is where about one-fourth of the world's supply of oranges is grown. While demand for orange juice is influenced somewhat by price, the major price determinant is the supply situation. Before taking a position, the trader should consider the main factors affecting the supply of oranges: production, imports, year-end carryover, and cold storage figures. Even when carryover stocks are at record levels, prudent traders will hesitate to establish short positions or bear spreads during the November-February period. The possibility that freezing temperatures could cause fruit damage makes those positions hazardous during the mentioned time frame. It must be noted that temperatures have to remain below 28 degrees Fahrenheit for at least 4-5 hours for significant fruit damage to occur. Cloud cover and wind velocity also must be taken into consideration.

***

Long September vs. Short January Orange Juice

This is an old crop/new crop spread. This inter-crop bull spread involves buying September and selling January (next year) at the beginning of the current calendar year. If a freeze, or freeze scare does occur, September will gain on the January contract. The spread should be liquidated late February. Unless a hurricane or other weather catastrophe destroys the crop, the September contract will decline prior to its expiration. If a real shortage is unlikely and September trades at an exorbitant premium above the January contract during the spring (inverted market), a bear spread involving the purchase of January (next year) against the sale of September (current) may offer a rare trading opportunity. This bear spread tends to perform best in mid-summer. Timing the entry is of paramount importance.

Many traders like to spread November against January. For the bull spread (long Nov/short Jan) the appropriate notes above apply. In case of the bear spread (short Nov/long Jan) the spread could be initiated late in August to mid-September and liquidated late October.

***

SUGAR #11

Two-thirds of the world's trade in sugar takes place in sheltered trading areas. The remaining third of the world supply is referred to as "world sugar" and the #11 sugar futures contract is the one written for "world" or, "free" sugar.

The crop year begins in October. Seasonally, October and November are usually the weakest months while April-May tend to be the strongest. The seasonality of sugar is a weak price factor when compared with other and stronger, influences. For example, high interest rates cause steep declines in world sugar prices because high rates discourage the holding of sugar inventories. World sugar prices are denominated in U.S. dollars and, therefore, when the dollar is strong, sugar prices are depressed. Sugar prices are also known to move relative to precious metal prices.

Long May vs. Short October SUGAR

This bull spread usually reaches its seasonal low between July and September. At that time a fairly reliable move favoring the May contract begins and extends until January. The two contract months are of the same calendar year, thus, in the fall of 1982 one would be long May '83 vs. short the October '83 sugar contract. The spread is normally traded between September 15 and January 15.

***

Short October vs. Long March SUGAR

Once the above May/Oct bull spread reaches its peak and the trader expects that bearish fundamentals will exert their influence, the Oct/March (next) bear spread may prove profitable if it is established in April-May and liquidated in August. The highs and lows for the spread have occured with little consistency in recent years because of widely fluctuating interest rates, oil prices, and dollar strength. These facts must be correlated with the traditional supply/demand considerations.

***

COMMODITY:	COCOA
EXCHANGE:	Coffee, Sugar and Cocoa Exch.
TRADING HOURS:	9:30 to 3:00 Eastern Time
DELIVERY MONTHS:	Mch, May, Jly, Sep, Dec.
TRADING UNIT:	30,000 lbs. (10 metric tons or 22,400 lbs. as of the December 1980 contract)
PRICE QUOTED IN:	¢/lb. ($/metric ton as of Dec. '80)
MINIMUM PRICE FLUCTUATION:	1/100¢/lb. ($1/ton as of Dec. '80)
VALUE OF MINIMUM FLUCTUATION:	$3.00 per contract unit ($10.00 as of Dec. '80)
FIRST DELIVERY DAY NOTICE:	Seven business days before 1st business day of delivery month
LAST TRADING DAY:	Seven business days prior to last business day of delivery mo.
CROP YEAR:	October 1 to September 30

COMMODITY:	COFFEE "C"
EXCHANGE:	Coffee, Sugar and Cocoa Exch.
TRADING HOURS:	9:45 to 2:30 Eastern Time
DELIVERY MONTHS:	Mch, May, Jly, Sep, Dec.
TRADING UNIT:	37,500 lbs.
PRICE QUOTED IN:	¢/lb.
MINIMUM PRICE FLUCTUATION:	1/100¢/lb.
VALUE OF MINIMUM FLUCTUATION:	$3.75 per contract unit
VALUE OF ONE CENT MOVE:	$375.00
DAILY LIMIT OF PRICE MOVE:	4¢ + or -
VALUE OF DAILY LIMIT:	$1,500.00
FIRST DELIVERY DAY NOTICE:	Five business days before 1st business day of delivery month
LAST TRADING DAY:	Five business days before last business day of contract month
CROP YEAR:	Coffee is grown around the world and is harvested year-round

COMMODITY:	ORANGE JUICE (FROZEN CONCENTRATED)
EXCHANGE:	Citrus Assoc., NY Cotton Exchange
TRADING HOURS:	10:15 to 2:45 Eastern Time
DELIVERY MONTHS:	Jan, Mch, May, Jly, Sep, Nov.
TRADING UNIT:	15,000 lbs.
PRICE QUOTED IN:	¢/lb.
MINIMUM PRICE FLUCTUATION:	5/100¢/lb. (1 pt. = $1.50)
VALUE OF MINIMUM FLUCTUATION:	$7.50 per contract unit
VALUE OF ONE CENT MOVE:	$150.00
DAILY LIMIT OF PRICE MOVE:	5¢ + or -
VALUE OF DAILY LIMIT:	$750.00
FIRST DELIVERY DAY NOTICE:	1st business day after last trading and at least 5 days before delivery
LAST TRADING DAY:	10th Business day prior to end of delivery month
CROP YEAR:	December 1 to November 30

COMMODITY:	SUGAR #11
EXCHANGE:	Coffee, Sugar and Cocoa Exchange
TRADING HOURS:	10:00 to 1:43 Eastern Time
DELIVERY MONTHS:	Jan, Mch, May, Jly, Sep, Dec.
TRADING UNIT:	50 long tons (112,000 lbs.)
PRICE QUOTED IN:	¢/lb.
MINIMUM PRICE FLUCTUATION:	1/100¢/lb. (1 pt. = $11.20)
VALUE OF MINIMUM FLUCTUATION:	$11.20 per contract unit
VALUE OF ONE CENT MOVE:	$1,120.00
DAILY LIMIT OF PRICE MOVE:	One cent
VALUE OF DAILY LIMIT:	$1,120.00
FIRST DELIVERY DAY NOTICE:	1st business day of delivery mo.
LAST TRADING DAY:	Last business day of month preceding delivery month
CROP YEAR:	October 1 to September 30

***

COCOA: DECEMBER / MARCH

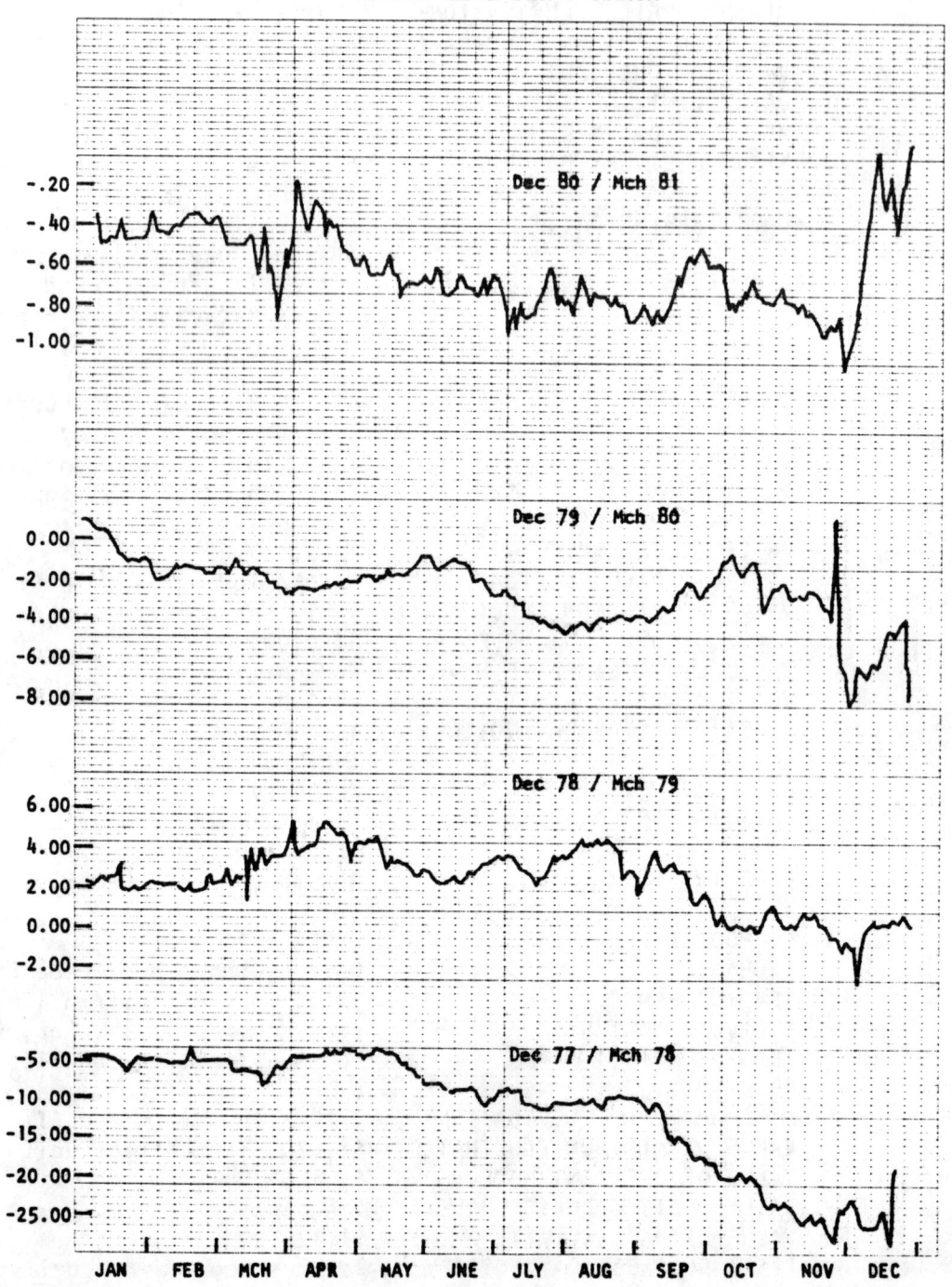

COFFEE: SEPTEMBER / DECEMBER

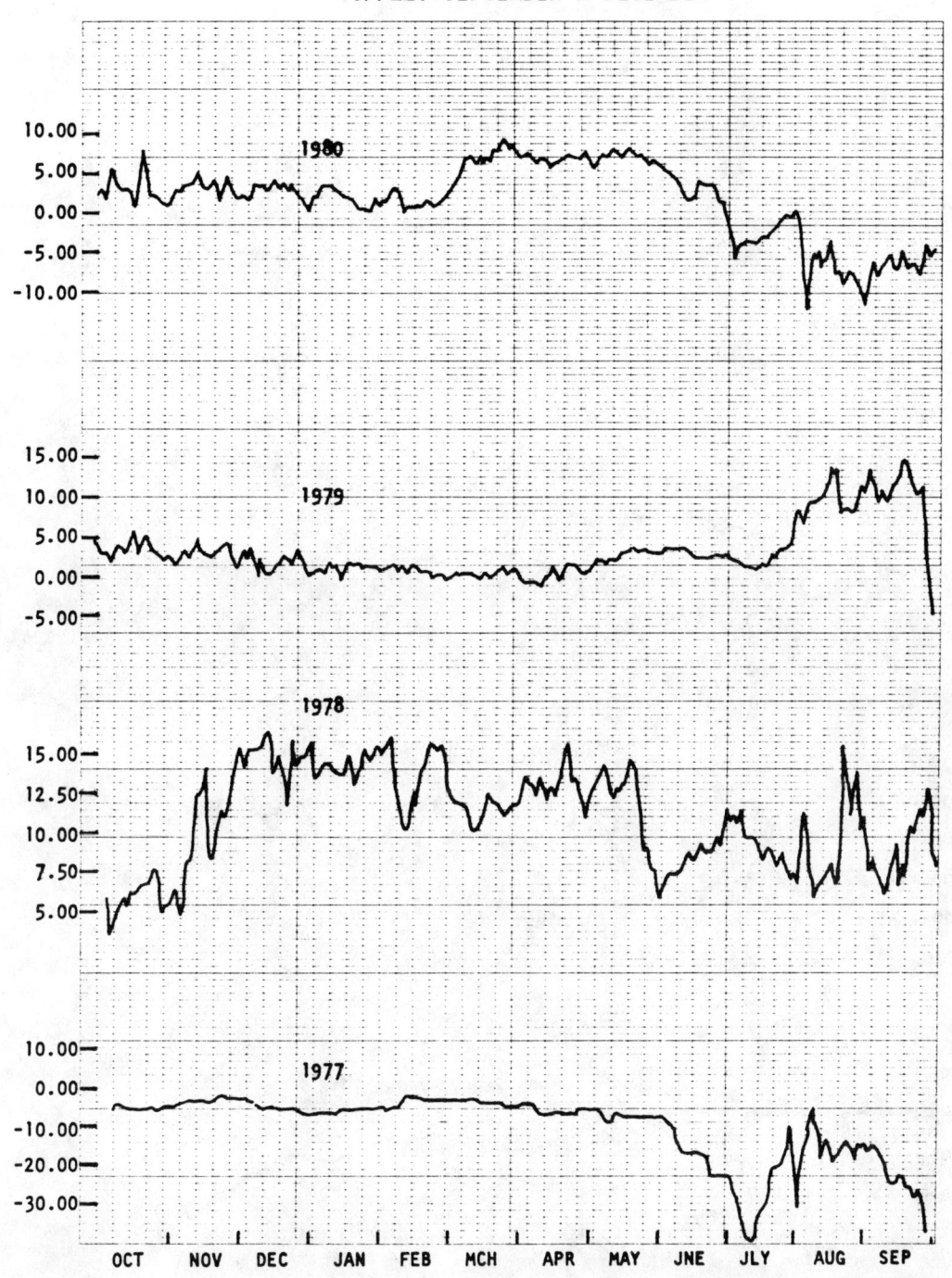

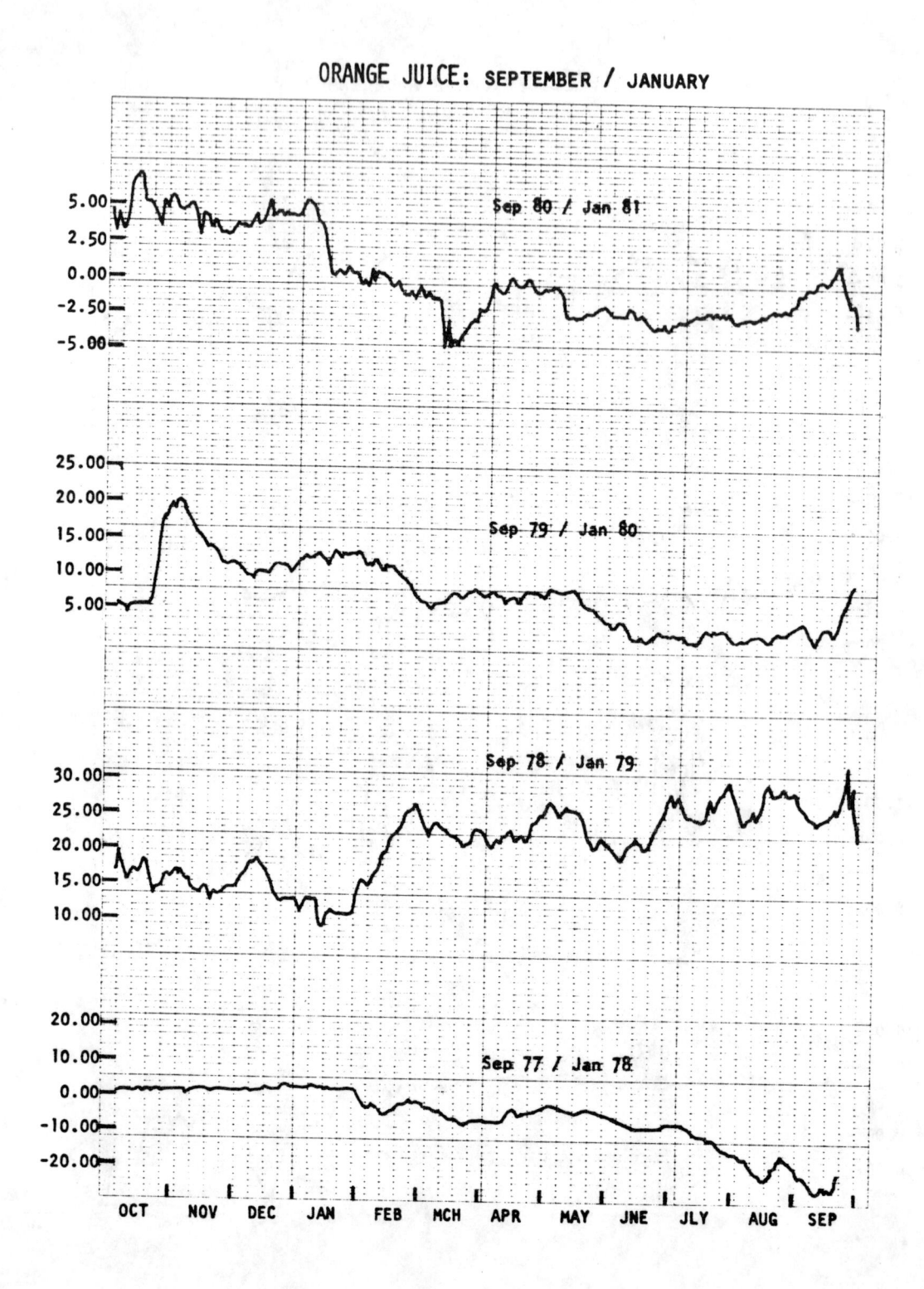

ORANGE JUICE: SEPTEMBER / JANUARY

SUGAR: OCTOBER / MARCH

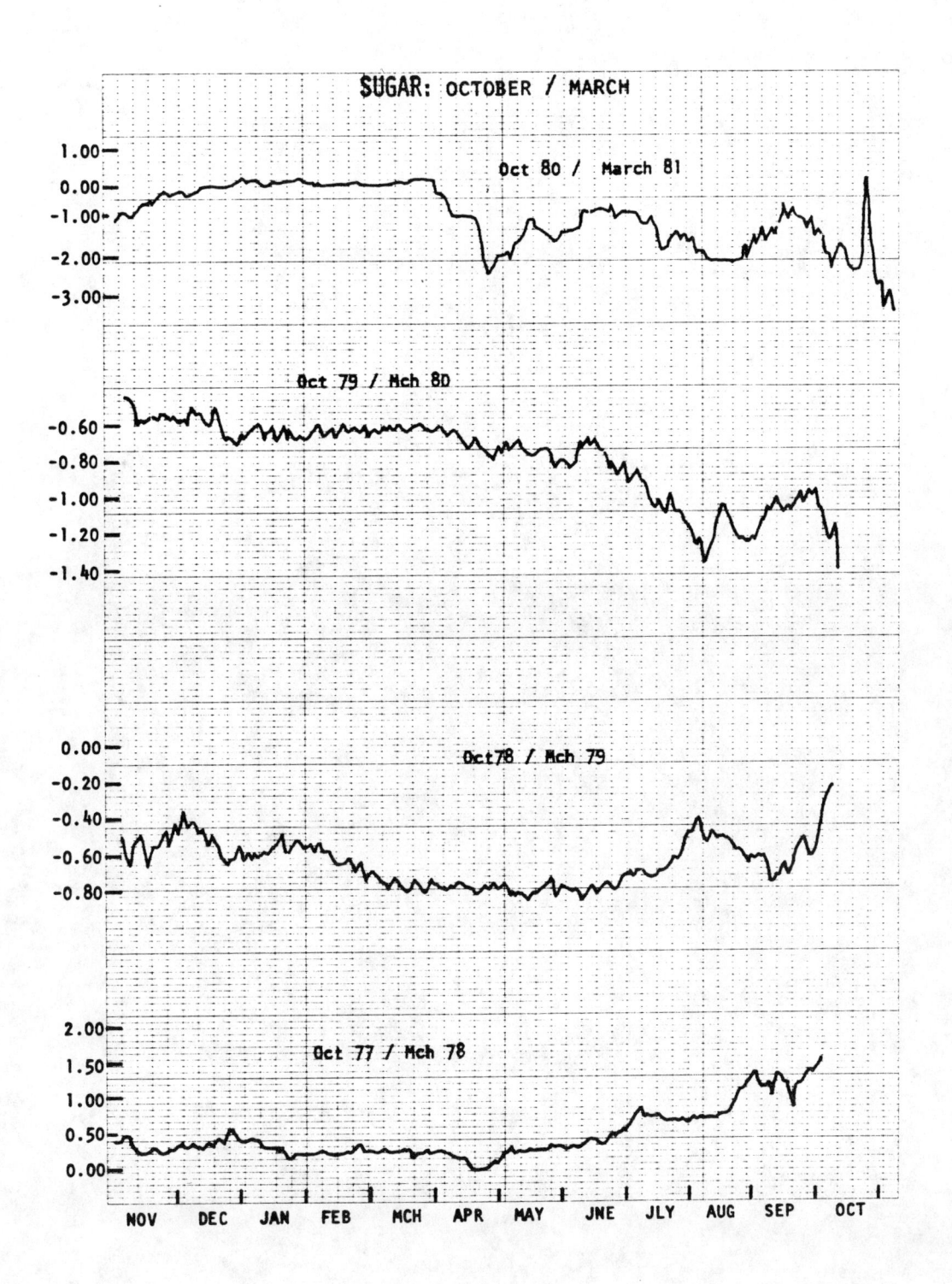

FIBER & FOREST PRODUCTS

COTTON No. 2

In the United States, most cotton is planted between March and May, and harvested during October and November. Weather is the big factor in cotton growth; hot and humid is best. The amount of rain also is important; too much or too little will mean a smaller crop.

During the harvest period, selling of the new crop causes price declines from August highs to October-November lows. During December-January a post-harvest rally may be created by heavy mill buying and heavy exports. After this short run up, however, the price declines steadily and reaches seasonal lows for the year during February-March. During planting season the price begins a slow up-trend. After May, the acreage actually planted becomes common knowledge and the price usually declines for a short time. Then, the uncertainty about both the weather and the condition of the planted acreage during the growing season tends to cause a price surge which lasts from June through August.

Since synthetic fibers require petroleum in their manufacture, the sharp increase in petroleum prices has resulted in the increased use of cotton. During the last oil embargo the price of cotton increased over 100%. It rose from about 40¢ per pound to about 85¢. When the embargo was lifted, cotton dropped back to 35¢ per pound.

China and Russia are the world's largest consumers of cotton. The U.S. ranks third.

***

December vs. March COTTON

If market fundamentals are strongly bullish, cotton bull spreads can be profitable and, in limited risk situations, these spreads will protect the trader against the violent shakeouts that so often happen in the cotton market. To set up a bull spread the trader goes long December cotton (December 1982 contract, for example) and short March cotton (March 1983 contract). He should try to buy December at a 100 to 200 point discount to March. This carrying charge spread can often be placed in May and liquidated late June or early July. Another possibility for long December vs. short March is to place the spread during September or October and liquidate it mid-November. In a strong bull market this spread can invert, with December moving to a 100+ point premium to March.

During an economic slowdown, users are reluctant to finance large inventories at much less than the carrying charge.

If cotton is plentiful, each expiring contract may move toward full carrying charges as it approaches maturity. Therefore, if a long March (1983) and short December (1982) cotton spread can be obtained at less than 50% carry (premium March), this bear spread may offer some limited potential. The spread should be initiated late August-early September, (year '82 in our example) and held until the third week in November.

Another possible bear spread would be to enter long March ('83) versus short December ('82) cotton, beginning January ('82) and holding until mid-March for a possible 100-200-point profit.

***

July vs. December Cotton

This is an old-crop/new-crop spread. July is the last futures contract of the current crop year, while December is the first contract offered after harvest is completed. Needless to say, this inter-crop spread is extremely volatile, as are all spreads that cut across crop years. Long July vs. short December bull spread may be profitable if initiated in October or November and held until the end of January. If export demand is strong, another opportunity is to enter the spread in March and hold it into May.

Between mid-April and the end of June, the July cotton contract often weakens after a bull market move. Just as old crop, July, rises swiftly over new crop, December, in a bull market, when the reaction arrives July plummets relative to December. It is hard to pinpoint the initiation period, but the July contract is expected to weaken considerably from early May through expiration.

***

October vs. December Cotton

Early summer is the time for a seasonal up-move in cotton. In a bullish market October cotton is expected to gain on December, perhaps as high as several hundreds of points premium. This spread is considered limited risk because both October and December are new crop contracts. October, however, is a swing month. An early crop will depress October, particularly if California and Texas crops are abundant, and October will go to discount relative to December cotton. On the other hand, if the crop is threatened and harvest is late, the October will behave more as an old crop month and the October contract will go to a high premium relative to the December contract. Late spring, thus, and early summer are the times to establish long October versus short December cotton bull spreads.

Even though October trades at a premium most of the year, as harvest time approaches, October frequently trades at a discount to December. Therefore, one has to watch the October/December spread chart in cotton for possible topping action, and to establish the long December vs. short October bear spread in the expectation that, before the expiration of October, the spread will go to even money. Or, perhaps October will sell at a discount under December during the month of September.

***

LUMBER

Lumber prices reflect the health of the housing industry. The trend depends on the pace of housing starts which, of course, are influenced by interest rates and the availability of money.

While lumber prices have strong seasonal tendencies, the interest rate factor can either magnify, cancel or reverse the seasonal price moves. If interest rates are high but steady, seasonal factors may still affect prices. However, when the prime rate soars from 15% to 20% and then plummets to 11% within a few months as it did in 1980, a reverse roller coaster movement affects the futures prices of T-bills, bonds and Ginnie Maes. And, along with the changes in these interest rate vehicles go the parallel fluctuations in lumber and plywood futures. Thus, in an era of high and volatile interest rates, the lumber and plywood futures markets are just another way of capitalizing on interest rate fluctuations.

From September to December lumber futures generally rise in anticipation of next year's building prospects. From December to March, inventory accumulations often force prices higher if there is strong demand for the cash products. This up-move is followed by a long down trend from March to September, as demand declines. Peak season for construction is the summer and the trader must watch for a sharp hike in late-summer prices. This summer rally is caused by additional demand from construction companies with inventories of lumber too low to sustain construction levels.

***

Long September vs. Short November LUMBER

The strongest seasonal relationship in lumber is the summer rally; the demand for lumber is often stronger during late summer than early winter. This bull spread should be initiated in late spring or the summer months. Attempt to enter it when September/November trades close to even money.

If market fundamentals are bullish enough, in a time span of
a few weeks September could move several hundred points premium over November. This spread may work even in a very bearish
situation: If in June the short term interest rates are high
and are expected to rise, and the spread is near its historically wide ground, it may offer a quick profit of a few hundred points. Caveat: lumber spreads are not limited risk
spreads and, therefore, carrying charges do not limit adverse
moves. Stop-loss protection is a must!

***

Short July vs. Long September LUMBER

This bear spread should be initiated during February or
March at approximately even money, plus-minus 50 points.
If the normal seasonal pattern holds, a good percentage
profit can be realized by late May.

***

Short March vs. Long May LUMBER

A bear spread that adheres to the seasonal pattern. Beginning
mid-December, May strengthens against March and the bear-trend lasts until March expires.

On the July/September and March/May bear spreads: Increases in
short-term interest rates would exact heavy pressure on the
deferred lumber contracts.

***

Note: The current, revised lumber contract became effective
with the January 1981 contract: The contract unit has been
increased in size from 100,000 to 130,000 board feet to accommodate the loading practices of Canadian mills. The new
contract increases the kinds of lumber that can be delivered
against the new contract. The Canadian provinces of Alberta
and British Columbia represent the largest source of lumber
deliverable against the contract. This introduces a new
variable and traders in lumber will have to watch the value
of the Canadian dollar in addition to housing starts, interest
rates and all the other factors that influence lumber prices.

***

In the event of an oil shortage, oil boycott, embargo, or a
Mideast war, there is a low-margin bull spread speculation:
The nearby and deferred lumber contracts should be six months
apart and the nearby contract should be 2-3 months forward
from the present.

Examples:

1. If an embargo occurs in October, buy January lumber and sell July lumber.
2. If a severe oil shortage develops in June or July, go long November and short May (next year) lumber contracts.

***

PLYWOOD

Plywood, like lumber, is heavily utilized in residential construction. As such, since it is a factor in production costs, it is highly sensitive to interest rates, to the level of housing starts, and the level of inflation.

Plywood is a good vehicle for the seasonal trader. It is less volatile than lumber, its risks are much lower and rewards only slightly lower. Bull spreads in plywood are safer than in lumber because plywood is a carrying charge commodity and, therefore, full carry protects the spread.

Plywood traditionally makes two major moves each year:

1. The seasonal up-move from October lows to the seasonal highs in March and,
2. The down-move from March to September if additional buying because of low inventories becomes necessary.

The seasonal up-move can be attributed to the construction industry's purchase of plywood during the fall and winter months. Builders accumulate inventories in advance for the next building season. Also, the seasonal bottom often comes in late June to early July.

***

Short July vs. Long November PLYWOOD

This is a bear spread: It is established about mid-February and liquidated in mid-April. If it shows a definite bear trend it should be kept on until the end of May. In March, the spread tends to test its highs. When the test of the previous highs results in a penetration of those highs, it indicates a contra-seasonal move. If that happens the spread should be reversed and a bull spread entered. Another possibility is to initiate the bear spread between March 15-25 and close it out before July 1. If just before the initiation of the spread a contra-seasonal move is indicated, abandon the idea of the bear spread and enter a bull spread.

***

Note: A bull spread in plywood is always safer than a bull spread in lumber. Plywood is a carrying charge commodity, and, therefore, the spread is protected by full carry, provided, of course, that interest rates remain stable during its life. Falling interest rates would benefit this bull spread.

In case of an oil embargo or shortage, the production of gasoline and the industrial uses of petroleum will be reduced. Plywood is constructed by glueing several sheets of thin wood together to form a board. Glue is a petroleum product and a shortage of it will restrict the production of plywood. A severe oil shortage would suggest a low-margin, very conservative bull spread speculation: Buy a nearby contract two to three months forward and sell a deferred contract nine months forward. For example, if an oil embargo is announced in April, the speculator would go long July plywood and short January (next year) plywood.

***

LUMBER vs. PLYWOOD

A popular inter-market spread in wood is lumber versus plywood. Lumber is traded on the Chicago Mercantile Exchange and the contract calls for delivery of 130,000 board ft. A price move of one dollar is equivalent to a profit or loss of $130 to the trader. Plywood is traded on the Chicago Board of Trade and the contract calls for delivery of 76,032 sq. ft. A price move of one dollar is equivalent to a profit or loss of about $76 to the trader.

Because the contracts are of different sizes, a spread between the two, to be approximately balanced, should consist of one lumber contract versus two plywood contracts. A 100-point move ($1) in lumber would be equivalent, as mentioned before, to $130 while a 100-point move ($1) for the two plywood contracts would amount to $152.

***

Long September LUMBER vs. Short September PLYWOOD

Because plywood is made of lower quality wood, lumber has a higher intrinsic value than plywood. During past bull moves in wood products, lumber has traded at several thousand points premium over plywood.

If one unit of lumber is spread against one unit plywood, profit or loss calculation is based on comparing contract values. This is called a 'money spread'. In the trade suggested above, one long unit of lumber is spread against two short plywood units. In this case each 100-point ($1) movement in the spread is worth about $140 change in equity. That is, one assumes a profit of about $140 for each 100 points lumber rises faster than plywood.

Most of the up and down moves in this spread seem to follow the action in the lumber market. Often this spread is in a down-trend between February and June; in July and August lumber tends to gain sharply on plywood. While there are short-term opportunities due to large day-to-day and week-to-week fluctuations, the spread often appears to be trendless until the last few weeks of trading. Follow this spread very closely. The risk factor is high.

***

COMMODITY:	COTTON No. 2
EXCHANGE:	New York Cotton Exchange
TRADING HOURS:	10:30 to 3:00 Eastern Time
DELIVERY MONTHS:	Mch, May, Jly, Oct, Dec.
TRADING UNIT:	50,000 lbs.
PRICE QUOTED IN:	¢/lb.
MINIMUM PRICE FLUCTUATION:	1/100¢/lb. (1 pt. = $5)
VALUE OF MINIMUM FLUCTUATION:	$5.00 per contract unit
VALUE OF ONE CENT MOVE:	$500.00
DAILY LIMIT OF PRICE MOVE:	Two cents + or -
VALUE OF DAILY LIMIT:	$1,000.00
FIRST DELIVERY DAY NOTICE:	5 full business days prior to 1st business day of delivery month
LAST TRADING DAY:	17th last business day of delivery month
CROP YEAR:	August 1 to July 31

***

COMMODITY:	LUMBER
EXCHANGE:	Chicago Mercantile Exchange
TRADING HOURS:	9:00 to 1:05 Central Time
DELIVERY MONTHS:	Jan, Mch, May, Jly, Sep, Nov.
TRADING UNIT:	130,000 board feet
PRICE QUOTED IN:	$/1,000 board feet
MINIMUM PRICE FLUCTUATION:	10¢/1,000 bd. ft. (10 pts = $13)
VALUE OF MINIMUM FLUCTUATION:	$13.00 per contract unit
VALUE OF ONE DOLLAR MOVE:	$130.00
DAILY LIMIT OF PRICE MOVE:	Five dollars + or -
VALUE OF DAILY LIMIT:	$650.00
FIRST DELIVERY DAY NOTICE:	Any business day after last trading day from 3rd to last business day of the month
LAST TRADING DAY:	Business day immediately preceding 16th day of the month

COMMODITY:	PLYWOOD
EXCHANGE:	Chicago Board of Trade
TRADING HOURS:	9:00 to 1:00 Central Time
DELIVERY MONTHS:	Jan, Mch, May, Jly, Sep, Nov.
TRADING UNIT:	76,032 square feet
PRICE QUOTED IN:	$/1,000 sq. ft.
MINIMUM PRICE FLUCTUATION:	10¢/1,000 sq. ft. (10 pts.=$7.60)
VALUE OF MINIMUM FLUCTUATION:	$7.60 per contract unit
VALUE OF ONE DOLLAR MOVE:	$76.03
DAILY LIMIT OF PRICE MOVE:	Seven dollars + or -
VALUE OF DAILY LIMIT:	$532.21
FIRST DELIVERY DAY NOTICE:	Last business day of month preceding delivery month
LAST TRADING DAY:	8th last business day of the contract month

***

COTTON: DECEMBER / MARCH

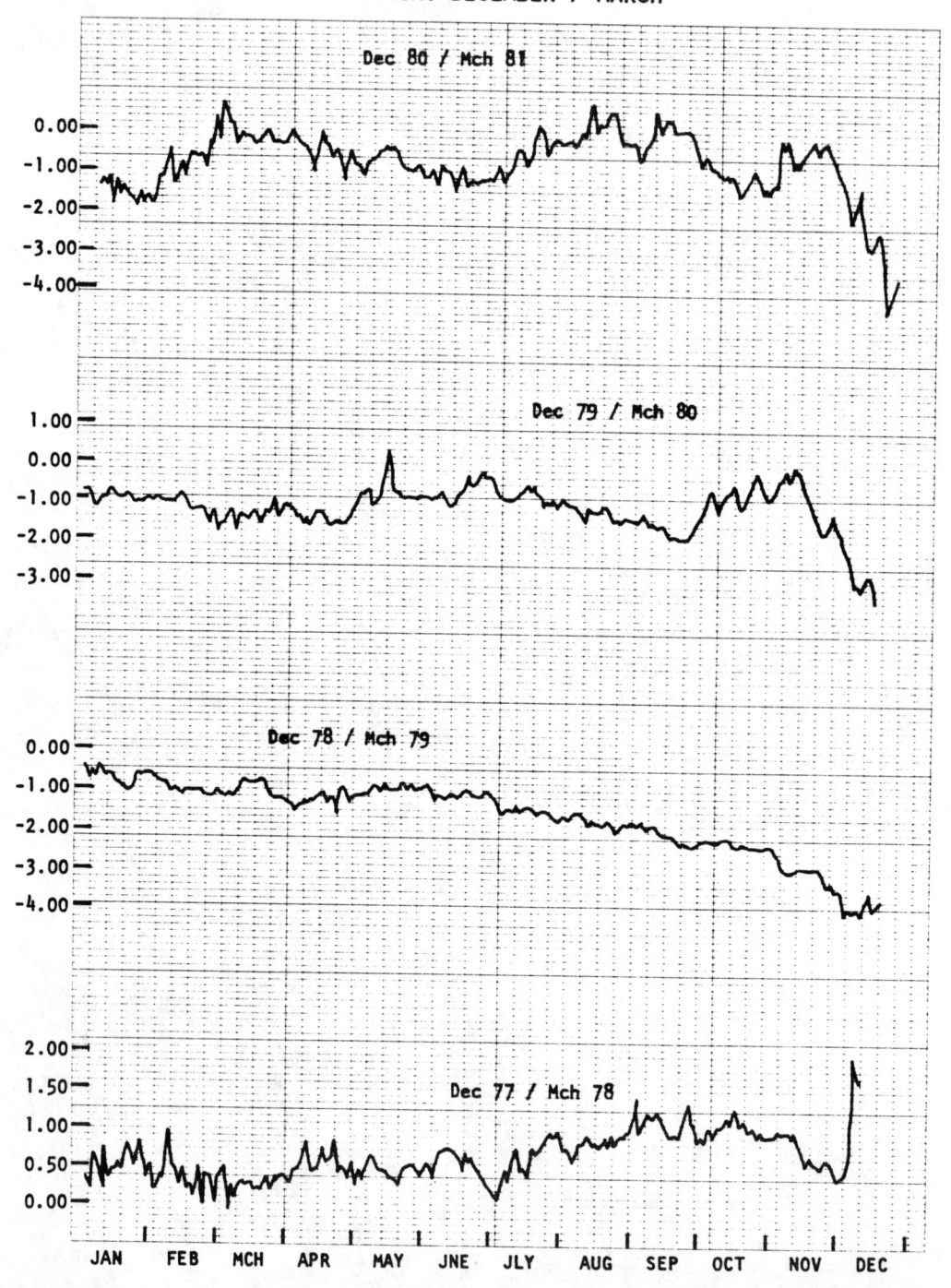

COTTON: JULY / DECEMBER

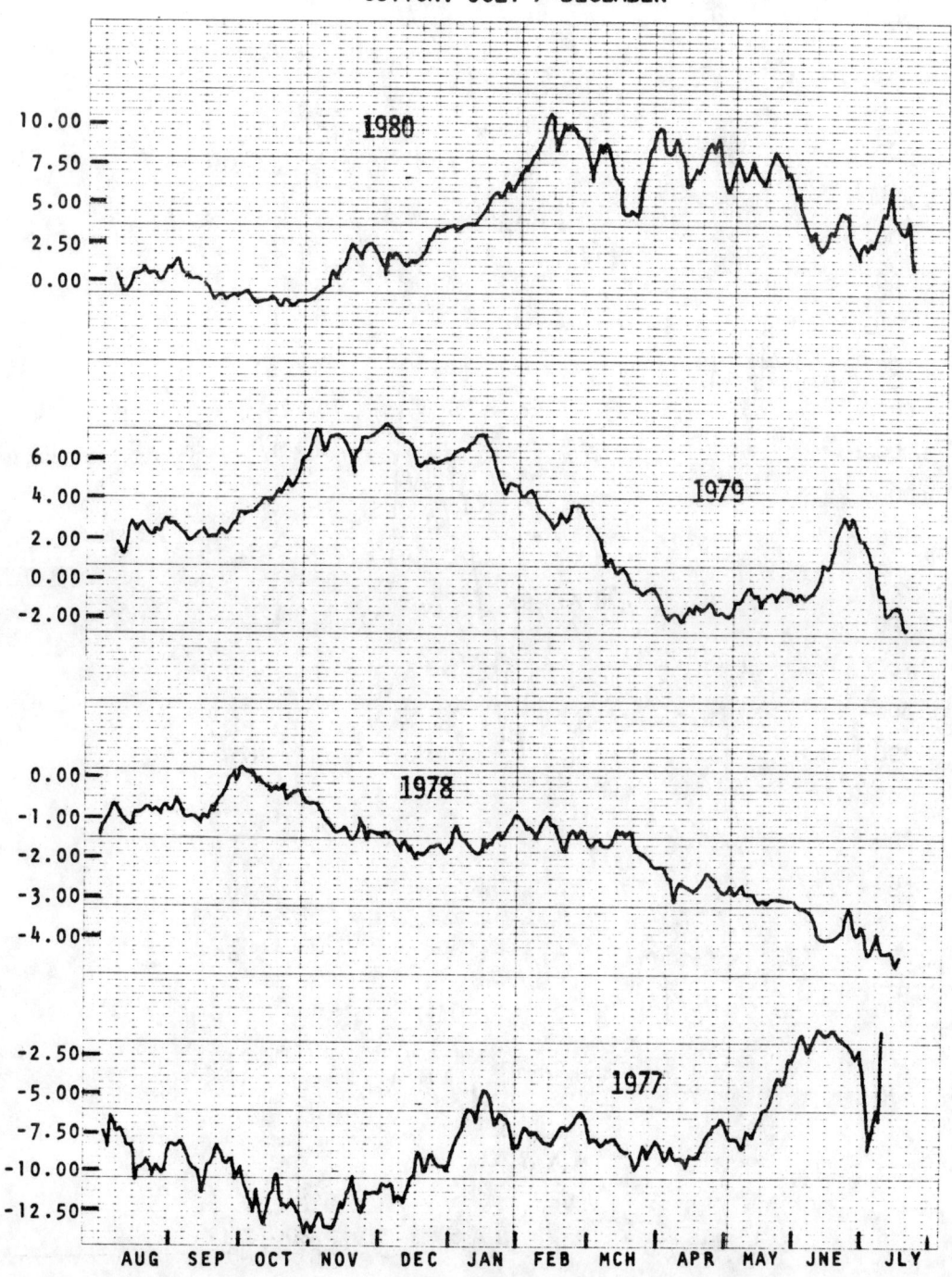

SPREAD SCOPE
Commodity Spread Charts

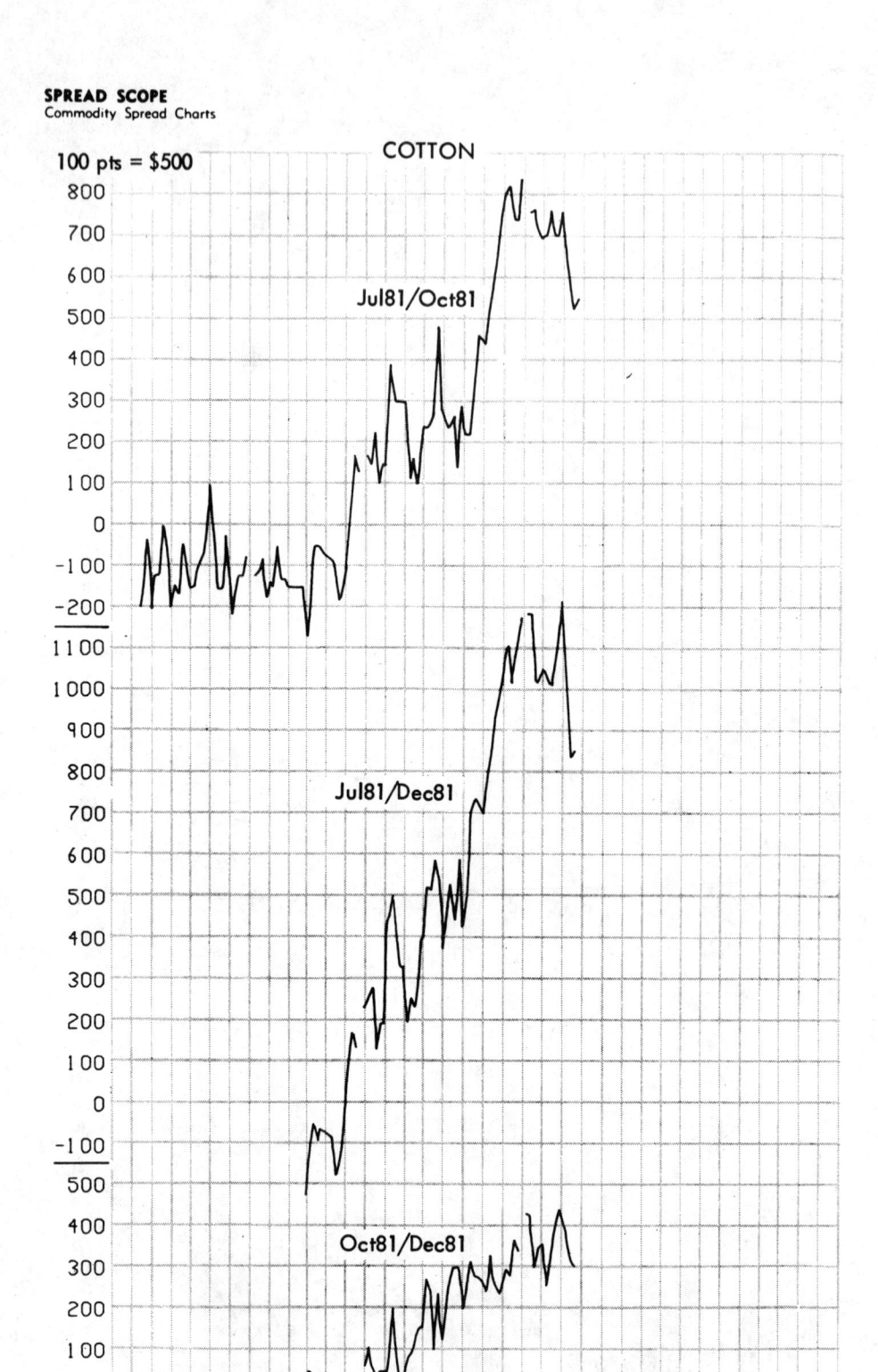

COTTON

Spread chart courtesy of Spread Scope, Inc.

144

LUMBER: SEPTEMBER / NOVEMBER

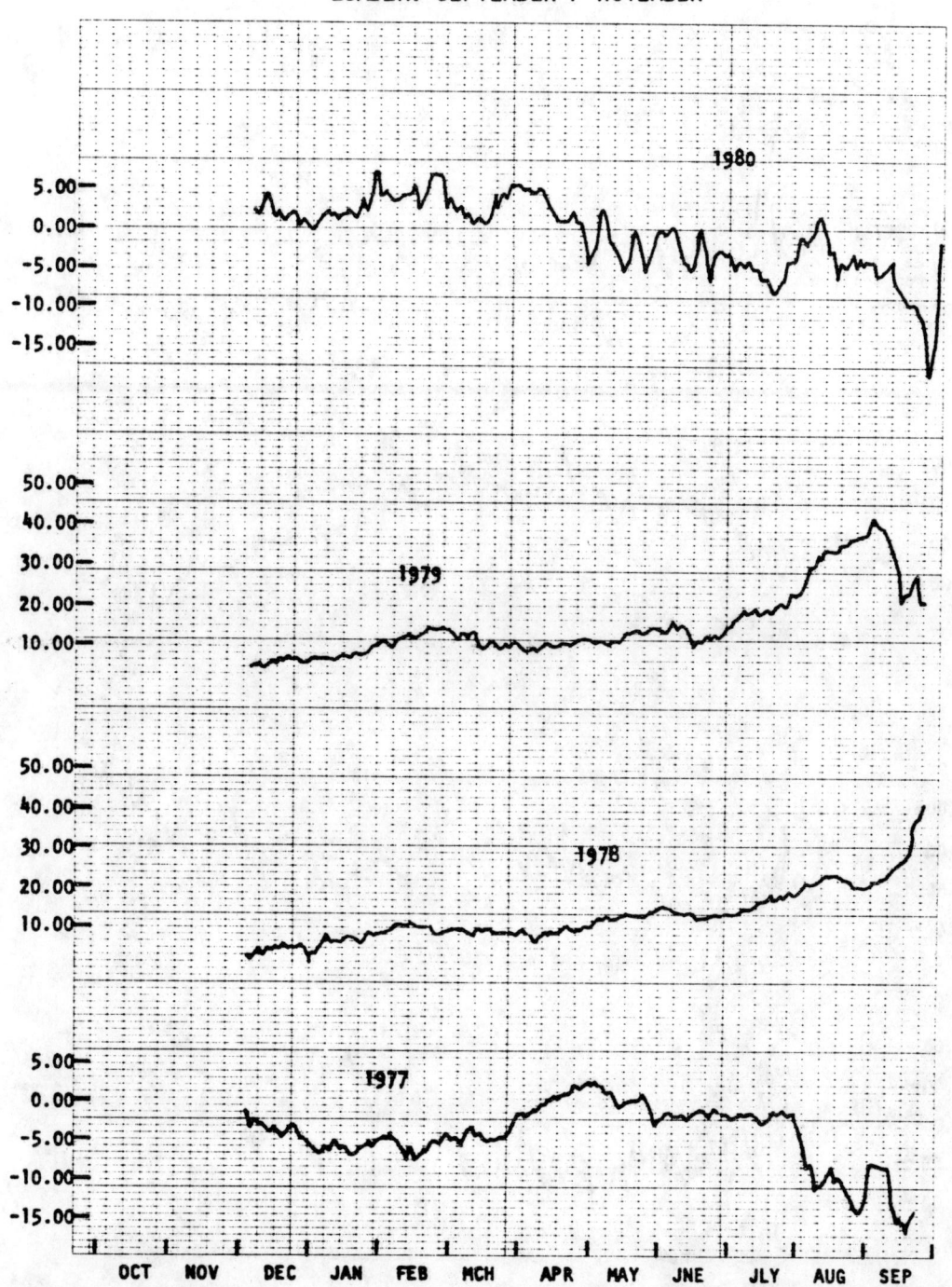

PLYWOOD: JULY / SEPTEMBER

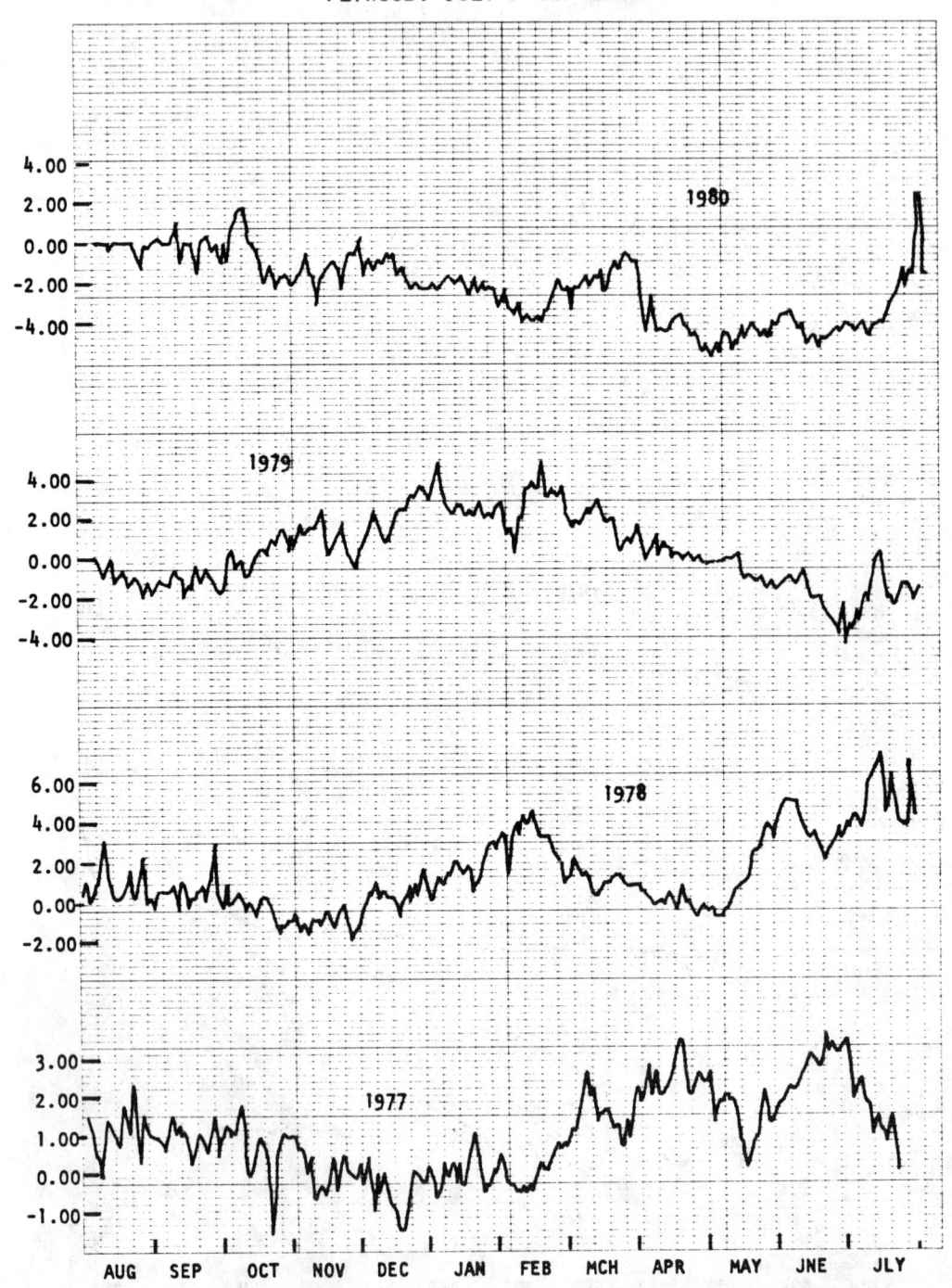

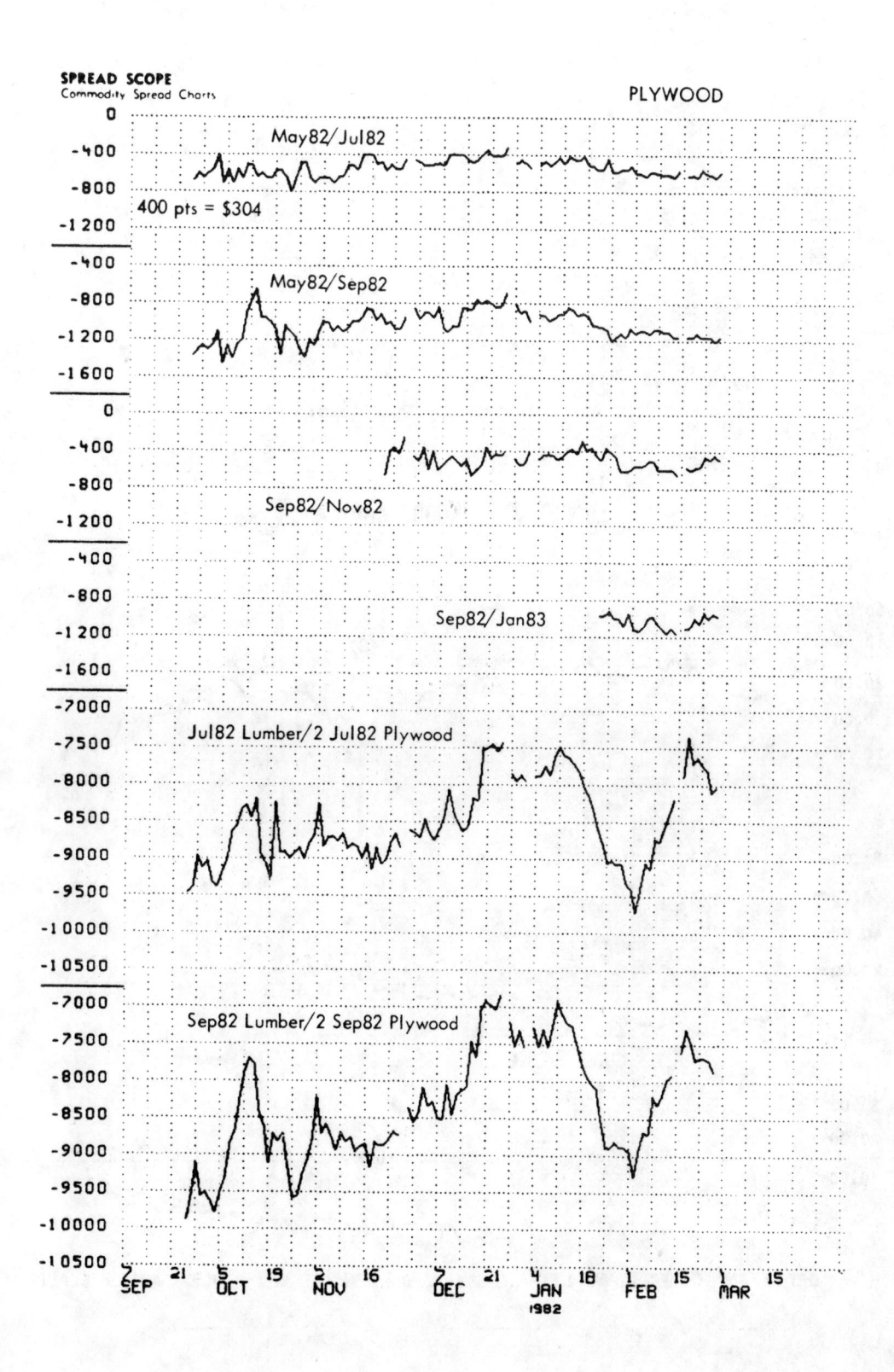

Spread chart courtesy of Spread Scope, Inc.

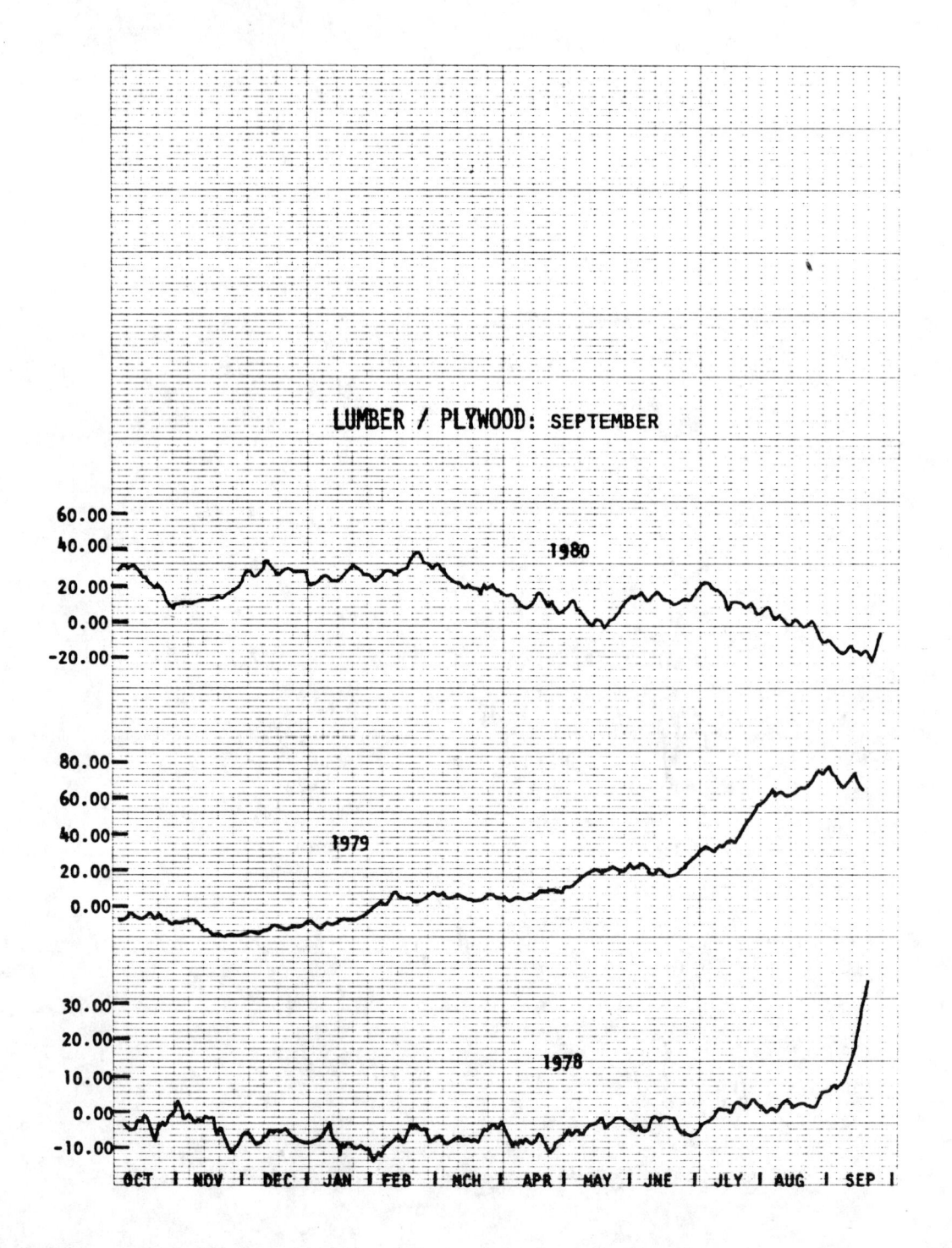

LUMBER / PLYWOOD: SEPTEMBER

LUMBER / PLYWOOD: JULY 1981

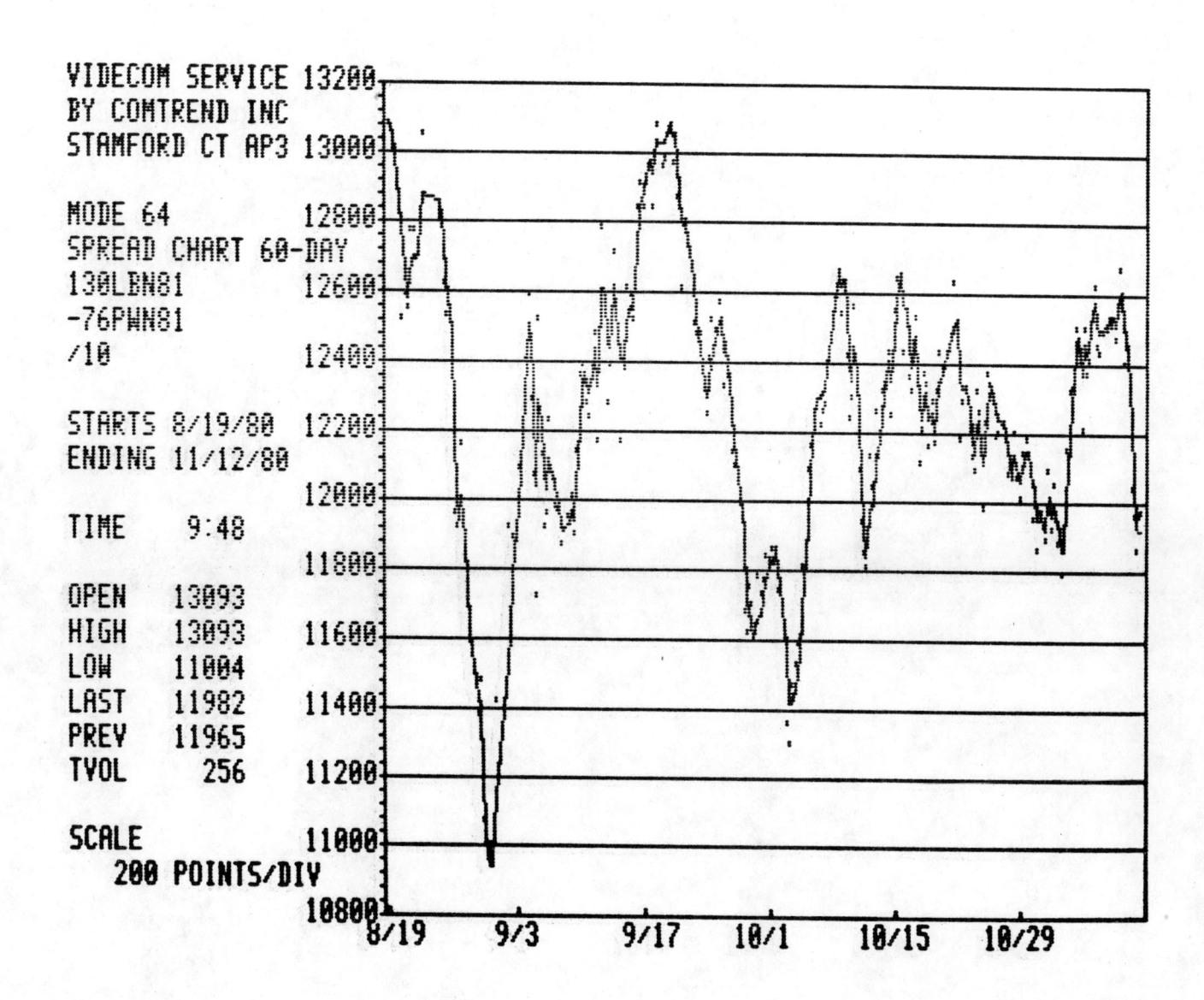

```
VIDECOM SERVICE
BY COMTREND INC
STAMFORD CT AP3

MODE 64
SPREAD CHART 60-DAY
130LBN81
-76PWN81
/10

STARTS 8/19/80
ENDING 11/12/80

TIME     9:48

OPEN    13093
HIGH    13093
LOW     11004
LAST    11982
PREV    11965
TVOL      256

SCALE
  200 POINTS/DIV
```

Videcom Spread Charts courtesy of ADP Comtrend.

METALS & PETROLEUM

COPPER

The housing and the automobile industries are the largest users of copper. Car manufacturers buy copper during the year's first quarter. The construction people buy during late winter and early spring. The large purchases made by these two users push copper prices up from December through March. Then, as the need declines, the season's lows are reached during October and November.

Copper seasonals are reliable. In normal years the price movements are long, strong and, within limits, predictable. Put on limited risk spreads in mid-winter; liquidate them in early spring and seasonal profits can be realized.

***

Long May vs. Short December COPPER

During the last few years copper spreads have become a function of price and interest rates. High interest rates have kept the copper spreads at historically wide levels.

Put on the long May vs. short December spread during the last week in December or the first week of January and hold it until mid-March to early April. Or, trade it by aiming at a 200-250-point profit and liquidating the spread if and when the hoped for profit is attained. Sharply increased industrial activity and/or falling interest rates will provide excellent profits, even a premium for the May contract if a true bull market in copper develops.

***

GOLD

The amount of the world's gold, above ground, has been estimated at 75,000 tons. Of this amount, about 20,000 tons in the form of bullion, is in private hands. Thirty-five thousand tons is owned by governments and official agencies. The balance, 20,000 tons has been fabricated into jewelry and religious articles. Because the annual supply of newly mined gold is barely 1,000 tons, the day-by-day fluctuation in the price of the metal is determined, for the most part, by transactions among the holders of large amounts of bullion.

The government of South Africa, the largest producer of gold in the free world, sometimes supports the price of the commodity by limiting the supply of new gold in the market.

Another control this government exerts over the price of gold is in the trades and swaps it arranges with other countries.

Other governments or agencies, with one or two exceptions, seldom enter into the gold pricing structure. The International Monetary Fund and the United States, for example, which used to sell gold from their stockpiles, no longer do so and there is no indication, at this writing, that they plan to in the future.

The largest, single factor which keeps the price of gold down in today's market may be the 80 to 250 tons sold annually by the Soviet Union. The Russian gold sale is made necessary by their perennial crop disasters. These force the Soviets to import large quantities of agricultural commodities from countries outside the communist block; the gold is used to raise the needed foreign exchange.

Other factors also weigh heavily on future gold (and silver) prices:

- Balance of payments: Large deficits are bullish.
- The dollar: A weak dollar is bullish.
- The U.S. budget: Large and/or record deficits are bullish.
- The economy: A credit crunch, serious recession, or a depression are all bearish and could cause a collapse of gold prices.
- Inflation: Expectation of increased inflation is bullish. However, as nominal interest rates rise above the inflation rate, investors tend to liquidate their gold/silver holdings in favor of financial investments. The real rates of return are the important factors, not merely the fact of rising or falling interest rates.
- Other bullish factors: Price controls; poor crops or crop failure; oil cartel price rises; banking system problems; tax cuts with no real spending cuts; an expanding money supply; the shutdown of South African gold mines; heavy Mid-Eastern buying; and last, but not least: war!

Investor demand for gold is low when interest rates are high, when a strong dollar attracts funds into dollar denominated assets and away from foreign currencies, gold coins, medals and bar investments none of which pays a return. Industrial users will allow their inventories to become depleted because of high financing costs. When inventories are low, however, and interest rates come down, fabricator demand and hedging operators, seeking to lock in on favorable prices, cause an upsurge in the price of gold. In simplest terms, the demand side is influenced, basically, by (1) the world's economy and (2) inflation psychology.

***

GOLD SPREADS

The price action in gold spreads is a function of:

    (a) Interest rates, and
    (b) the price of gold.

For example, sharply higher interest rates and higher gold prices will cause distant gold futures contracts to gain on the nearby futures. Thus, in a bull market the carrying charges - whose primary determinant is interest rates - will tend to increase and result in the deferred months gaining ground on the nearbys. This situation is the exact opposite to what we have seen in grains, oilseeds, pork bellies and other carrying charge, limited risk commodities. As completely storable commodities, the rule for gold (and silver) is:

(1) Buy the distant contract and sell short the nearby to take advantage of a bull market.
(2) Buy the nearby and sell the distant contract to take advantage of a bear market.

If there is a seasonal tendency for gold to advance it is expected to begin in September.

***

SILVER

The late winter---early spring price rise in silver is based on its use as an industrial commodity. The demand for silver follows a pattern similar to the demand for copper. Silver prices tend to move up in sympathy with the winter run-up of copper. Also, silver is strongly influenced by the price action of gold.

***

SILVER SPREADS

As a completely storable commodity, silver follows the rule noted for gold: In bull markets sell the nearby contracts and buy the distants. In a bear market, do the opposite: Buy the nearbys and sell the distant contracts. This in expectation that carrying charges will narrow if the market declines and cause the distant month's price to fall faster then the nearby's. There is one exception to this rule and it occurs when a short squeeze develops. This is a rare situation but when it does happen the nearbys will rise faster than the distant months. In general, silver spreads work poorly, even in strong bull markets - unless interest rates soar.

GOLD vs. SILVER SPREADS

The price of gold compared to silver has fluctuated widely on an historical basis. Spreading precious metals is risky but, of course, the profit opportunities are commensurately great.

The gold/silver price ratio is the number of silver ounces it takes at any given time to buy one ounce of gold. For example, when gold sells for $450 and silver sells for $9 at the same time, the gold/silver ratio is then 50:1.

During the early days of the United States the ratio between gold and silver varied from about 10:1 to 16:1. When in the late 1800s silver was demonetized in Europe and was eliminated from coinage in the U.S., the ratio rose to 40:1. During the economic depression of the 1930s silver's price plummeted and in 1932 the ratio soared to an all-time high of 70:1. In 1966 when gold was still $35 per troy ounce and silver was priced at $1.29 per troy ounce, the gold/silver ratio was 27:1. When gold peaked at $850 and silver also peaked at $48 per ounce late January in 1980, the ratio was a bit over 17:1. Subsequently, precious metals prices plunged and by March 1980 the ratio widened out to 44:1. Further erosion of prices during '81 widened the ratio out to 49:1 on July 1 ($414 gold and $8.33 silver). The ratio then narrowed to 40:1 but then came the announcement that the U.S. government will sell 1.25 million ounces of silver at regular intervals from the national defense stockpile. The severe market reaction pushed the ratio to 51:1. By the end of March '82 the ratio was 45.6:1 (gold at $318.50 and silver at $6.97).

The 50:1 ratio of July and September 1981 may be a double top and in that area one would buy a 5,000-ounce silver contract and sell one 100-ounce gold contract in the expectation of another narrowing of the ratio. The margin for this spread would be the sum of the margins required for the two units separately. The trader would also pay two commissions, one for each individual commodity.

A less expensive trade would be the mini-contracts on the MidAmerica Commodity Exchange, using a 33.2-ounce gold contract versus a 1,000-ounce silver contract.

Whenever the ratio approaches the lower limits, the strategy is: Buy gold and sell silver. While the ratio must be favorable for a given spread, one must keep in mind at all times that silver is basically an industrial metal and its usage is dependent on the health of the economy.

***

PLATINUM vs. GOLD SPREADS

Although each metal trades on its respective fundamentals, the two metals usually move in tandem. The automobile and petroleum industries account for about 70% of platinum sales. U.S. production of platinum is negligible. Imports from South Africa and the USSR provide 60% and 20% of U.S. imports, respectively. Current government stockpiles are less than ½-million troy ounces of platinum, well below the U.S. government goal of 1.3 million troy ounces.

During 1975, platinum's discount to gold reached $40. It was a year when the automobile industry, the largest user of platinum, was severely depressed. The Japanese jewelry industry is another large platinum user but the year 1981 has seen a sharp decline of demand from Japan. The discount of $55 under gold was recorded more than once in 1981. On the other hand, in March 1980 when platinum reached its historically high price of $1,085 per ounce, its <u>premium</u> over gold was $420 which is $110 higher per ounce than platinum's price was in March 1982!

While platinum participates in all precious metals' rallies, one must still remember it is an industrial metal. As the economy accelerates, therefore, platinum tends to gain on gold. Also, a drop in interest rates favors platinum. It is also true, however, that sustained high interest rates would fail to stimulate heavier industrial activity and stockpiling platinum.

Provided the outlook for the platinum/gold spread is favorable on the basis of expanding industrial activity, the trader may consider two seasonal patterns:

First, platinum often makes substantial gains on gold beginning late March. To take advantage of this move, buy two (2) units of July platinum versus the short sale of one (1) unit of September gold. (Platinum on NY Merc., gold on Chicago Merc.)

Second, platinum tends to gain on gold from mid-October to early January. In this instance the trader would go long two units of April platinum (NY Merc.) versus short one unit of April gold (Comex). These trades should be initiated as platinum nears support levels relative to gold.

***

No. 2 HEATING OIL

Within four years of its inception, in 1982, the No. 2 Heating Oil contract joined the twenty most actively traded commodities. There are many people and industries trading No. 2 contracts. To name a few, there are refiners, oil dealers, jobbers, wholesalers; consumers of oil products, utilities, trucking companies, school systems, apartment complexes, airlines, glass and chemical companies, etc. Almost everybody in the production/distribution chain is exposed to price risk, thus, hedgers account for a large portion of market participants.

The heating oil market is ideal for futures trading. The price is volatile and responds to many influences. Among these are:

- The weather
- Inventories
- Seasonal price fluctuations
- OPEC meetings
- U.S. energy and conservation measures
- Economic conditions
- Political developments, both domestic and international.

Like a crop, heating oil is weather sensitive and its price is seasonal. However, while weather affects the supply of a crop, with heating oil it influences demand.

Usage: Because heating oil is used mainly in the winter, demand starts to increase in the fall and reaches its peak in January or February.

Supply: The end of the heating season is in March or April and at that time stocks are lowest. Stocks start to increase during the second quarter and peak early in the fourth quarter.

Prices: On seasonal demand basis heating oil prices bottom in late spring or early summer and then increase, until they peak, in October of November, the start of the winter heating season.

There is a seeming contradiction in the two previous paragraphs dealing with supply and price patterns. Note, there is a seasonal peak in distillate oil stocks during the fourth quarter. Prices also peak about the same time. This unusual situation is due, probably, to anticipation of winter demand, to inflation and to the resulting automatic price increases by the OPEC, and to political tensions in the Mideast.

Since each one-cent move per gallon is worth $420 gain or loss per contract this market can be quite risky.

Long January vs. Short March HEATING OIL

A bull spread consisting of long January versus short March contracts established in late August, or right after Labor Day, and liquidated during the second week of December could work profitably.

This is an interesting spread but additional study of this market is needed. Future editions of this book or its supplements will bring further details. Heating oil is one of the 'survival' commodities, like gold and silver, that floor traders buy promptly at even the serious threat of war. Because oil is a cartel-controlled commodity, the prudent trader will trade only net long positions. The possibility of war, and oil embargo, or the imposition of price controls is ever present and the trader must keep in mind that oil products are storable commodities. There is, however, relatively little storage space available for long-term holding. This limited storage space capacity for crude oil and its products explains, in part, the volatility of oil prices. A glut of products can back up the whole production chain and thus the industry is extremely vulnerable to declines in product offtake. These factors in addition to changes in world crude market supplies, can disturb the seasonal pattern.

***

COMMODITY:	C O P P E R
EXCHANGE:	N.Y. Commodity Exchange, Inc.
TRADING HOURS:	9:50 to 2:00 Eastern Time
DELIVERY MONTHS:	Jan, Mch, May, Jly, Sep, Dec.
TRADING UNIT:	25,000 lbs.
PRICE QUOTED IN:	¢/lb.
MINIMUM PRICE FLUCTUATION:	5/100¢/lb.
VALUE OF MINIMUM FLUCTUATION:	$12.50 per contract unit
VALUE OF ONE CENT MOVE:	$250.00 per contract
DAILY LIMIT OF PRICE MOVE:	Five cents + or -
VALUE OF DAILY LIMIT:	$1,250.00
FIRST DELIVERY DAY NOTICE:	Next to last business day of the month prior to delivery month
LAST TRADING DAY:	The third to last business day of delivery month

COMMODITY:	G O L D (COMEX)
EXCHANGE:	N.Y. Commodity Exchange, Inc.
TRADING HOURS:	9:25 to 2:30 Eastern Time
DELIVERY MONTHS:	Feb, Apr, Jne, Aug, Oct, Dec.
TRADING UNIT:	100 troy ounces
PRICE QUOTED IN:	$/troy ounce
MINIMUM PRICE FLUCTUATION:	10¢/troy oz. (10 pts. = $10.00)
VALUE OF MINIMUM FLUCTUATION:	$10.00 per contract unit

VALUE OF ONE DOLLAR MOVE:	$100.00
DAILY LIMIT OF PRICE MOVE:	$25.00 + or -
VALUE OF DAILY LIMIT:	$2,500.00
FIRST DELIVERY DAY NOTICE:	Next to last business day of the month prior to delivery month
LAST TRADING DAY:	The third to last business day of delivery month

COMMODITY:	G O L D (IMM)
EXCHANGE:	International Monetary Market, Chicago Mercantile Exchange
TRADING HOURS:	8:25 to 1:30 Central Time
DELIVERY MONTHS:	Jan, Mch, Apr, Jne, Jly, Sep, Oct, Dec.
TRADING UNIT:	100 troy ounces
PRICE QUOTED IN:	$/troy oz.
MINIMUM PRICE FLUCTUATION:	10¢/troy oz. (10 pts. = $10)
VALUE OF MINIMUM FLUCTUATION:	$10.00 per contract unit
VALUE OF ONE DOLLAR MOVE:	$100.00
DAILY LIMIT OF PRICE MOVE:	$50.00 + or -
VALUE OF DAILY LIMIT:	$5,000.00
FIRST DELIVERY DAY NOTICE:	First business day of delivery mo.
LAST TRADING DAY:	Day prior to fifth to the last business day of contract month

COMMODITY:	G O L D (MidAm)
EXCHANGE:	MidAmerica Commodity Exchange
TRADING HOURS:	8:25 to 1:40 Central Time
DELIVERY MONTHS:	Mch, Jne, Sep, Dec.
TRADING UNIT:	33.2 troy ounces
PRICE QUOTED IN:	$/troy oz.
MINIMUM PRICE FLUCTUATION:	2½¢/troy oz. (10 pts. = $3.32)
VALUE OF MINIMUM FLUCTUATION:	83 cents per contract unit
VALUE OF ONE DOLLAR MOVE:	$33.20
DAILY LIMIT OF PRICE MOVE:	$10.00 + or -
VALUE OF DAILY LIMIT:	$332.00
LAST TRADING DAY:	Day prior to fifth to the last business day of delivery month

COMMODITY:	S I L V E R (COMEX)
EXCHANGE:	N.Y. Commodity Exchange, Inc.
TRADING HOURS:	9:40 to 2:15 Eastern Time
DELIVERY MONTHS:	Jan, Mch, May, Jly, Sep, Dec.
TRADING UNIT:	5,000 troy ounces
PRICE QUOTED IN:	¢/troy ounce
MINIMUM PRICE FLUCTUATION:	1/10th ¢ (10 pts. = $5.00)
VALUE OF MINIMUM FLUCTUATION:	$5.00 per contract unit
VALUE OF ONE CENT MOVE:	$50.00
DAILY LIMIT OF PRICE MOVE:	20¢ + or -
VALUE OF DAILY LIMIT:	$1,000.00
FIRST DELIVERY DAY NOTICE:	Next to the last business day of

LAST TRADING DAY: the month prior to deliv. month
The third to the last business day of delivery month

COMMODITY: S I L V E R   (CBT)
EXCHANGE: Chicago Board of Trade
TRADING HOURS: 8:40 to 1:25 Central Time
DELIVERY MONTHS: Feb, Apr, Jne, Aug, Oct, Dec.
TRADING UNIT: 5,000 troy ounces
PRICE QUOTED IN: ¢/troy ounce
MINIMUM PRICE FLUCTUATION: 1/10¢/troy oz. (10 pts. = $5)
VALUE OF MINIMUM FLUCTUATION: $5.00 per contract unit
VALUE OF ONE CENT MOVE: $50.00
DAILY LIMIT OF PRICE MOVE: 20¢/oz. + or -
VALUE OF DAILY LIMIT: $1,000.00
LAST TRADING DAY: 4th last business day of contract month

COMMODITY: S I L V E R   (MidAm)
EXCHANGE: MidAmerica Commodity Exchange
TRADING HOURS: 8:40 to 1:40 Central Time
DELIVERY MONTHS: Feb, Apr, Jne, Aug, Oct, Dec.
TRADING UNIT: 1,000 troy ounces
PRICE QUOTED IN: ¢/troy oz.
MINIMUM PRICE FLUCTUATION: .05¢/troy oz. (10 pts. = $1.00)
VALUE OF MINIMUM FLUCTUATION: 50¢ per contract unit
VALUE OF ONE CENT MOVE: $10.00
DAILY LIMIT OF PRICE MOVE: 20¢/oz. + or -
VALUE OF DAILY LIMIT: $200.00
LAST TRADING DAY: 3rd last business day of contract month.

COMMODITY: P L A T I N U M
EXCHANGE: N.Y. Mercantile Exchange
TRADING HOURS: 9:30 to 2:30 Eastern Time
DELIVERY MONTHS: Jan, Apr, Jly, Oct.
TRADING UNIT: 50 troy ounces
PRICE QUOTED IN: $/troy ounce
MINIMUM PRICE FLUCTUATION: 10¢/troy oz. (10 pts. = $5.00)
VALUE OF MINIMUM FLUCTUATION: $5.00 per contract unit
VALUE OF ONE DOLLAR MOVE: $50.00
DAILY LIMIT OF PRICE MOVE: $10/oz. + or -
VALUE OF DAILY LIMIT: $500.00
FIRST DELIVERY DAY: The second business day of the delivery month
LAST TRADING DAY: The fourth business day prior to the end of the delivery month

COMMODITY:	No. 2 HEATING OIL
EXCHANGE:	N.Y. Mercantile Exchange
TRADING HOURS:	10:30 to 2:45 Eastern Time
DELIVERY MONTHS:	All months
TRADING UNIT:	42,000 U.S. gallons (1,000 U.S. barrels)
PRICE QUOTED IN:	$ and ¢ per gallon
MINIMUM PRICE FLUCTUATION:	$.0001 (.01¢) per gallon
VALUE OF MINIMUM FLUCTUATION:	$4.20 per contract unit
VALUE OF ONE CENT MOVE:	$420.00
DAILY LIMIT OF PRICE MOVE:	2¢/gallon + or -
VALUE OF DAILY LIMIT:	$840.00
FIRST DELIVERY DAY:	6th business day of deliv. month
LAST TRADING DAY:	Last business day of month prior to the delivery month

***

GOLD CASH PRICE LONDON

WEEKLY HIGH, LOW & CLOSE
(BASED ON DAILY EARLY & AFTERNOON QUOTE)

Prepared by Commodity Research Bureau, Inc.
ONE LIBERTY PLAZA, NEW YORK, N.Y. 10006

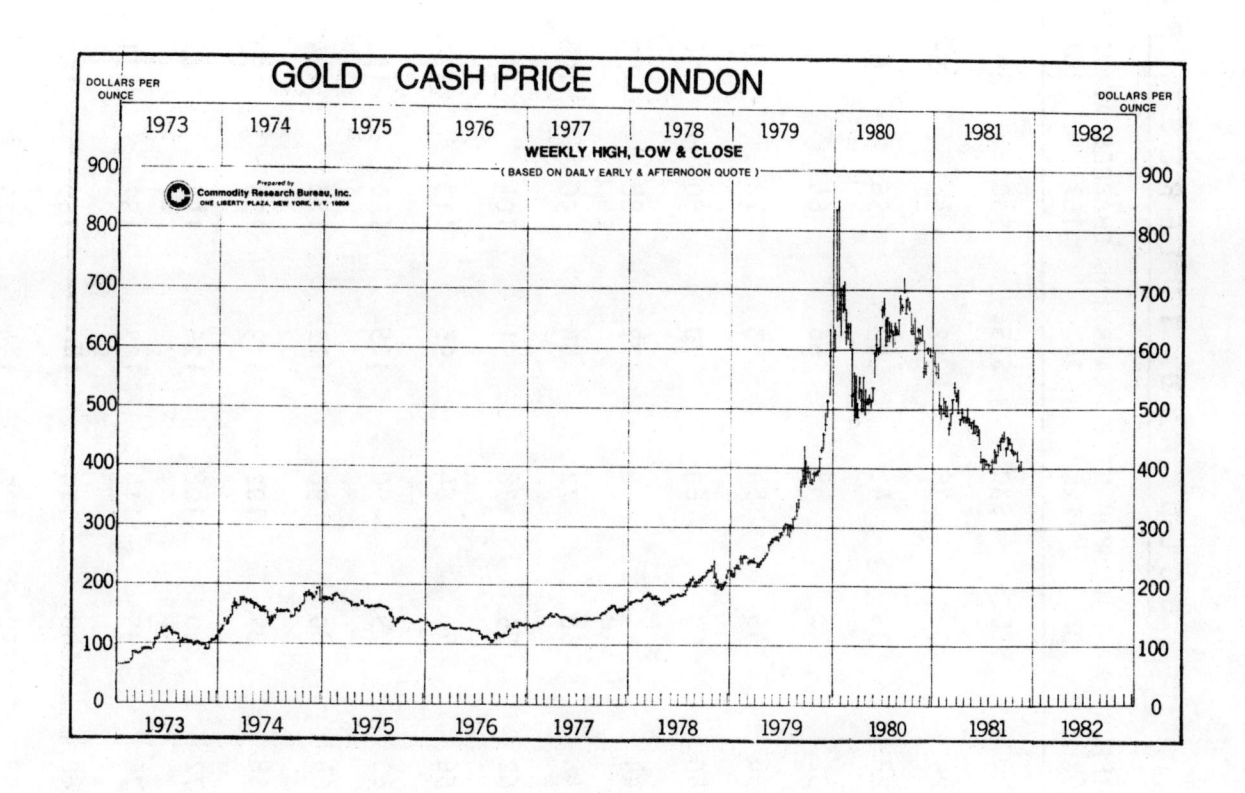

CHART REPRINTED FROM:
Commodity Chart Service
A Weekly Publication of
COMMODITY RESEARCH BUREAU, INC.
1 Liberty Plaza, New York, N. Y. 10006

GOLD AND INTEREST RATES

INTEREST RATE COMPONENT OF CARRYING CHARGES AT VARIOUS GOLD PRICES & INTEREST RATES:

GOLD PRICE: $/oz.	8%	10%	12%	14%	16%	18%	20%	22%	24%
$250	$20.-	$25.-	$30.-	$35.-	$40.-	$45.-	$50.-	$55.-	$60.-
300	24	30	36	42	48	54	60	66	72
350	28	35	42	49	56	63	70	77	84
400	32	40	48	56	64	72	80	88	96
450	36	45	54	63	72	81	90	99	108
500	40	50	60	70	80	90	100	110	120
550	44	55	66	77	88	99	110	121	132
600	48	60	72	84	96	108	120	132	144
650	52	65	78	91	104	117	130	143	156
700	56	70	84	98	112	126	140	154	168
750	60	75	90	105	120	135	150	165	180
800	64	80	96	112	128	144	160	176	192
850	68	85	102	119	136	153	170	187	204
900	72	90	108	126	144	162	180	198	216
950	76	95	114	133	152	171	190	209	228
1,000	80	100	120	140	160	180	200	220	240
1,100	88	110	132	154	176	198	220	242	264

(Interest rate = Prime rate + 1%)

SILVER AND INTEREST RATES

SILVER PRICE: CENTS/OZ.	INTEREST RATE COMPONENT OF CARRYING CHARGES AT VARIOUS SILVER PRICES & INTEREST RATES:								
	8%	10%	12%	14%	16%	18%	20%	22%	24%
650¢	52¢	65¢	78¢	91¢	104¢	117¢	130¢	143¢	156¢
700	56	70	84	98	112	126	140	154	168
750	60	75	90	105	120	135	150	165	180
800	64	80	96	112	128	144	160	176	192
850	68	85	102	119	136	153	170	187	204
900	72	90	108	126	144	162	180	198	216
950	76	95	114	133	152	171	190	209	228
1,000	80	100	120	140	160	180	200	220	240
1,100	88	110	132	154	176	198	220	242	264
1,200	96	120	144	168	192	216	240	264	288
1,300	104	130	156	182	208	234	260	286	312
1,400	112	140	168	196	224	252	280	308	336
1,500	120	150	180	210	240	270	300	330	360
2,000	160	200	240	280	320	360	400	440	480
2,500	200	250	300	350	400	450	500	550	600
3,000	240	300	360	420	480	540	600	660	720

(Interest rate = Prime rate + 1%)

COPPER: MAY / DECEMBER

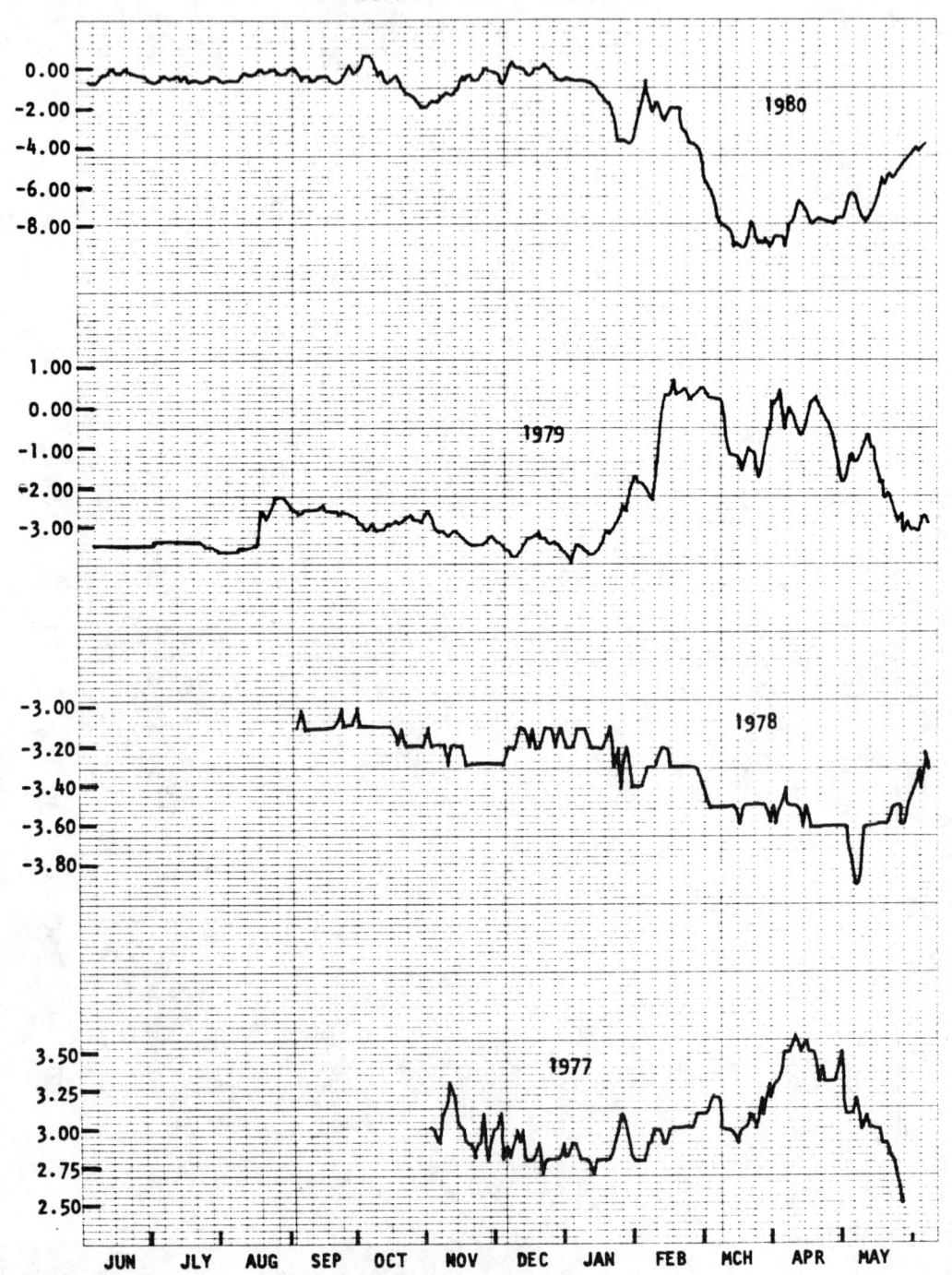

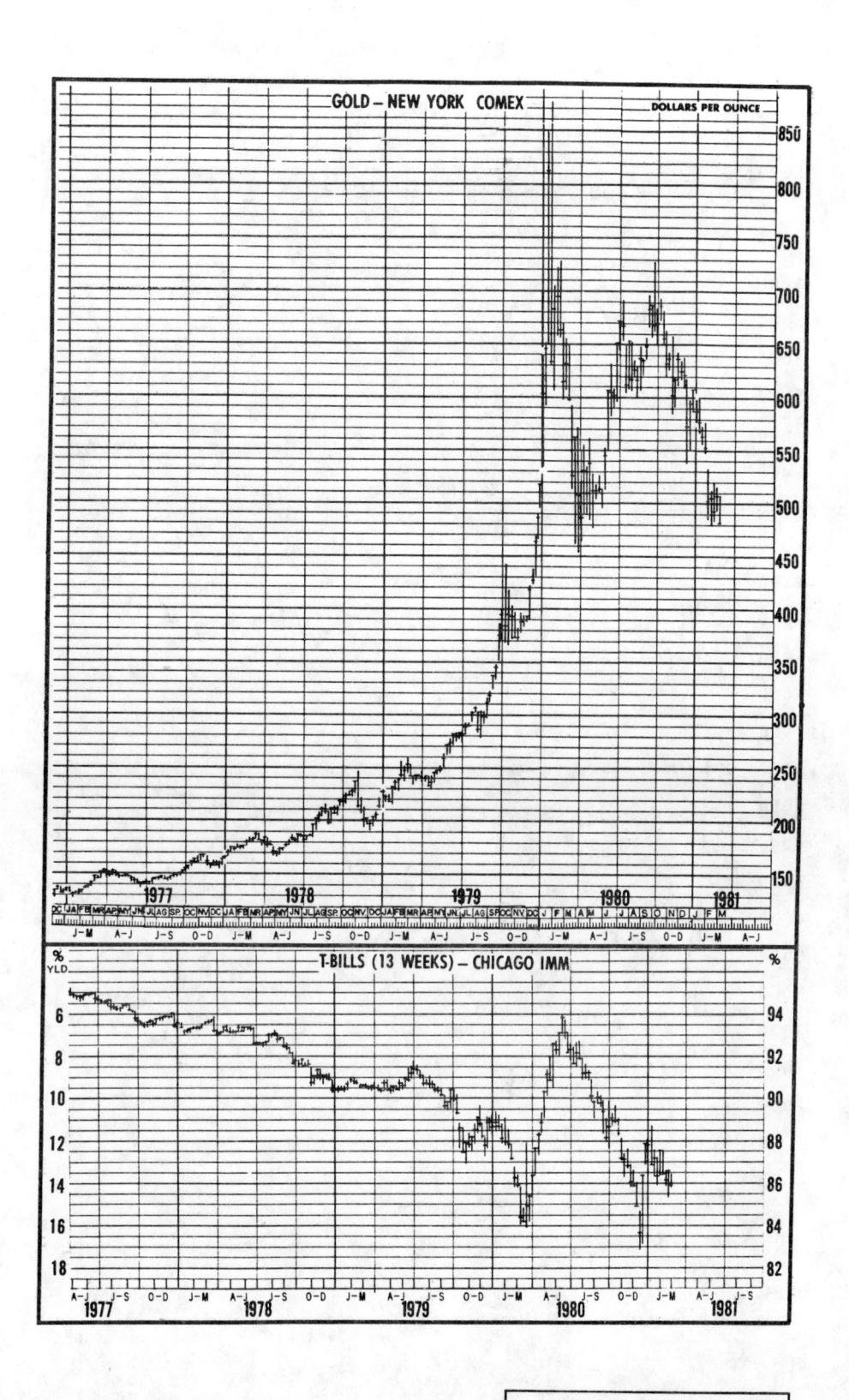

CHART REPRINTED FROM:
Commodity Chart Service
A Weekly Publication of
COMMODITY RESEARCH BUREAU, INC.
1 Liberty Plaza, New York, N.Y. 10006

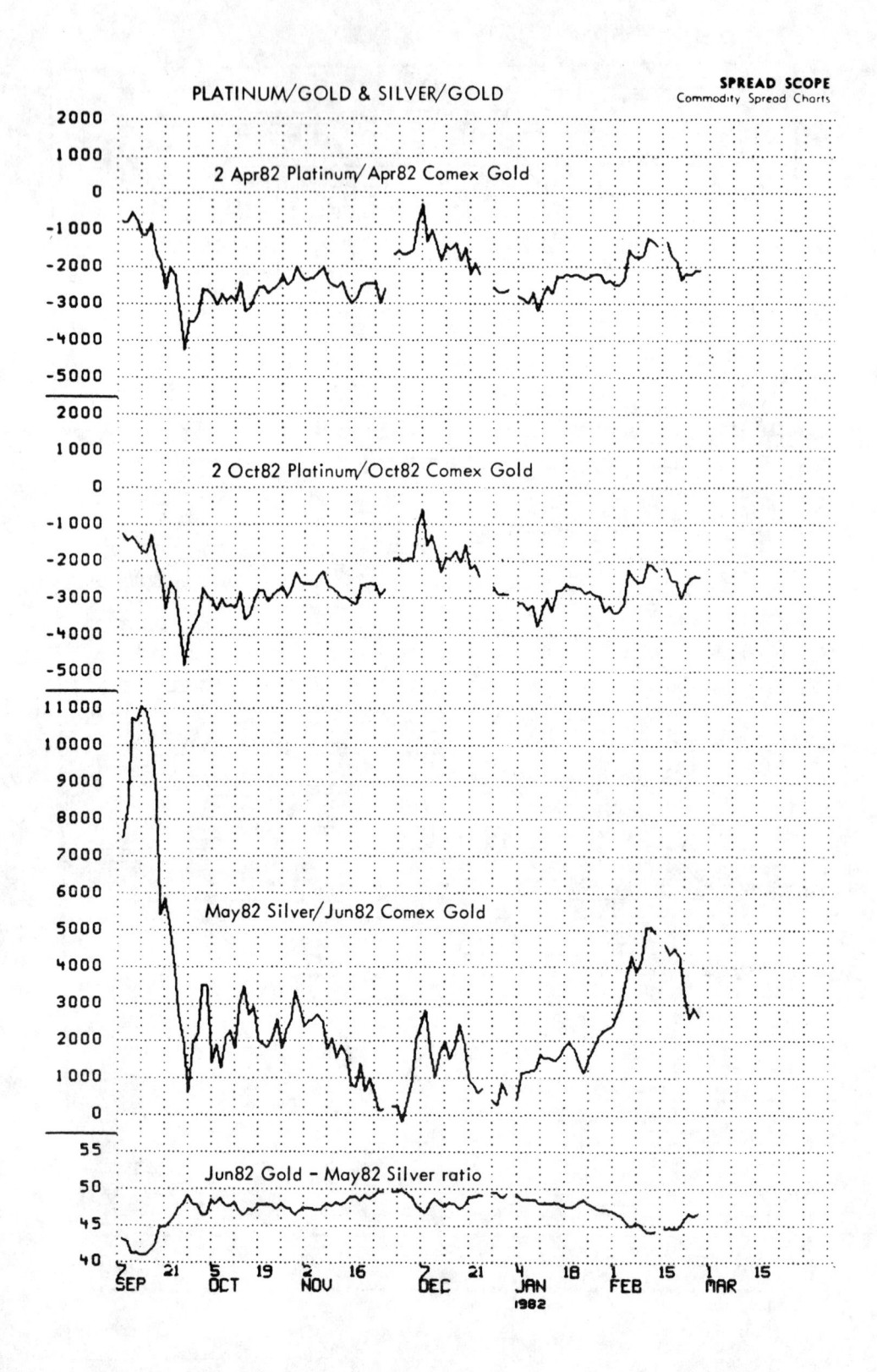

Spread chart courtesy of Spread Scope, Inc.

HEATING OIL

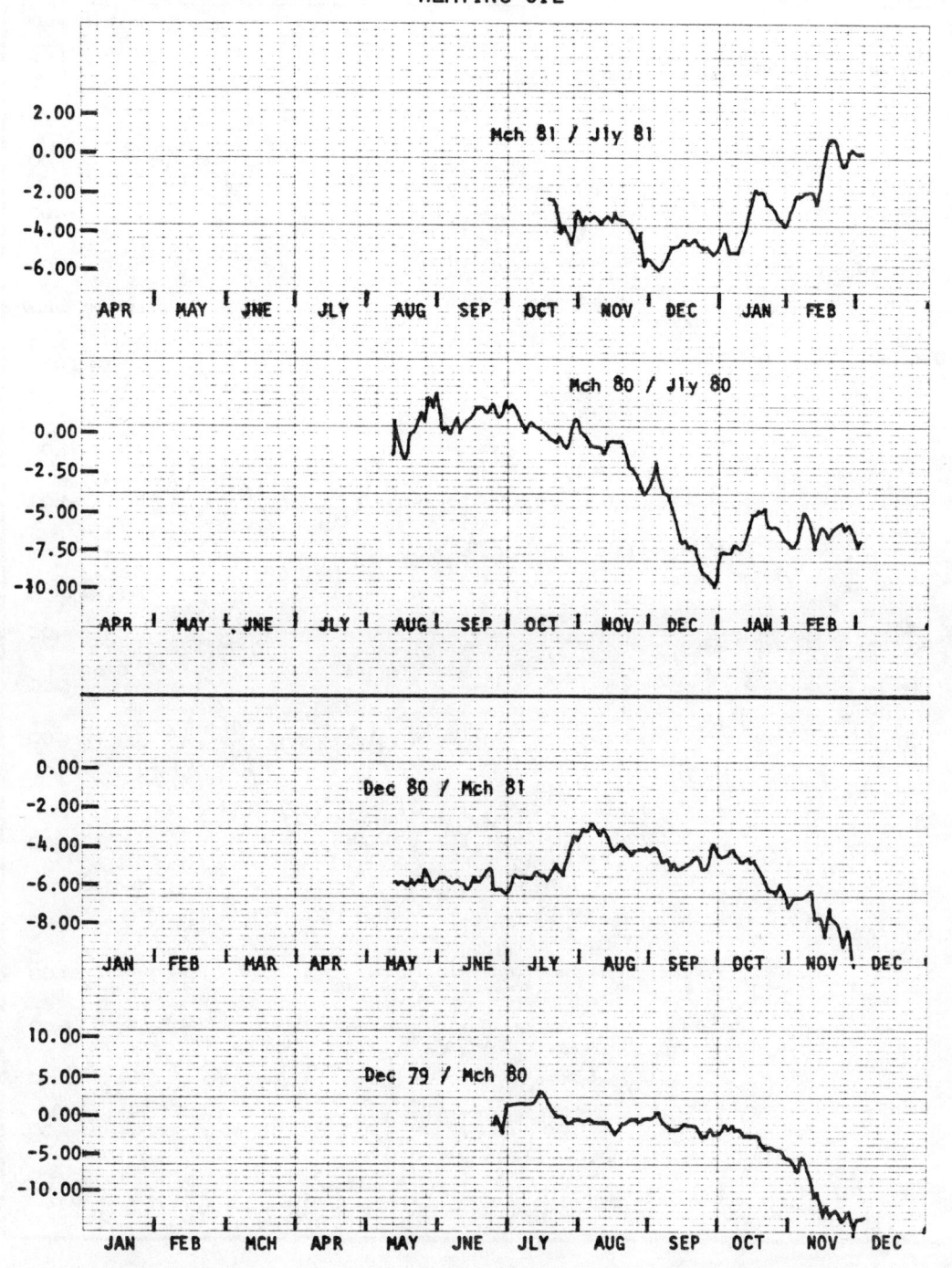

HEATING OIL NO.2
SPREADS

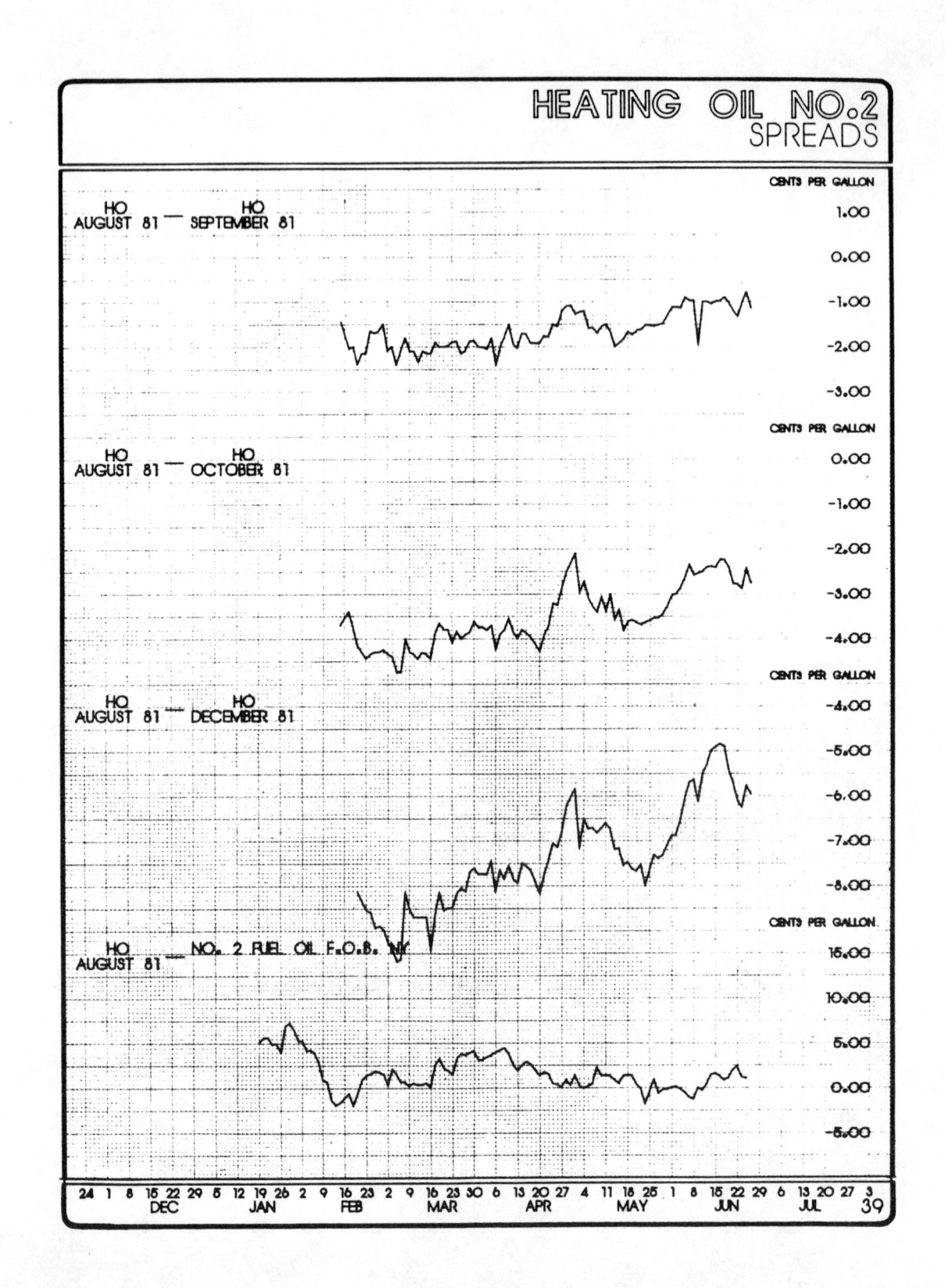

Chart courtesy Data Lab Corp., Chicago, IL

168

CURRENCIES

Currency prices are always quoted in relation to another currency, in terms of how many units of one currency it will take to buy one unit of the other. The International Monetary Market Division of the Chicago Mercantile Exchange quotes in terms of the U.S. dollar. An example...

CURRENCY:	*U.S.$/unit of currency:
BP (British pound)...	$1.7920
CD (Canadian dollar)...	$.8106
DM (Deutsche mark)...	$.4204
JY (Japanese yen)...	$.4132
SF (Swiss franc)...	$.5287

* Settlement prices on March 29, 1982 for June 1982 futures.

The BP, CD, DM, and SF quotes have four digits to the right of the decimal point. The JY has four digits to the right of the decimal point after dropping the first two digits (00) for ease of electronic data transmission. Thus, the actual price of the JY in the example given above is U.S.$.004132/yen.

With the present floating currency rate system, which began in 1973, price fluctuations reflect the changing supply and demand picture. The fundamental factors that influence foreign exchange rates are:

- <u>The economic health</u> of the country. This is reflected in the country's interest rates, inflation rate, unemployment, price levels, monetary reserves, money supply, flow of funds, balance of payments, balance of trade, productivity and many other indicators. To this list add political factors such as:

- <u>Government actions</u> on exchange controls, import and export duties, taxation, treaties with other governments and political stability.

- <u>Extraordinary events</u> which influence the value of a currency. For example: wars, oil shortages, embargoes, labor strikes, major bank failures, etc.

- <u>Interest rate differentials</u>: The highest interest rate country attracts enormous amounts of 'hot money', which is always attracted to the currency with the highest rates.

- <u>Expectations</u> of future interest rates. They play an even more important role in determining exchange rates than do current interest rates.

- <u>Seasonal influences</u>: High demand during peak export season; increased supply during peak import season.

***

INTERDELIVERY CURRENCY SPREADS

An interdelivery currency spread is defined as being long one futures maturity versus short another futures maturity in the same currency. When the trader's expectation is for a shift to a greater interest rate, he would buy the deferred contract and sell the nearby. If a decrease in the interest rate was anticipated, he would establish a long nearby versus short deferred futures position. The purpose of an interdelivery currency spread is to have the price difference (spread) between the two contract maturities either widen or narrow in accord with the intent of the established position. The positions would be liquidated at a profit if the interest rate shifts as per the trader's expectations.

Interdelivery currency spread trading is very similar to other spreading operations which function on an interest rate basis. The futures market in metals could be used as one example; money market instruments will be covered in the next section.

A spread position in silver or gold futures could be profitably established by buying deferred contracts versus the sale of nearby maturities, if the trader's presumption of a sharp rise in interest rates becomes a reality. The rise in interest rates would increase the carrying charge and thus widen the price spread between the two contract months. If the interest rate outlook was for a sharp decline, the spread would be set up in reverse: long nearby versus short deferred contracts - in anticipation of a narrowing price difference.

EXAMPLE: A three-month interdelivery currency spread of

Short December vs. Long March CANADIAN DOLLARS.

The trader expects interest rates to increase and thus the spread to widen. Each futures contract is for 100,000 CDs.

On July 25, 1980;   Step I:
   Sell December '80 CD   and   Buy March '81 CD
   @ $.8579   @ $.8560

On September 5, 1980; Step II:
   Buy December '80 CD   and   Sell March '81 CD
   @ $.8610   @ $.8650

LOSS: 31 points   GAIN: 90 points

Net profit: 90 - 31 = 59 pts. X $10/pt. = $590.- per spread

SHORTCUT: In practice, the trader would use a kind of shorthand to calculate his profit or loss rather than the formalized approach used in the example. First, he would deduct the number of spread points at the time the position was established ($.8579 - $.8560 = +19 points) from the spread points at liquidation ($.8610 - $.8650 = -40 points) to arrive at a profit of 59 points. Since the Canadian Dollar contract is written for 100,000 CDs, the second step is:
$$(CD\$100,000 \times \$.0059)$$
which amounts to U.S.$590.- profit on each spread.

To sum up: Interdelivery spreads for a currency reflect expectations about interest rate differentials at a future date. For example, if three-month interest rates in Japan are 7% and in the U.S. are at 12%, then the forward discount rate on U.S. dollars is expected to be about 5%. The difference between the March Japanese yen futures and the June Japanese yen futures reflects expectations about what this three-month interest rate differential between the U.S. and Japan will be in March.

***

STRATEGY: Some guidelines to follow when trading interdelivery currency futures:

- Buy the nearby futures and sell the deferred futures, if:
  (a) You expect interest rate differentials to decline when the forward prices are at a premium, or
  (b) You expect interest rate differentials to increase when the forward prices are at a discount.

- Buy the deferred futures and sell the nearby futures, if:
  (c) You expect interest rate differentials to increase when the forwards are at a premium, or
  (d) You expect interest rate differentials to decrease when the forwards are at a discount.

Note 1: Nearbys will gain on deferreds in interdelivery currency spreads when there is weakness in the U.S. interest rates, and relative strength in the foreign country's interest rates.

Note 2: When foreign interest rates are higher than the U.S. rates, interdelivery spreads in the foreign currency futures are inverted.

***

CROSS RATES

The word 'spread' in forex (foreign exchange) jargon refers to the tactic of buying and selling a single currency for delivery at different times in the future. In other words, reference is made to an interdelivery spread trade, such as the December vs. March Canadian dollar spread described earlier. Cross rates are the price relationships between foreign currencies, - between yen and pounds, or marks and francs, and other combinations. A cross-rate position is like an intercommodity spread in which the trader simultaneously buys one currency future and sells another currency future short; usually the same delivery month for both currencies. Some crosses are well established and heavily traded, such as the

DEUTSCHE MARK vs. SWISS FRANC SPREAD.

In times of dollar weakness, the Swiss franc usually rises more than other European currencies against the dollar, and falls faster in times of dollar strength. This is the traditional pattern. However, early in 1981 when the dollar was rising, the Deutsche mark fell faster than the Swiss franc because of Germany's troubled economy. Over 60% of Swiss exports go to Germany. Government intervention attempts to fine tune exchange rates so as to keep imports relatively cheap without restricting exports. Past experience shows that ever since the Swiss franc was pegged against the Deutsche mark, this spread fluctuated between 300 and 1,100+ points. One can only say (based on past experience) that, if the differential (spread) is near the upper limits one would go long DM and short the SF. Conversely, when the differential retreats to 350 points or less, then the position should be reversed: long SF vs. short DM. This intercurrency spread trends well, that is, bull or bear trends are of quite long duration and chart patterns tend to adhere to chart formation theories better than in most other markets.

***

INTERCURRENCY SPREADS

Intercurrency spreads, like the above mentioned DM vs. SF spread, fluctuate mainly in response to changes in carrying charges. The carrying charge in currency spreads is the difference in interest rates between the two countries involved. A person who wants to carry currencies must first figure his cost of borrowing U.S. dollars to buy the foreign currency and then calculate the interest he will earn when he deposits the foreign currency just purchased. The difference between the two interest rates is the carrying charge which, naturally, can be a positive or a negative value, depending on which country has the higher interest rates.

As has been shown, an intercurrency spread using currency futures is a position involving long one currency (for ex. Dec. SF) versus short another (Dec. DM). Usually the trader will use the same contract maturity for each side of the spread. If the spread is between SF and DM, low margin will be required for the trade because the price history of these two currencies show parallel movement vis-a-vis the dollar. In practical terms, to set up the cross, the trader will be asked to put up only the higher of the two net margins. The price movements of CD, BP and JY fluctuate independently against each other and against the dollar. Thus, they are perceived as higher risk spreads and margin may be required on both legs of the position.

***

As mentioned, the DM and SF trend together against the dollar, but within this broad trend susteain separate price variances versus the dollar. This variance is exploited by the alert trader.

EXAMPLE:

Step I:
On March 28, 1980;
   BUY Dec. '80 SF @ $.5852   and   SELL Dec. '80 DM @ $.5455

Step II:
On May 16, 1980;
  SELL Dec. '80 SF @ $.6178   and   BUY Dec. '80 DM @ $.5641
      PROFIT: + .0326   LOSS: -(.0186)

(+326 pts.) x $12.50/pt. = $4,075

                  (-186 pts.) x $12.50/pt. = -$2,325

    Net profit on the spread: $4,075 - $2,325 = $1,750

SHORTCUT:

Spread (price diff.) at liquidation: 6178 - 5641 = 537 pts.
   "   ("   ")when established: 5852 - 5455 = 397 pts.
                                       GAIN: 140 pts.

Both SF and DM contracts are for 125,000 currency units, so that each point of price movement is worth $12.50. Therefore,
    profit on the spread: 140 pts. x $12.50 = $1,750

The above profit figure is, of course, exclusive of commissions.

***

INTERCURRENCY 'MONEY SPREADS'

In the previous example it was possible to use the shortcut because currency contracts were written for the same number of currency units (125,000). But, assume one wanted to spread Deutsche marks against British pounds. Since there are 125,000 marks in the DM contract and 25,000 pounds in the BP contract, two multiplications and a subtraction must be carried out in order to get the dollar difference between the two contracts. (Remember: foreign currencies are always quoted in terms of U.S. dollars.)

DEUTSCHE MARK vs. BRITISH POUND SPREAD

Suppose the March '82 DM futures are trading at $.4238 on February 17, 1982 and on the same day and at the same time the March '82 BP futures are quoted at $1.8544. The dollar difference (money spread) between contract values is found as follows;

Value of DM contract   -   Value of BP contract = money spread
  (125,000 x $.4238)   -   (25,000 x $1.8544) =
       $52,975   - $46,360   = $6,615

The money spread is calculated twice: Once when it is established and again when it is liquidated. The change in the money spread will indicate directly the dollar amount of profit or loss.

***

COMMODITY:	BRITISH POUND
EXCHANGE:	International Monetary Market, Div. Chicago Mercantile Exch.
TRADING HOURS:	7:30 to 1:24 Central Time
DELIVERY MONTHS:	Mch, Jne, Sep, Dec.
TRADING UNIT:	25,000 Pounds Sterling
PRICE QUOTED IN:	U.S.$/BP
MINIMUM PRICE FLUCTUATION:	5 pts. ($.0005/pound sterling)
VALUE OF MINIMUM FLUCTUATION:	$12.50 per contract unit
VALUE OF ONE CENT MOVE:	$250.00
DAILY LIMIT OF PRICE MOVE:	500 pts. = 5¢/BP + or -
VALUE OF DAILY LIMIT:	$1,250.00
DELIVERY DAY:	The 3rd Wed. of delivery month
LAST TRADING DAY:	3rd Monday of delivery month

COMMODITY: C A N A D I A N   D O L L A R
EXCHANGE: International Monetary Market,
                                   Div. Chicago Mercantile Exch.
TRADING HOURS: 7:30 to 1:22 Central Time
DELIVERY MONTHS: Mch, Jne, Sep, Dec.
TRADING UNIT: 100,000 Canadian Dollars
PRICE QUOTED IN: U.S.$/CD
MINIMUM PRICE FLUCTUATION: 1 pt. ($.0001/CD)
VALUE OF MINIMUM FLUCTUATION: $10.00 per contract unit
VALUE OF ONE CENT MOVE: $1,000.00
DAILY LIMIT OF PRICE MOVE: 75 pts. = 3/4¢/CD + or -
VALUE OF DAILY LIMIT: $750.00
DELIVERY DAY: The 3rd Wed. of delivery month
LAST TRADING DAY: 3rd Tuesday of delivery month

COMMODITY: D E U T S C H E   M A R K
EXCHANGE: International Monetary Market,
                                   Div. Chicago Mercantile Exch.
TRADING HOURS: 7:30 to 1:20 Central Time
DELIVERY MONTHS: Mch, Jne, Sep, Dec.
TRADING UNIT: 125,000 Deutsche Marks
PRICE QUOTED IN: U.S.$/DM
MINIMUM PRICE FLUCTUATION: 1 pt. ($.0001/DM)
VALUE OF MINIMUM FLUCTUATION: $12.50 per contract unit
VALUE OF ONE CENT MOVE: $1,250.00
DAILY LIMIT OF PRICE MOVE: 100 pts. = 1¢/DM + or -
VALUE OF DAILY LIMIT: $1,250.00
DELIVERY DAY: The 3rd Wed. of delivery month
LAST TRADING DAY: 3rd Monday of delivery month

COMMODITY: J A P A N E S E   Y E N
EXCHANGE: International Monetary Market,
                                   Div. Chicago Mercantile Exch.
TRADING HOURS: 7:30 to 1:26 Central Time
DELIVERY MONTHS: Mch, Jne, Sep, Dec.
TRADING UNIT: 12,500,000 Japanese Yen
PRICE QUOTED IN: U.S.¢/JY
MINIMUM PRICE FLUCTUATION: 1 pt. = $.000001/JY + or -
VALUE OF MINIMUM FLUCTUATION: $12.50 per contract unit
VALUE OF ONE CENT MOVE: $1,250.00
DAILY LIMIT OF PRICE MOVE: 100 pts. = 1/100¢/JY
VALUE OF DAILY LIMIT: $1,250.00
DELIVERY DAY: The 3rd Wed. of delivery month
LAST TRADING DAY: 3rd Monday of delivery month

COMMODITY: S W I S S   F R A N C
EXCHANGE: International Monetary Market,
                                   Div. Chicago Mercantile Exch.
TRADING HOURS: 7:30 to 1:16 Central Time
DELIVERY MONTHS: Mch, Jne, Sep, Dec.

TRADING UNIT:	125,000 Swiss Francs
PRICE QUOTED IN:	U.S.$/SF
MINIMUM PRICE FLUCTUATION:	1 pt. ($.0001/SF)
VALUE OF MINIMUM FLUCTUATION:	$12.50 per contract unit
VALUE OF ONE CENT MOVE:	$1,250.00
DAILY LIMIT OF PRICE MOVE:	150 pts. = 1½¢/SF + or -
VALUE OF DAILY LIMIT:	$1,875.00
DELIVERY DAY:	The 3rd Wed. of delivery month
LAST TRADING DAY:	3rd Monday of delivery month

***

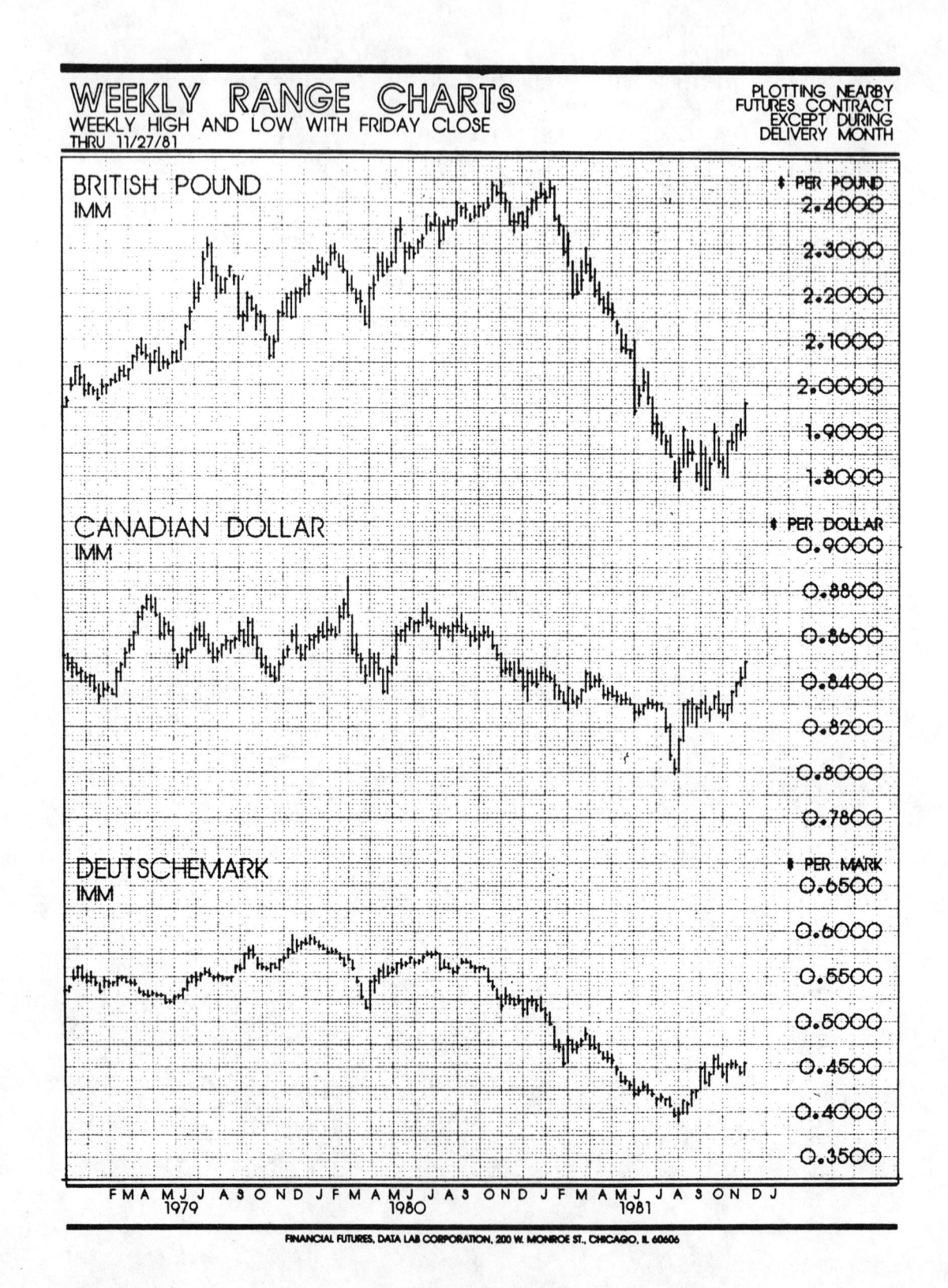

Chart courtesy Data Lab Corp., Chicago, IL

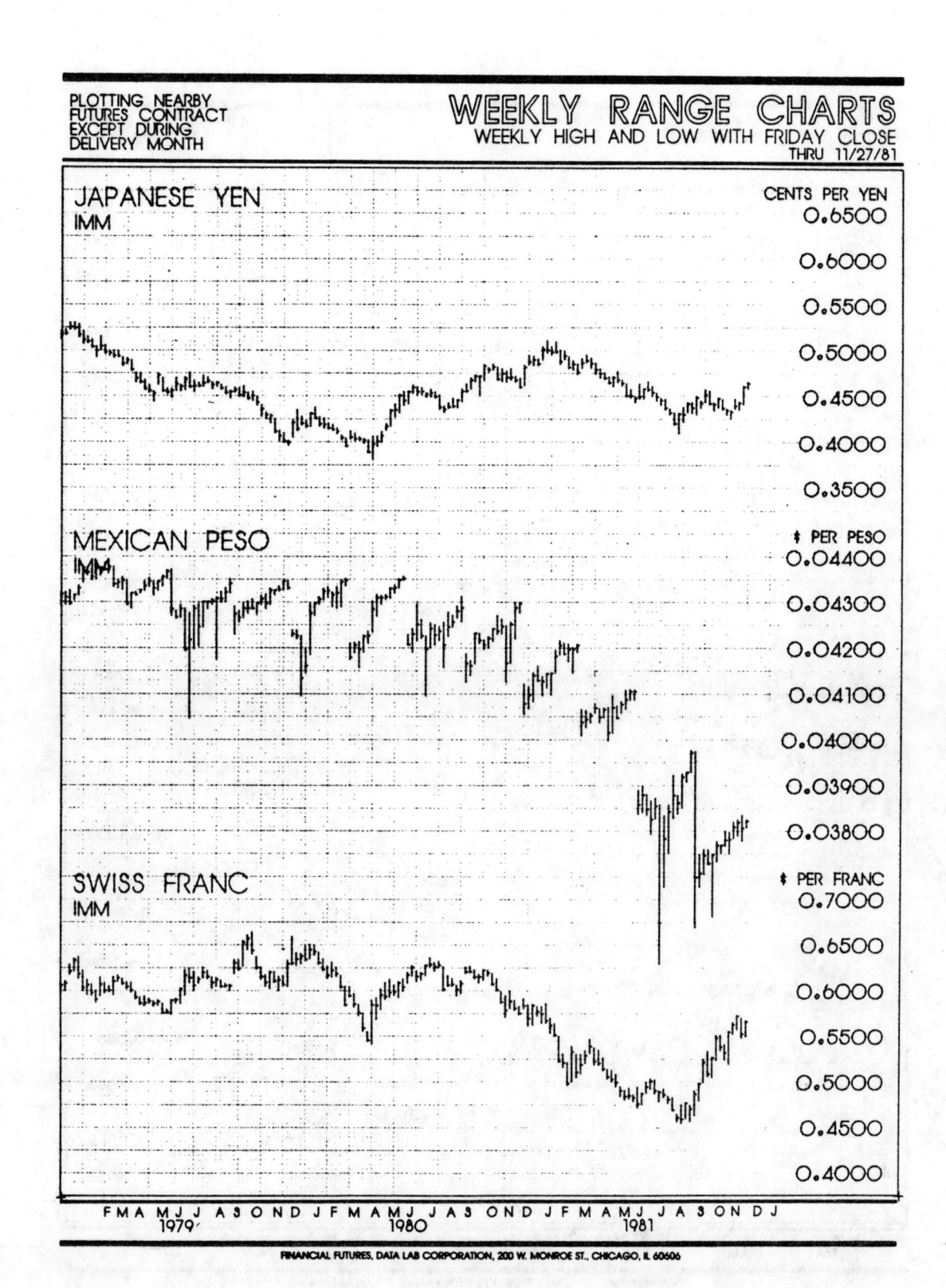

WEEKLY RANGE CHARTS
WEEKLY HIGH AND LOW WITH FRIDAY CLOSE
THRU 11/27/81

PLOTTING NEARBY FUTURES CONTRACT EXCEPT DURING DELIVERY MONTH

JAPANESE YEN — IMM (CENTS PER YEN)

MEXICAN PESO — IMM ($ PER PESO)

SWISS FRANC — IMM ($ PER FRANC)

FINANCIAL FUTURES, DATA LAB CORPORATION, 200 W. MONROE ST., CHICAGO, IL 60606

Chart courtesy Data Lab Corp., Chicago, IL

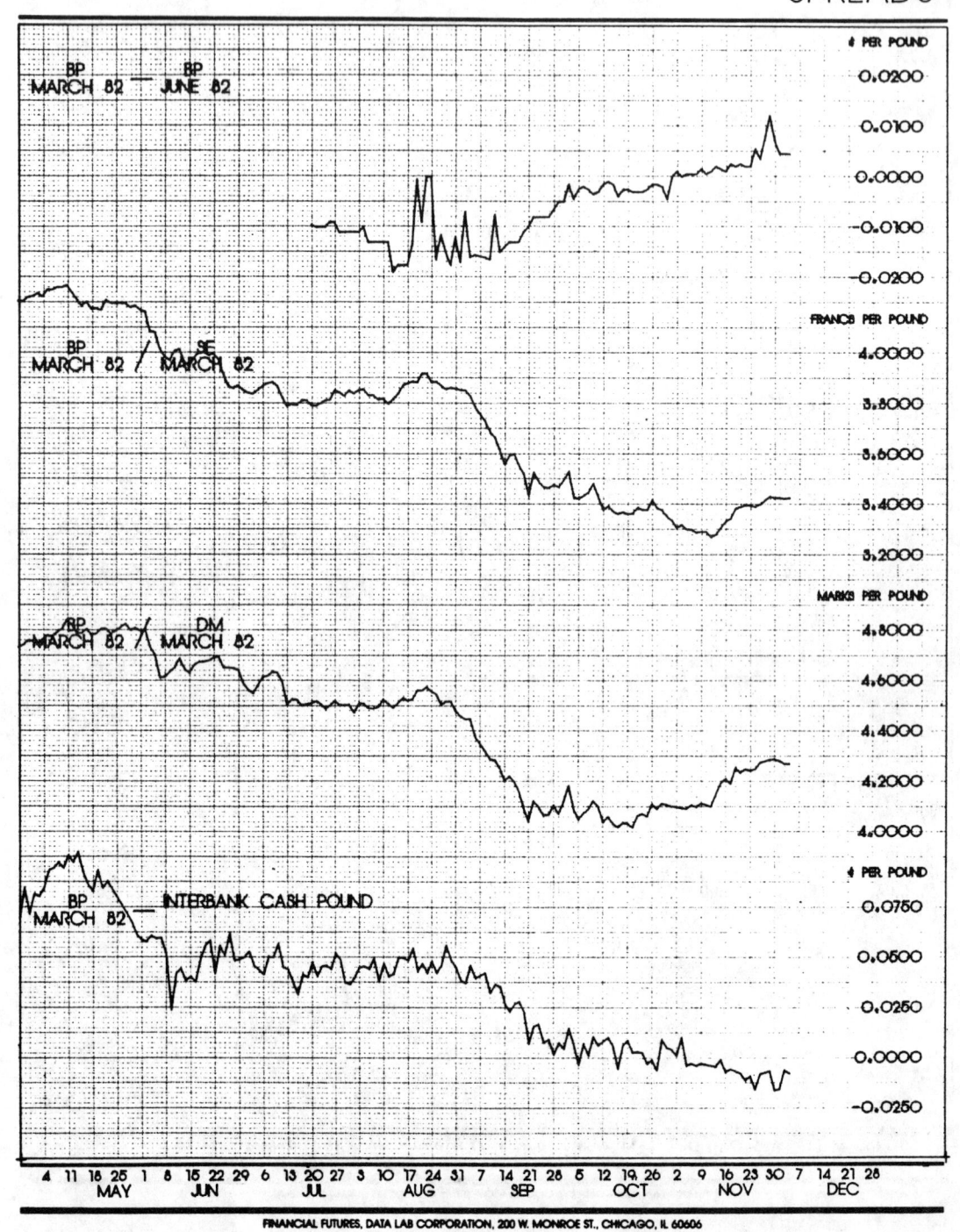

Chart courtesy Data Lab Corp., Chicago, IL

Chart courtesy Data Lab Corp., Chicago, IL

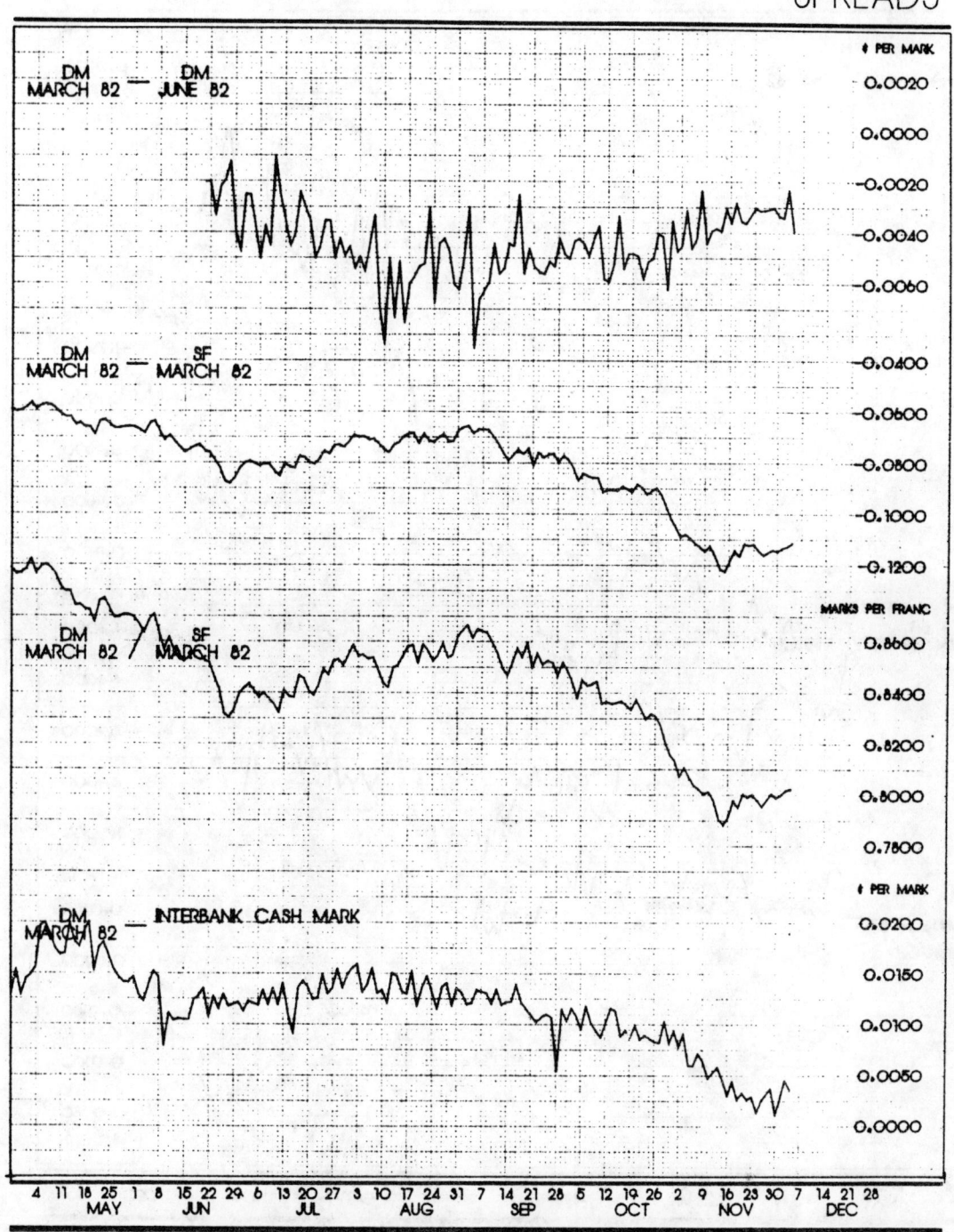

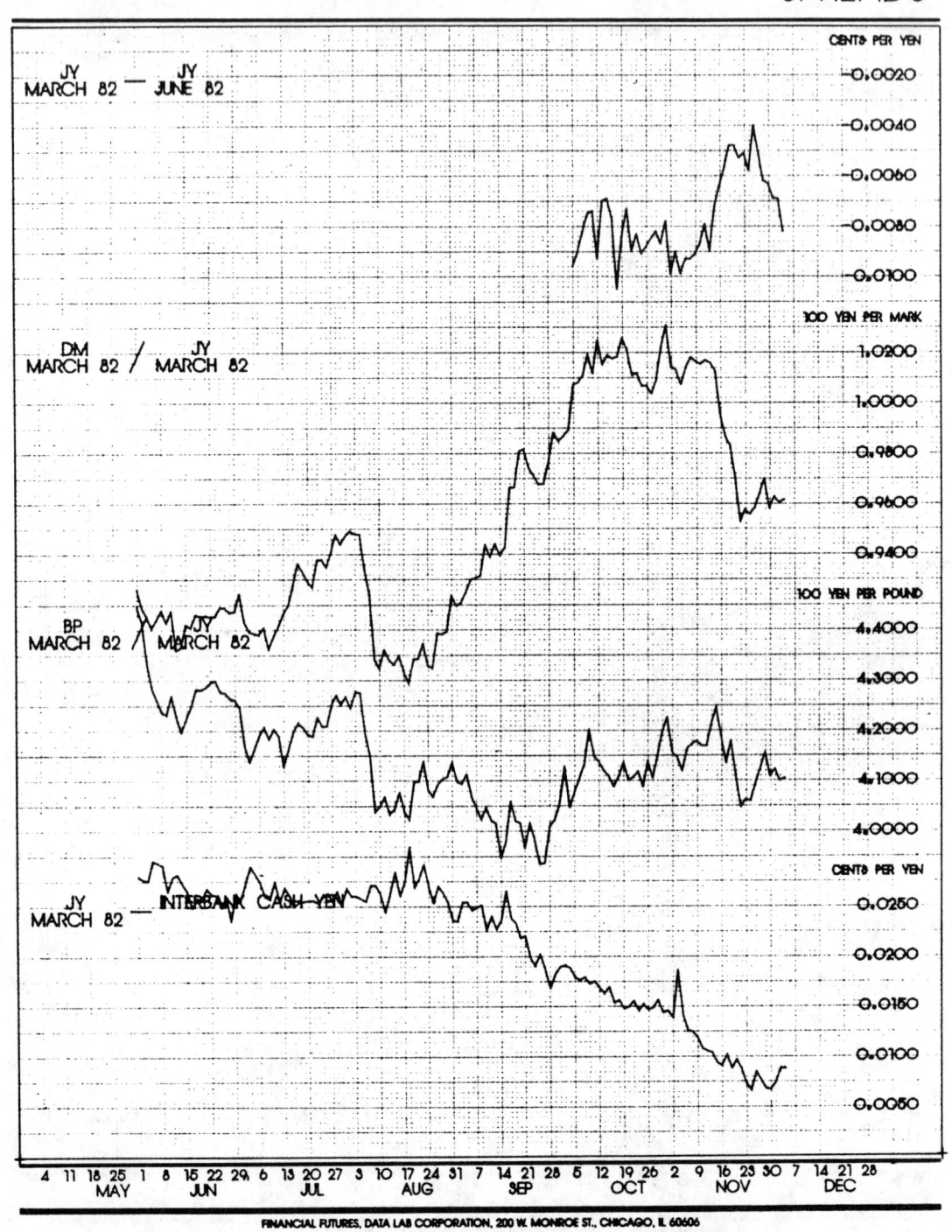

Chart courtesy Data Lab Corp., Chicago, IL

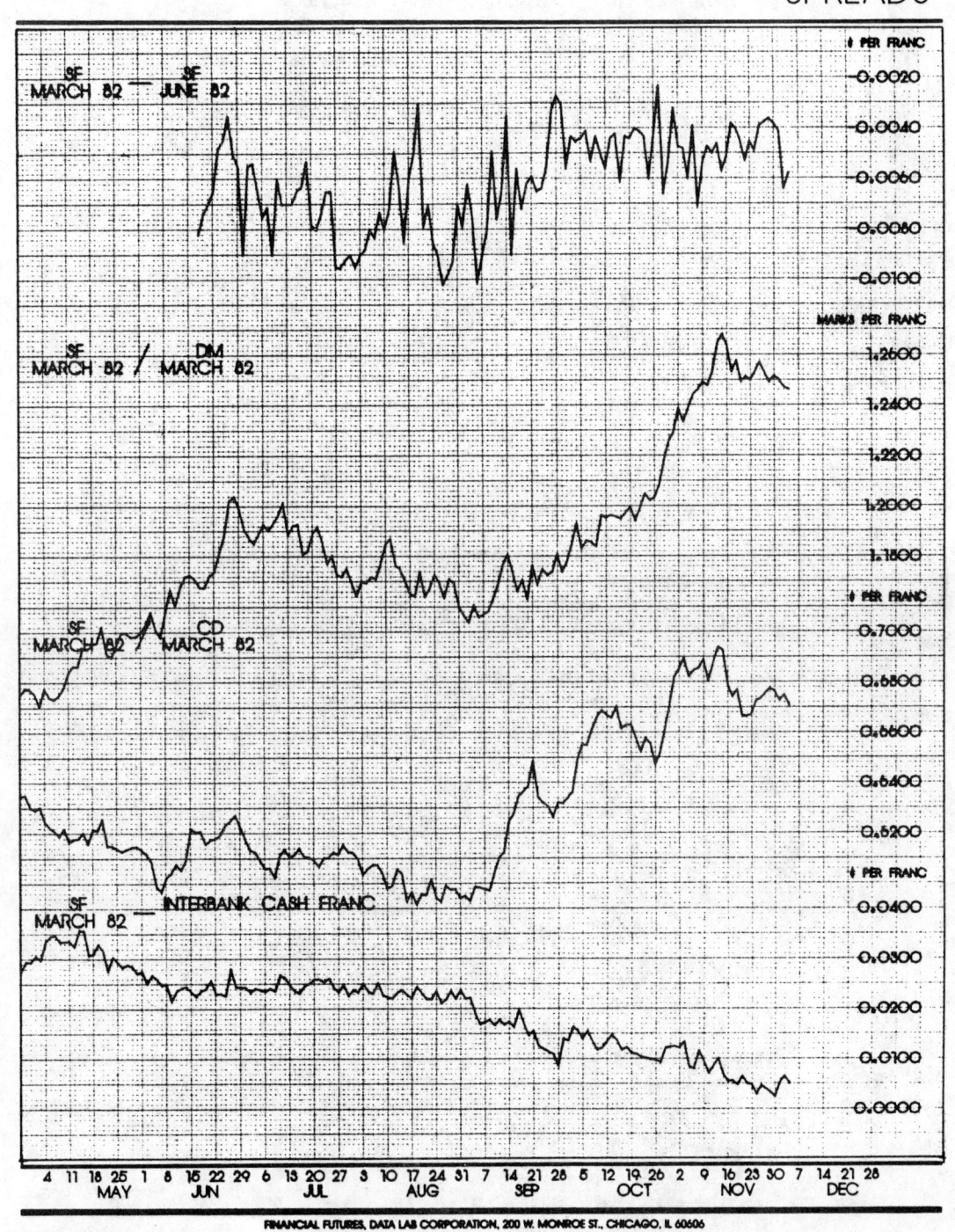

Chart courtesy Data Lab Corp., Chicago, IL

SWISS FRANC / DEUTSCHE MARK: DECEMBER

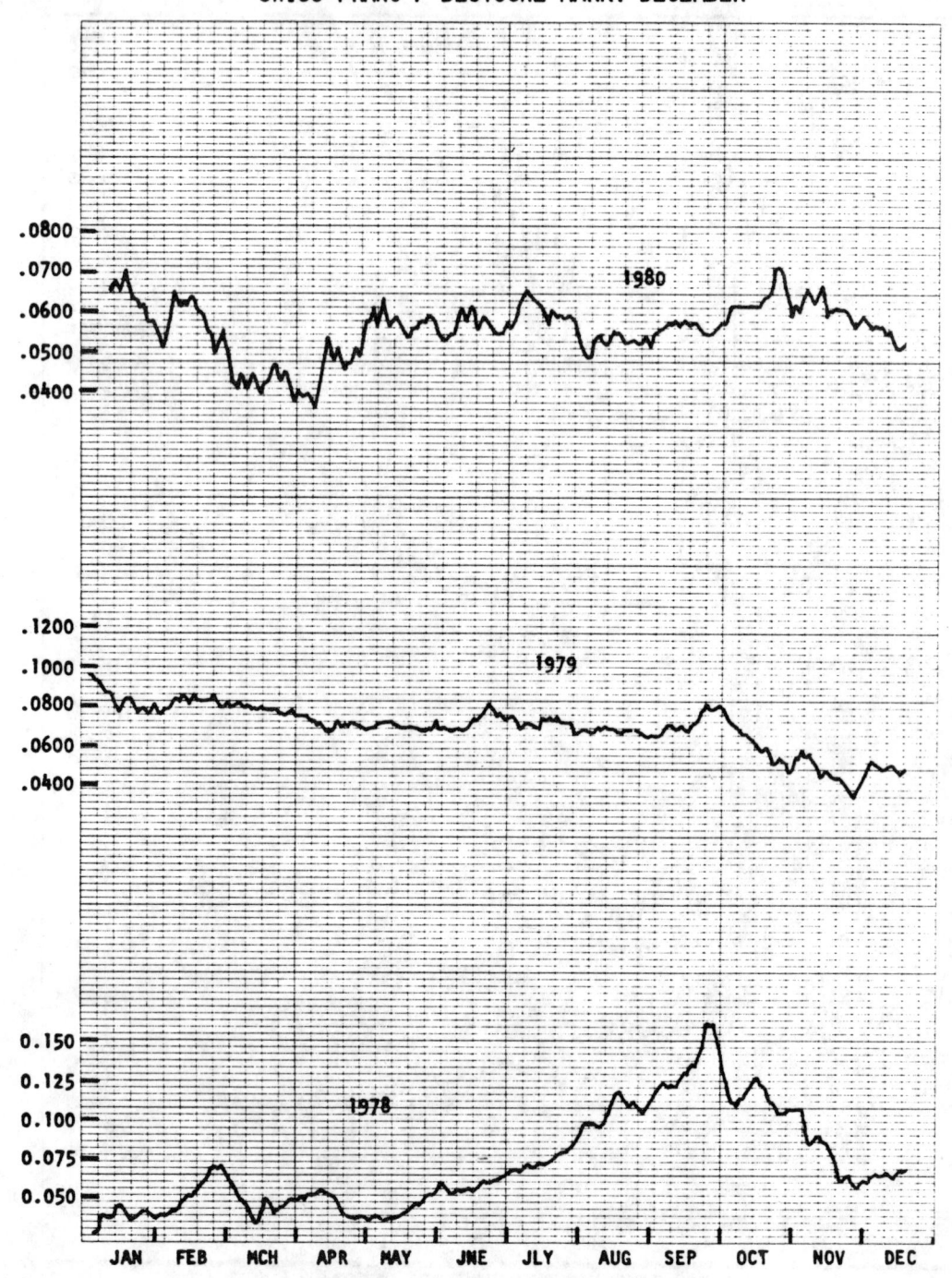

December '81 Swiss Franc / December '81 Deutsche Mark

Spread chart courtesy of Spread Scope, Inc.

FINANCIAL INSTRUMENTS

INTEREST RATE FUTURES

Trading in interest rate, or financial instrument futures, began a short seven years ago. The first contract was for GNMA certificates, a new mortgage-backed contract, based on the premise that money, or rather the cost of money, could be considered, as merely another commodity.

Because the price of money varies according to the laws of supply and demand, there is risk involved when dealing in it. Businessmen and money managers, therefore, welcomed the hedging opportunity offered in financial futures.

Here, a brief look will be taken at the three most popular financial futures contracts: 90-day U.S. Treasury bills, long-term U.S. Treasury bonds, and General National Mortgage Association (GNMA, or Ginnie Mae) certificates, which last represent pools of home mortgages. These contracts trade on federally regulated exchanges, and are growing in popularity. Already, some two dozen additional contracts await approval by the Commodity Futures Trading Commission.

FINANCIAL FUTURES BASICS

The contracts are written for delivery quarterly, in March, June, September, and December, these being the last months of each calendar quarter. To buy a December T-bill futures contract is a promise to accept delivery of $1 million worth of 90-day T-bills to be auctioned by the Treasury in December.

The T-bond contract specifies a $100,000 face amount with an 8% coupon. Auctions are held periodically.

Ginnie Mae certificates with a principal balance of $100,000 and a stated interest rate of 8% are the basic trading unit of their futures contract. Ginnie Maes are issued constantly. Selling any of these futures contracts short is a promise to deliver the specified securities.

PRICE CHANGES

Price changes in financial futures contracts reflect the movement of interest rates. In the case of T-bills, prices fluctuate in 1/100 of 1% of the face amount of $1 million. This is known as a *basis point*. It amounts to $100 per annum, but because the bills run for three months the minimum price fluctuation, known as a *tic*, is worth $25.

For T-bonds and Ginnie Maes, the minimum price change, or tic, is 1/32nd of 1% of the face value which is $100,000 for each. Thus, a tic for these futures is worth $31.25.

OUTRIGHT POSITIONS

Risks are large but, of course, the potential for loss coexists with the potential for large profits. An outright long or short position will be taken by the speculator based on his perception of interest rate trends. When one considers the leverage factor created by the small amount of initial margin required to establish a position, plus the volatility of financial futures, a speculator's capital position can be drastically altered in a single market session.

THE RISK FACTOR

Let's assume the speculator deposits $1,500 initial margin for a 90-day T-bill futures contract. He now controls $1 million (paper value). A 1% interest rate change is worth $2,500. The Exchange, however, puts a limit on daily price swings of 60 basic points on T-bills. This means that even one trading day's limit move can give the trader a 100% profit, (60 basic pts. X $25/pt = $1,500) or, his margin money can be wiped out if he guesses wrong. If the 1% interest rate change occurs and the speculator guessed right he has a $2,500 profit, and this profit may be withdrawn from his account. Remember, however, if he guessed wrong, he lost the $1,500 margin and owes his broker an additional $1,000 plus the commission. In a bad market the daily limits may be reached for several consecutive days, and then the Exchange extends the daily limits. In other words, outright positions are extremely high-risk investments even for the experienced and well financed trader. Treasury bonds and other financial futures contracts have different price changes for each 1% change in interest rates, but outright positions are high-risk speculations in all financial futures.

FINANCIAL FUTURES SPREADS

Spreads, as we already know, are the simultaneous purchase and sale of futures contracts. The spread trader bases his position on the belief that one contract will outperform another. Even though, in most instances, both contracts move in the same direction, there is an expected quantitative change in the price differential (spread) during the life of the trade. The trader who spots an abnormal relationship between the yields and prices of two financial futures contracts establishes the spread position and hopes to profit when the normal relationship is restored.

TYPES OF SPREADS

The most common spread situation occurs when the trader buys one contract delivery month and simultaneously sells another contract delivery month of the same interest rate instrument, such as a spread between March versus June T-bills. When the trader buys the nearby March contract and sells the more distant June contract, the strategy is known as a bull spread. When the bull spread is initiated it is referred to as "buying the spread." The opposite of this trategy is the bear spread when the nearby contract is sold and the more distant contract bought. This is called "selling the spread." Whenever the spread is set up between two different delivery months within the same market, it is known as an *interdelivery spread*.

If a spread is set up between two financial instruments such as Treasury bond contracts and GNMA contracts, it is referred to as an *intercommodity spread*. Both these last contracts trade on the Chicago Board of Trade.

A spread between T-bills and T-bonds is called an *intermarket spread* because T-bills are traded on both the Chicago Mercantile Exchange (IMM) and the New York Futures Exchange, while T-bonds are traded on the Chicago Board of Trade.

INTEREST RATE FLUCTUATIONS

Traders who anticipate a rise in interest rates sell (go short) interest rate futures; while traders who anticipate a decline purchase (go long) interest rate futures. The difficulty, of course, comes from anticipating correctly how and when short- and long-term interest rates will change over a period of time, and then how the change will be reflected in the market price of interest rate futures. It is important always to keep in mind that yield is the inverse of price; thus, the higher the yield on an interest-bearing instrument, the lower its price, and ice versa. When yields rise, prices fall; when yields decline, prices rise.

The object of futures spread trading is to have the price differential between the two contracts either increase or decrease so that a profit is made. In his search for promising spread trading strategies the trader should use *yield curve analysis*.

WHAT ARE YIELD CURVES?

In financial markets yield refers to the annual rate of return on an investment. The interest rate, the price paid, and the remaining life of the investment are interrelated to determine the yield. Knowledge of yield is important because it reflects interest rates which link stock and bond markets, the mortgage market and the commodity and money markets. Money moves quickly from one market to another as it seeks the highest rate of return. This return is reflected in the yield. A *yield curve* is constructed by plotting yields of various treasury securities or any other related group of securities against their various maturities. Time, or maturity dates are plotted on the horizontal scale of the chart and yields (in %) on the vertical scale. There are four basic yield curves and their shapes change with time to reflect changing market conditions and the economy as it moves through a business cycle. Figures 1A, 2A, 3A and 4A are typical cash market yield curves. One can also develop curves for the financial futures markets. These last are called futures price *discount curves* and examples are shown in Figs. 1B, 2B, 3B and 4B.

***

Figure 1A shows the cash market yield curve and Fig. 1B the corresponding futures price discount curve.

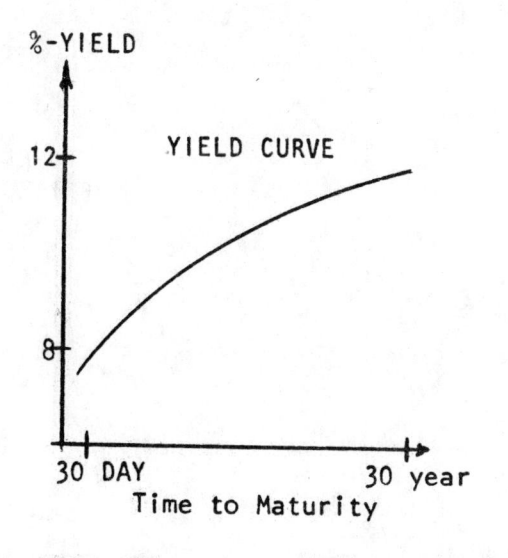

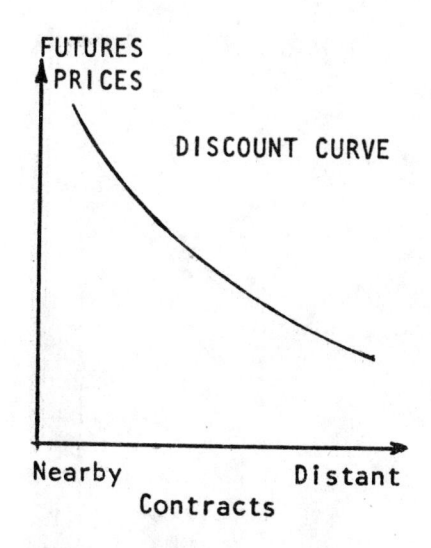

Fig. 1A

Fig. 1B

When short-term rates are less than long-term rates, the yield curve (1A) will be upward sloping and the discount curve downward sloping. This type of yield curve shows a 'normal' or 'positive carry' market. In normal times bond yields follow a gentle upslope because the longer the maturity the greater the risk, and that demands a greater premium for the risk. In general, this type of curve indicates that demand for credit is slack.

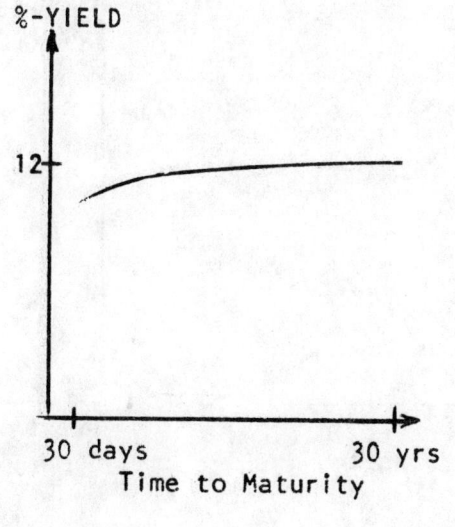

Fig. 2A

Fig. 2B

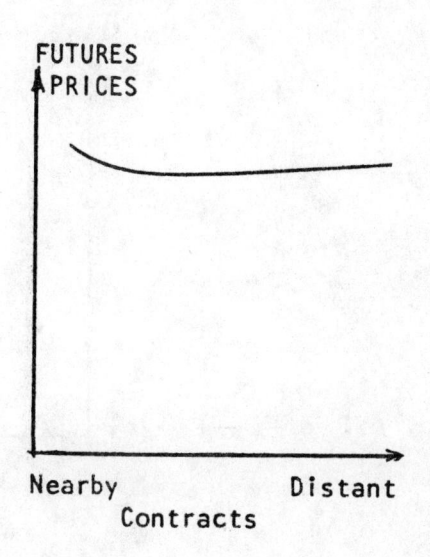

The yield curve flattens when yields are close along the entire range of maturities. In other words, if 3-month T-bills and 30-year Treasury bonds each pay about 12%, the yield curve is flat (Fig. 2A). This type of curve indicates that the market is in transition from easy credit to tighter credit.

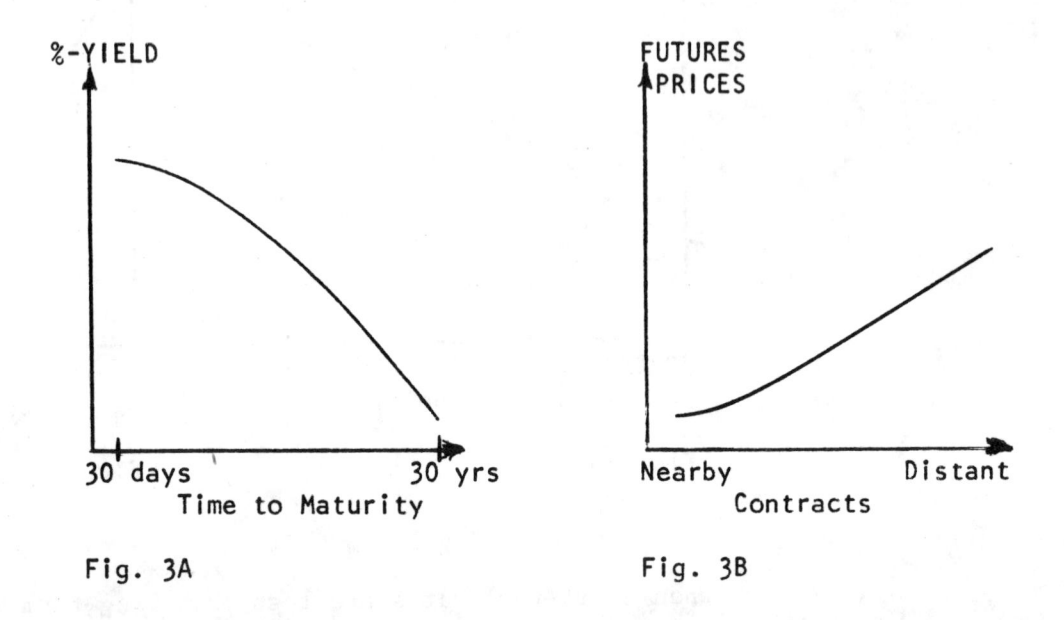

Fig. 3A

Fig. 3B

As money gets tighter, the yield curve may show a reversal and short-term interest rates will go higher than long-term. This type of yield curve (3A) shows an 'inverted' or 'negative carry' market. It goes with tight credit and the yield curve often inverts when credit demand is at, or approaching, its peak.

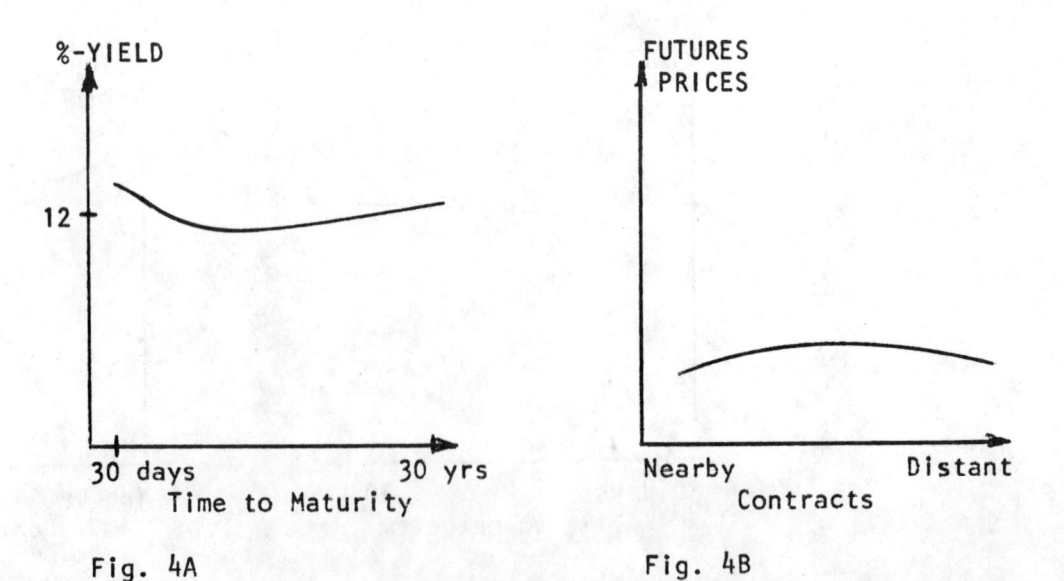

Fig. 4A

Fig. 4B

Figure 4A illustrates the flattening of the curve due to lower interest rates and a decreasing demand for short-term funds. It indicates the transition to easier credit.

The discount curve shows the market price for each of the contract months traded, for a particular interest rate instrument on a given day. The discount curve is a good representation of the collective thinking of market participants and often it gives a clue to the timing when the investment community expects a fundamental change in market sentiment. For example, the occurrence of a critical interest rate peak may show up as a 'hump-back' in the discount curve (4B) when the market goes through a transition to easier credit.

Remember: The discount curve is a snapshot which portrays the consensus of traders in financial futures at a given moment. The spread trader develops strategies to 'ride the discount curve' by anticipating changes in the shape of the curve and taking spread positions to profit from the changes. The curve may change from positive to negative, from flat to negative, from slightly negative to very negative, from negative to positive, etc.

INTERDELIVERY SPREADS

The trader makes a choice between the following spread positions:

1. Money gets tighter; interest rates go up; yield curve is changing shape from Fig. 1 towards Fig. 3. Under these conditions a bear spread of long the deferred and short the nearby contract deliveries could be initiated.

2. If a change from tight credit (Fig. 3) toward easier credit (Fig. 4 or even Fig. 1) is expected, a bull spread of long nearby versus short the deferred contract could be initiated.

The profitability of the two spreads above depends on correctly guessing the shape of the changing yield curve. One can make a large return by correctly calling the shift of the yield curve, but large scale shifts occur infrequently, and then only gradually, and over a long period of time.

COST OF CARRY

Interdelivery spreads offer potentially profitable situations due to movements in short-term financing costs. Short-term interest rates (and financing costs) are less than yields on longer-term debt during periods of easy money. In contrast, toward the end of a business expansion, when money is tight, short-term interest rates exceed those of longer maturities. The price spread depends on the 'net cost of carry' which is the amount of money earned from a cash security minus financing costs. In times of easy money the cost of carry (interest earned minus financing costs) will be positive, and during times of tight money it will be negative. Spread traders try to anticipate how financing costs will move and trade accordingly.

- If short-term financing costs are expected to increase, the trader will sell the nearby and buy the distant contract (bear spread).
- If the trader believes that short-term financing costs will decrease, he will buy a nearby contract and sell a more distant one (bull spread).

YIELD CURVES AND TRADING STRATEGIES

An understanding of how and why yield curves take on the shape they do and why they move from one level to another becomes the basis for developing trading strategies - particularly those strategies based on spreads.

With interest rate futures it is possible to do spreads that involve movements between different yield curves - e.g. purchasing June futures and selling September futures of the same financial instrument, or utilizing spreads involving movements along a single yield curve, like buying T-bond futures and selling GNMA futures. As the illustration shows, these two instruments are located at different points on the yield curve.

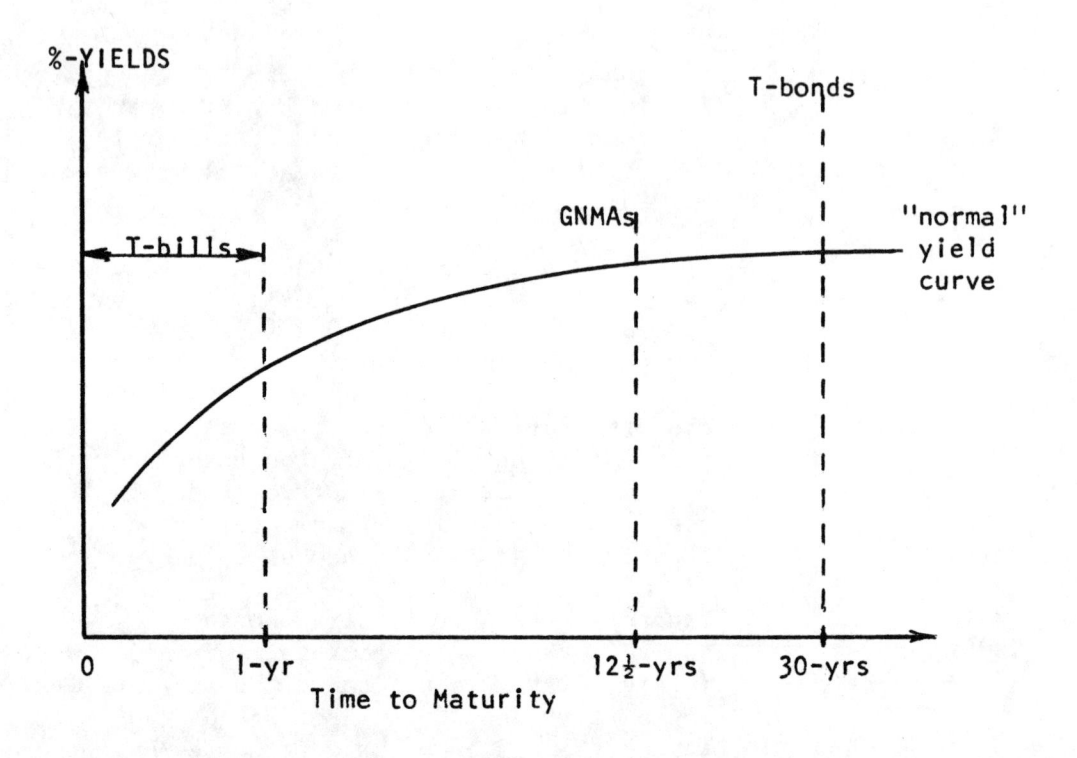

The figure above shows that the shape of a yield curve affects each financial futures contract (T-bills, GNMAs, T-bonds). Interdelivery price spreads for T-bills will be influenced by the front part of the curve; GNMA and T-bond price spreads will be affected by other sections of the curve, further to the right.

***

T-BILLS

Treasury bills are direct obligations of the U.S. Treasury. Banks, corporations, foreign governments, and individuals purchase 3-month (also called 13-week or 90-day) T-bills because they are the nearest thing to cash and, also, are an earning asset.

T-bills are sold every Monday by the Federal Reserve Board at an auction. They are sold on a discount basis, below their face value, and are redeemed at maturity at par. The difference represents interest. The buyer of a T-bill contract, let us say, for December delivery, agrees to accept delivery during December of a contract for U.S. Treasury bills worth one million dollars. It would mature 90 days later; after the T-bills were actually received.

If short-term interest rates rise, 3-month T-bills must fall in price (as yields rise, prices decline and vice versa). If a T-bill is to be sold at a greater yield, the price of the bill will be lower. Because of this inverse relationship between yield and price the bid price is higher than the asked (offered) price. This is contrary to normal practice when trading stocks and commodities, where the bid price is lower than the asked price.

I.M.M. INDEX The International Monetary Market (IMM), a Division of the Chicago Mercantile Exchange, developed a system of quoting T-bill futures prices that conforms to traditional methods of trading in stocks and commodity futures. The IMM Index is based on the difference between the actual T-bill discount rate and 100.00. Thus, a T-bill discount rate of 12.5% would be quoted via the IMM Index as 87.50. If a trader bought a June T-bill contract at 87.50, and a month later the futures market was forecasting a yield of 11.80% for June, then, in terms of the IMM Index, T-bills would be quoted at 88.20 (100.00 - 11.80 = 88.20). If the June futures contract was covered at this price there would be a gross profit of 70 basis points, or $1,750 (70 basis pts. X $25/pt.) less round-turn commission. With this quotation system, if one is long in futures and the IMM Index goes up, the trader has a profit, as in other futures markets. Thus, if the trader expects interest rates to rise he will sell T-bill futures, since the cash dollar price of the bill, and the IMM Index quoted futures price of the bill, will decline as interest rates go up.

T-bill futures do not exhibit carrying charges; they are similar to non-carrying charge commodities such as live cattle or live hogs. The reason for this is that T-bill futures are deliverable only once, and there is only one deliverable T-bill.

T-BILL SPREADS

Treasury bill futures spreads are based on the market's perception of where interest rates will be at different times as represented by the yield curve. When the yield curve is normal, rates in the near-term are lower than those in the more distant future. Prices are higher, because market participants demand a higher rate of return on their money for longer periods. In addition, investors are willing to pay more (accept lower yield) for shorter maturities in order to minimize the risk of loss from price movements.

Reduced credit demands coupled with prospects for an easier monetary policy might cause nearby T-bills to gain on the deferreds, and result in a narrowing of the spread. For example:

In expectation of easier credit, the trader purchased March '82 T-bill futures and sold September '82 T-bill futures:

	March '82 T-bill futures:	September '82 T-bill futures:	Spread (Mch - Sep):
On June 19,'81:	BOT @ 87.93	SLD @ 88.09	-.16
On July 31,'81:	SLD @ 86.95	BOT @ 87.35	-.40
	98 x $25	74 x $25	- 24 pts. (wider!)
	LOSS: $2,450.-	GAIN: $1,850.-	

<u>NET LOSS: $600.-</u>

Result: The bull spread did not work out. Mid-June it appeared that the prime rate was topping out. After a false signal it went still higher and as a result T-bill prices dropped, the long March contract losing more than the short September contract gained.

***

T-BONDS

Treasury bonds are long-term obligations of the U.S. government. They are issued by the Treasury to fund government debt and pay interest semi-annually. The interest payment (coupon rate) is pre-determined when the bond is issued. At maturity, the principal, plus the final interest payment is paid to the holder.

The agricultural trader who used to trade on the grain markets will feel comfortable with T-bond futures. It is a carrying charge market and the configuration of the spreads is quite familiar.

T-BOND SPREAD EXAMPLE: Let's say that the Federal Reserve Board takes steps to tighten credit and raise short-term interest rates. In response, one would expect short-term interest rates to rise relative to longer-term rates. In case of the March versus September T-bond spread one would expect that prices for both contracts would fall, but that the nearby contract (March) would drop further in price than the deferred (September) contract. In a situation like this, the strategy, therefore, is to sell the March futures and buy the September futures, thus setting up a bear spread.

When the expectation is that the yield curve will return to normal, i.e., short-term rates will be lower than the long-term rates, therefore, one would buy the nearby March and sell short the more distant September contract, in the expectation that the spread will narrow. As the normal yield curve keeps getting steeper, the price of the March T-bond contract should appreciate increasingly in comparison to the September T-bond contract.

	March '82 T-bond futures:	September '82 T-bond futures:	S P R E A D (Mch - Sep):
On Sep. 11, '81:	BOT @ 60-06	SLD @ 61-02	-28/32
On Nov. 20, '81:	SLD @ 64-23	BOT @ 64-24	- 1/32
	4-17	3-22	27/32
	= 145/32 x $31.25	= 118/32 x $31.25	(narrower)
	GAIN: $4,531.25	LOSS: $3,687.50	

<u>NET PROFIT: $843.75</u>

<u>Result</u>: Short-term interest rates declined sharply, bond prices gained, the nearby March gained more than the more distant September contract. The bull spread was successful.

***

GINNIE MAE

GNMAs are mortgage-backed certificates guaranteed by the Government National Mortgage Association. The security of a 'Ginnie Mae' is equally strong as that of a Treasury bond. When issued, GNMAs have a life of 30 years, but experience has shown that the average life of GNMAs is 12½ years.

The basic trading unit of this futures contract is a GNMA

certificate with a principal balance of $100,000 and a stated interest rate of 8%, assuming a 30-year mortgage prepaid in the 12th year. Ginnie Mae and T-bond futures prices are quoted as a percentage of par; e.g., 100-00 is 100% of par. A price of 65-12 would indicate a price of 65-12/32 or 65.375% of par. Digits to the right of the dash are 32nds of a percent, as with T-bonds. Minimum price fluctuation is 1/32nd of a point = #31.25 per contract ($100,000 ÷ 100 ÷ 32 = = $31.25).

EQUIVALENCY TABLE:

1/32 =	.03125	17/32 =	.53125
2/32 =	.0625	18/32 =	.5625
3/32 =	.09375	19/32 =	.59375
4/32 =	.125	20/32 =	.625
5/32 =	.15625	21/32 =	.65625
6/32 =	.1875	22/32 =	.6875
7/32 =	.21875	23/32 =	.71875
8/32 =	.25	24/32 =	.75
9/32 =	.28125	25/32 =	.78125
10/32 =	.3125	26/32 =	.8125
11/32 =	.34375	27/32 =	.84375
12/32 =	.375	28/32 =	.875
13/32 =	.40625	29/32 =	.90625
14/32 =	.4375	30/32 =	.9375
15/32 =	.46875	31/32 =	.96875
16/32 =	.50	32/32 =	1.00000

When mortgage interest rates rise, the prices of futures contracts fall. Thus, if interest rates are expected to increase, one goes short the futures; long if one expects them to decrease.

INTERMARKET SPREADS

Changes in the money supply, activities of the Federal Reserve, and economic activity affect all segments of the money markets. However, long-term interest rates are affected differently than short-term; they may even move in a divergent direction from short-term rates. It would not be wise, therefore, to attempt spread transactions between T-bills and GNMAs unless you are capable of analyzing the many factors affecting these two separate markets.

INTERCOMMODITY SPREADS

In an intercommodity spread, futures contracts traded on the same exchange for the same delivery month are spread between two different commodities which are economically related, such as the popular December GNMA versus December Treasury bond futures.

Note: the GNMA vs. T-bond intercommodity spread usually behaves in a predictable fashion: bond prices fall faster than GNMA prices as yields rise; bond prices rise faster than GNMA prices as yields fall.

Example: The trader expects interest rates to go down, futures prices to go up, and the spread to narrow:

	December '81 GNMA futures:	December '81 T-bond futures:	S P R E A D (GNMA - T-bonds):
On Sep. 18, '81:	BOT @ 59-05	SLD @ 60-06	-33/32
On Nov. 6, '81:	SLD @ 61-15	BOT @ 61-05	+10/32
	74/32 x $31.25	31/32 x $31.25	43/32 (1-11) (narrower)
	GAIN: $2,312.50	LOSS: $968.75	

NET PROFIT: $1,343.75

Result: The transaction is a profitable one. Note: Even if prices had gone up, as long as the spread narrowed a profit would have still resulted.

SEASONALITY

The GNMA/T-bond spread has been traded for only a few years. While its history is short, some seasonal tendencies are already evident.

- T-bonds tend to gain on the GNMAs from mid-August until the middle of September. The average gain is about 32 tics. Then from late September to the first week of November the situation is reversed: GNMAs tend to gain on T-bonds. The average gain is 32-64 tics.

- Ginnie Maes are produced to provide money for mortgages. When housing starts are low, there is less need to produce GNMAs. The winter months are the low point in actual housing starts and, therefore, in GNMA production.

- The quarterly Treasury refunding and large budget deficits force the U.S. Treasury to borrow heavily to meet its commitments. The large supply of T-bonds weighs more on the T-bonds than the GNMAs.

YIELD-INDIFFERENT SPREADS

A spread of one GNMA vs. one T-bond will vary as the *level of yields* fluctuates, even if the *yield differential* between the two instruments remains unchanged. This is true, because T-bonds have a longer maturity than GNMAs and, therefore, an equivalent yield change for both will alter the T-bond price by a greater amount. A one-to-one spread is quite complex to analyze because the success of the position will depend upon the direction of interest rate change and, also, on the relative yield change between GNMAs and T-bonds. Since the spread trader is interested only in the *relative yield*, the spread must be implemented in such a futures ratio that the spread will be *yield-indifferent*. At this writing, four GNMAs versus three T-bonds would be the smallest yield-indifferent spread position. Each full point move in this 4/3 spread represents a $1,000 change in equity. The Wall Street Journal lists daily prices and also yields for GNMA and T-bond futures. The GNMA vs. T-bond yield spread can be calculated by taking the difference between the listed GNMA yield and T-bond yield.

ADDITIONAL NOTES REGARDING G.N.M.A. vs. T-BOND SPREADS:

- As a matter of habit, most spread traders put on the long and short leg of a GNMA/T-Bond spread in the same futures delivery month. However, to maximize the return it often improves profitability to go long a nearby T-bond contract (like March) and go short a more distant GNMA, (like June or September) or vice versa. If properly set up, such a spread may give profit from the shift in the cash yield curve as well as from a shift in the futures discount curve.

- As mentioned before in connection with seasonality, at the beginning of every February, May, August and November quarterly Treasury refundings occur and large amounts of T-bonds are sold. It is often profitable to sell the T-bonds and buy the GNMAs one or two weeks before the refunding period and liquidate the spread a few weeks after the refunding.

***

COMMODITY:	TREASURY BILLS
EXCHANGE:	International Monetary Market, Div. Chicago Mercantile Exch.
TRADING HOURS:	8:00 to 1:40 Central Time
DELIVERY MONTHS:	Mch, Jne, Sep, Dec.
TRADING UNIT:	$1 million (90-day T-bills)
PRICE QUOTED IN:	I.M.M. INDEX
MINIMUM PRICE FLUCTUATION:	1 basis pt. (.01 of 1%)
VALUE OF MINIMUM FLUCTUATION:	$25.00 per contract unit
VALUE OF ONE PERCENT MOVE:	$2,500.00
DAILY LIMIT OF PRICE MOVE:	60 points + or -
VALUE OF DAILY LIMIT:	$1,500.00
DELIVERY DAY:	3rd Thursday of delivery month
LAST TRADING DAY:	3rd Wednesday of delivery month

COMMODITY:	TREASURY BONDS
EXCHANGE:	Chicago Board of Trade
TRADING HOURS:	8:00 to 2:00 Central Time
DELIVERY MONTHS:	Mch, Jne, Sep, Dec.
TRADING UNIT:	Long-term U.S. Treasury bonds with $100,000 face value
PRICE QUOTED IN:	Pts. & 32nds of 100%
MINIMUM PRICE FLUCTUATION:	1/32 of 1 pt. per unit
VALUE OF MINIMUM FLUCTUATION:	$31.25 per contract unit
VALUE OF ONE POINT MOVE:	$1,000.00
DAILY LIMIT OF PRICE MOVE:	64/32 (2 points) + or -
VALUE OF DAILY LIMIT:	$2,000.00
FIRST DELIVERY DAY:	1st business day of the current delivery month
LAST TRADING DAY:	The 8th business day from the end of current delivery month

COMMODITY:	G I N N I E M A E - CDR
EXCHANGE:	Chicago Board of Trade
TRADING HOURS:	8:00 to 2:00 Central Time
DELIVERY MONTHS	Mch, Jne, Sep, Dec.
TRADING UNIT:	Ginnie Mae with $100,000 principal balance and stated interest of 8 percent
PRICE QUOTED IN:	Points and 32nds of 100%
MINIMUM PRICE FLUCTUATION:	1/32nd of 1 pt. per unit
VALUE OF MINIMUM FLUCTUATION:	$31.25
VALUE OF ONE POINT MOVE:	$1,000.00
DAILY LIMIT OF PRICE MOVE:	64/32 (2 points) + or -
VALUE OF DAILY LIMIT:	$2,000.00
FIRST DELIVERY DAY:	The first business day of the current delivery month
LAST TRADING DAY:	Eight business day from the end of the current delivery month

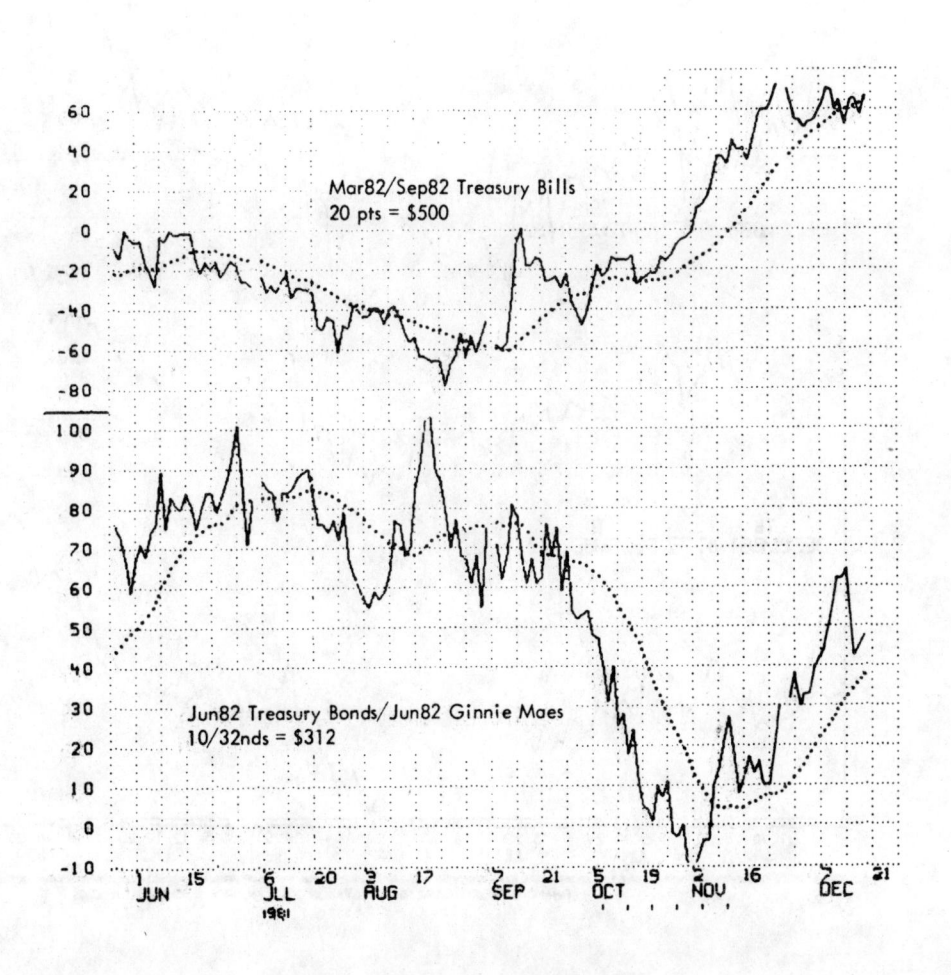

***

Spread chart courtesy of Spread Scope, Inc.

TREASURY BILL SPREADS

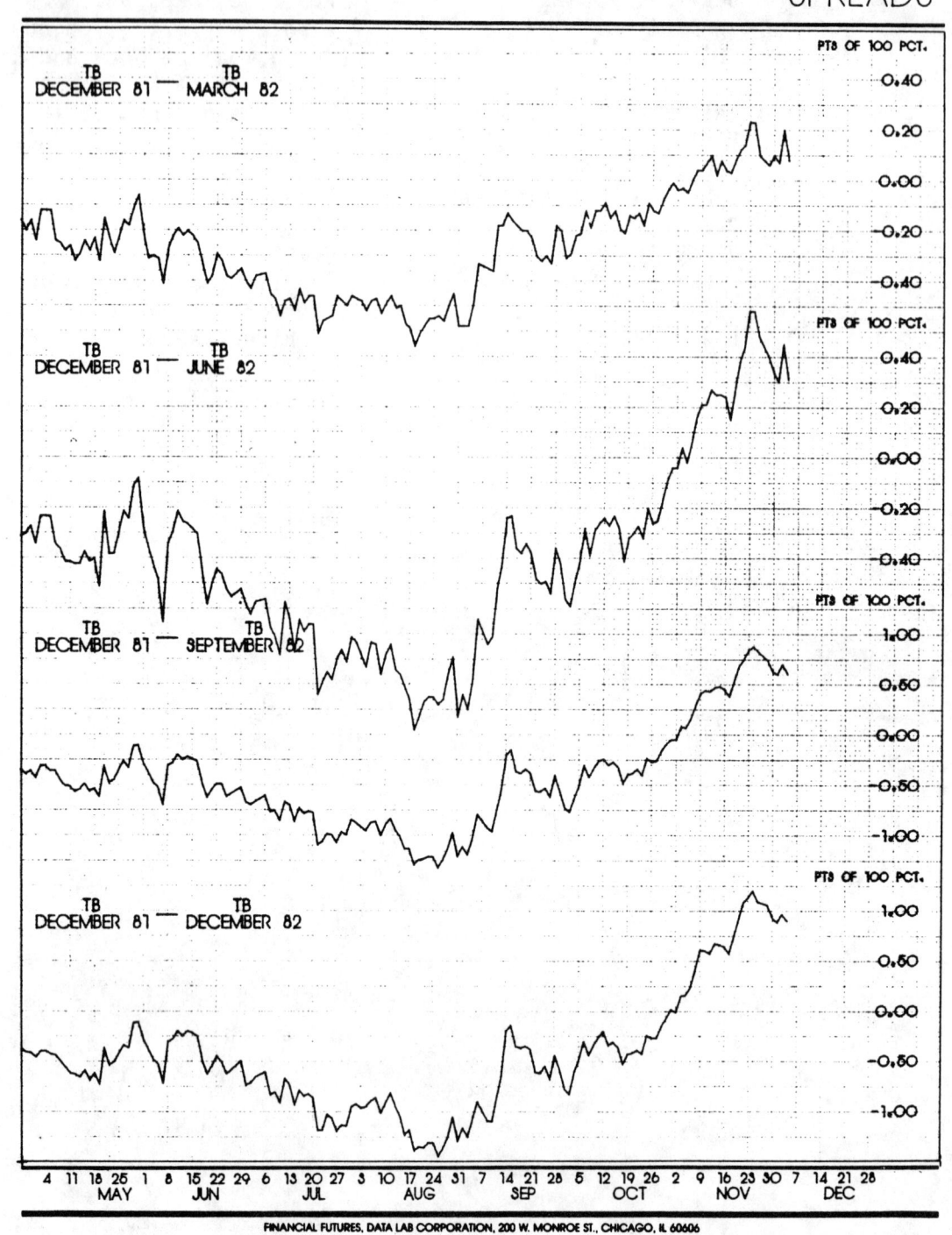

Chart courtesy Data Lab Corp., Chicago, IL

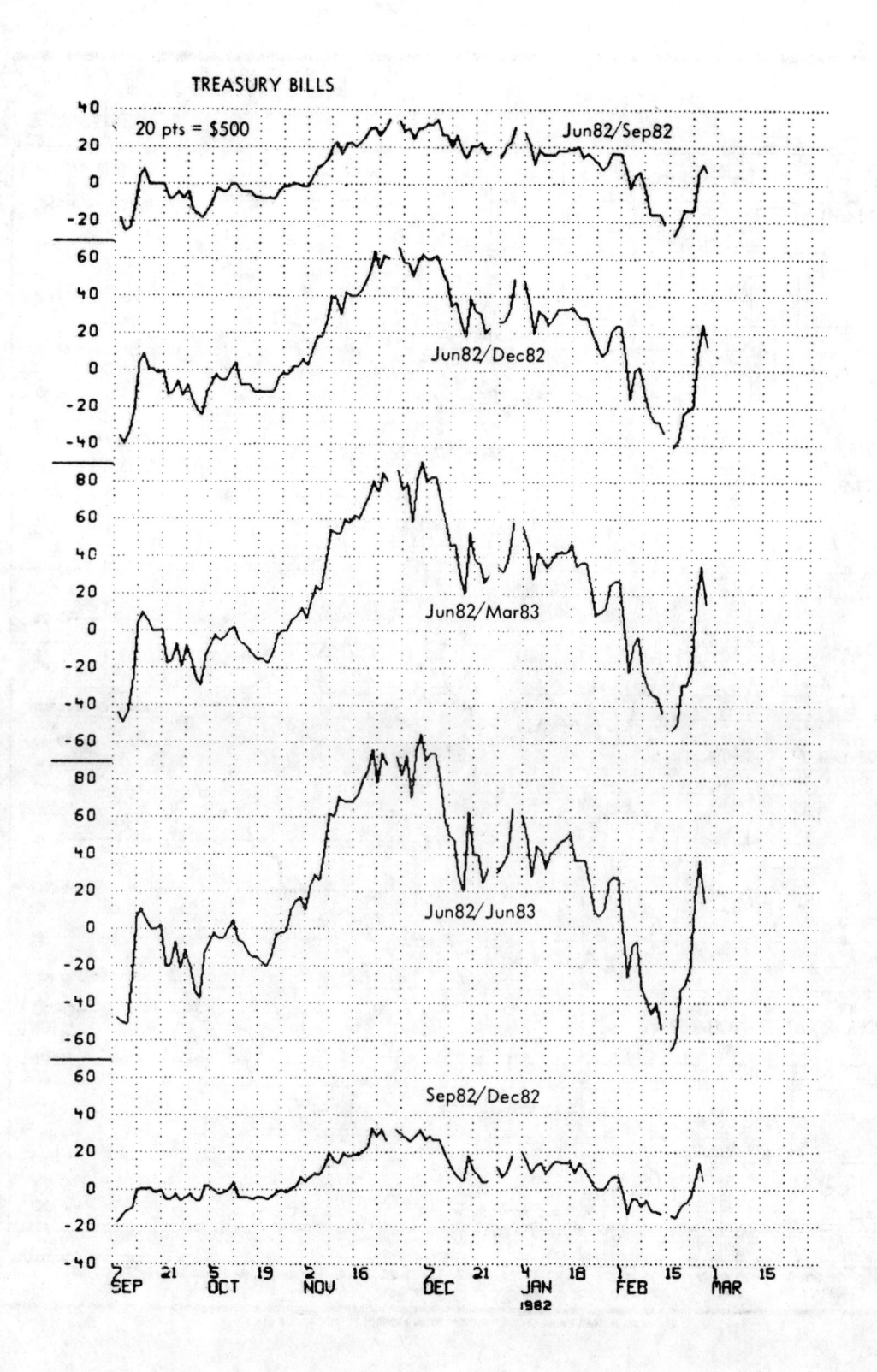

Spread chart courtesy of Spread Scope, Inc.

TREASURY BOND SPREADS

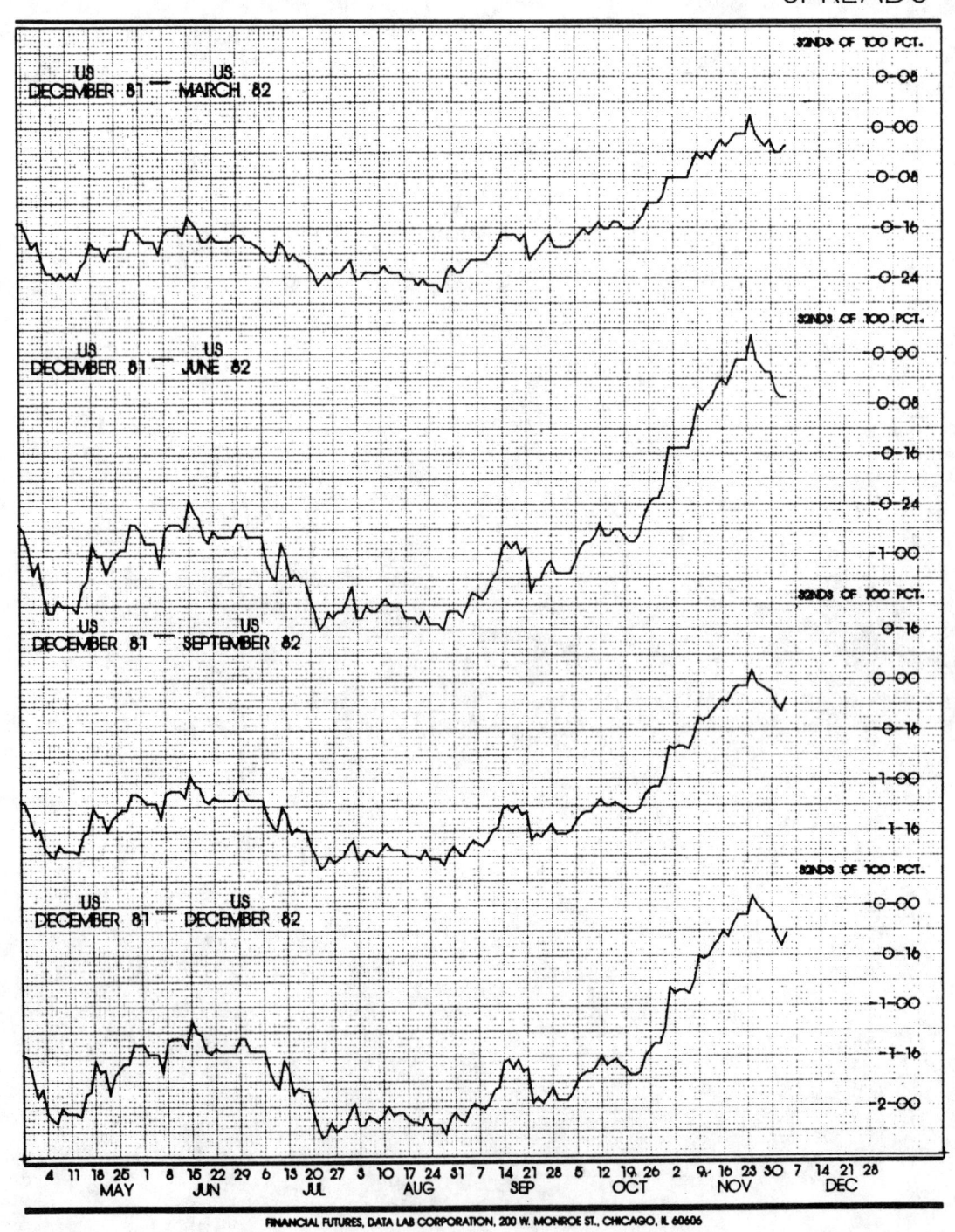

Chart courtesy Data Lab Corp., Chicago, IL

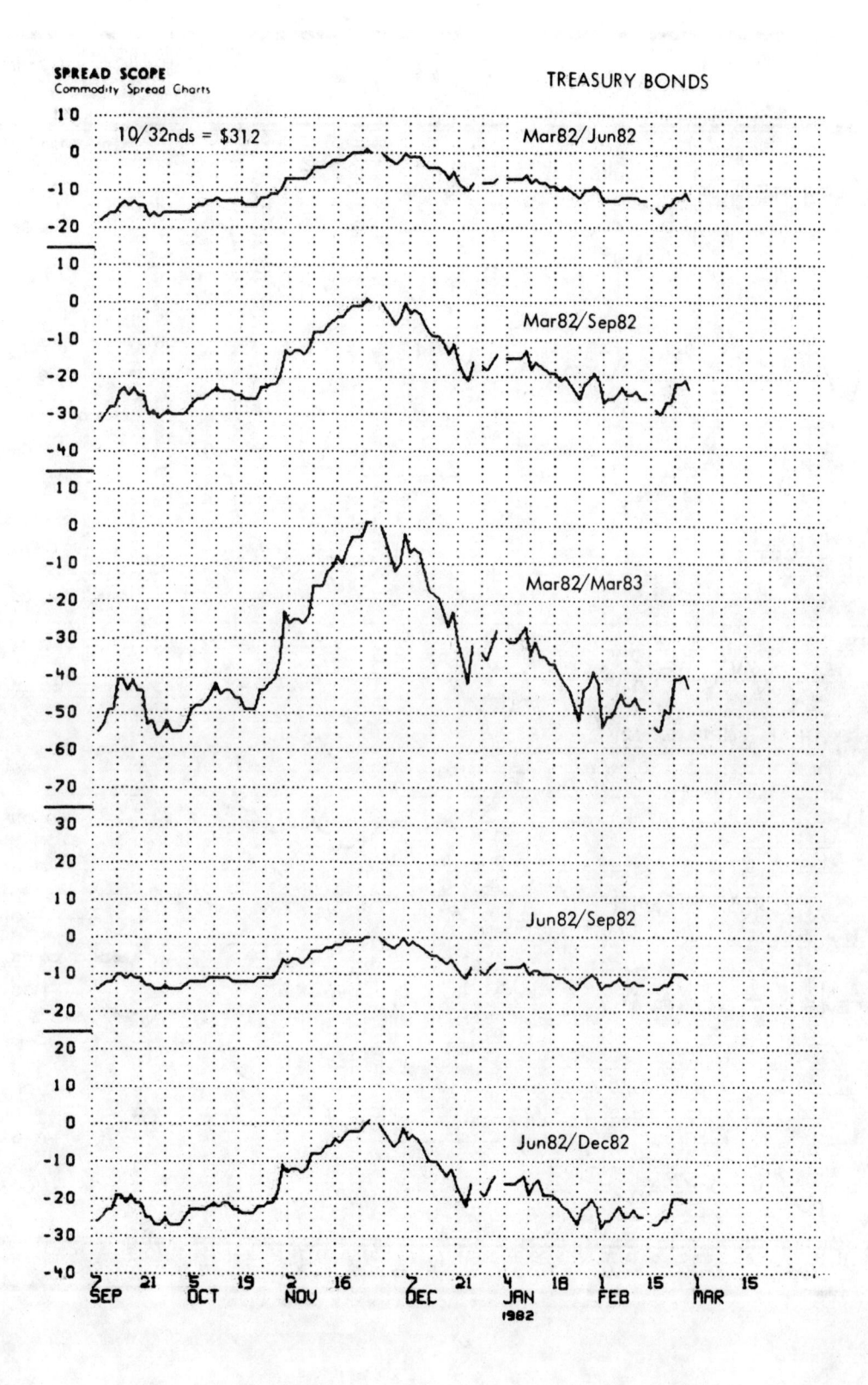

Spread chart courtesy of Spread Scope, Inc.

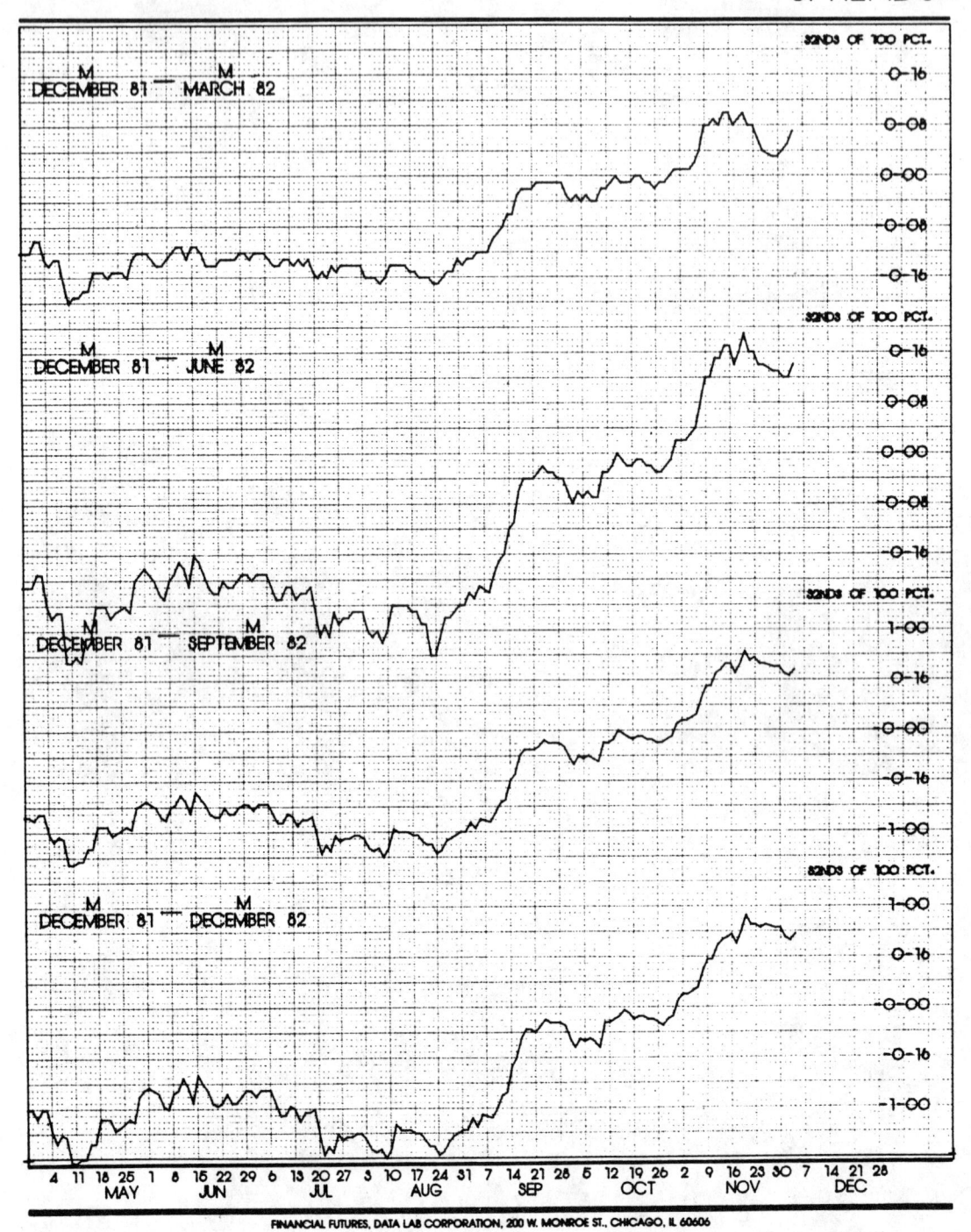

Chart courtesy Data Lab Corp., Chicago, IL

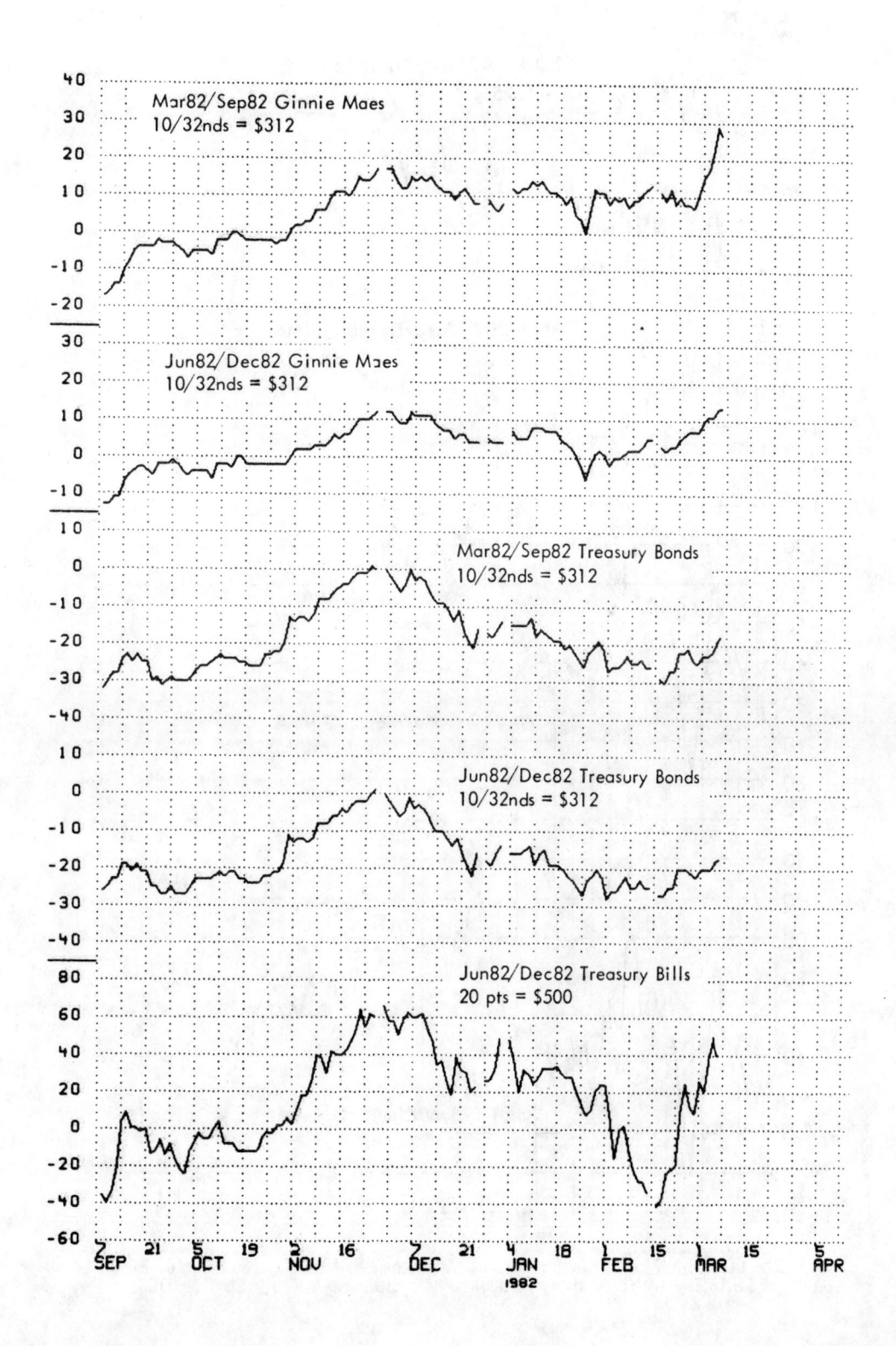

Spread chart courtesy of Spread Scope, Inc.

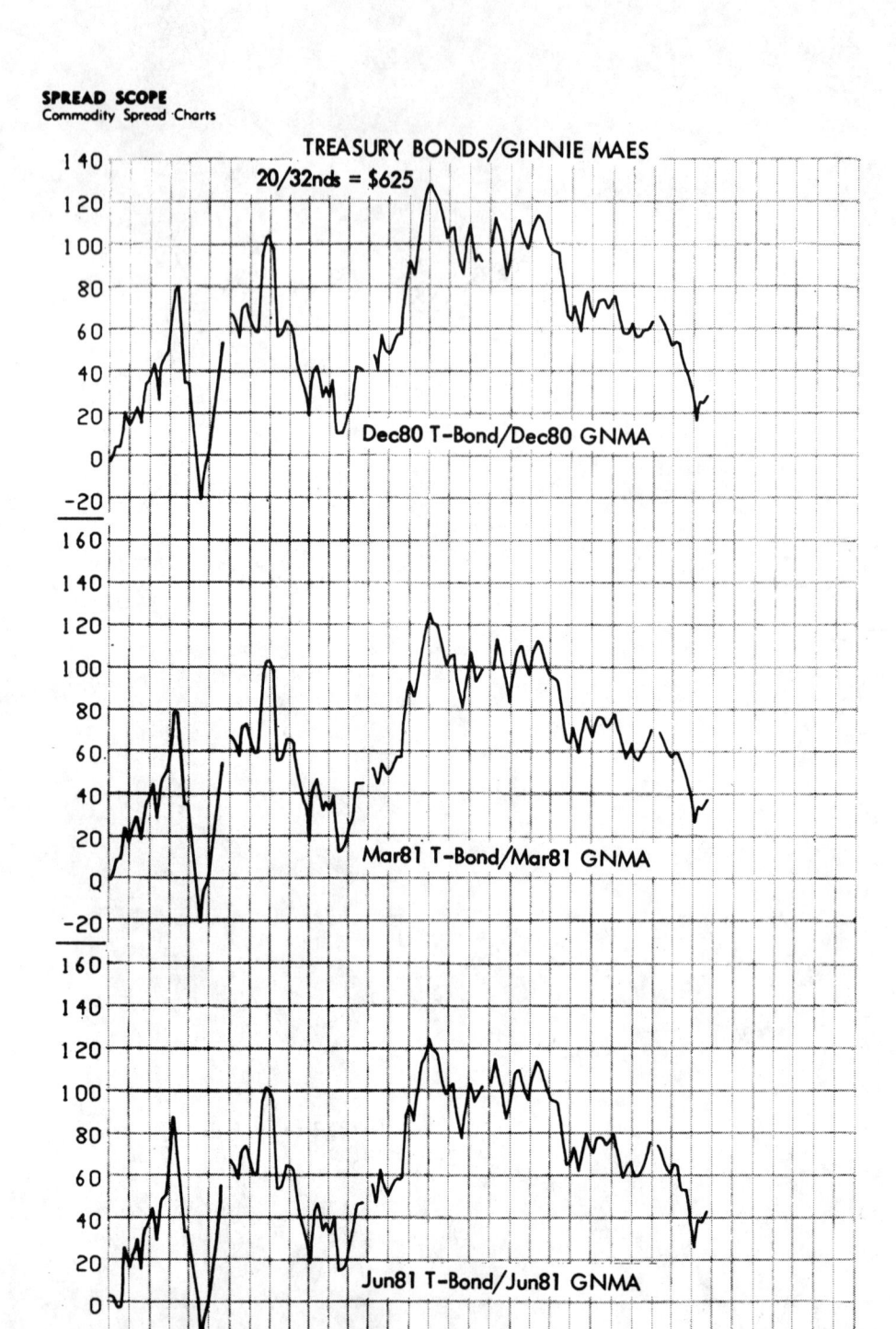

SPREAD SCOPE
Commodity Spread Charts

TREASURY BONDS/GINNIE MAES
20/32nds = $625

Dec80 T-Bond/Dec80 GNMA

Mar81 T-Bond/Mar81 GNMA

Jun81 T-Bond/Jun81 GNMA

Spread chart courtesy of Spread Scope, Inc.

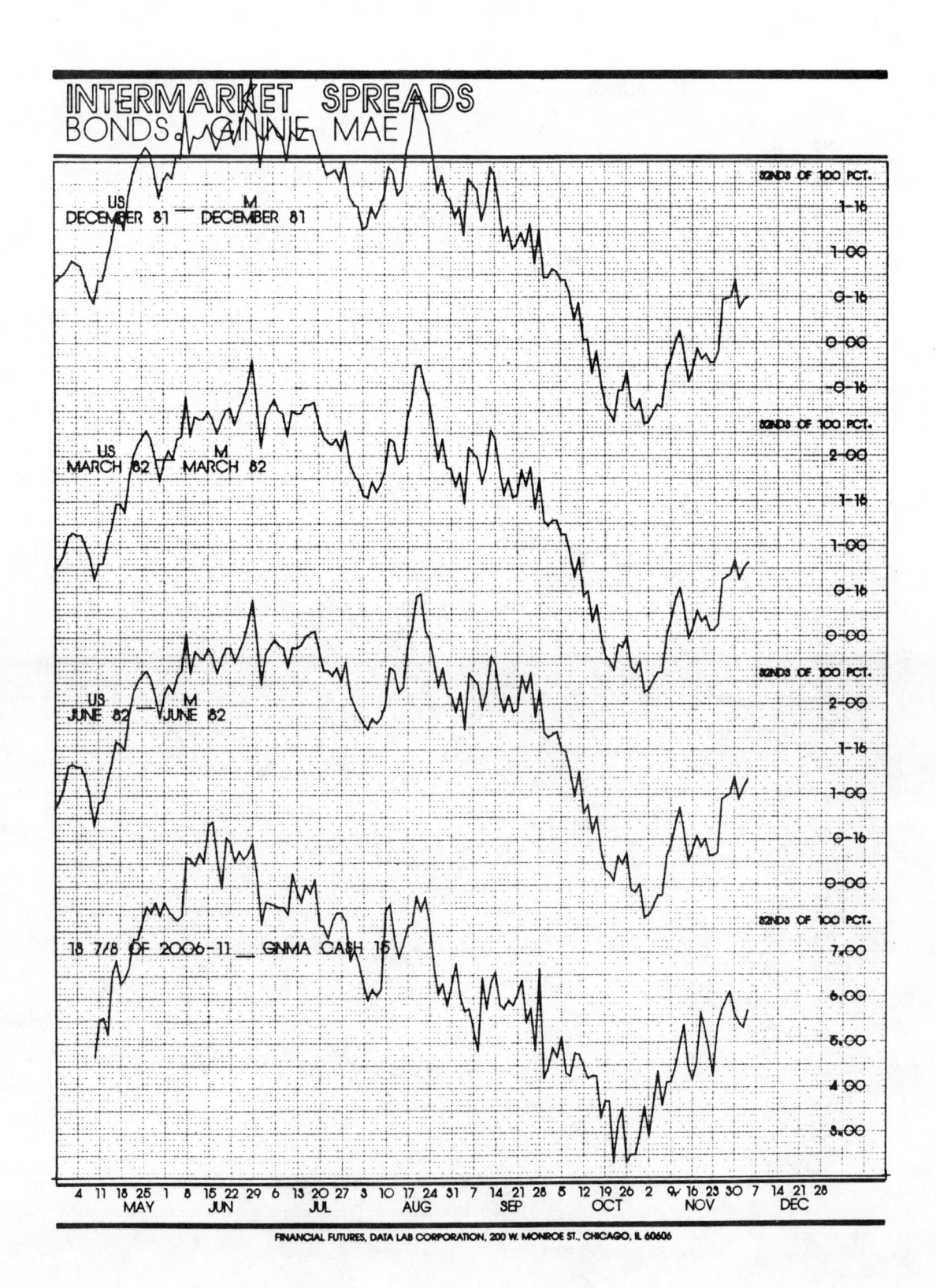

Chart courtesy Data Lab Corp., Chicago, IL.

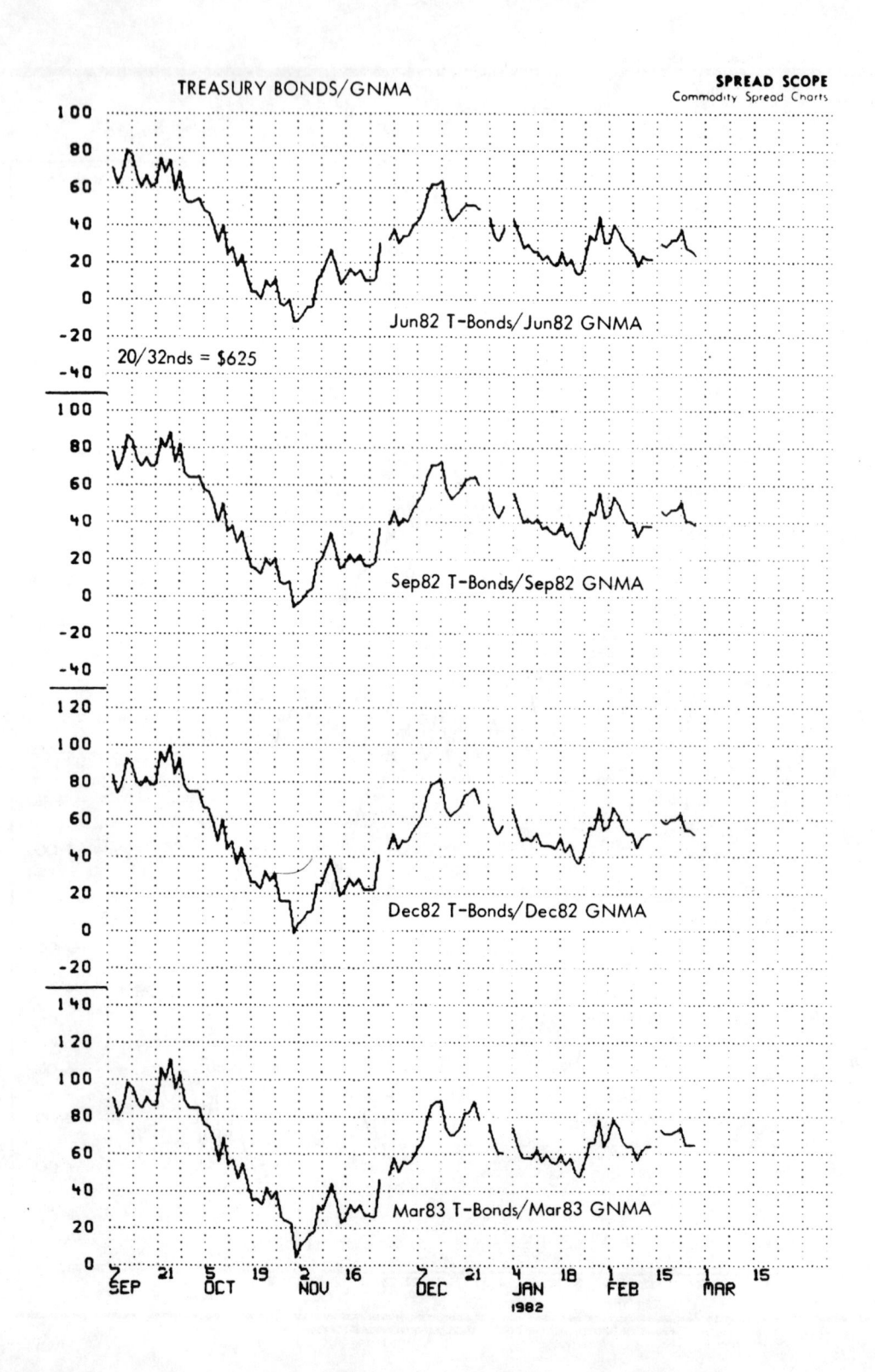

Spread chart courtesy of Spread Scope, Inc.

A YEAR-ROUND PROGRAM FOR SPREAD TRADERS

FIRST QUARTER: JAN - FEB - MCH

SOYBEAN OIL: Buy Sep. - Sell Dec.

Enter: Beginning calendar year.
Exit: Between mid-Feb and late Mch.
Note: This is a bull spread.

ORANGE JUICE: Buy Sep. - Sell Jan.(next)

Enter: Beginning of calendar year.
Exit: Late February.
Note: Intercrop spread. Success depends on freeze or freeze scare (see page 125).

CATTLE: Buy June - Sell October

Enter: In January.
Exit: About mid-May.
Note: Try to initiate spread with Oct. at a premium (see p104).

SOYBEAN MEAL: Buy Sep. - Sell Dec.

Enter: Late in January.
Exit: In May or earlier (in some years even in March).

HOGS: Sell April - Buy July

Enter: Before mid-February.
Exit: Late March or early April.
Note: Quite reliable bear spread. Try to initiate spread at less than 150 points premium July.

HOGS: Buy June - Sell October

Enter: From mid-Feb. to end of March.
Exit: During mid-May.
Note: Initiate if June has less than 50 points premium at entry. In case of October premium, add extra positions.

PLYWOOD: Sell July - Buy November

Enter: Between mid-Feb and mid-March.
Exit: Mid-April (in strong bear trend hold spread until June).
Note: See text (p138) re possible contra-seasonal move. This is a bear spread.

CORN: Buy May - Sell July

Enter: Late February or early March.
Exit: Last week of April.
Note: Entry level even money, or preferably July premium.

LUMBER: Sell July - Buy September

Enter: February or March.
Exit: Late May.
Note: Initiate this bear spread about even money: + or - 50 points.

WHEAT: Buy July (Chi) - Sell July (K.C.)

Enter: Beginning March.
Exit: Late June.
Note: Historical spread range Chi +30¢ over K.C. to 35¢ under.

HOGS: Buy July - Sell December

Enter: After the March Hogs & Pig Rpt.
Exit: Late June or early July.
Note: This bull spread is similar to June/October.

COFFEE: Buy September - Sell December

Enter: During March-May lows.
Exit: During July-August highs.
Note: Initiate in bullish situations, when September trades at least 100 points under December.

213

Buy Dec. CORN - Sell Dec. WHEAT (Chi)

Enter: During first quarter after spread tops out in chart.
Exit: In May/June period.
Note: Watch seasonals (see p71).

CORN: Buy July - Sell December

Enter: March to mid-April.
Exit: Late May to mid-June.
Note: Watch for bottom formation in spread chart.

SECOND QUARTER: APR - MAY - JUNE

Buy 3 July PORK BELLIES and Sell 4 July LIVE HOGS

Enter: Mid-April (for seasonal move).
Exit: Mid-June.
Note: Initiate whenever the price of July PB approaches the price of July Hogs.

COCOA: Buy July - Sell December

Enter: April to May.
Exit: Late in June.

LUMBER: Buy September - Sell November

Enter: April or May.
Exit: In June-July period.
Note: Attempts to enter this bull spread close to even money. High-risk!

SUGAR: Sell October - Buy March (next yr)

Enter: In April or May.
Exit: In August.
Note: Initiate when bearish fundamentals are expected to exert their influence (see p126).

SOYBEANS: Sell July - Buy November

Enter: During May.
Exit: Last trading day in June.
Note: This is a bear spread. Often works even in contra-seasonal years.

Buy 1 Dec. CORN - Sell 2 Dec. OATS

Enter: In April-June.
Exit: July-August.
Note: See text re corn/oats spreads.

COTTON: Buy December - Sell March

Enter: In May.
(Second opportunity Sep-Oct).
Exit: Late June or early July.
(Second opportunity mid-Nov.)

COCOA: Buy December - Sell May (next)

Enter: Early May.
Exit: Between mid-Oct. and early Nov.
Note: Fairly reliable bull spread.

SOYBEANS: Sell September - Buy Nov.

Enter: Late May or early June.
Exit: Mid-September at even money or a premium November.
Watch: Enter at sizeable premium Sept.

SOYBEAN COMPLEX: January Reverse Crush
Buy Jan. Products - Sell Jan. Beans

Enter: During May-June. Can also be entered in September which is less risky but tends to be less profitable.
Exit: During November-December.
Note: Establish spread at 30¢ or less, premium products.
(See text on p90).

Buy Dec. WHEAT (Chi) - Sell Dec. CORN

Enter: May or June.
Exit: During peak in the Oct-Dec. period.
Note: See p70-71.

SOYBEANS: Buy September - Sell Nov.

Enter: June or July.
Exit: Early September.
Note: See p86.

COTTON: Buy October - Sell December

Enter: Between late spring and early summer.
Exit: Watch spread chart for topping out action.
Note: Initiate if the crop is threatened and harvest is late.
Note 2: Upon topping action reverse spread: Sell Oct & Buy Dec. See p136.

THIRD QUARTER: JLY - AUG - SEP

Buy Dec. OIL - Sell Dec. MEAL

Enter: In July.
Exit: Between late Aug.-early Oct.

CATTLE: Sell October - Buy December

Enter: Early in August.
Exit: About mid-September.
Note: Initiate only if Oct. trades at 50 points or more premium over December. (This is a bear spr.)

WHEAT (Chi): Buy May - Sell July

Enter: During the summer months.
Exit: November or later.
Note: See p68.

SOYBEAN OIL: Sell December - Buy May

Enter: Early August.
Exit: Between mid-September and early October. In strong bear trend hold spread till November.
Note: May = next year. Bear spread!

CORN: Sell December - Buy July (next)

Enter: Mid-August.
Exit: End of October.
Note: See p66.

Buy 2 Dec. OATS - Sell 1 Dec. CORN

Enter: About mid-August.
Exit: During November.
Note: Wait for seasonal low to initiate spread.

PORK BELLIES: Buy March - Sell July

Enter: Late August.
Exit: In February.
Note: Similar to Feb/May spread. This is also a bull spread. A quick seasonal upmove is possible in mid-November.

WHEAT (Chi): Buy Dec. - Sell March (next)

Enter: End of August or in September.
Exit: Mid-December.
Note: Carrying charges, interest rates, and chance of a bull move must be watched. The May contract is often used instead of March.

SUGAR: Buy May - Sell October

Enter: During seasonal low in Aug-Sep.
Exit: Between December and mid-January.
Note: See p126.

215

PORK BELLIES: Buy February - Sell May

Enter: During August-September.
Exit: Early October.

WHEAT: Buy May (Chi) - Sell May (Minn.)

Note: Minneapolis tends to lose on Chicago and K.C. during summer.

WHEAT: Buy May (Minn.) - Sell May (Chi or K.C.)

Note: Minneapolis tends to gain on Chicago and K.C. from September through next June.

CATTLE: Sell December - Buy Feb. (next)

Enter: In late Sep. or Oct. with the December contract at a premium.
Exit: As Dec. cattle approaches maturity.
Note: Enter if statistics are bearish.

FOURTH QUARTER: OCT - NOV - DEC

CORN: Sell July - Buy December

Enter: During fourth quarter of the current year.
Exit: Late March or during April following year.
Note: Enter only if Dec. trades at a sharp discount to July.

SOYBEANS: Buy July - Sell November

Enter: During the fourth quarter of current calendar year.
Exit: In April or May next year.
Note: Intercrop spread. Dynamic and risky. See text on this bull spread on p85.

SOYBEAN MEAL: Buy Jan. - Sell Mch.(or May)

Enter: Early October.
Exit: Mid- or late-December.
Note: Limited-risk spread. Watch prices and interest rates. Enter only if Jan. sells at good discount to Mch (May) during September.

CATTLE: Sell December - Buy April (next)

Enter: During October.
Exit: Near the end of Nov. or early Dec.
Note: Enter only if bear-trend confirmed.

WHEAT: Buy March (Chi) - Sell March (KC)

Enter: October.
Exit: End of January.
Note: See p70.

SOYBEAN OIL: Buy March - Sell September

Enter: Early November. Dip in January can be used to add to positions.
Exit: Before expiration of Mch. contract.

HOGS: Buy February - Sell April

Enter: Late in October.
Exit: Near the end of January.
Note: Feb. hogs are expected to gain on April into the new year.

COTTON: Buy July - Sell December

Enter: Oct. or Nov.
(Second opportunity in March)
Exit: End of Jan.
(Second opportunity if export demand is strong: exit in May those spreads which were set up in March).
Note: Buy July when it is trading at a discount to December.

LUMBER: Sell March - Buy May

Enter: Mid-December.
Exit: Late February.
Note: A bear spread that adheres to
       the seasonal pattern.

Buy July CORN - Sell July WHEAT (Chi)

Enter: In December (if price moves in
       favor of corn).
Exit: May or early June.
Watch: For seasonal high between Nov.
       and Feb. High-risk trade.

WHEAT (Chi): Sell May - Buy December

Enter: During December-January.
Exit: Before the end of April (next).
Note: Be alert to bullish news events.
       This is a bear spread!
       See text on p68-69.

WHEAT (Chi): Sell May - Buy July

Enter: Near the end of December.
Exit: During March or April if a strong
       bear trend exists. Otherwise,
       exit late Jan. or early Feb.

ORANGE JUICE: Buy November - Sell Jan.

Enter: December-January.
Exit: Late February.
Note: See p125.

COPPER: Buy May - Sell December

Enter: Last week of December or
       beginning of January.
Exit: Mid-March or early April.
Note: Copper spreads are a function of
       price and interest rates.
       Seasonals are reliable but often
       overpowered by the above factors.

BIBLIOGRAPHY

1. Aldrich, Samuel R., Walter O. Scott and Earl R. Leng. MODERN CORN PRODUCTION. 2nd ed. Champaign, IL, A & L Publications, 1975.

2. Aliber, Robert A. THE INTERNATIONAL MARKET FOR FOREIGN EXCHANGE. New York, Praeger, 1969.

3. Aliber, Robert Z. NATIONAL MONETARY POLICIES AND THE INTERNATIONAL FINANCIAL SYSTEM. Chicago, University of Chicago Press, 1974.

4. Aliber, Robert Z. THE INTERNATIONAL MONEY GAME, 2nd ed. New York, Basic Books, 1976.

5. Allen, R.C. HOW TO USE THE 4 DAY, 9 DAY, AND 18 DAY MOVING AVERAGE TO EARN LARGER PROFITS FROM COMMODITIES. Chicago, Best Books, 1974.

6. Anderson, Keith B., Michael P. Lynch, and Jonathan D. Ogur. THE U.S. SUGAR INDUSTRY. Washington, U.S. Federal Trade Commission, 1975.

7. Anderson, B. Ray. HOW YOU CAN USE INFLATION TO BEAT THE I.R.S. New York, Harper & Row, 1981.

8. Angell, George. COMPUTER-PROVEN COMMODITY SPREADS.- The 24 Most Consistently Profitable Low-Risk Trades. Brightwaters, N.Y., Windsor Books, 1981.

9. Angrist, Stanley W. SENSIBLE SPECULATING IN COMMODITIES; OR, HOW TO PROFIT IN THE BELLIES, BUSHELS, AND BALES MARKET. New York, Simon & Schuster, 1972.

10. Appel, George. WINNING MARKET SYSTEMS, OR 83 WAYS TO BEAT THE MARKET. Rev. 2nd ed. Great Neck, N.Y., Signalert, 1974.

11. Appleman, Mark J. THE WINNING HABIT: HOW YOUR PERSONALITY MAKES YOU A WINNER OR A LOSER IN THE STOCK MARKET. New York, McCall Publishing, 1970.

12. Armour, Lawrence A. THE YOUNG MILLIONAIRES. Chicago, IL, Playboy Press, 1973.

13. Arms, Richard W. PROFITS IN VOLUME. Larchmont, N.Y., Investors Intelligence, 1971

14. Arthur, Henry B. COMMODITY FUTURES AS A BUSINESS MANAGEMENT TOOL. Boston, Harvard University Press, 1971.

15. Bakken, Henry H. (ed.) FUTURES TRADING LIVESTOCK. Madison, W.I., Mimir Publishers, 1970.

16. Barnes, Robert M. TAMING THE PITS; A TECHNICAL APPROACH TO COMMODITY TRADING. New York, John Wiley, 1979.

17. Barnes, Robert M. 1981 TECHNICAL COMMODITY YEARBOOK. New York, Van Nostrand Reinhold, 1980.

17A. Barnes, Robert M. COMMODITY PROFITS THROUGH TREND TRADING: A Price Model and Strategies. New York, John Wiley, 1982.

18. Beckman, R.C. SUPERTIMING: THE UNIQUE ELLIOTT WAVE SYSTEM. Los Angeles, The Library of Investment Study.

19. Belveal, L. Dee. COMMODITY SPECULATION WITH PROFITS IN MIND. Wilmette, IL, Commodities Press, 1967.

20. Belveal, L. Dee. CHARTING COMMODITY MARKET PRICE BEHAVIOR. Wilmette, IL, Commodities Press, 1969.

21. Bernstein, Jake. M.B.H. SEASONAL FUTURES CHARTS. Winnetka, IL, MBH Commodity Advisors.

22. Bernstein, Jake. SEASONAL CHART STUDY 1953-1976: AN ANALYSIS OF SEASONAL CASH COMMODITY PRICE TENDENCIES. Winnetka, IL, MBH Commodity Advisors, 1977.

23. Bernstein, J., and D. Madej. SEASONAL CHART STUDY II. COMMODITY SPREADS. Winnetka, IL, MBH Commodity Advisors, 1978.

24. Bernstein, Jacob. THE INVESTOR'S QUOTIENT. The Psychology of Successful Investing In Commodities And Stocks. New York, John Wiley, 1980.

24A. Bernstein, Jacob. THE HANDBOOK OF COMMODITY CYCLES. New York, John Wiley, 1982.

25. Bernstein, Peter L. A PRIMER ON MONEY, BANKING AND GOLD, 2nd ed. New York, Random House, 1968.

26. Besant, Lloyd, Dana Kellerman and Gregory Monroe (eds.). COMMODITY TRADING MANUAL (4th ed.). Chicago, Chicago Board of Trade, 1980.

27. Blumenthal, Earl. CHART FOR PROFIT: POINT & FIGURE TRADING. Larchmont, NY, Investors Intelligence, 1975.

28. Bolton, A. Hamilton. THE ELLIOTT WAVE PRINCIPLE: A CRITICAL APPRAISAL. Hamilton, Bermuda, Monetary Research, 1970.

29. Brown, Brendon. MONEY HARD AND SOFT ON THE INTERNATIONAL CURRENCY MARKETS. New York, Halsted Press (Wiley), 1978.

30. Browne, Harry. HOW YOU CAN PROFIT FROM THE COMING DEVALUATION. New Rochelle, NY, Arlington House, 1970.

31. Browne, Harry. YOU CAN PROFIT FROM A MONETARY CRISIS. New York, Macmillan, 1974.

32. Browne, Harry. HARRY BROWNE'S COMPLETE GUIDE TO SWISS BANKS. New York, McGraw-Hill, 1976.

33. Browne, Harry. NEW PROFITS FROM THE MONETARY CRISIS. New York, Morrow, 1978.

34. Browne, Harry and Terry Coxon. INFLATION-PROOFING YOUR INVESTMENTS. New York, William Morrow and Company, 1981.

35. Brownstone and Franck. THE V.N.R. INVESTOR'S DISCTIONARY. New York, Van Nostrand, 1981.

36. Butts, Allison (ed.). SILVER: ECONOMICS, METALLURGY, AND USE. Reprint of 1967 edition. Huntington, NY, Krieger, 1975.

37. Caldwell, B.E. (ed.). SOYBEANS: IMPROVEMENT, PRODUCTION, AND USES. Madison, WI, American Society of Agronomy, 1973.

38. Canterbery, E.R. FOREIGN EXCHANGE, CAPITAL FLOWS & MONETARY POLICY. Princeton, NJ, Princeton University, 1965.

39. Carabini, Louis E. (ed.). EVERYTHING YOU NEED TO KNOW ABOUT GOLD AND SILVER. New Rochelle, NY, Arlington House, 1974.

40. Carroll McEntee & McGinley. HANDBOOK OF U.S. TREASURY AND FEDERAL AGENCY SECURITIES, INCLUDING OTHER SHORT-TERM MONEY MARKET INSTRUMENTS. 2nd ed. New York, Street Publishing, 1977.

41. Charles River Associates. ECONOMIC ANALYSIS OF THE SILVER INDUSTRY. Cambridge, MA, 1969.

42. Chicago Board of Trade. GRAINS: PRODUCTION, PROCESSING, MARKETING. 2nd rev. ed. Chicago, Chicago Board of Trade, 1977.

43. Chicago Board of Trade. COMMODITY FUTURES TRADING: A BIBLIOGRAPHY, CUMULATIVE THROUGH 1976. Chicago, Chicago Board of Trade, 1978 (annual)

44. Christner, Ronald Charles. RETURN, RISK AND DIVERSIFICATION ASPECTS OF THE NEW MARKETS FOR LUMBER AND PLYWOOD FUTURES. Ph.D. dissertation, University of Minnesota, 1973. Ann Arbor, MI, University Microfilms, 1974.

45. Clawson, Marion. DECISION MAKING IN TIMBER PRODUCTION, HARVEST AND MARKETING. Washington, Resources for the Future, 1977.

46. Clendenning, E. Wayne. EURO-DOLLAR MARKET. London: Oxford University Press, 1970.

47. Cohen, A.W. HOW TO USE THE THREE-POINT REVERSAL METHOD OF POINT-AND-FIGURE CHARTING. Larchmont, NY, Chartcraft, 1972.

48. Cohen, A.W. TECHNICAL INDICATOR ANALYSIS BY POINT-AND-FIGURE TECHNIQUE. Larchmont, NY, Chartcraft, 1977.

49. Commission on Critical Choices for Americans. VITAL RESOURCES. Lexington, MA, Lexington Books, 1977.

50. Commodity Perspective. ENCYCLOPEDIA OF HISTORICAL CHARTS. Chicago, Investor Publishing, 1977. (annual supplements)

51. Commodity Research Bureau. COMMODITY YEARBOOK.
New York, Commodity Research Bureau (annual).

52. Commodity Research Bureau. UNDERSTANDING THE COMMODITY FUTURES MARKET.
New York, Commodity Research Bureau, 1973.

53. Coninx, Raymond, G.F. FOREIGN EXCHANGE TODAY.
New York, Halstead Press (Wiley), 1980.

54. Cook, Timothy Q. (ed.). INSTRUMENTS OF THE MONEY MARKET. 4th ed.
Richmond, VA, Federal Reserve Bank of Richmond, 1977.

55. Coombs, Charles A. THE ARENA OF INTERNATIONAL FINANCE.
New York, John Wiley, 1976.

56. Cox, Houston A. A COMMON SENSE APPROACH TO COMMODITY FUTURES TRADING.
New York, Reynolds Securities, 1972.

57. Cox, Houston A. CONCEPTS ON PROFITS IN COMMODITY FUTURES TRADING.
New York, Reynolds Securities, 1972.

58. Crocraft, Perry J. LONDON OPTIONS ON COMMODITIES: A PRIMER FOR AMERICAN SPECULATORS. Chicago, IL, Contemporary Books, 1977.

59. Crowe, Kenneth. AMERICA FOR SALE. New York, Doubleday & Co., 1978.

60. Darst, David. THE COMPLETE BOND BOOK, A GUIDE TO ALL TYPES OF FIXED-INCOME SECURITIES.

61. Davies, David M. COMMODITY TRADING FOR THE INVESTOR. 2nd ed.
London, Financial Research Associates, 1971.

62. Dean, William, and David S. Evans (eds.). TERMS OF THE TRADE: A HANDBOOK FOR THE FOREST PRODUCTS INDUSTRY.
Eugene, OR, Random Lengths Publications, 1978.

63. Dewey, Edward R. CYCLES, SELECTED WRITINGS.
Pittsburgh, PA, Foundation for the Study of Cycles, 1970.

64. Dewey, Edward R. CYCLES: THE MYSTERIOUS FORCES THAT TRIGGER EVENTS.
New York, Hawthorne Books, 1971.

65. Dines, James. HOW THE AVERAGE INVESTOR CAN USE TECHNICAL ANALYSIS FOR STOCK PROFITS. New York, Dines Chart Corp., 1973.

66. Dobson, Edward D. COMMODITIES: A CHART ANTHOLOGY.
Greenville, SC, Edward D. Dobson (Annual).

67. Dobson, Edward D. COMMODITY SPREADS: A HISTORICAL CHART PERSPECTIVE.
Greenville, SC, Edward D. Dobson, 1974.

68. Dobson, Edward D. THE TRADING RULE THAT CAN MAKE YOU RICH.
Greenville, SC, Traders Press, 1979.

69. Dominick, B.A., and F.W. Williams. FUTURES TRADING AND THE FLORIDA ORANGE INDUSTRY. Gainesville, University of Florida, Agri. Exper. Sta., 1965.

70. Dominguez, John R. DEVALUATION AND FUTURES MARKETS. Lexington, MA, Lexington Books, 1972.

71. Donoghue, William E., with T. Tilling. COMPLETE MONEY MARKET GUIDE. New York, Harper & Row, 1981.

72. Doyle, Thomas L., Jr. LIVE CATTLE, LIVE HOGS AND FROZEN PORK BELLIES. Los Altos, CA, Futures Research Co., 1976.

73. Dufey, Gunter and Ian H. Giddy. THE INTERNATIONAL MONEY MARKET. Englewood Cliffs, NJ, Prentice-Hall, 1978.

74. Dunn, Dennis D. CONSISTENT PROFITS IN JUNE LIVE BEEF CATTLE. Lafayette, IN, Dunn & Hargitt, 1972.

75. Dunn, Dennis D. RESULTS OF TRADING METHOD WRITTEN BY ROBERT D. TAYLOR. West Lafayette, IN, Dunn & Hargitt, 1972.

76. Dunn & Hargitt. CONSISTENT PROFITS IN PORK BELLIES. Lafayette, IN, Dunn & Hargitt, n.d.

77. Dushek, Charles and Carol Harding. TRADING IN FOREIGN CURRENCIES: SPECULATIVE PRACTICES AND TECHNIQUES. Chicago, American TransEuro, 1978.

78. Edwards, Robert D., and John Magee. TECHNICAL ANALISYS OF STOCK TRENDS. 5th ed. Springfield, MA, John Magee, 1966.

79. Einzig, Paul. A DYNAMIC THEORY OF FORWARD EXCHANGE. New York, St. Martin's Press, 1968.

80. Einzig, Paul. FOREIGN EXCHANGE CRISES, 2nd ed. New York, St. Martin's Press, 1970.

81. Einzig, Paul. THE CASE AGAINST FLOATING EXCHANGES. New York, St. Martin's Press, 1970.

82. Einzig, Paul. THE HISTORY OF FOREIGN EXCHANGE, 2nd ed. New York, St. Martin's Press, 1970.

83. Einzig, Paul. THE DESTINY OF GOLD. New York, St. Martin's Press, 1972.

84. Einzig, Paul and Brian S. Quinn. THE EURO-DOLLAR SYSTEM: PRACTICE AND THEORY OF INTERNATIONAL INTEREST RATES. 6th ed.

85. Elliott, R.N. THE WAVE PRINCIPLE. Hamilton, Bermuda, Monetary Research, '69.

86. Ensminger, M.E. POULTRY SCIENCE. Danville, IL, Interstate, 1971.

87. Ensminger, M.R. BEEF CATTLE SCIENCE, 5th ed. Danville, IL, Interstate, 1976.

88. Ensor, Richard and Boris Antl (eds.). THE MANAGEMENT OF FOREIGN EXCHANGE RISK. London, Euromoney, 1978.

89. Epstein, Eugene. MAKING MONEY IN COMMODITIES. New York, Praeger, 1976.

90. Evitt, H.E. A MANUAL OF FOREIGN EXCHANGE (7th ed. revised by R.F. Pither). London, Pitman, 1971.

91. Federal Reserve Bank of Philadelphia. DEFENDING THE DOLLAR (rev. ed.). Philadelphia, PA, Federal Reserve Bank, 1974.

91A. Federal Reserve Bank of New York. HOW TO READ U.S. GOVERNMENT SECURITIES QUOTES (Fedpoints 7). New York, Federal Reserve Bank of N.Y., 1977.

91B. Federal Reserve Bank of New York. BASIC INFORMATION ON TREASURY NOTES AND BONDS. New York, Federal Reserve Bank of N.Y., 1980.

91C. Federal Reserve Bank of New York. BASIC INFORMATION ON TREASURY BILLS. New York, Federal Reserve Bank of N.Y., 1981.

92. Feldman, Jill B. THE PRICE EFFECTS OF FUTURES TRADING IN RELATION TO INTERNATIONAL COFFEE AND COCOA MARKETS. South Hadley, MA, Mount Holyoke College, 1973.

93. First Boston Corporation. HANDBOOK OF SECURITIES OF THE UNITED STATES GOVERNMENT AND FEDERAL AGENCIES AND RELATED MONEY MARKET INSTRUMENTS. (28th ed.). New York, First Boston Corp., 1978.

94. Fisher, Bart S. THE INTERNATIONAL COFFEE AGREEMENT: A STUDY IN COFFEE DIPLOMACY. New York, Praeger, 1972.

95. Friedman, Milton. THE EURO-DOLLAR MARKET, SOME FIRST PRINCIPLES. Chicago, University of Chicago (n.d.).

96. Friedman, Milton and Rose D. FREE TO CHOOSE. New York, Harcourt Brace Jovanovich, 1980.

97. Gann, W.D. HOW TO MAKE PROFITS TRADING IN COMMODITIES (rev. ed.). Pomeroy, WA, Lambert-Gann Publishing, 1951.

98. Garretty, M.D. MAKING MONEY IN THE FUTURES MARKET IN AUSTRALIA. Blackburn, Victoria, Australia, Acacia Press (n.d.).

99. Gibson-Jarvie, Robert. THE LONDON METAL EXCHANGE: A COMMODITY MARKET. Waterloo, IA, Investor Publications, 1976.

100. GNMA Mortgage-Backed Securities Dealers Association. THE GINNIE MAE MANUAL. Homewood, IL, Dow-Jones-Irwin, 1978.

101. Gold, Gerald. MODERN COMMODITY FUTURES TRADING (7th rev. ed.). New York, Commodity Research Bureau, 1975.

102. Gold, Gerald. FINANCIAL SURVIVAL IN THE 70s WITH GOLD, SILVER AND PLATINUM. New York, RHM Press, 1975.

102A. Gonczy, Anne-Marie L. ABCs OF FIGURING INTEREST. Readings in Economics and Finance. Chicago, Federal Reserve Bank of Chicago, 1979.

103. Goss, B.A. A THEORY OF FUTURES TRADING. London and Boston, Routledge and Kegan, 1972.

104. Goss, B.A. THE ECONOMICS OF FUTURES TRADING. New York, John Wiley, 1976.

105. Gould, Bruce G. DOW JONES-IRWIN GUIDE TO COMMODITIES TRADING. Homewood, Dow Jones-Irwin, 1973.

106. Gould, Bruce G. BRUCE GOULD'S MY MOST SUCCESSFUL TECHNIQUE FOR MAKING MONEY. Seattle, WA, Bruce Gould Publications, 1975.

107. Gould, Bruce G. BRUCE GOULD'S COMMODITY TRADING MANUAL. Seattle, WA, Bruce Gould Publications, 1976.

108. Gould, Bruce G. $65 COMMODITY TRADING MANUAL. Seattle, WA, Bruce Gould Publications, 1976.

109. Granger, C.W.J. GETTING STARTED IN LONDON COMMODITIES. Columbia, MD, Investor Publications, 1975.

110. Gray, Roger W. THE FEASIBILITY OF ORGANIZED FUTURES TRADING IN RESIDENTIAL MORTGAGES. Washington, DC, Federal Home Loan Morgage Corporation, 1974.

111. Green, Timothy. HOW TO BUY GOLD. New York, Walker & Co., 1975.

112. Grennes, Thomas, Paul R. Johnson and Marie Thursby. THE ECONOMICS OF WORLD GRAIN TRADE. New York, Praeger, 1978.

113. Grishcow, Jack and Courtney Smith. PROFITS THROUGH SEASONAL TRADING. New York, John Wiley, 1980.

114. Hammonds, Timothy M. THE PRODUCER'S AND LENDER'S GUIDE TO FUTURES TRADING. Corvallis, OR, Conrad Press, 1974.

115. Hardy, C. Colburn. INVESTOR'S GUIDE TO TECHNICAL ANALYSIS. New York, McGraw-Hill, 1978.

116. Harris Bank. THE U.S. GOVERNMENT SECURITIES MARKETS (3rd ed.). Chicago, Harris Trust & Savings Bank, 1976.

117. Hayden, Jack J. WHAT MAKES YOU A WINNER OR A LOSER IN THE STOCK AND COMMODITY MARKETS? Larchmont, NY, Investors Intelligence, 1970.

118. Heller, H. Robert. INTERNATIONAL MONETARY ECONOMICS. Englewood Cliffs, NJ, Prentice-Hall, 1974.

119. Hendra, Tony, Christopher Cerf and Peter Elbling (eds.). THE 80s: A LOOK BACK AT THE TUMULTUOUS DECADE, 1980-1989. Workman Press, 1979.

120. Henning, Charles N. et al. FINANCIAL MARKETS AND THE ECONOMY. New York, Prentice-Hall, 1975.

121. Hieronymus, Thomas A. ECONOMICS OF FUTURES TRADING FOR COMMERCIAL AND PERSONAL PROFIT (2nd ed.). New York, Commodity Research Bureau, 1977.

122. Hill, J.R. STOCK & COMMODITY MARKET TREND TRADING BY ADVANCED TECHNICAL ANALYSIS. Hendersonville, NC, Commodity Research Institute, 1977.

123. Hill, Lowell D. (ed.). WORLD SOYBEAN RESEARCH CONFERENCE. Champaign, IL, 1975, Proceedings. Danville, IL, Interstate, 1976.

124. Hoel, Arline. A PRIMER ON THE FUTURES MARKETS FOR TREASURY BILLS. New York, Federal Reserve Bank of New York, 1977.

125. Homer, Sidney. A HISTORY OF INTEREST RATES (2nd rev. ed.). New Brunswick, NJ, Rutgers University, 1977.

126. Horn, Frederick. TRADING IN COMMODITY FUTURES (2nd ed.). New York, New York Institute of Finance, 1979.

127. Houck, James P. SOYBEANS AND THEIR PRODUCTS: MARKETS, MODELS, POLICY. Minneapolis, University of Minnesota Press, 1972.

128. Horwitz, Paul. MONETARY POLICY AND THE FINANCIAL SYSTEM. Englewood Cliffs, NJ, Prentice-Hall, 1969.

129. Hurst, James Willard. A LEGAL HISTORY OF MONEY IN THE U.S. 1774-1970. Lincoln, NE, University of Nebraska Press, 1973.

130. Ibbotson, Roger G. and Rex A. Sinquefield. STOCKS, BONDS, BILLS, AND INFLATION: THE PAST (1926-1976) AND THE FUTURE (1977-2000). Chicago, Financial Analysts Research Foundation, 1977.

131. Inglett, George E. (ed.). CORN: CULTURE, PROCESSING, PRODUCTS. Westport, CT, Avi, 1970.

132. Inglett, George E. (ed.). WHEAT: PRODUCTION AND UTILIZATION. Westport, CT, Avi, 1974.

133. Inglett, George E. (ed.). SYMPOSIUM: SEED PROTEINS. Westport, CT, Avi, 1972

134. Jacque, Laurent L. MANAGEMENT OF FOREIGN EXCHANGE RISK. Lexington, MA, Heath, 1978.

135. Jastram, Roy W. THE GOLDEN CONSTANT, THE ENGLISH AND AMERICAN EXPERIENCE 1560-1976. New York, Wiley, 1977.

136. Jastram, Roy W. SILVER: THE RESTLESS METAL. New York, Wiley, 1981.

137. Jiler, Harry. GUIDE TO COMMODITY PRICE FORECASTING. New York, Commodity Research Bureau, 1967.

138. Jiler, Harry (ed.). FORECASTING COMMODITY PRICES: HOW THE EXPERTS ANALYZE THE MARKET. New York, Commodity Research Bureau, 1975.

139. Jiler, William L. (ed.) FORECASTING COMMODITY PRICES. New York, Commodity Research Bureau, 1975.

140. Johnson, D.G. FORWARD PRICES FOR AGRICULTURE. Chicago, University of Chicago Press, 1967.

141. Johnson, H.G. MONEY, TRADE AND ECONOMIC GROWTH. Cambridge, MA, Harvard University Press, 1967.

141A. Johnson, Philip McB. COMMODITIES REGULATION (vols. 1 & 2). Boston, Little, Brown & Co., 1982.

142. Kallard, Thomas. MAKE MONEY IN COMMODITY SPREADS! New York, Optosonic Press, 1974.

143. Kaufman, Perry J. COMMODITY TRADING SYSTEMS AND METHODS. New York, Wiley, 1979.

144. Kaufman, Perry J. (ed.) TECHNICAL ANALYSIS IN COMMODITIES. New York, Wiley, 1980.

145. Keltner, Chester W. HOW TO MAKE MONEY IN COMMODITIES. Kansas City, MO, Keltner Statistical Service, 1969.

146. Kemp, Jack. AN AMERICAN RENAISSANCE: A STRATEGY FOR THE 80s. New York, Harper & Row, 1979.

147. Kessel, Reuben A. THE CYCLICAL BEHAVIOR OF THE TERM STRUCTURE OF INTEREST RATES. New York, National Bureau of Economic Research, 1965.

148. Kindleberger, C.P. THE DOLLAR AND WORLD LIQUIDITY. New Haven, CT, Yale University, 1966.

149. Kroll, Stanley and Irwin Shishko. THE COMMODITY FUTURES MARKET GUIDE. New York, Harper & Row, 1973.

150. Kroll, Stanley. THE PROFESSIONAL COMMODITY TRADER: LOOK OVER MY SHOULDER. New York, Harper & Row, 1974.

151. Kubarych, Roger M. FOREIGN EXCHANGE MARKETS IN THE UNITED STATES. New York, Federal Reserve Bank, 1978.

152. Labys, Walter C., and C.W.J. Granger. SPECULATION, HEDGING, AND COMMODITY PRICE FORECASTING. Lexington, MA, Heath Lexington Books, 1970.

153. Labys, Walter C. DYNAMIC COMMODITY MODELS: SPECIFICATION, ESTIMATION, AND SIMULATION. Lexington, MA, Lexington Books, 1973.

154. Labys, Walter C. QUANTITATIVE MODELS OF COMMODITY MARKETS. Cambridge, MA, Ballinger, 1975.

155. Lange, Elmer. THE GOLDEN FLEECE. Hicksville, NY, Exposition, 1976.

156. Lasch, Christopher. THE CULTURE OF NARCISSISM: AMERICAN LIFE IN AN AGE OF DIMINISHING EXPECTATIONS. Norton, 1978.

157. Law, Alton D. INTERNATIONAL COMMODITY AGREEMENTS: SETTING, PERFORMANCE AND PROSPECTS. Lexington, MA, D.C. Heath, 1975.

158. Lawrence, James C. YOUR FORTUNE IN FUTURES: A GUIDE TO COMMODITY FUTURES TRADING. New York, St. Martin's Press, 1976.

159. Lecomber, Richard. THE ECONOMICS OF NATURAL RESOURCES. New York, Halstead Press (Wiley), 1980.

160. Leslie, Conrad. CONRAD LESLIE'S GUIDE FOR SUCCESSFUL SPECULATION: STOCKS, COMMODITIES, GOLD. Chicago, Dartnell Press, 1970.

161. Lietaer, Bernard A. FINANCIAL MANAGEMENT OF FOREIGN EXCHANGE: An Operational Technique to Reduce Risk. Cambridge, MA, M.I.T. Press, 1971.

162. Lindow, Wesley. INSIDE THE MONEY MARKET. New York, Random House, 1975.

163. Lindsay, Charles. TRIDENT, A TRADING STRATEGY (2nd ed.). Waterloo, IA, Investor Publications, 1977.

164. Little, James M. FINANCIAL FUTURES HEDGING GUIDE. Chicago, IL, Clayton Brown & Associates, 1979.

165. Longstreet, Roy W. VIEWPOINT OF A COMMODITY TRADER. New York, Frederick Fell Publishers, 1968.

166. Loosigian, Allen M. INTEREST RATE FUTURES: A MARKET GUIDE FOR HEDGERS AND SPECULATORS. Princeton, NJ Dow Jones Books, n.d.

167. Lowell, Fred R. PROFITS IN SOYBEANS. Kansas City, MO, Keltner Statistical Service, 1966.

168. Lowell, Fred R. THE WHEAT MARKET. Kansas City, MO, Keltner Statistical Service, 1968.

169. Malkiel, Burton Gordon. THE TERM STRUCTURE OF INTEREST RATES: EXPECTATIONS AND BEHAVIOR PATTERNS. Princeton, NJ, Princeton Univ. Press, 1966

170. Mamis, Justin and Robert Mamis. WHEN TO SELL. New York, Farrar Straus Giroux, 1977.

171. Massino, John P. THE POINT AND FIGURE METHOD OF COMMODITY FUTURES TRADING. Madison, WI, Comchart, 1972.

172. Maxwell, Joseph R., Sr. COMMODITY FUTURES TRADING WITH MOVING AVERAGES. Port Angeles, WA, Speer Books, 1975.

173. Maxwell, Joseph R., Sr. COMMODITY FUTURES TRADING ORDERS. Port Angeles, WA, Speer Books, 1975.

174. Maxwell, Joseph R., Sr. COMMODITY FUTURES TRADING WITH STOPS.
Port Angeles, WA, Speer Books, 1977.

175. Maxwell, Joseph R., Sr. COMMODITY FUTURES TRADING WITH POINT AND FIGURE CHARTS. Cupertino, CA, Speer Books, 1978.

176. McCoy, John H. LIVESTOCK AND MEAT MARKETING (2nd ed.).
Westport, CT, Avi Publishers, 1979.

177. McMaster, R.E., Jr. TRADER'S NOTEBOOK 1978.
Phoenix, AZ, The Reaper, 1978.

178. Meadows, Dennis L. DYNAMICS OF COMMODITY PRODUCTION CYCLES.
New York, Wiley, 1970.

179. Meek, Paul. OPEN MARKET OPERATIONS.
The Federal Reserve Bank of New York, 1973.

180. Mendelsohn, M.S. MONEY ON THE MOVE: The Modern International Capital Market. New York, NY, McGraw-Hill, 1981.

181. Merrill, Arthur A. FILTERED WAVES, BASIC THEORY: A TOOL FOR STOCK MARKET ANALYSIS. Chappaqua, NY Analysis Press, 1977.

182. Merrill Lynch, Pierce, Fenner & Smith, Inc. HOW TO BUY AND SELL COMMODITIES. New York, Merrill Lynch, 1972.

183. Milner, Arthur R. GRAIN MARKETING, PRICING TRANSPORTATION.
Westville, OH, West-Camp Press, 1970.

184. Miracle, Diane J.S. THE ROLE OF THE EGG FUTURES MARKET IN THE EGG ECONOMY: 1940-1966.
Ph.D dissertation, Stanford University, 1971.

185. Monhollon, Jimmie R. and Picou, Glenn (eds.). INSTRUMENTS OF THE MONEY MARKET. Federal Reserve Bank of Richmond, Richmond, VA, 1974.

186. Munn, Glenn G. GLENN G. MUNN'S ENCYCLOPEDIA OF BANKING AND FINANCE (7th revised and enlarged edition by F.L. Garcia) Boston, Bankers Publishing,'73.

187. Neill, Humphrey B. THE ART OF CONTRARY THINKING (4th ed.).
Caldwell, OH, Caxton, 1963.

188. Nelson, Charles R. THE TERM STRUCTURE OF INTEREST RATES.
New York, Basic Books, 1972.

189. Ney, Richard. MAKING IT IN THE MARKET. New York, McGraw-Hill, 1975.

190. Nofri, Eugene and Jeanette Nofri Steinberg. SUCCESS IN COMMODITIES... THE CONGESTION PHASE SYSTEM. New York, Pageant Poseidon Press, 1975.

191. O'M. Bockris, John. ENERGY OPTIONS. New York, Halstead Press (Wiley),'80.

192. Oster, Merrill J.   COMMODITY FUTURES FOR PROFIT.
Cedar Falls, IA, Professional Farmers of America, 1979.

193. Oster, Merrill J.   MULTIPLY YOUR MONEY...A BEGINNER'S GUIDE TO COMMODITY SPECULATION.   Waterloo, IA, Investor Publications, 1979.

194. Paarlberg, Don.   FARM AND FOOD POLICY ISSUES OF THE 1980s.
University of Nebraska Press, Lincoln, Nebraska,

195. Paris, Alexander.   THE COMING CREDIT COLLAPSE. An Update for the 1980s.
Barrington Hills, IL, HMR Publishing Co., 1980.

196. Parris, Frank G. and Joseph J. Tedesco.   THE COMMODITY MARKET - HOW IT WORKS. (rev. ed.).   Ft. Lauderdale, FL, Parris & Company, 1976.

197. Payer, Cheryl.   COMMODITY TRADE OF THE THIRD WORLD.
New York, Halstead (Wiley), 1976.

198. Peck, Anne E (ed.).
VIEWS FROM THE TRADE: SELECTED WRITINGS OF HOLBROOK WORKING, Book I (1977),
VIEWS FROM THE TRADE: SELECTED WRITINGS ON FUTURES MARKETS. Book II (1977),
VIEWS FROM THE TRADE: READINGS IN FUTURES MARKETS, Book III (1978).
Chicago, Published by the Chicago Board of Trade.

199. Persons, Robert H.   THE INVESTOR'S ENCYCLOPEDIA OF GOLD, SILVER AND OTHER PRECIOUS METALS: HOW TO INVEST SUCCESSFULLY IN ALL FORMS OF PRECIOUS METALS.   New York, Random House, 1974.

200. Pick, Franz.   PICK'S CURRENCY YEARBOOK, New York, Pick Publishing (annual).

201. Powers, Mark J.   GETTING STARTED IN COMMODITY FUTURES TRADING (2nd ed.).
Waterloo, IA,   Investor Publications, 1977.

202. Powers, Mark J. and David J. Vogel.   INSIDE THE FINANCIAL FUTURES MARKETS.
New York, Wiley, 1981.

203. Prather, Charles L.   MONEY AND BANKING (9th ed.).
Homewood, IL, Richard D. Irwin, 1969.

204. Prechter, Robert Jr. (ed.).   THE MAJOR WORKS OF R.N. ELLIOTT.
Chappaqua, NY, New Classic Library.

205. Pring, Martin J.   HOW TO FORECAST INTEREST RATES.
New York, McGraw-Hill, 1980.

206. Pring, Martin J.   TECHNICAL ANALYSIS EXPLAINED: An Illustrated Guide for the Investor.   New York, McGraw-Hill, 1981.

206A. Pugh, Burton H.   MASTERING COTTON. Pomeroy, WA, Lambert-Gann Publ.

206B. Pugh, Burton H.   SCIENCE AND SECRETS OF WHEAT TRADING.
Pomeroy, WA, Lambert-Gann Publ.

207. Quinn, Brian S. THE NEW EUROMARKETS: A THEORETICAL AND PRACTICAL STUDY OF INTERNATIONAL FINANCING IN THE EUROBOND, EUROCURRENCY AND RELATED FINANCIAL MARKETS. New York, Halsted Press, 1975.

208. Rapson, W.S. and T. Groenewald. GOLD USAGE.
New York, Academic Press, 1978.

209. Reidy, Brian and John Edwards (eds.). GUIDE TO WORLD COMMODITY MARKETS (2nd ed.). New York, Nichols, 1980.

210. Reinach, Anthony M. THE FASTEST GAME IN TOWN: TRADING COMMODITY FUTURES. New York, Commodity Research Bureau, 1973.

211. Riehl, H. and R.M. Rodriguez. FOREIGN EXCHANGE MARKETS: A GUIDE TO FOREIGN CURRENCY OPERATIONS.
New York, McGraw-Hill Book Co., 1977.

212. Robinson, Roland I. and Dwayne Wrightsman. FINANCIAL MARKETS: THE ACCUMULATION AND ALLOCATION OF WEALTH.
New York, McGraw-Hill, 1974.

213. Rolfe, Sidney E. and James L. Burtle. THE GREAT WHEEL: THE WORLD MONETARY SYSTEM - A REINTERPRETATION. New York, McGraw-Hill, 1975.

214. Roll, Richard. THE BEHAVIOR OF INTEREST RATES.
New York, Basic Books, 1970.

215. Rosen, Lawrence R. DOW JONES-IRWIN GUIDE TO INTEREST: WHAT YOU SHOULD KNOW ABOUT THE TIME VALUE OF MONEY. Homewood, IL, Dow Jones-Irwin, 1974.

216. Rosen, Lawrence R. WHEN AND HOW TO PROFIT FROM BUYING AND SELLING GOLD.
Homewood, IL, Dow Jones-Irwin, 1975.

217. Ruck, Dan (ed.). THE DOW JONES COMMODITIES BOOK.
Chicopee, MA, Dow Jones Books, annual.

218. Rudolf Wolff Co. WOLFF'S GUIDE TO THE LONDON METAL EXCHANGE.
London, Metal Bulletin Books, 1977.

219. Sarnoff, Paul. SILVER BULLS - The Great Silver Boom and Bust.
Westport, CT, Arlington House Publ., 1980.

220. Sawyer, Gordon. THE AGRIBUSINESS POULTRY INDUSTRY: A HISTORY OF ITS DEVELOPMENT. New York, Exposition, 1971.

221. Schultz, Harry. WHAT THE PRUDENT INVESTOR SHOULD KNOW ABOUT SWITZERLAND.
New Rochelle, NY Arlington House, 1970.

222. Schulz, John W. THE INTELLIGENT CHARTIST.
New York, WRSM Financial Service, 1962.

223. Schwarz, Edward W. HOW TO USE INTEREST RATE FUTURES CONTRACTS.
Homewood, IL, Dow Jones-Irwin, 1979.

224. Scott, Walter O. and Samuel R. Aldrich.   MODER SOYBEAN PRODUCTION.
Champaign, IL, S & A Publications, 1970.

225. Shaw, John E.B.   A PROFESSIONAL GUIDE TO COMMODITY SPECULATION.
West Nyack, NY, Parker Publsihing, 1972.

226. Shepherd, Geoffrey S. and Gene A. Futrell.   AGRICULTURAL PRICE ANALYSIS.
Ames, IA, Iowa State University Press, 1969.

227. Shepherd, Geoffrey S. and Gene A. Futrell,   MARKETING FARM PRODUCTS (6th ed.).   Ames, IA, Iowa State University Press, 1976.

228. Shulman, Morton.   ANYONE CAN STILL MAKE A MILLION.
New York, Stein & Day, 1973.

229. Sinclair, James E. and Harry D. Schultz.   HOW THE EXPERTS BUY AND SELL GOLD BULLION, GOLD STOCKS AND GOLD COINS.   New York, Arlington House, '75.

230. Sinclair, John.   PRODUCTION, MARKETING, AND CONSUMPTION OF COTTON.
New York, Praeger, 1968.

231. Sklarew, Arthur.   TECHNIQUES OF A PROFESSIONAL COMMODITY CHART ANALYST.
New York, Commodity Research Bureau, 1980.

232. Smyth, David and Laurance F. Stuntz.   THE SPECULATOR'S HANDBOOK.
Chicago, Henry Regnery, 1974.

233. Solomon, Robert.   THE INTERNATIONAL MONETARY SYSTEM 1945-1976: AN INSIDER'S VIEW.   New York, Harper & Row, 1977.

234. Sprinkel, Beryl W.   MONEY AND MARKETS: A MONETARIST VIEW.
Homewood, IL, Richard D. Irwin, Inc., 1971.

235. Sprinkel, Beryl W. and Robert J. Genetski.   WINNING WITH MONEY: A GUIDE FOR YOUR FUTURE.   Homewood, IL, Dow Jones-Irwin, 1977.

236. Starr, Roger.   HOUSING AND THE MONEY MARKET.
New York, Basic Books, 1975.

237. Stigum. Marcia.   THE MONEY MARKET: MYTH, REALITY, AND PRACTICE.
Homewood, IL, Dow Jones-Irwin, 1978.

238. Stoken, Dick A.   CYCLES: WHAT THEY ARE, WHAT THEY MEAN, HOW TO PROFIT BY THEM.   New York, McGraw-Hill, 1978.

239. Story, Harry Joe.   AN ECONOMIC ANALYSIS OF THE PLYWOOD FUTURES MARKET.
Ph.D. dissertation, University of Oregon, 1975
Ann Arbor, MI, University Microfilms, 1975.

240. Sutton, Anthony. THE WAR ON GOLD. Seal Beach, CA, Seventy-Six Press, 1977.

241. Tew Brian.   THE EVOLUTION OF THE INTERNATIONAL MONETARY SYSTEM, 1945-1976.
New York, Wiley, 1977.

242. Teweles, Richard J., Charles V. Harlow, and Herbert L. Stone. THE COMMODITY FUTURES TRADING GUIDE: THE SCIENCE AND THE ART OF SOUND COMMODITY TRADING. New York, McGraw-Hill, 1969.

243. Teweles, Richard J., Charles V. Harlow, and Herbert L. Stone. THE COMMODITY FUTURES GAME: WHO WINS? WHO LOSES? WHY? New York, McGraw-Hill, 1974.

244. Thiel, Charles C. and Robert E. Davis. POINT AND FIGURE COMMODITY TRADING: A COMPUTER EVALUATION. West Lafayette, IN, Dunn & Hargitt, 1970.

245. Thies, Terry. TECHNICAL TRADING OF FINANCIAL MARKETS. Chicago, American TransEuro, 1978.

246. Tomek, William G. and Kenneth L. Robinson. AGRICULTURAL PRODUCT PRICES. Ithaca, NY, Cornell University Press, 1972.

247. Toffler, Alvin. FUTURE SHOCK. New York, Random House, 1970.

247A. Trainer, Richard D.C. THE ARITHMETIC OF INTEREST RATES. Public Information Dept., Federal Reserve Bank of New York, 1981.

248. Trevithick, J.A. and C. Mulvey. THE ECONOMICS OF INFLATION. New York, Halstead Press (Wiley), 1979.

248A. Tucker, James F. BUYING TREASURY SECURITIES AT FEDERAL RESERVE BANKS. Richmond: Federal Reserve Bank of Richmond, 1980.

249. Turnbull, Roderick. TURNBULL ON GRAIN. Danville, IL, Interstate, 1978.

250. Turner, Dennis, and Stephen H. Blinn. TRADING SILVER - PROFITABLY. New York, Arlington House, 1975.

251. Tylecote, Andrew. THE CAUSES OF THE PRESENT INFLATION. New York, Halstead Press (Wiley), 1980.

252. Underwood, Trevor (ed.). FOREIGN EXCHANGE YEARBOOK - 1980 edition. New York, Halstead Press (Wiley), 1980.

253. Vichas, Robert. GETTING RICH IN COMMODITIES, CURRENCIES AND COINS - BEFORE OR DURING THE NEXT DEPRESSION. New York, Arlington House, 1975.

254. Walker, Townsend. A GUIDE FOR USING THE FOREIGN EXCHANGE MARKET. New York, John Wiley, 1981.

255. Wasserman, Paul. COMMODITY PRICES: A SOURCE BOOK AND INDEX. Detroit, Gale Research, 1974.

256. Watling, Tom F. and Jonathan Morley. SUCCESSFUL COMMODITY FUTURES TRADING: HOW YOU CAN MAKE MONEY IN COMMODITY MARKETS. London, Business Books, 1974.

257. Watson, Donald S. and Mary A. Holman. PRICE THEORY AND ITS USES (4th ed.). Boston, Houghton Mifflin, 1976.

258. Weberman, Ben. INTEREST RATE FUTURES - PROFITS AND PITFALLS.
New York, Ben Weberman, 1980.

259. Weiss, Theodore J. FOOD OILS AND THEIR USES. Westport, CT, Avi, 1970.

260. Weymar, F. Helmut. THE DYNAMICS OF THE WORLD COCOA MARKET.
Cambridge, MA, M.I.T. Press, 1968.

261. Wheelan, Alexander H. STUDY HELPS IN POINT AND FIGURE TECHNIQUE.
New York, Morgan, Rogers and Roberts, 1966.

262. White, Walter E. and Russell L. Hall. THE ELLIOTT WAVE PRINCIPLE OF MARKET BEHAVIOR. Hamilton, Bermuda, Monetary Research, 1968.

263. Wilder, J. Wells, Jr. NEW CONCEPTS IN TECHNICAL TRADING SYSTEMS.
Greensboro, NC, Trend Research, 1978.

264. Williams, Larry R. HOW I MADE ONE MILLION DOLLARS IN THE COMMODITY MARKET LAST YEAR. Carmel Valley, CA, Conceptual Management, 1974.

265. Williams, Larry R. and Michelle L. Noseworthy. SURE THING COMMODITY TRADING: HOW SEASONAL FACTORS INFLUENCE COMMODITY PRICES.
Brightwaters, NY, Windsor Books, 1977.

266. Willis, Parker B. THE FEDERAL FUNDS MARKETS: ITS ORIGIN AND DEVELOPMENT.
Boston, MA, Federal Reserve Bank of Boston, 1970.

267. Willis, W.E. TIMBER FROM FOREST TO CONSUMER.
New York, International Publications Service, 1968.

268. Wills, Walter J. AN INTRODUCTION TO GRAIN MARKETING.
Danville, IL, Interstate, 1972.

269. Wilson, Louise L. CATALOG OF CYCLES.
Pittsburgh, PA.: Foundation for the Study of Cycles, 1964.

270. Winikates, James. GNMA MORTGAGE FUTURES MARKET: A FINANCIAL MANAGER'S GUIDE. Chicago, Financial Manager's Society for Savings Institutions, '77.

271. Working Holbrook. SELECTED WRITINGS OF HOLBROOK WORKING.
Chicago, Chicago Board of Trade, 1977.

272. Woy, James B. COMMODITY FUTURES TRADING: A BIBLIOGRAPHIC GUIDE.
New York, R.R. Bowker Co., 1976.

273. Wyckoff, Peter (ed.). INTERNATIONAL STOCK AND COMMODITY EXCHANGE DIRECTORY.
Canaan, NH, Phoenix Publishing, 1974 (supplement 1976).

274. Youngquist, Walther. INVESTING IN NATURAL RESOURCES (2nd ed.).
Homewood, IL, Dow Jones-Irwin, 1980.

275. Zieg, Kermit C. Jr. and Perry J. Kaufman. POINT AND FIGURE COMMODITY TRADING TECHNIQUES: ALSO STOCKS, BONDS AND INTERNATIONAL CURRENCY.
Larchmont, NY, Investors Intelligence, 1975.

276. Zieg, Kermit C., Jr. and William E. Nix. THE COMMODITY OPTIONS MARKET: DYNAMIC TRADING STRATEGIES FOR SPECULATION AND COMMERCIAL HEDGING. Homewood, IL, Dow Jones-Irwin, 1978.

277. Zieg, Kermit C., Jr. and Susannah H. Zieg. COMMODITY OPTIONS. Larchmont, NY, Investors Intelligence, 1974.

+ + + +

CATCHWORD INDEX

BANKING:	#25, 179, 180, 203
BIBLIOGRAPHY:	#43, 272
CATTLE (LIVE):	#72, 74, 87
COMMODITY PRICES (historical):	#255
CONTRARY THINKING:	#187
CHARTS & CHARTING:	#20, 21, 22, 23, 27, 47, 48, 50, 66, 67, 222, 231
COCOA:	#92, 260
COFFEE:	#92, 94
COMMODITY OPTIONS:	#58, 276, 277
CORN:	#1, 42, 131, 249
COTTON:	#206A, 230
CREDIT:	#195
CURRENCY MARKETS:	#29, 200, 211, 254
CYCLES:	#24A, 63, 64, 147, 178, 238, 269
DEVALUATION:	#30, 70
DICTIONARY (for investors):	#35, 186
ELLIOTT WAVE PRINCIPLE:	#18, 28, 85, 204, 262
EURODOLLAR MARKETS:	#46, 84, 95, 207
FEDERAL RESERVE SYSTEM:	#91, 91A, 91B, 91C

FINANCIAL FUTURES: #164, 166, 202, 223, 245, 258

FIXED INCOME SECURITIES: #60, 91A, 248A

FOREIGN EXCHANGE: #2, 4, 38, 53, 73, 77, 80, 81, 82, 88, 90, 91, 118, 134, 151, 161, 211, 252, 254

GENERAL READING: #9, 12, 16, 19, 26, 52, 56, 57, 61, 89, 96, 97, 98, 101, 103, 104, 105, 107, 119, 121, 126, 129, 130, 140, 141, 142, 145, 146, 148, 149, 150, 153, 154, 155, 156, 157, 158, 160, 165, 177, 179, 182, 189, 191, 192, 193, 194, 196, 197, 198, 201, 209, 210, 212, 213, 225, 227, 228, 232, 233, 234, 241, 242, 243, 247, 253, 256, 264, 266, 271, 273

GINNIE MAEs: #100, 110, 236, 270

GOLD: #25, 39, 83, 102, 111, 135, 199, 208, 216, 229, 240

GRAIN TRADING: #112, 183, 268

HARD MONEY: #29

HEDGING: #14, 114, 152, 164, 166

HOGS (LIVE): #72

INFLATION: #7, 34, 130, 248, 251

INTEREST RATES: #84, 102A, 125, 147, 169, 188, 205, 214, 215, 223, 247A, 248A 258.

LIVESTOCK:	#15, 72, 176
LONDON COMMODITIES:	#99, 109, 218
LONDON OPTIONS:	#58
LUMBER:	#44, 45, 62, 267
MONETARY CRISIS:	#31, 33
MONETARY POLICY:	#3, 38, 128
MONEY:	#25, 203, 235
MONEY MARKET INSTRUMENTS:	#40, 54, 71, 93, 116, 120, 124, 162, 180, 185, 236, 237
MOVING AVERAGES:	#5, 172
OILSEEDS:	#259
ORANGE JUICE:	#69
PLATINUM:	#102
PLYWOOD:	#44, 62, 239
POINT AND FIGURE CHARTING:	#27, 47, 48, 171, 244, 261, 275
PORK BELLIES:	#72, 76
POULTRY & EGGS:	#86, 184, 220
PRICE FORECASTING:	#137, 138, 139, 152, 205, 226, 246, 257
REGULATIONS:	#141A
RESOURCES:	#49, 159, 274
SEASONALS:	#21, 22, 23, 113, 265
SILVER:	#36, 39, 41, 102, 136, 199, 219, 250
SOYBEANS:	#37, 123, 127, 133, 167, 224
SPREAD TRADING:	#8, 23, 142
SUGAR:	#6

SWITZERLAND & SWISS BANKS: #32, 221

TREASURY BILLS: #91C, 248A

TAXES: #7

TECHNICAL ANALYSIS: #17A, 78, 115, 122, 138, 144, 181, 206, 231

TECHNICAL TRADING METHODS: #5, 10, 13, 16, 17, 17A, 27, 65, 68, 75, 106, 108, 113, 122, 143, 163, 170, 172, 173, 174, 190, 245, 261, 263, 275

WINNERS AND LOSERS: #11, 24, 117

WHEAT: #42, 132, 168, 206B, 249

YEARBOOKS: #17, 51, 200, 217, 252

+ + + + +

GLOSSARY OF TERMS

There are terms peculiar to the commodity markets, constantly used but little understood by the general public. The glossary following is included to help the uninitiated understand the jargon of the commodity market.

The definitions are not intended to state or suggest the legal significance or meaning of any word or term.

ACCOUNT EXECUTIVE: The executive who deals directly with customers in a commission house.

ACCUMULATION: The process of adding to a commodity position at predetermined intervals or price levels.

ACREAGE ALLOTMENT: A voluntary limitation on acreage farmers may plant and still receive government price supports and financial assistance. Purpose: to stimulate production of certain crops and curtail production of others.

ACTUALS: The physical or cash commodities as distinguished from commodity futures contracts which are promises to deliver in the future.

AFLOATS: Commodities on vessels en route to destination. May also refer to loaded boats in harbor and ready to sail. It does not apply to cargoes on vessels already at their destination.

ALLOY: A substance composed of two or more metals.

AMORTIZE: An artificial method of allocating, over the life of the instrument, income received or given up at maturity.

ANIMAL vs. PRODUCT SPREAD: Example: hogs versus pork bellies.

ANNUALIZE: To figure on an annual basis. Interest rates, for example, are quoted on a yearly basis. Also, a profit of $5 on a 6-month investment of $100 would be 10% on an annualized basis.

APPRECIATION: An increase in value. For example, if the Swiss Franc appreciates relative to the U.S. dollar, it will take more dollars to buy the same amount of Swiss francs.
(See also: REVALUATION.)

ARBITRAGE: In commodities arbitrage is the simultaneous buying and selling of futures contracts of the same commodity in two markets in different locations. It is used to take advantage of a temporary disparity in prices. For example, silver in New York and silver in Chicago; or, New York sugar versus London sugar. The term is sometimes used interchangeably with spreads and straddles.

ASSAY: To analyze a metal in order to determine its purity.

AT THE MARKET: An order to buy or sell at the best price obtainable at the time an order reaches the trading pit or ring.

BACKSPREADING: Buying distant (also called back or deferred) delivery months versus selling nearbys. Entering this type of spread involves theoretically unlimited risk (See PREMIUM SPREADS.)

BACKWARDATION: A market situation when prices are progressively lower in the distant delivery months. For example: if the cotton quotation for July delivery is 74¢ per lb. and that for October delivery is 71¢ per lb. then the backwardation for three months against July is 3¢ per lb. Backwardation is the opposite of CONTANGO. (See also INVERTED MARKET and PREMIUM SPREADS.)

BAG: The basic unit of trading for silver coins. Each bag contains $1,000 face value in dimes or quarters.

BALANCE OF PAYMENTS: A recording of the value of all the economic transactions by residents, business firms, institutions and the government of one country against the rest of the world. Usually reported on a quarterly or annual basis.

BALANCE OF TRADE: The difference between the total value, exclusively, of merchandise exported and imported (excluding gold bullion). If exports are less than imports, it is called a trade deficit, if more, a trade surplus.

BANK RATE: The rate a government's central bank charges for loans to member banks.

BANKERS ACCEPTANCES: A draft or bill of exchange accepted by a bank which then guarantees payment. Used extensively in foreign trade transactions.

BARREL: The standard of measurement for volume used in the international petroleum trade. A petroleum barrel is equivalent to 42 U.S. gallons.

BARTER: The exchange of one commodity for another without the use of money or money substitutes.

BASIS: The difference between the spot (cash) price and the price of futures. Basis also refers to the difference between the cash market price at a given local point and current delivery-point prices. Thus, statements of basis may apply to location as well as time. Sometimes basis is used synonimously with cash commodity as in the phrases 'long the basis' or 'short the basis', meaning that one has bought or sold the cash (actual) commodity.

BASIS GRADE: The grade of a commodity used as the standard of the contract.

BASIS POINT (BP): A measure of the yield change for fixed-income securities. One basis point equals 1/100 of 1 percent.

BEAR: One who believes prices will move lower. (See BULL.)

BEAR MARKET: A market in which prices are declining.

BEAR SPREAD: Buying (long) a distant contract vs. selling (short) a nearby.

BEARER SECURITY: A security which promises to pay the holder of the security on demand.

BEARISH and BULLISH: When conditions suggest lower prices in the future a bearish situation exists. The expectation of higher prices suggest a bullish situation.

BID: An offer to purchase a specific quantity of a commodity at a specified price. (See OFFER.)

BID & ASK: One can sell at the bid price and buy at the asked price.

BLACK MARKET: A free market operating without government sanction.

BOARD OF TRADE: Any exchange or association of persons engaged in buying and selling commodities are receiving them for sale on consignment.

B.O.M. SPREAD: Soybeans (B) versus soybean oil (O) and soybean meal (M). (See CRUSH SPREAD and REVERSE CRUSH SPREAD.)

BOND: A promissory note to repay a loan, with interest, in a specified period of time.

BREAK: A rapid, sharp price decline.

BROAD TAPE: News wires that carry exchange prices and trading information to subscribers.

BROKER: A person or firm which fills the buy and sell orders of a customer for a commission.

BROKERAGE: A fee charged by a broker for execution of a transaction.

Btu- (British thermal unit): The amount of heat necessary to raise the temperature of one pound of water one degree Fahrenheit.

BULGE: A rapid advance in cash or futures prices.

BULL: One who expects prices to rise. (See BEAR.)

BULL MARKET: A market in which prices are rising.

BULL SPREAD: Long a nearby contract vs. short a more distant one.

BULLION: Silver or gold in bars or ingots of a specified fineness.

BUTTERFLY SPREAD: A tree-legged spread in which the short (long) month is couched between two long (short) months.

BUY IN: To cover, offset or close out a short position. (See OFFSET and also COVER.)

BUY ON CLOSE: To buy at the end of the trading session at a price within the closing range.

BUY ON OPENING: To buy at the beginning of a trading session at a price within the opening range.

BUYER'S MARKET: A condition of the market in which there is an abundance of goods available and hence buyers can afford to be selective and may be able to buy at less than the price that had previously prevailed.

BUYING: The act of initiating or taking a new long position.

BUYING HEDGE: A hedging transaction in which futures contracts are bought to protect against possible increased cost of commodities. Also called 'long hedge.'

C & F: Cost and Freight paid to ship actual commodities to port of destination.

CALL MONEY: The charge on loans to brokers on stock exchange collateral.

CAPITAL: Financial assets, land, facilities and equipment used in business.

CAPITAL EXPENDITURES: Money spent for property or other fixed assets used in business - land, buildings machinery and other equipment.

CARAT: A term used to express the proportionate fineness of gold. Gold of twenty-four carats is pure gold; gold of sixteen carats has eight parts of alloy. (Same as KARAT.)

CARGO: In grains, usually 350,000 bushels.

CARLOAD: A load of a commodity aboard a railroad car usually from 1,800 to 2,000 bushels of grains.

CARRY: The cost of financing (borrowing to buy) a position in financial instruments.

CARRY (NEGATIVE): The condition where the cost of financing (the short-term rate of interest) is above the current return of the instrument.

CARRY (POSITIVE): The condition where the cost of financing (the short-term rate of interest) is less than the current return of the instrument.

CARRYING CHARGE SPREAD: Same crop or industrial commodity spreads. Long nearbys, short distant futures: nearbys at a discount to more distant futures. Risk usually limited to the cost of carrying the commodity, including storage and interest. (See CARRYING CHARGES.)

CARRYING CHARGES: The cost of storing a physical commodity over a period of of time, such as storage, insurance, inspection and interest charges on borrowed working capital, and any other incidentals. It is a carrying charge market when there are higher futures prices for each successive contract maturity. If the carrying charge is adequate to reimburse the holder, it is called a full carrying charge.

CARRYOVER: That part of current supplies of a commodity left over from previous production or marketing seasons.

CASH: (a) The absence of credit; (b) money substitutes in paper form.

CASH COMMODITY: The actual physical commodity as distinguished from a futures commodity.

CASH FORWARD MARKET: A market made by GNMA dealers who trade in GNMA mortgage-backed securities maturing in 30 to 180 days.

CASH MARKET: Market for immediate delivery and payment of commodities.

CASH PRICE: The price in the market place for physical commodities to be delivered via normal market channels.

C.C.C.: Commodity Credit Corporation.

CENTRAL BANK: A government agency in each country which manages that country's currency in foreign exchange markets and domestic money markets and also regulates domestic banking activities. In the U.S. the Federal Reserve System is the central bank.

CENTRAL BANK INTERVENTION: Official buying of domestic currency versus the sale of other currencies, or vice versa. These transactions are made in the open exchange market to maintain desired price relationships with other currencies.

CENTRAL RATE: A monetary exchange rate set by the country of issuance and ratified by the International Monetary Fund. (I.M.F.)

CERTIFICATES OF DEPOSIT (C.D.'s): A deposit for a fixed time period at a fixed rate of interest.

CERTIFICATED STOCK: Stocks of a commodity available for delivery against futures contracts, as per exchange regulations.

CFTC: See Commodity Futures Trading Commission.

CHARTS and CHARTING: The process whereby price, volume and open interest is transferred from mathematical data to graphs and charts to be used in technical analysis of futures markets.

CHEAP: The term for a fixed-income security that is underpriced relative to similar securities. If overpriced, it is called 'rich'.

CHURNING: Excessive trading which permits the broker to derive a profit while disregarding the best interests of the customer.

CIF: Price including Cost, Insurance and Freight paid to port of destination and included in the price quoted.

CLEARINGHOUSE: An adjunct to a commodity futures exchange through which transactions executed on the floor of the exchange are settled through a process of matching purchases and sales. A clearing organization is also charged with the proper conduct of delivery procedures and the adequate financing of the entire operation.

CLEARING MEMBER: A member firm of the clearing house or association. All trades of a non-clearing member must be registered and eventually settled through a clearing member.

CLEARING PRICE: See SETTLEMENT PRICE.

CLOSE, The: The period at the end of the trading session. Sometimes used to refer to the closing price. (See OPENING, The.)

CLOSING RANGE (or RANGE): The closing price (or price range) recorded during the period designated by the exchange as the official close. (See SETTLEMENT PRICE.)

COIN GOLD: Silver and copper alloyed with gold form coin gold. The extra metals are added to increase the alloy's hardness and durability.

COLD STORAGE: Refrigerated warehouses where perishable commodities are stored. These warehouses are secondary sources of commodities that are not immediately available from the producers.

COLLATERALIZED DEPOSITORY RECEIPTS (CDRs): The CDR GNMA mortgage interest rate futures contract does not allow for direct delivery of GNMA certificates in the settlement of a futures position. Instead, the contract calls for the delivery of a negotiable instrument called a collateralized depository receipt. The CDR is a document prepared, signed, and dated by a depository bank: it is similar to a warehouse receipt.

COMMERCIAL: A company that merchandises or processes cash grain and other commodities.

COMMERCIAL PAPER: Short term promissory notes calling for the payment of money on demand or at some future date; they are issued in large denominations by the major corporations in their commercial transactions.

COMMISSION (or ROUND-TURN): The one-time fee charged by a broker to a customer when a position is liquidated either by offset or delivery.

COMMISSION HOUSE: An organization that buys or sells for clients. Also known as a brokerage house or a wire house. Its income is generated by the commission charged to their clients.

COMMITMENT: A trader is said to have a commitment when he assumes the obligation to accept or make delivery on a futures contract. (See OPEN INTEREST.)

COMMODITIES: Goods that are used in trade or industry and can be transported. Wheat, corn, soybeans, copper, lumber and sugar are examples.

COMMODITY CREDIT CORPORATION (CCC): A government-owned corporation established in 1933 to assist U.S. agriculture. The major operations of the CCC are price support programs and assistance in foreign exports of agricultural commodities.

COMMODITY EXCHANGE AUTHORITY (CEA): A regulatory agency of the U.S. Dept. of Agriculture established in 1936 to administer the Commodity Exchange Act, forerunner of Commodity Futures Trading Commission (CFTC).

COMMODITY FUTURES CONTRACT: An agreement to deliver or take delivery of a given quantity of a commodity at a fixed price on a specified date in the future.

COMMODITY FUTURES TRADING COMMISSION (CFTC): An independent federal agency created by Congress (effective April 21, 1975) to regulate commodity futures trading. Previously, futures trading had been regulated by the Commodity Exchange Authority (CEA) of the U.S. Dept. of Agriculture (USDA).

CONGESTION: (1) A congested market situation where shorts attempting to cover their positions are not likely to find longs willing to liquidate or by new sellers wishing to enter the market, except at sharply higher prices. (2) In technical analysis, an era of repetitious and limited price fluctuations.

CONTANGO: A British term referring to carrying charge markets. Contango is the opposite of BACKWARDATION.

CONTRACT: A term of reference applied to a unit of trading for a commodity (or financial) future. Also, as defined by an exchange, a bilateral agreement between the buyer and seller of a futures transaction.

CONTRACT GRADE: The grade of the actual cash commodity which may be delivered against a futures contract as officially approved by an exchange.

CONTRACT MONTH: The month in which futures contracts may be fulfilled by making or accepting delivery. The word 'option' is sometimes used as a synonym for contract month.
(See DELIVERY MONTH.)

CONTRACT TRADING VOLUME:
See VOLUME.

CONTRACT UNIT: The specific amount of the commodity represented by the futures contract: e.g., 100 troy ounces is the contract unit for gold futures traded on COMEX.

CONVERTIBILITY: The ability to receive gold in exchange for currency from the agency that issued the currency.

CORNER: (1) To secure sufficient control of a commodity so that its price can be manipulated. (2) Accumulating contracts for delivery of more commodities than are available.

CORPORATE BOND: An instrument evidencing indebtedness of a corporation.

CORRELATION COEFFICIENT: Correlation is the degree to which yield and price fluctuations of one security or money market instrument are reflected by another. The more accurate the correlation, the larger the correlation coefficient. A correlation coefficient of 100 denotes a perfect relationship.

COST OF PRODUCTION SPREAD:
Example Hogs vs. corn.

COUNTRY ELEVATOR: A storage facility in the farming community.

COUPON: A fixed amount, stated as a percentage of principal value, payable at regular intervals upon presentation by the instrument's owner.

COVER: To offset a previous futures transaction with an equal and opposite transaction. Short covering is buying in on a previously established short position. Liquidation is the sale of a previously established long position.

COVERED INTEREST ARBITRAGE: Interest arbitrage transaction that is hedged against exchange rate fluctuations.

CROP REPORTS: Reports issued periodically by the U.S. Dept. of Agriculture (USDA) describing the current status of the specific commodity which is to be planted or is growing in the fields. Similar reports are made on livestock.

CROP YEAR: The period of time from one harvest or storage cycle to the next. Varies with each commodity.

CROSS HEDGE: The buying or selling of an interest rate futures contract to protect the value of a cash position of a similar, but not identical, instrument. This type of hedging is a measured risk since the outcome of such a transaction is a function of the price correlation of the securities being hedged.

CROSS-RATE: The price relationship of two currencies (one in terms of the other) where neither currency is the home currency of the user.

CRUSH: The process of reducing the raw, unusable soybean into its two major components, oil and meal. The 'crush margin' is the gross profit that a processor makes from selling oil and meal minus the cost of buying soybeans.

CRUSH SPREAD: A spreading operation whereby that trader will buy futures contracts of soybeans and sell futures contracts os soybean meal and soybean oil. (See REVERSE CRUSH SPREAD.)

CURRENCY: An I.O.U. for real money in storage. In present practice synonymous with 'paper money,' which may or may not be backed by real money. (See FIAT MONEY.)

CURRENCY DEVALUATION: Action by a government or by market forces that reduces the value of a currency in relation to the currencies of other nations.

CURRENT DELIVERY (MONTH): The futures that is closest to expiration. Also called SPOT (DELIVERY) MONTH.

CURRENT YIELD: The amount of money received (currently) divided by the instrument purchase price.

CUSTOMER'S MAN: An employee of a commission house, also called an associated person, a broker, account executive, solicitor, or registered representative. One who solicits, or accepts and handles orders for commodity futures transactions.

DAY ORDER: An order which must be filled during that day's trading session. If the order cannot be filled that day, it is automatically cancelled.

DAY TRADE: The purchase and sale of a futures contract on the same day.

"DEAD LEG" SPREAD: In case of a definitely strong (weak) price trend buy (sell) the strongest (weakest) delivery month and spread it against a quiet delivery month. This reduces margin requirements and might offer some protection against adverse price movement.

DEBENTURE: A debt instrument whose backing lies in the goodwill of the issuer rather than on any tangible assets.

DEFAULT: Failure to perform on a futures contract as required by exchange rules, such as failure to meet a margin call, or to make or take delivery.

DEFERRED FUTURES: Those contracts which will mature beyond the current (spot) delivery month. Also called deferred deliveries, distant or back contracts. (Contrasted with NEARBYS.)

DEFICIT: In balance of payments, the implication that more of a country's currency went abroad than foreign currencies came into the country in a given period.

DEFLATION: A protracted decline in the general price level.

DELIVERABLE GRADE: See CONTRACT GRADE.

DELIVERY: The tender of the actual commodity in fulfillment of a short position. Tendering of the physical commodity is in the form of a warehouse receipt or other negotiable instrument to the floor of the exchange during the delivery month.

DELIVERY MONTH: A specified month within which delivery may be made under the terms of the futures contract.

DELIVERY NOTICE: Written notice from the clearing house of a seller's intention to make delivery of the physical commodity against his open, short futures position on a particular date.

DELIVERY POINTS: Those locations designated by commodity exchanges at which a commodity covered by a futures contract may be delivered in fulfillment of the contract.

DELIVERY PRICE: The price fixed by the Clearing House at which deliveries on futures are invoiced and also the price at which the futures contract is settled when deliveries are made.

DEPOSITORY RECEIPT: A document issued by a bank or warehouse indicating ownership of a commodity stored in a bank depository or warehouse. This document can be used by the 'short' to fulfill an expiring futures contract's delivery requirement. (Also called WAREHOUSE or ELEVATOR RECEIPT.)

DEPRECIATE: A currency depreciates in value when its price or exchange rate, in terms of other currencies, goes down.

DEPRESSION: A protracted period of greatly reduced business activity characterized by widespread unemployment and low production.

DEVALUATION: A formal decrease in the exchange rate, made with International Monetary Fund agreement, or unilaterally by a country.

DEVALUATION SPREAD: Buying a commodity in the weak monetary country and selling the same commodity in the strong monetary country. (See also ARBITRAGE and DEVALUATION.)

DIRTY FLOAT: Intervention by a central bank in the foreign exchange markets while the government officially denies the action.

DISCOUNT: The price differences between futures of different delivery months. For example, 'July at a discount to October' means that the price of the July future is lower than that of October. (See PREMIUM.)

DISCOUNT PRICE: The price of a bond trading at less than par. (Par is 100 cents on the dollar of its face value.)

DISCOUNT RATE: The interest that Federal Reserve banks charge on funds borrowed by commercial member banks.

DISCRETIONARY ACCOUNT: An arrangement by which the holder of the account gives written power of attorney to another, often his broker, to make buying and selling decisions without notification to the holder; often referred to as a managed account, or controlled account.

DISINTERMEDIATION: The process wherein monies are withdrawn from the banking system because of noncompetitive returns, uncertainty, or a variety of other reasons. It results in a shrinkage of credit for the system as a whole.

DOMESTIC vs IMPORTED COMMODITY SPREADS: Example: Domestic sugar vs. World sugar.

DOMINANT FUTURE: The futures month which has the largest number of open contracts.

DUMPING: Selling goods in a foreign country cheaper than they are sold in the country of origin.

DUTCH AUCTION: Method of sale whereby the lowest price at which the entire issue can be sold is established as the uniform price for the entire issue.

EASE OFF: A minor and/or slow decline in the prices of a market.

ECONOMETRICS: The use of statistical and mathematical methods in the field of economics to verify and develop economic theories.

ELASTICITY: A characteristic of commodities which describes the interaction of the supply, demand, and price of a commodity. The supply of a commodity is said to be elastic when a change in price creates change in the production of the commodity.

EQUITY: The residual dollar value of a futures trading account, assuming its liquidation at the going market price.

ERRATIC: A market that moves rapidly, changes direction quickly and is irregular in its action.

EUROCURRENCY: C.D.'s, bonds, deposits, or any capital market instrument issued outside of the national boundaries of the currency in which the instrument is denominated.
(See also EURODOLLARS.)

EURODOLLARS: Funds denominated in U.S. dollars placed in banks in European market-oriented countries. Analogous funds also exist in banks in major Asian financial centers such as Hong Kong and Singapore.

EVEN LOT: A unit of trading in a commodity established by an exchange.

EVENING UP: Buying or selling to offset or liquidate an existing market position. (See COVER and LIQUIDATION.)

EXCHANGE: A membership association of persons engaged in buying or selling any commodity or receiving the same for sale on consignment.

EXCHANGE CONTROLS: Any government measure to restrain and manipulate foreign exchange transactions. Undertaken to assure the use of available foreign exchange in accordance with public policy.

EXCHANGE RATE: The amount of one currency that is traded for another currency by bankers and dealers. (See FOREIGN EXCHANGE RATE.)

EXCHANGE RATE FUTURES: Futures contracts for currencies.

EX-PIT TRANSACTIONS: Transactions made outside the ring or pit.

FACE VALUE: The legal tender value of a coin, banknote, token, or certificate.

FARM PRICES: The prices received by farmers for their products, as published by the USDA, as of the 15th of each month.

FEDERAL FUNDS: Member banks' deposits held by the Federal Reserve; also reserves traded among commercial banks for overnight use in amounts of $1 million or more.

FEDERAL FUNDS RATE: The rate of interest charged for the use of federal funds.

FEDERAL HOME LOAN BANK: One of twelve federally chartered banks which regulates credit to its member institutions.

FEDERAL HOUSING ADMINISTRATION (FHA): A division of HUD; it insures residential mortgage loans and sets construction standards as its principal activities.

FEDERAL NATIONAL MORTGAGE ASSOCIATION (FNMA): A corporation created by Congress to support the secondary mortgage market; it purchases and sells residential mortgages insured by the FHA or guaranteed by the Veterans Administration.

FEDERAL RESERVE SYSTEM: A quasi governmental organization of twelve regional banks and a governing board of directors. The Federal Reserve Bank has discretionary powers over the volume of credit in the U.S. The System seeks to actively manage the U.S. economy by influencing monetary variables.

FEED RATIOS: The variable relationships of the cost of feeding animals to market weight to sales prices, expressed as ratios, such as the hog/corn ratio. These indicators show the profit return (or lack of it) in feeding animals to market weight.

FIAT MONEY: Paper money without gold or silver backing. Qualified as legal tender by government fiat or edict.

FILL-OR-KILL ORDER: A commodity order which demands immediate execution or cancellation.

FINANCIAL INSTRUMENTS: Currency, securities, and indices of their value. Examples include shares, mortgages, commercial paper and Treasury bills, bonds and notes.

FINENESS: Refers to the purity of gold or silver bullion. Gold bullion of .995 fineness means that 99.5% of the total weight is pure gold.

FIRST NOTICE DAY: The first date, varying by contracts and exchanges, on which notices may be given by the shorts to the longs of their intention to deliver actual commodities against futures contracts.

FIXED EXCHANGE RATES: Currency exchange rates prevented from fluctuation by government purchases and sales of the currencies involved.

FLOATING (EXCHANGE RATES): The establishment of exchange rates by free market forces. So called dirty floats involve government manipulation of the price. Clean floats mean no government intervention to manipulate exchange rates.

FLOOR BROKER: A member who, on the exchange floor, executes orders for the purchase or sale of any commodity for future delivery.

FLOOR TRADER: A member who generally trades only for his own account, for an account controlled by him or who has such a trade made for him. Also referred to as a 'local.'

F.O.B.: Free-on-Board, meaning that the commodity will be placed aboard the shipping vehicle at no cost to the purchaser, but thereafter the purchaser must bear all shipping costs.

FOREIGN EXCHANGE: On the foreign exchange market, foreign currency is bought and sold for immediate or forward (future) delivery.

FOREIGN EXCHANGE RATE: The price of a currency as expressed in units of another currency.

FORWARD: In the future.

FORWARD CONTRACTING: A cash transaction common to many industries. In commodity merchandising, the buyer and seller agree to delivery of a specified quality and quantity of goods at a specified future date.

FORWARD EXCHANGE: Contract for future delivery of foreign currency whose maturities are usually for periods of 30, 60, and 90 days; often referred to as 'forward rates.'

FORWARD MARKET: Refers to informal (non-exchange) trading of commodities to be delivered at a future date.

FORWARD MONTHS: Futures contracts, of those currently traded, calling for a later or distant delivery. Also described as DEFERRED CONTRACTS or DEFERRED FUTURES.

FREE ENTERPRISE: An economic system in which every person has the right to own property and engage in economic activities of his own choice, for his own profit.

FREE MARKET: A market free from government intervention.

FREE SUPPLY: The storage supply of a commodity not restricted by government ownership or control and is readily available for commercial sale.

FULL CARRYING CHARGE: See CARRYING CHARGES.

FUNDAMENTAL ANALYSIS: A study of market behavior which stresses underlying factors of supply and demand of a particular commodity in the belief that such analysis will enable one to profit from being able to anticipate price trends. (See also TECHNICAL ANALYSIS.)

FUTURE: The term used to designate futures contracts maturing during a specified month, e.g., the 1982 May wheat 'future.'

FUTURES: A term used to designate any or all standardized contracts made on an exchange and subject to its rules.

FUTURES CONTRACT: See FUTURES.

FUTURES PRICE: The price of a given commodity unit determined by public auction on a futures exchange.

GASOHOL: In the U.S. a mixture of 90% unleaded gasoline and 10% ethyl alcohol.

GASOIL: European designation for No. 2 heating oils and diesel fuel.

GINNIE MAE: See GNMA.

GNMA: See GOVERNMENT NATIONAL MORTGAGE ASSOCIATION.

GOLD PURITY VALUES: Gold purity in percentages as identified in karats: 24K = 100%, 22K = 91%, 18K = 75%, 14K = 58%, and 10K = 41%.

GPM: Gross Processing Margin refers to the difference between the cost of soybeans and the combined sales income from the soybean meal and oil resulting from the processing (crushing) of soybeans. Other industries have similar raw materials versus finished products relationships.

GOVERNMENT NATIONAL MORTGAGE ASSOCIATION (GNMA): A quasi government organization. GNMA administers and guarantees mortgage-backed securities.

GOVERNMENT NATIONAL MORTGAGE ASSOCIATION SECURITIES (Ginnie Maes): Securities backed by an underlying pool of insured guaranteed mortgages. These securities carry the full faith and credit of the U.S. government.

GRAIN: As used in coin weights: There are 15.432 grains to a gram, and 480 grams to a troy ounce.

GRAM: A metric unit of mass and weight. A gram equals approximately 1/32 troy ounce and is used in troy weight to measure gold.

GROSS NATIONAL PRODUCT (GNP): The market value of a nation's total output of goods and services.

GROSS PROCESSING MARGIN (GPM): The difference between the cost of soybeans and the combined sales income of the soybean meal and oil that results from processing soybeans.

G-T-C: Good-'Til-Cancelled order. An open order that remains in force until the customer explicitly cancels the order, until the futures contract expires or until the order is filled. (See OPEN ORDER.)

HARD MONEY: Gold or silver. Synonymous with 'real money.'

HARDENING: Describes a price which is gradually stabilizing; a term indicating a slowly advancing market.

HEATING OIL: Generic term for oils used exclusively for home heating. Widely used as a synonym for No. 2 fuel.

HEDGER: One who hedges.

HEDGING: The establishment of a position in the futures market opposite from that held in the spot market. Used as a means of risk protection against the possibility of adverse price fluctuations.

HIGH: Highest price at which a commodity is sold during the market day.

HUD: Department of Housing and Urban Development.

IMF: See INTERNATIONAL MONETARY FUND.

INFLATION: A protracted rise in the general price level over a significant period of time. This price rise is usually associated with an increase of the currency in circulation, government budget deficits, greater capital spending, less consumer savings, and an expansion of credit. These and other factors result in a fall in the value of the inflated currency.
(See FIAT MONEY.)

INITIAL MARGIN: The amount of margin capital required by a brokerage firm to establish a new position in the futures market. (See ORIGINAL MARGIN.)

INTER-COMMODITY SPREADS: Examples: plywood versus lumber; live hogs vs. live cattle.

INTER-CROP SPREADS: Between two subsequent annual crops - same grain. Example: May (old crop) vs. July (new crop) Chicago wheat.

INTER-GRAIN SPREADS: Examples: wheat vs. corn; corn vs. oats, - same crop or intercrop.

INTER-MARKET SPREADS: Example: Chicago wheat vs. Kansas City wheat, - old or new crop.

INTEREST: The amount a borrower pays in return for use of a lender's money.

INTERNATIONAL MONETARY FUND (IMF): An organization established by the Bretton Woods Agreement with the objective of promoting exchange stability, exchange arrangements among its members, and eliminating exchange restrictions on international trade.

INTRA-MARKET SPREADS: A spread involving the purchase of one month of a commodity and the simultaneous sale of another month of the same commodity. For example: long Fenruary vs. short March pork bellies.

INVENTORIES: The supply of raw materials and unsold goods that a business keeps on hand to meet production and customer needs as they arise.

INVERSE CARRYING CHARGES: The market is described as inverted when the spot price is greater than the futures price, or when the futures price for the near months is greater than the futures price for distant months.

INVERTED MARKET: A futures market in which the nearer delivery months are selling at premiums to the more distant delivery months due to a heavy near-term demand for the cash commodity in which supplies are in shortage. (See PREMIUM SPREADS and BACKWARDATION.)

INVISIBLE SUPPLY: Stocks of a commodity in the hands of wholesalers, manufacturers, producers, and consumers which cannot be counted accurately.

KARAT: A measure of the fineness of gold on a scale of 1-24. One Karat is 1/24 pure gold, 24 Karats gold (24K) is 100% pure gold. 12K gold is 50% pure (or fine).

LARGE TRADERS: One who holds or controls a position in any one commodity futures or all futures of one commodity combined on any one market equalling or exceeding the reporting level.

LAST NOTICE DAY: The final day on which notices of intent to deliver on futures contracts may be issued.

LAST TRADING DAY: The final day under an exchange's rules during which trading may take place in a particular delivery futures month. Futures contracts outstanding at the end of the last trading day must be settled by delivery of the actual physical commodity, or by agreement for monetary settlement if the former is impossible.

LIFE OF CONTRACT: The period of time between the beginning of trading in a particular futures contract and the expiration of trading at the end of the last trading day. Usually less than one year but in some cases up to 18 months.

LIFTING A LEG: Liquidating one side (leg) of a spread, leaving an outright position open.

LIMIT (UP or DOWN): The maximum price advance or decline from the previous days settlement price permitted in one trading session. (Also PRICE LIMITS.)

LIMIT MOVE: The maximum price advance or decline for a given commodity permitted by exchange rules for any one day's trading. (See also MAXIMUM PRICE FLUCTUATION.)

LIMIT ORDER: A price or time restriction placed on an order by the customer. Generally, an order to buy or sell at the price given in the order or better.

LIMIT PRICE: (See LIMIT MOVE and MAXIMUM PRICE FLUCTUATION.)

LIMITED RISK SPREADS: (See CARRYING CHARGE SPREADS.)

LIQUID MARKET: A market in which transactions are numerous and easily made. A large number of buyers and sellers, all eager to trade makes for a liquid market.

LIQUIDATION: Same as evening up or offset. Any transaction that offsets or closes out a long or short position. (See EVENING UP, OFFSET.)

LOAN PRICES: The prices at which producers may obtain loans for their crops from the government.

LOAN PROGRAM: The primary means of government agricultural price support operations.

LONG: (1) One who has bought a futures contract to establish a market position. (2) A market position which obligates the holder to take delivery. (3) One who owns an inventory of commodities. (The opposite of SHORT.)

LONG HEDGE: The purchase of a futures contract to offset the forward sale of an equivalent quantity of a commodity not yet owned. Used as protection against an advance in the cash market price. (Also called BUYING HEDGE.)

LONG TERM or LONG PULL: A period of time, usually lasting several months over which some specific price action is expected to occur.

LONG THE BASIS: See BASIS.

LOT: Usually any definite quantity of a commodity of unifirm grade. In the futures market: the standard unit of trading.

LOW: Lowest price at which a commodity is sold during the market day.

MAINTENANCE MARGIN: Money, usually less than, but part of, the original deposit or margin, which the customer must maintain on deposit at all times. Should a customer's equity in any futures position drop to, or under, the maintenance margin level, the broker must issue a margin call for the amount of money required to restore the customer's equity in the account to its original margin level. (See MARGIN CALL.)

MARGIN: The cash amount of funds the customer must put up as a 'good faith deposit' with the broker for each futures contract. Minimum margin requirements are set by the exchanges, usually from 5% to 15% of the total value of the commodity contract. Also called SECURITY DEPOSIT.

MARGIN CALL: A demand by a brokerage firm for additional cash funds when (because of an adverse price movement) the customer's equity in any futures position drops to or below the maintenance margin level. (See MAINTENANCE MARGIN.)

MARK TO MARKET: The daily process of debiting and crediting a customer account to reflect price movements.

MARKET ORDER: An order to buy or sell futures contracts as soon as possible at the best obtainable price. (See also LIMIT ORDER.)

MATURITY: The period between the first notice day and the last trading day within which a futures contract can be settled by delivering the actual physical commodity.

MAXIMUM PRICE FLUCTUATION: As fixed by Exchange rules, the maximum amount the futures contract price can change, up or down, during one trading session. (See LIMIT PRICE.)

MEMBER'S RATE: Commission charged for

the execution of an order for a person who is a member of the exchange.

MINIMUM PRICE FLUCTUATION: Smallest increment of price movement possible in trading a given contract. Set by the exchange. (See POINT.)

M-I-T: Market-If-Touched. A price order which automatically becomes a market order if the price is reached.

MONETARY POLICY: Management of the money supply by the Federal Reserve System to keep the amount of available credit in line with the needs of the economy in order to influence its course.

MONEY SPREADS: Examples: Soybean oil vs. soybean meal; hogs vs. pork bellies; lumber vs. plywood; silver vs. gold, etc. - these are not considered spreads for margin purposes. Spread differentials are calculated on the basis of the dollar value of the contracts.

MONEY SUPPLY, Measures of, -
 M1-A = currency plus demand deposits.
 M1-B = M1-A plus NOW type accounts.
 M2   = M1-B plus overnight repurchase agreements plus savings deposits at banks and thrifts plus small time deposits plus overnight Eurodollar deposits at offshore branches held by foreigners plus money market mutual fund shares.
 M3   = M2 plus large C.D.'s and term RPs.
 L   = M3 plus other liquid assets such as commercial paper, Treasury bills, U.S. savings bonds, and some bankers acceptances.

MORTGAGE: A conveyance of interest in real property given as security for the payment of debt.

NEARBYS: The delivery month closest to maturity, as opposed to a DEFERRED month which is farther into the future.

NET POSITION: The difference between the open long contracts and the open short contracts held by any individual or group in any one commodity.

NEW CROP: The supply of a commodity available after harvest.

NOMINAL PRICE: Price quotation on futures for a period in which no actual trading took place. Usually the average between the bid and asked prices.

NOTE: One of a variety of debt securities. Treasury notes refer to coupon securities with a maturity of one to ten years; municipal notes are short-term promissory notes.

NOTICE DAY: See FIRST NOTICE DAY.

NORMAL MARKET: Nearby futures contracts are at a discount compared to distant months. The premium on the distants reflects partial or full carrying charges.

O-C-O: One-Cancels-the-Other. Placing orders on both sides of the trading range with the stipulation that whichever order is filled first will automatically cancel the other.

OFFER: An indication of willingness to sell at a given price.
(The opposite of BID.)

OFFSET: See COVER, EVENING UP and LIQUIDATION.

OLD CROP: The supply of a crop from previous harvests.

OMNIBUS ACCOUNT: An account carried by one futures commission merchant with another in which the transactions of two or more persons are combined rather than executed separately.

ON THE CLOSE: An order given by a customer to his broker to execute a transaction within the closing minutes of the trading session.

ON THE OPEN: An order given by a

customer to his broker to execute a transaction within the first five minutes of the trading session.

OPEC: The Organization of Petroleum Exporting Countries. Thirteen nations that aim at developing common oil-marketing policies.

OPEN CONTRACTS: Contracts which have been bought or sold without the transaction having been completed by subsequent sale or purchase. Or, making or taking actual delivery of the actual physical commodity or financial instrument.

OPEN INTEREST: Number of open futures contracts. Refers to unliquidated purchases or sales but never to their combined total.

OPEN ORDER: An order to a broker that is good until it is cancelled or executed. (See G-T-C)

OPEN OUTCRY: Method of public auction required for making bids and offers in the trading pits or rings of commodity exchanges.

OPENING, The,: That period at the beginning of the trading session officially designated by the Exchange during which all transactions are considered made 'at the opening.' (See CLOSE, The.)

OPENING PRICE (or RANGE): The price (or range) recorded during the period designated by the Exchange as the official opening.

ORIGINAL MARGIN: The margin needed to cover a specific new position. (See INITIAL MARGIN.)

OVERBOUGHT: A term used to express the opinion that prices have risen too high and too fast and, therefore, will decline as traders liquidate their positions.

OVERSOLD: Analogous to 'overbought' except that prices have fallen too far and too fast and so will probably rebound.

P & S: Purchase & Sale Statement. A statement provided by the broker which shows the change in customer's net ledger balance after the offset of a previously established position(s).

PAPER PROFITS: Profits that would exist at a given moment of one closed a transaction. Or, profits figured on paper, but not yet realized by offset.

PAR: A particular price, 100 per cent of principal value. In foreign exchange, an exchange rate arbitrarily set by the country of issuance and ratified by the IMF.

PAR or BASIS GRADE: The grade or grades specified in a given futures contract for delivery. A contract may permit deviations from the par grade subject to appropriate premiums or discounts.

PARITY: The difference at a given time between the price of contracts at two futures markets or in the same market for different futures. (See SPREAD.)

PARITY RATE: Official exchange rate between the currencies of two countries, making the purchasing power of one currency equal to that of the other.

PENNYWEIGHT: A unit of weight for gold. Twenty pennyweights equal one troy ounce.

PER ANNUM: Per year. Usually refers to interest rates.

PIT: A specially constructed area on the trading floor of some exchanges where trading in futures is conducted. On other exchanges, the term ring designates the trading area for a commodity.

PIT BROKER: See FLOOR BROKER.

POINT: (a) A dollar amount equal to one percent of principal value of a note ot other debt instrument.
(b) The smallest monetary unit, set by the exchange, in which the price

movement of a given commodity may be expressed. It is equal to 1/100 of one cent in most futures traded in decimal units. In grains it is 1/4 of one cent. (See MINIMUM PRICE FLUCTUATION.)

PORK BELLIES: One of the major cuts of the hog carcass that, when cured, becomes bacon.

POSITION: An interest in the market, either long or short, in the form of open contracts. (See OPEN CONTRACTS.)

POSITION LIMIT: The maximum number of speculative futures contracts one can hold. Determined by the Commodity Futures Trading Commission and/or the Exchange upon which the contract is traded. (Also called TRADING LIMIT.)

POSITION TRADING: An approach to trading in which the trader either buys or sells contracts and holds them for an extended period of time.

PREMIUM: The excess of a cash commodity price over a futures contract price or over another cash commodity price. Also, the excess of one futures contract price over another. In foreign exchange - the amount the forward rate is above the spot price. (See DISCOUNT.)

PREMIUM SPREADS: When demand in nearbys is extremely strong (any commodity) the premium of nearbys is theoretically unlimited over deferred delivery months. (See also SHORT SQUEEZE.)

PRICE LIMITS: The maximum price advance or decline permitted for a futures contract in one trading session as compared to the previous day's settlement price. Determined by the Exchange upon which the contract is traded.

PRICING: Eaxample: GNMAs and government securities prices are expressed in points and 32ds, as in 97-01, with digits to right of the dash being 32ds. The points reflect a percentage of par, thus 100-00 is 100 percent of par. A price of 94-08 would indicate a price of 94-8/32 percent of par. Price changes do not occur with the same magnitude as yield changes. There is no straight-line relationship. the remaining maturity of a bond has a major effect on the relative changes of prices and yields.

PRIMARY MARKET: The principal underlying market for a financial instrument. Also, the distribution centers to which farmers bring crops for sale, such as country grain elevators.

PRIME RATE: The interest rate charged by banks on business loans to their largest and most credit-worthy customers.

PRINCIPAL: The outstanding balance of a loan.

PRIVATE WIRES: Wires leased by various firms and news agencies for the transmission of information to branch offices and subscriber clients.

PROTECTIVE STOP: A better name for 'stop-loss' because placing of a stop does not always prevent a loss. Also called 'money management stop.'

PUBLIC: In trade parlance, non-professional speculators as distinguished from hedgers and professional speculators or traders.

PUBLIC ELEVATORS: Grain elevators in which bulk storage of grain is provided for the public for a fee.

PURCHASE & SALE STATEMENT: See P & S.

PYRAMIDING: The practice of using accrued paper profits to margin additional trades.

QUOTATION: The actual price or the bid or asked price of either cash commodities or futures contracts.

RALLY: An upward movement of prices following a decline; the opposite of a REACTION.

RANGE: The highest and lowest prices recorded during a specified time; i.e., day, week, month, or year.

RAW MATERIAL vs. ONE PRODUCT SPREAD: Example: Soybeans vs. either soybean oil or meal.

REACTION: A decline in prices following an advance; the opposite of a RALLY.

REALIZING: Taking profits.

RECESSION: An economic downturn, less severe than a depression and is market by two or more calendar quarters of reduced gross national product. Calculated after adjusting the dollar values to eliminate the effects of inflation.

RECIPROCAL: Any number divided into "1". In foreign exchange - a means of expressing currency prices in terms of each other. For example, if one British pound = $2.40, then $1.00 = 1 ÷ 2.40 = .4166 British pounds.

RECOVERY: Usually describes a price advance following a decline. (See RALLY.)

REGISTERED COMMODITY REPRESENTATIVE (RCR): A member or nonmember of an exchange registered with it to solicit and handle commodity customers business for a fee.

REGULATED COMMODITIES: Since 1975 U.S. futures markets in all commodities became regulated under the Commodity Exchange Act as amended by the Commodity Futures Trading Act of 1974. Trading on foreign futures markets, such as London sugar, copper, silver, etc. is not regulated.

REPORTING LEVEL or LIMIT: Size of positions set by the exchange and/or the CFTC at, or above which, commodity traders must make daily reports as to the size of the position by both commodity and delivery month. Also, whether the position is speculative or a hedge must be stated.

REPURCHASE AGREEMENT (REPO): The selling of a security by a dealer to another party at the same time that the other party enters into an agreement to resell the securities to the dealer at a predetermined price and date.

RESERVE: That portion of a resource that has been discovered and available but not yet exploited. It is assumed to be technically and economically extractable.

RESERVES: The gross official monetary holdings of a country maintained with its central bank. Composed mainly of convertible foreign currencies and gold, its value is periodically reported in terms of the equivalent amount of home currency. The U.S. dollar is a primary reserve currency.

RESISTANCE ZONE: A price range, above the current price, where a rising price movement is likely to meet resistance to a continuation of the same price trend. (See SUPPORT ZONE.)

RESTING ORDER: (See DAY ORDER, G-T-C, and OPEN ORDER.)

RETENDER: The right of holders of futures contracts who have been tendered a delivery notice, to offer the notice for sale on the open market and liquidate their obligation to take delivery under the contract. Applicable only to certain commodities within a specified period of time.

REVALUATION: A formal, official increase in the exchange rate of a currency made with IMF agreement, or, one made unilaterally by a country.

REVERSE CRUSH SPREAD: A spreading operation involving the purchase of soybean oil and soybean meal futures contracts against the sale of soybean futures contracts.

REVERSE REPURCHASE AGREEMENT (REVERSE REPO): The sale of a security by an investor or mortgage banker to a dealer while the investor simultaneously agrees to repurchase the security at a specific price and date. It is used to temporarily borrow against collateral.

RICH: Slang for a security that is relatively overpriced.

RING: A circular platform on the trading floor of an exchange, consisting of steps upon which traders and brokers stand while executing futures trades. (See PIT.)

ROLL-OVER: A special spread trading procedure which involves the shift of one month of a spread into another month, while holding the remaining contract month. The shift can take place in either the long or short leg of the spread.

ROUND LOT: A quantity of a commodity equal in size to the corresponding futures contract for the commodity, as distinguished from a job lot, which may be larger or smaller than the contract.

ROUND-TURN: A procedure whereby the long or short position of an individual is offset by an opposite transaction, or by acceptance or making delivery of the physical commodity or financial instrument. Commission fees for commodities transactions cover the 'round-turn.'

RULES: The principles for government of the exchange.

SAFE SPREADS: None exists. Even full carrying charge spreads can get out of line due to government actions, such as price controls, credit controls, export/import controls, etc.

SCALE DOWN (or UP): To purchase or sell on scale down means to buy or sell at regular price intervals in a declining market. To buy or sell on a scale up means to buy or sell at regular price intervals as the market advances.

SCALP: To trade for small gains. Normally involves establishing and liquidating a position quickly, usually within the same day.

SEASONAL SPREADS: Can be any commodity showing seasonal patterns. Not a 'safe' spread because patterns are broken every few years.

SECURITY: Common or preferred stock; a bond of a corporation, government, or quasi-government body.

SECURITY DEPOSIT: See MARGIN.

SELLER'S MARKET: A condition of the market in which there is a scarcity of goods available and hence sellers can obtain better conditions of sale or higher prices.

SELLING: The act of closing or getting out of a long position by selling a futures contract. When initiating or taking a new short position, the term 'shorting' is more properly used.

SELLING HEDGE: Selling futures contracts to protect against possible price drops of commodities owned. (Also called SHORT HEDGE.)

SETTLEMENT DATE: Date on which ownership and funds are transferred between buyer and seller for a securities or commodity transaction.

SETTLEMENT PRICE: The daily price at which the Clearing House clears all trades. The settlement price of each day's trades is based upon their closing range. Settlement prices are used to determine margin calls and invoice prices for deliveries. (See CLOSING RANGE.)

SHAKEOUT: A healthy technical correction of an overbought situation, characterized by a comparatively short but sharp decline in prices.

SHOGUNS: Wealthy Japanese feudal class, which, toward the end of the 17th century, issued receipts - the predecessors of futures - against rice being grown in the fields.

SHORT: One who has sold a futures contract to establish a market position hoping for a price decline. (The opposite of LONG.)

SHORT COVERING: See COVER.

SHORT HEDGE: The sale of futures contracts to reduce the possible decline in value of an approximately equal amount of the physical commodity held.

SHORT SELLING: See SHORTING.

SHORT SQUEEZE: A situation in which the lack of supplies tends to force shorts to cover their positions by offset at higher prices.

SHORT THE BASIS: See BASIS.

SHORTING: The act of initiating or taking a short position with a commodity futures contract.

SMALL TRADERS: Traders not required to file reports of futures transactions or positions. Their positions are derived by subtracting large traders' commitments from the total open interest. Accordingly, the number of small traders is unknown.

SOFT: A description of a price which is gradually weakening.

SOLD-OUT MARKET: A merket in which liquidation of weakly held contracts has been largely completed and offerings are scarce.

SOLID GOLD: Any article that is 10K or finer and does not have a hollow center. This definition was adopted in 1967 by the Federal Trade Commission.

SPECIE: Gold or silver

SPECULATOR: One who anticipates price changes and through market activities attempts to make profits. A speculator is not involved in the production, processing, marketing or handling of the physical commodity.

SPOT COMMODITY: The actual cash commodity. (Same as ACTUALS.)

SPOT DELIVERY MONTH: The nearest delivery month on all contracts traded at any time.

SPOT PRICE: The price at which the actual commodity is traded in the cash market.

SPREADING: (1) In general terms, it means the simultaneous purchase of a futures contract against the sale of another futures contract to take advantage of and profit from the fluctuation of the price differentials between the two futures contracts. (2) In monetary markets - the difference in the prices of a currency between various future deliveries, or between the spot market and a future delivery. In some markets the terms 'straddle', 'switch' and 'arbitrage' are used synonymously.

SQUEEZE: A situation in which the lack of deliverable supplies force those traders who are short in the market to cover their positions while prices are rapidly advancing.

STOP LIMIT ORDER: A stop limit order is an order that goes into force as soon as there is a trade at the specified price. The order, however, can only be filled at the stop limit price or better.

STOP ORDER: An order to be executed when the market reaches a designated price level, or price differential if the order is a spread. Done usually to protect a profit or limit a loss. It can also be used to initiate a new position.

STOPPED OUT: The market situation in which a customer's position, long or short, was closed out, liquidated or covered as the result of an existing stop order executed and filled at either the stop price, above it or below it.

STRADDLE: See SPREADING.

STRADDLE-UP SPREADS: Usually done ahead of crop reports or to reduce margins. One might be forced to straddle-up by margin calls.

STRONG HANDS: This, in a trading context, refers to the ownership of security or commodity as being a source of considerable financial strength.

SUPPORT ZONE: A price range, below the current price, where descending price movement is likely to encounter resistance. (See RESISTANCE ZONE.)

SURPLUS: The excess of a commodity on hand over actual or prospective requirements; in refernce to balance of payments, income exceeds total payment to foreigners.

SWITCHING: Liquidating an existing position and simultaneously reinstating that position in another contract month of the same commodity or financial instrument. (Also see SPREADING.)

SYNFUELS: Fuels synthesized from sources other than crude oil or natural gas.

TECHNICAL ANALYSIS: An approach to analysis of futures markets and commodity prices which examines the technical factors behind market activity. The technical analyst examines patterns of price change, rates of change, volume of trading and open interest. Charts are often used to help predict future trends.

TECHNICAL POSITION: Term used to indicate internal market conditions. When the market is sold out or is over-sold, its technical position is said to be strong. Conversely, after a sharp advance when the market is clearly over-bought, its technical position is said to be weak.

TECHNICAL RALLY (or DECLINE): A price movement resulting from conditions developing within the futures market itself, which include changes in open interest, volume, the extent of recent price movement and the approach of the first notice day.

TENDER: When the seller of futures contracts (the short) gives notice of intention to deliver the physical commodity in satisfaction of the futures contract. (See also RETENDER.)

TERMINAL ELEVATOR: An elevator located at a point of greatest accumulation in the movement of agricultural products which stores the commodity or moves it to the processors.

TICK: A change in price, either up or down. (See POINT.)

TICKER TAPE: A continuous paper tape transmission of commodity or security prices, volume, and other trading and market information, which operates on private leased wires by the exchanges and is available to their member firms and other interested parties on a subscription basis.

T.N.: Transferable Notice. (See also DELIVERY NOTICE.)

TOPPING OUT: Denotes loss of upside energy at the top after a long price run-up.

TRADE BALANCE: The net amount of goods exported and imported.

TRADER: (1) A merchant involved in cash commodities; (2) A professional speculator who trades for his own account.

TRADING LIMIT: (1) The limit on the trading range in one trading session, under the rules of the Exchange. (See MAXIMUM PRICE FLUCTUATION.) (2) The maximum number of contracts anyone is permitted to own or control during one trading day. (3) The maximum futures position an individual is allowed to hold at any time under commodity exchange and CFTC regulations.

TRADING SESSION: The period of time from the opening of trading until the closing of trading during a single day.

TRADING VOLUME: See VOLUME.

TRAILING STOP: A progressively changed protective stop order that follows the profitable price move of a futures position, thus locking in most of the profit gained.

TRANSFERABLE NOTICE: See RETENDER.

TREASURY BILLS: Government debt obligations sold at less than their face value, the differnce, thereby, being the yield. For example, a one-year T-Bill worth $10,000 at maturity may sell at $8,900. The $1,100 difference would be the yield, which is 12.36% (1,100 divided into 8,900). T-Bills are considered a good barometer of interest rates.

TREASURY BONDS: Medium or long term obligations of the U.S. government. If not callable these bonds pay interest semi-annually until they mature, at which time the principal and the final interest payment is paid to the investor. If they are callable, the Treasury can call the bond back in advance of maturity, paying accrued interest to the investor at that time. Until such time as the bond is called the semi-annual interest is paid.

TREND: The general direction of the market.

TROY OUNCE: A measure of weight. There are twelve troy ounces to one troy pound. Gold is measured worldwide in troy weights.

UNDERWRITER: A firm that purchases new issues and distributes them. Until the issue is distributed, it trades on a 'when, as, and if issued' basis.

UNWINDING: Liquidating a spread.

USDA: U.S. Department of Agriculture.

VARIABLE LIMIT MARGIN: In periods of extreme price volatility, some exchanges permit trading at price levels that exceed regular daily limits.

VENDOR: A seller.

VENTURE CAPITAL: Monies not needed for routine living expenses which are available for purposes of investing and speculating.

VISIBLE SUPPLY: The quantity of a commodity that can be counted and computed accurately. Includes port stocks, stocks afloat, farm stocks and stocks in licensed warehouses.

VOLUME OF TRADE: The number of transactions of a futures contract made during a specified period: day, week, month or year. A transaction consists of a purchase and matching sale or vice versa.

WEAK HANDS: In a trading context, refers to the owners of securities or commodities who are relatively weak financially and, therefore, unable to withstand pressures such as margin calls.

WIDENING: When the distant month of a spread gains on the nearby.

WINTER WHEAT: Wheat that is planted in the fall, lies dormant during the winter and is harvested beginning about May of the next year.

WIRE HOUSE: An organization operating a private wire to its own branch offices, or to other firms, commission houses and brokerage houses.

YIELD: A measure of the annual return on an investment expressed as a percentage. Yield to maturity: The current yield augmented or decreased by the amortized difference between the purchase price and the maturity value.

APPENDICES

SIMPLIFIED SPREAD CALCULATIONS

WHEAT VS. CORN SPREAD

Price of December wheat: 5.06-1/4 dollars per bushel
Contract size: 5,000 bushels

Price of December corn: 3.57-1/4 dollars per bushel
Contract size: 5,000 bushels

Spread: 506.25¢ - 357.25¢ = +149 cents.

***

2 OATS VS. 1 CORN SPREAD

Price of September oats: 1.93½ dollars per bushel
Contract size: 5,000 bushels
Value of 2 contracts: (193.5 x 50) x 2 = $19,350.-

Price of September corn: 3.48¼ dollars per bushel
Contract size: 5,000 bushels
Value of contract: (348.25 x 50) = $17,412.50

$ Spread: $19,350 - $17,412.50 = +$1,937.50

Spread in ¢: (193.5¢ x 2) - 348.25 =
              387¢   - 348.25 = 38.75 cents spread.

***

SOYBEAN MEAL VS. CORN SPREAD

Price of May SB meal: 261.80 dollars per ton
Contract size: 100 tons
Value of contract: $26,180.-

Price of May corn: 3.72 dollars per bushel
Contract size: 5,000 bushels
Value of contract: (372 x 50) = $18,600

$ Spread: $26,180 - $18,600 = $7,580.-

***

SOYBEAN OIL VS. SOYBEAN MEAL SPREAD

Price of July SB oil: 29.55 dollars per 100 lbs.=¢/lb.
Contract size: 60,000 lbs.
Value of contract: (2955 x 6) = $17,730.-

Price of July SB meal: 259.80 dollars per ton
Contract size: 100 tons
Value of contract: $25,980.-

$ Spread: $17,730 - $25,980 = -$8,250.-

***

SOYBEAN REVERSE CRUSH SPREAD (1-1-1)

Price of January oil: 28.63 $/100 lbs. = ¢/lb.
Price of January meal: 258.80 $/ton
Price of January beans: 8.92 $/bushel

Crush Margin: Oil (28.63 x .11) = $3.1493
              + Meal (258.80 x .024)= $6.2112
                                      $9.3605
              - Price of beans   -$8.9200
                                      $0.4405

Crush Margin: +44¢ per bushel.

***

SOYBEAN REVERSE CRUSH (BALANCED: 9-12-10)

1. Multiply the price of oil by 5,400 (28.63 x 5,400) = $154,602.- (for nine contracts of oil)
2. Multiply the price of meal by 1,200 (258.80 x 1,200) = $310,560.- (for twelve meal contracts)

3. Add the value of all oil contracts and all meal contracts:
   $154,602 + $310,560) = $465,162.-
4. Multiply the price of soybeans by 50,000 (8.92 x 50,000) =
   $446,000.- (for ten soybeans contracts)
5. Subtract the value of the soybean contracts from the
   combined value of the products:
   $465,162 - $446,000 = $19,162.-

Result: Nine oil contracts plus twelve meal contracts are
         worth $19,162 more than ten (January) bean contracts.

***

FEEDER CATTLE VS. LIVE CATTLE SPREAD

   Price of May feeders: 75.62 cents per lb.
   Contract size: 42,000 lbs.
   Value of contract: (7562 x 4.2) = $31,760.40

   Price of Oct fat cattle: 68.25 cents per lb.
   Contract size: 40,000 lbs.
   Value of contract: (6825 x 4) = $27,300.-

$ Spread: $31,760.40 - $27,300 = +$4,460.40

***

LIVE CATTLE VS. LIVE HOGS SPREAD

   Price of February cattle: 72.20 cents per lb.
   Contract size: 40,000 lbs.
   Value of contract: (7220 x 4) = $28,880.-

   Price of April hogs: 53.80 cents per lb.
   Contract size: 30,000 lbs.
   Value of contract: (5380 x 3) = $16,140.-

$ Spread: $28,880 - $16,140 = +$12,740.-

***

PORK BELLIES VS. LIVE HOGS SPREAD

   Price of February pork bellies: 71.57 cents per lb.
   Contract size: 38,000 lbs.
   Value of contract: (7157 x 3.8) = $27,196.60

   Price of February hogs: 54.85 cents per lb.
   Contract size: 30,000 lbs.
   Value of contract: (5485 x 3) = $16,455.-

$ Spread: $27,196.60 - $16,455 = +$10,741.60

***

GOLD VS. SILVER SPREAD

    Price of December gold: 377.70 dollars per troy ounce
    Contract size: 100 troy ounces
    Value of contract: $37,770.-

    Price of December silver: 819.0 cents per troy ounce
    Contract size: 5,000 troy ounces
    Value of contract: (8190 x 5) = $40,950.-

$ Spread: $37,770 - $40,950 = -$3,180.-

***

PLYWOOD VS. LUMBER SPREAD

    Price of January plywood: 206.40 dollars per 1,000 sq.ft.
    Contract size: 76,032 sq. ft.
    Value of contract: (20640 x .76032) = $15,693.-

    Price of January lumber: 190.20 dollars per 1,000 bd. ft.
    Contract size: 130,000 bd. ft.
    Value of contract: (19020 x 1.3) = $24,726.-

$ Spread: $15,693 - $24,726 = -$9,033.-

***

SWISS FRANC VS. DEUTSCHE MARK SPREAD

    Price of September SF: .5336 American dollars/franc
    Contract size: 125,000 francs
    Value of contract: (5336 x 12.5) = $66,700.-

    Price of September DM: .4259 American dollars/mark
    Contract size: 125,000 marks
    Value of contract: (4259 x 12.5) = $53,237.50

$ Spread: $66,700 - $53,237.50 = +$13,462.50

Another method: (5336 - 4259) = 1077 (differential)
               1077 x 12.50 = $13,462.50 ($ spread)

***

DEUTSCHE MARK VS. BRITISH POUND SPREAD

    Price of June DM: .4196 American dollars / mark
    Contract size: 125,000 marks
    Value of contract: (4196 x 12.5) = $52,450.-

    Price of June BP: 1.7730 American dollars/pound sterling
    Contract size: 25,000 pounds sterling
    Value of contract: (17730 x 2.5) = $44,325.-

$ Spread: $52,450 - $44,325 = +$8,125.-

               ***

BRITISH POUND VS. JAPANESE YEN SPREAD

    Price of September BP: 1,7800 American dollars/pound sterling
    Contract size: 25,000 pounds sterling
    Value of contract: (17800 x 2.5) = $44,500.-

    Price of September JY: .004176 percentage of one cent
    Contract size: 12,500,000 yen
    Value of contract: (4176 x 12.5) = $52,200.-

$ Spread: $44,500 - $52,200 = -$7,700.-

               ***

G.N.M.A. VS. T-BONDS SPREAD

    Price of December GNMA: 59-26 pts., 32nds of 100%
    Contract size: $100,000 principal
    Value of contract: $59,812.50

    Price of December T-Bonds: 61-31 pts., 32nds of 100%
    Contract size: $100,000 principal
    Value of contract: $61,968.75

$ Spread: $59,812.50 - $61,968.75 = -$2,156.25

Another method:
    59-26 minus 61-31 = -(2-5) =-69/32 = -(69x$31.25)=$2,156.25

               ***

TELEPHONE INFORMATION

FARMERS' NEWSLINE (U.S. Department of Agriculture: Summary of
major reports.)
1-(900) 976-0404

COFFEE, SUGAR & COCOA EXCHANGE, INC.:

    (212) 938-2847   Opening prices   11:00 a.m. (EST)
                              Closing prices   4:00 p.m. (EST)

MINNEAPOLIS GRAIN EXCHANGE:

    (612) 340-9438   Previous day's data   11:30 a.m. (CST)
                              Settlement prices   2:00 p.m. (CST)

NEW YORK MERCANTILE EXCHANGE: Prices & volume (24-hrs. service)

    (212) 938-2679   Potatoes; Beef; Currencies
    (212) 938-2680   Metals; Platinum; Gold
    (212) 938-2681   Petroleum

CHICAGO BOARD OF TRADE:

    (312) 922-7885   Opening ranges   9:45 a.m. (CST)
                              Commentary & prices   10:30 a.m.
                              Prices for all CBT commodities
                                except GNMAs and T-bonds...2:30 p.m.
                              Including GNMAs & T-bonds...3:15 p.m.

    (312) 922-9110   Price update on agri futures
    (312) 922-9120   Price update on financial instruments

CHICAGO MERCANTILE EXCHANGE:

                                                          (CST):
    (312) 648-1013   Settlement prices (IMM) 2 p.m.-6 p.m.
    (312) 648-0836   Settlement prices (CME) 2 p.m.-6 p.m.
    (312) 648-1199   London gold: 3:40 p.m. (CST)
                              N.Y. T-bill close: 3:40 p.m. (CST)

* * *

COMMODITY EXCHANGES

Many books, brochures and other materials are available from the commodity exchanges free upon request. They cover futures trading, contract specifications and the fundamental factors that affect the prices of specific commodities.

CHICAGO BOARD OF TRADE
141 W. Jackson Blvd.
Chicago, IL 60604

CHICAGO MERCANTILE EXCHANGE
444 W. Jackson Blvd.
Chicago, IL 60606

COFFEE, SUGAR & COCOA EXCHANGE, INC.
Four World Trade Center
New York, NY 10048

COMMODITY EXCHANGE, INC.
Four World Trade Center
New York, NY 10048

INTERNATIONAL MONETARY MARKET
Div. Chicago Mercantile Exchange
444 W. Jackson Blvd.
Chicago, IL 60606

KANSAS CITY BOARD OF TRADE
4800 Main Street, Suite 274
Kansas City, MO 64112

MIDAMERICA COMMODITY EXCHANGE
175 W. Jackson Blvd.
Chicago, IL 60604

MINNEAPOLIS GRAIN EXCHANGE
150 Grain Exchange Bldg.
Minneapolis, MN 55145

NEW ORLEANS COMMODITY EXCHANGE
308 Board of Trade Place
New Orleans, LA 70130

NEW YORK COTTON EXCHANGE
Four World Trade Center
New York, NY 10048

NEW YORK FUTURES EXCHANGE
20 Broad Street
New York, NY 10005

NEW YORK MERCANTILE EXCHANGE
Four World Trade Center
New York, NY 10048

SOURCES OF BOOKS

CONSENSUS
30 W. Pershing Road
Kansas City, MO 64108

INVESTOR PUBLICATIONS, INC.
Box 6
Cedar Falls, Iowa 50613

SPREADSCOPE, INC.
P.O. Box 5841
Mission Hills, CA 91345

TRADERS PRESS
P.O. Box 10344
Greenville, SC 29603

PERIODICALS, NEWSPAPERS AND NEWSLETTERS

AGRI FINANCE
5520 Touhy Avenue
Skokie, IL 60076

AMERICAN BANKER
525 W. 42nd Street
New York, NY 10036

AMERICAN GOLD NEWS
P.O. Box 457
Ione, CA 95640

AMERICAN METAL MARKET
7 E. 12th Street
New York, NY 10003

BANK CREDIT ANALYST, THE
1010 Sherbrooke Street, West
Suite 1203
Montreal, Que. H3A 2R7
Canada

BANKERS MONTHLY
601 Skokie Blvd.
Northbrook, IL 60062

BARRON'S
22 Cortland Street
New York, NY 10007

BOND MARKET ROUNDUP
Salomon Brothers
One New York Plaza
New York, NY 10004

BULLETIN
Credit Suisse
P.O. Box
CH-8021 Zurich
Switzerland

BUSINESS WEEK
1221 Avenue of the Americas
New York, NY 10020

CANADIAN MINING JOURNAL
310 Victoria Avenue
Westmount, Que. H3Z 2M9
C a n a d a

CAPITAL INTERNATIONAL
15 rue du Cendrier
CH-1201 Geneva
S w i t z e r l a n d

CASEY ADVISORY, THE
P.O. Box 9925
Atlanta, GA 30319

COMMENTS ON CREDIT
Salomon Brothers
One New York Plaza
New York, NY 10004

COMMERCE
130 S. Michigan Avenue
Chicago, IL 60603

COMMERCIAL and FINANCIAL CHRONICLE
Suite 1515
120 Broadway
New York, NY 10005

COMMODITIES
219 Parkade
Cedar Falls, IA 50613

COMMODITIES REPORT
219 Parkade
Cedar Falls, IA 50613

COMMODITY CLOSEUP
Box 6
Cedar Falls, IA 50613

COMMODITY JOURNAL
9 Mill Lane
New York, NY 10004

COMMODITY SPREAD LETTER
Spread Scope, Inc.
P.O. Box 5841
Mission Hills, CA 91345

COMMODITY SPREAD TRADER
Hadady Publication
P.O. Bin 91
Pasadena, CA 91109

CONSENSUS
30 W. Pershing Road
Kansas City, MO 64108

CORN PRO
219 Parkade
Cedar Falls, IA 50613

CROW'S FOREST PRODUCTS DIGEST
Terminal Sales Building
Portland, Oregon 97205

CYCLES
124 So. Highland Avenue
Pittsburgh, PA 15206

DAILY COMMODITY TRANSCRIPT, THE
801 Second Avenue
New York, NY 10017

DINES LETTER, THE
P.O. Box 22
Belvedere, CA 94920

DOANE'S AGRICULTURAL REPORT
8900 Manchester Road
St. Louis, MO 63144

DUN'S REVIEW
666 Fifth Avenue
New York, NY 10103

ECONOMIST, THE
527 Madison Avenue
New York, NY 10022

EUROMONEY
Suite 1120
527 Madison Avenue
New York, NY 10022

FARM FUTURES
225 E. Michigan
Milwaukee, WI 53202

FARM JOURNAL
230 W. Washington Square
Philadelphia, PA 19105

FEEDSTUFFS
P.O. Box 67
Minneapolis, MN 55440

FINANCIAL ANALYSTS JOURNAL
1633 Broadway
New York, NY 10019

FINANCIAL TIMES OF CANADA
1885 Leslie Street
Don Mills, Ontario
Canada

FINANCIAL TIMES (LONDON)
75 Rockefeller Plaza
New York, NY 10019

FINANCIAL TIMES WORLD BUSINESS WEEKLY
P.O. Box 979
Farmingdale, NY 11737

FINANCIAL WORLD
150 East 58th Street
New York, NY 10155

FORBES
60 Fifth Avenue
New York, NY 10011

FOREIGN EXCHANGE LETTER
Journal of Investment Finance
286 Fifth Avenue
New York, NY 10011

FORTUNE
1271 Avenue of the Americas
New York, NY 10020

FREE MARKET PERSPECTIVES
P.O. Box 471
Barrington Hills, IL 60010

GOLD NEWSLETTER
N.C.M.R.
8422 Oak Street
New Orleans, LA 70118

GRAIN AGE
3055 N. Brookfield Road
Brookfield, WI 53005

HAL COMMODITY CYCLES
P.O. Box 40070
Tucson, AZ 85717

HARVARD BUSINESS REVIEW
P.O. Box 3000
Woburn, MA 01888

INSTITUTIONAL INVESTOR
488 Madison Avenue
New York, NY 10022

INTEREST RATE FUTURES NEWSLETTER
Chicago Board of Trade
LaSalle at Jackson
Chicago, IL 60604

INTERNATIONAL ADVISOR, THE
P.O. Box 2729
Seal Beach, CA 90740

INTERNATIONAL BANK CREDIT ANALYST
Butterfly Building
Front Street
Hamilton
Bermuda

INTERNATIONAL CURRENCY REVIEW
11 Regency Place
London, SW1P 2EA
England

INTERNATIONAL FINANCIAL STATISTICS
by the International Monetary Fund
Publications Unit
Washington, DC 20431

INTERNATIONAL HARRY SCHULTZ LETTER, THE
Xebex, P.O. Box 134
Princeton, NJ 08540

INTERNATIONAL MONETARY REPORT, THE
G.H. Miller & Co., publisher
222 So. Riverside Plaza, Ste. 444
Chicago, IL 60606

INTERNATIONAL MONEYLINE
25 Broad Street
New York, NY 10004

INVESTMENT BULLETIN
50 Stockbridge Road, P.O. Box 567
Great Barrington, MA 01230

JOURNAL OF COMMERCE, THE
110 Wall Street
New York, NY 10005

JOURNAL OF BUSINESS, THE
The University of Chicago Press
5801 Ellis Avenue
Chicago, IL 60637

JOURNAL OF FINANCE
100 Trinity Place
New York, NY 10006

JOURNAL OF FINANCIAL RESEARCH, THE
College of Business Administration
Texas Tech University
P.O. Box 4320
Lubbock, TX 79409

JOURNAL OF FUTURES MARKETS, THE
John Wiley & Sons
605 Third Avenue
New York, NY 10158

MBH MONEY MARKET STRATEGIES
P.O. Box 353
Winnetka, IL 60093

McKEEVER STRATEGY LETTER, THE
P.O. Box 4130
Medford, Oregon 97501

METALS WEEK
1221 Avenue of the Americas
New York, NY 10020

MONEY
Time & Life Building
Rockefeller Center
New York, NY 10020

MONEY MANAGER, THE
1 State Street Plaza
New York, NY 10004

MONEY MARKET INVESTOR
P.O. Box 67433
Los Angeles, CA 90067

MYERS' FINANCE & ENERGY
642 Peyton Building
Spokane, WA 99201

NATION'S BUSINESS
1615 H Street, N.W.
Washington, DC 20062

OIL & GAS JOURNAL, THE
PenWell Publishing Co.
1421 S. Sheridan Road, Box 1260
Tulsa, Oklahoma 74101

NEW YORK TIMES, THE
229 West 43rd Street
New York, NY 10036

PARRIS & COMPANY
Commodity Service Letter
649 West Oakland Park Blvd.
Fort Lauderdale, FL 33311

Pensions & Investments
708 Third Avenue
New York, NY 10017

PETROLEUM ECONOMIST
107 Charterhouse Street
London, EC1M 6AA
E n g l a n d

PICK'S WORLD CURRENCY REPORT
Pick Publishing Corp.
21 West Street
New York, NY 10006

PORK PRO
219 Parkade
Cedar Falls, IA 50613

PRO FARMER
219 Parkade
Cedar Falls, IA 50613

PROFIT ALERT
219 Parkade
Cedar Falls, IA 50613

RANDOM LENGTHS
Box 867
Eugene, OR 97401

RUFF TIMES, THE
Target Publishers, Inc.
P.O. Box 2000
2411 Old Crow Canyon Road
San Ramon, CA 94583

SILVER & GOLD REPORT
P.O. Box 325
Newtown, CT 06470

SPREAD TRADING SERVICE
Commodity Publications, Inc.
407 So. Dearborn Street
Chicago, IL 60605

STATISTICAL BULLETIN
The Conference Board, Inc.
845 Third Avenue
New York, NY 10022

SUCCESSFUL FARMING
1716 Locust Street
Des Moines, IA 50336

TIMES OF LONDON, THE
Gray's Inn Road
London, WC1
E n g l a n d

TONY HENFREY'S GOLD LETTER
P.O. Box 5577
Durban 4000
Republic of South Africa

U.S. NEWS & WORLD REPORT
2300 N Street, N.W.
Washington, DC 20062

WALL STREET JOURNAL, THE
22 Cortland Street
New York, NY 10007

WALL STREET REVIEW OF BOOKS, THE
Redgrave Publishing Company
430 Manville Road
Pleasantville, NY 10570

WEEKLY INTELLIGENCE LETTER
S.J. Rundt and Associates
130 East 63rd Street
New York, NY 10021

WHARTON MAGAZINE, THE
P.O. Box 581, Martinsville Center
Martinsville, NJ 08836

WORLD BUSINESS WEEKLY
Financial Times of London
75 Rockefeller Plaza
New York, NY 10019

WORLD FINANCIAL MARKETS
Morgan Guaranty Trust Company
of New York
23 Wall Street
New York, NY 10015

WORLD MARKET PERSPECTIVE
ERC Publishing Co.
P.O. Box 91491
West Vancouver, B.C. V7V 3P2
C A N A D A

WORLD MINING
500 Howard Street
San Francisco, CA 94105

CHART SERVICES

COMMODITY CHART SERVICE
Commodity Research Bureau, Inc.
1 Liberty Plaza
New York, NY 10006
(Weekly chart service; all commodities; bar charts, moving averages, swing oscillators; 12-16 spread charts/week.)

COMMODITY PERSPECTIVE
327 South LaSalle Street
Chicago, IL 60604
(Weekly; all commodities; includes about 2-3 dozen spreads.)

COMMODITY PRICE CHARTS
219 Parkade
Cedar Falls, IA 50613
(Weekly; bar, p&f, moving average charts; some grain and livestock spreads.)

FINANCIAL FUTURES
Data Lab Corporation
200 West Monroe
Chicago, IL 60606
(Weekly: financial instruments, foreign currencies, precious metals; many spreads in each group.)

FINANCIAL CHART SERVICE
520 N. Michigan, Ste. 904
Chicago, IL 60611
(Five foreign currencies and four financial instruments updated weekly. Also some spread charts.)

FINANCIAL PERSPECTIVE
Investor Publishing, Inc.
327 S. LaSalle Street
Chicago, IL 60604
(Weekly charting service: financial instruments, currencies and metals.)

GRAPHIX COMMODITY CHARTS
Suite 1432, 30 W. Washington Street
Chicago, IL 60602
(52 issues per year; every 8 weeks long-term charts; every four weeks selection of spread charts.)

HARRISCHARTS
Harris Trust and Savings Bank
111 W. Monroe Street
Chicago, IL 60690
(Monthly economic chart service.)

SPREAD SCOPE
Commodity Spread Charts
P.O. Box 5841
Mission Hills, CA 91345
(Weekly; most comprehensive spread chart coverage; also closing prices, moving average data, cash prices and basis charts.)

VIDECOM Quotation System
Comtrend, Inc.
25 Third Street
Stamford, CT 06905
(Tic-by-tic point & figure, trendline and bar charts on a TV screen. Any Videcom chart display can be transferred from the TV screen to hard copy up-to-the-minute printout. Price spreads between any two contracts are retrievable on a real-time basis.)

PERIODIC REPORTS

BUSINESS CONDITIONS DIGEST
U.S. Dept. of Commerce
Washington, DC

COMMITMENTS OF TRADERS IN COMMODITY FUTURES, WITH MARKET CONCENTRATION RATIOS.
Commodity Futures Trading Commission
233 So. Wacker Drive, 46th Floor
Chicago, IL 60606

ECONOMIC REVIEW
Federal Reserve Bank of San Francisco
P.O. Box 7702
San Francisco, CA 94120

FEDERAL RESERVE BULLETIN
Board of Governors,
Federal Reserve System
Washington, DC 20551

FOREIGN EXCHANGE BULLETIN
Bank of Tokyo
40 North Dearborn Street
Chicago, IL 60606

INTERNATIONAL FINANCIAL STATISTICS
International Monetary Fund
19th & H Streets, N.W.
Washington, DC 20431

INTERNATIONAL LETTER
Federal Reserve Bank of Chicago
P.O. Box 834
Chicago, IL 60690

INTERNATIONAL MONEY MARKERTS & FOREIGN EXCHANGE RATES
Harris Trust & Savings Bank
111 West Monroe Street
Chicago, IL 60690

MONETARY TRENDS
Federal Reserve Bank of St. Louis
P.O. Box 442
St. Louis, MO 63166

MONTHLY REVIEW
Federal Reserve Bank of Kansas City
10th St. & Grand Avenue
Kansas City, MO 64198

MONTHLY REVIEW
Federal Reserve Bank of St. Louis
P.O. Box 442
St. Louis, MO 63166

NATIONAL ECONOMIC TRENDS
Federal Reserve Bank of St. Louis
P.O. Box 442
St. Louis, MO 63166

QUARTERLY REVIEW
Federal Reserve Bank of New York
33 Liberty Street
New York, NY 10045

OVERSEAS BUSINESS REPORTS
Superintendent of Documents
Government Printing Office
Washington, DC 20402

CONSTRUCTION REVIEW;
ECONOMIC INDICATORS;
HOUSING STARTS;
FOREIGN AGRICULTURE;
TREASURY BULLETIN;
WEEKLY BUSINESS STATISTICS.
Superintendent of Documents
U.S. Government Printing Office
Washington, DC 20402

AGRICULTURAL PRICE REPORTS;
FIELD CROPS AND STOCKS REPORTS;
LIVESTOCK AND PRODUCTS REPORTS;
POULTRY AND EGG REPORTS;
SEED CROP REPORTS;
OTHER REPORTS.
Crop Reporting Board
U.S. Department of Agriculture
Room 0005,
Washington, DC 20250

SITUATION REPORTS AND SUPPLY DEMAND
 ESTIMATES REPORT;
OTHER REPORTS.
ESCS Information Staff
Publications Unit, Room 0054-South
U.S. Department of Agriculture
Washington, DC 20250

FOREST SURVEY REPORTS
Forest Service
U.S. Department of Agriculture
Washington, DC 20250

FOREST PRODUCTS REVIEW
U.S. Department of Commerce
Superintendent of Documents
U.S. Government Printing Office
Washington, DC 20402

FOREIGN ECONOMIC TRENDS AND THEIR
 IMPLICATIONS FOR THE UNITED STATES
U.S. Department of Commerce
Superintendent of Documents
Washington, DC 20402

INDEX TO FOREIGN MARKET REPORTS
U.S. Dept. of Commerce, N.T.I.S.
5285 Port Royal Road
Springfield, Virginia 22161

BUSINESS CONDITIONS DIGEST;
CURRENT INDUSTRIAL REPORTS
Bureau of Census
U.S. Department of Commerce
Suitland, MD 20233

MONTHLY PETROLEUM STATISTICS REPORT, THE
U.S. Department of Energy
Superintendent of Documents
U.S. Government Printing Office
Washington, DC 20402

MINERALS & MATERIALS
Bureau of Mines
U.S. Department of the Interior
2401 E. Street, N.W.
Washington, DC 20241

COPPER PRODUCTION;
GOLD & SILVER
PLATINUM
U.S. Department of Interior
Bureau of Mines
Washington, DC 20241

STATISTICAL SOURCES

BALANCE OF PAYMENTS YEARBOOK
International Monetary Fund
Washington, DC 20431

COMMODITY YEARBOOK
Commoditiy Research Bureau, Inc.
One Liberty Plaza
New York, NY 10006

FEDERAL RESERVE BULLETIN
Federal Reserve System
Washington, DC 20551

INTERNATIONAL FINANCIAL STATISTICS
International Monetary Fund
Washington, DC 20431

INTERNATIONAL MONETARY
 MARKET YEARBOOK
International Monetary Market division
of the Chicago Mercantile Exchange
444W JacksonBlvd.
Chicago, IL 60606

METAL STATISTICS
American Metal Market
7 East 12th Street
New York, NY 10003

MINERALS YEARBOOK
U.S. Bureau of Mines
Department of the Interior
Washington, DC 20240

STATISTICAL ANNUAL GRAINS, METALS
 AND FOREST PRODUCTS.
Chicago Board of Trade
141 W. Jackson Blvd.
Chicago, IL 60604

STATISTICAL ANNUAL FINANCIAL INSTRUMENTS
 FUTURES.
Chicago Board of Trade
141 W. Jackson Blvd.
Chicago, IL 60604

STATISTICAL YEARBOOK
United Nations Publications
Room A-3315
New York, NY 10017

THE WORLD IN FIGURES
The Economist Newspaper Ltd.
Publications Department
25 St. James's Street
London, SW1A 1GH
E n g l a n d

THE YEARBOOK OF THE AMERICAN BUREAU
 OF METAL STATISTICS
50 Broadway
New York, NY 10004

U.S. FINANCIAL DATA
Federal Reserve Bank of St. Louis
P.O. Box 442
St. Louis, MO 63166

* * *

EXAMPLES OF MAY, 1982 DELIVERIES

	FIRST NOTICE DAY	LAST TRADING DAY New York Time	LAST NOTICE DAY
CHICAGO			
Grains	4/30/82	5/19/82 1:00 PM	5/27/82
Soybeans	4/30/82	5/19/82 1:00 PM	5/27/82
Soybean Oil	4/30/82	5/19/82 1:00 PM	5/27/82
Soybean Meal	4/30/82	5/19/82 1:00 PM	5/27/82
Plywood	4/30/82	5/19/82 1:15 PM	5/20/82
Treasury Bonds	4/30/82	5/19/82 1:00 PM	5/27/82
Cattle, Feeders	4/30/82	5/20/82 12:45 PM	5/27/82
Pork Bellies	5/03/82	5/21/82 1:00 PM	5/28/82
Lumber	5/17/82	5/14/82 1:05 PM	5/25/82
KANSAS CITY Wheat	4/30/82	5/19/82 2:15 PM	5/27/82
MINNEAPOLIS Wheat	4/30/82	5/19/82 1:00 PM	5/27/82
MIDAMERICA			
Grains	4/30/82	5/19/82 1:15 PM	5/27/82
Silver	4/30/82	5/25/82 1:15 PM	5/27/82
Gold	4/30/82	5/25/82 1:40 PM	5/27/82
Soybeans	4/30/82	5/19/82 1:15 PM	5/27/82
N.Y. FUTURES			
British Pound	5/18/82	5/17/82 10:20 AM	5/18/82
Canadian Dollars	5/18/82	5/18/82 10:19 AM	5/18/82
Deutsche Marks	5/18/82	5/17/82 10:18 AM	5/18/82
Japanese Yen	5/18/82	5/17/82 10:21 AM	5/18/82
Swiss Francs	5/18/82	5/17/82 10:16 AM	5/18/82
20-Year T-Bonds	5/17/82	5/19/82 11:00 AM	5/19/82
NEW YORK			
Cotton #2	4/26/82	5/06/82 12:30 PM	5/13/82
Orange Juice	5/03/82	5/17/82 10:00 N	5/21/82
Coffee "C"	4/22/82	5/18/82 2:45 PM	5/18/82
Sugar #11	5/03/82	4/30/82 1:45 PM	5/03/82
Cocoa	4/22/82	5/19/82 12:00 N	5/19/82
Silver CMX	4/29/82	5/25/82 2:15 PM	5/26/82
Copper CMX	4/29/82	5/25/82 2:00 PM	5/26/82
Gold CMX	4/29/82	5/25/82 2:30 PM	5/26/82
GNMA CMX	5/21/82	5/20/82 12:00 N	5/21/82
90-Day T-Bills	5/19/82	5/19/82 12:00 N	5/19/82
Platinum	5/03/82	5/25/82 2:15 PM	5/27/82
N.Y. Heating Oil	5/04/82	4/30/82 2:45 PM	5/04/82

* * *

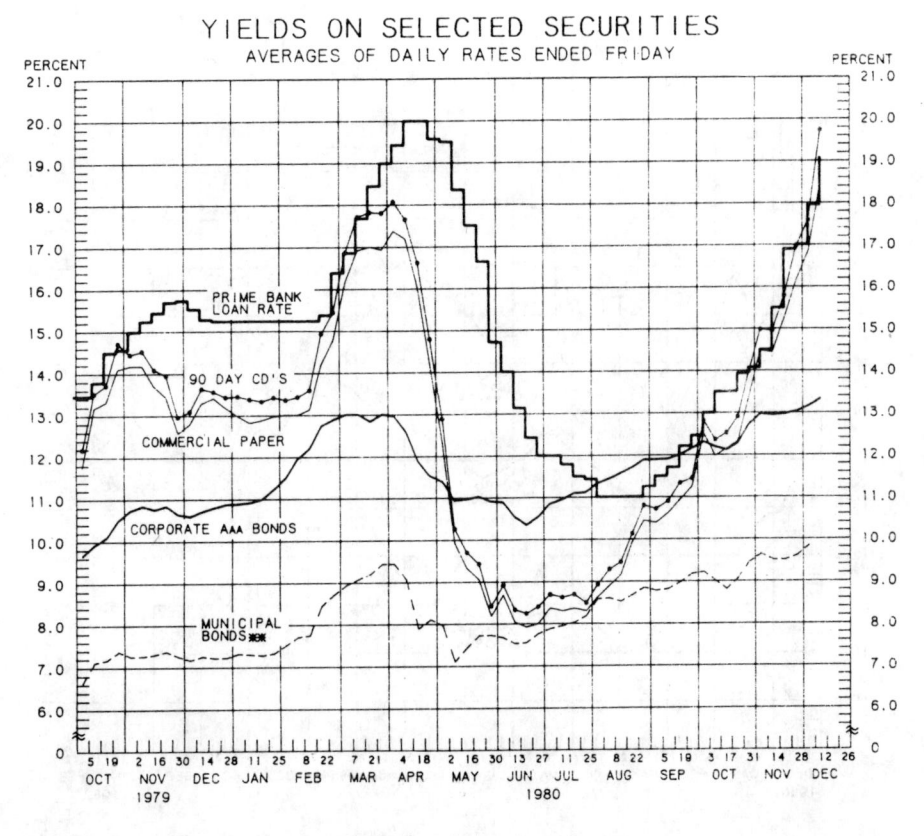

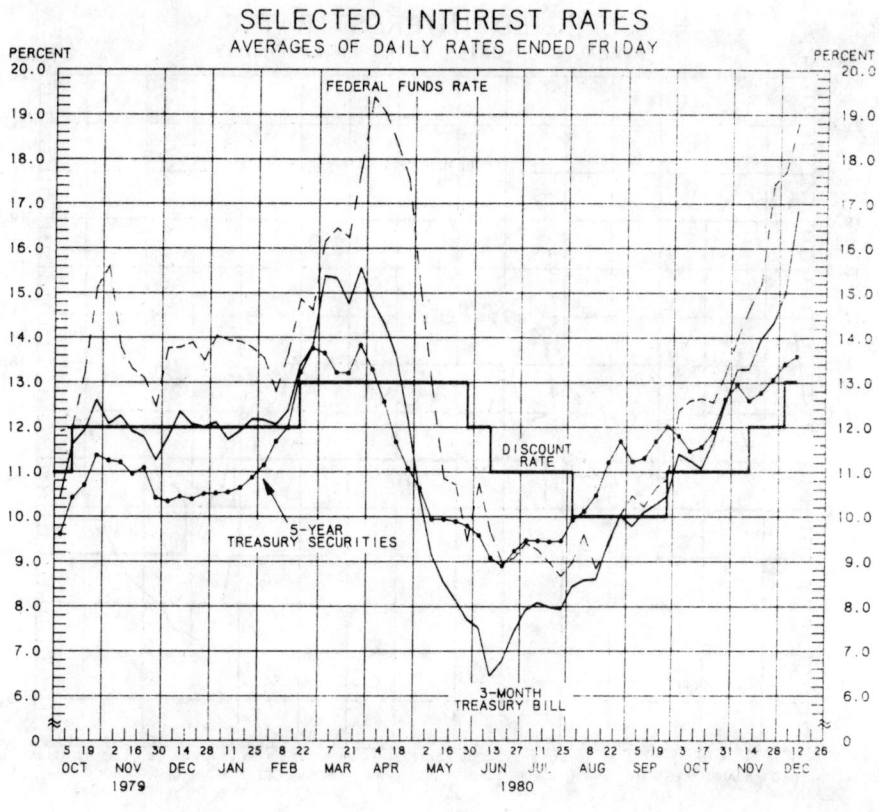

YIELDS ON SELECTED SECURITIES
AVERAGES OF DAILY RATES ENDED FRIDAY

SELECTED INTEREST RATES
AVERAGES OF DAILY RATES ENDED FRIDAY

Prepared by Federal Reserve Bank of St. Louis

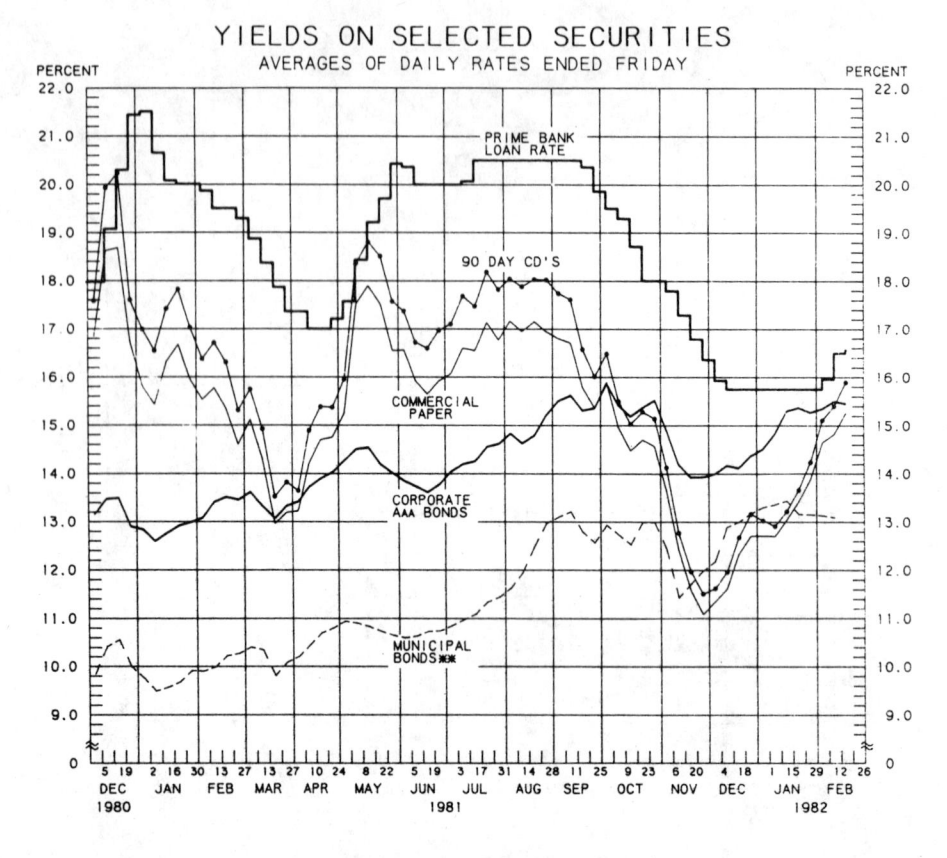

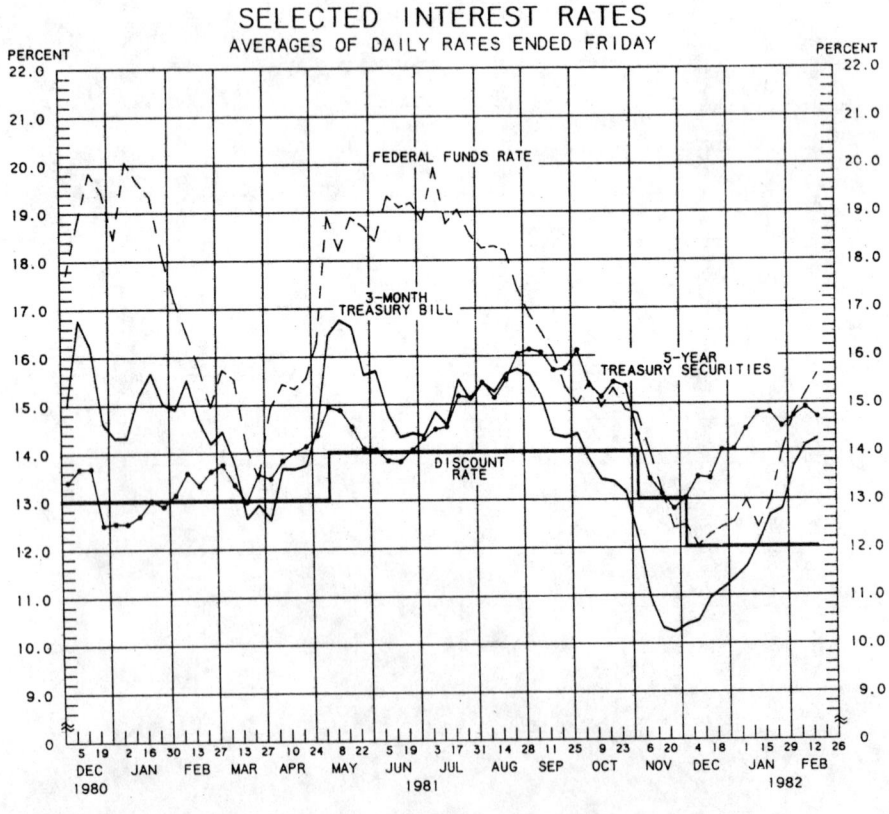

YIELDS ON SELECTED SECURITIES
AVERAGES OF DAILY RATES ENDED FRIDAY

SELECTED INTEREST RATES
AVERAGES OF DAILY RATES ENDED FRIDAY

Prepared by Federal Reserve Bank of St. Louis

PRIMARY LEADING INDICATORS

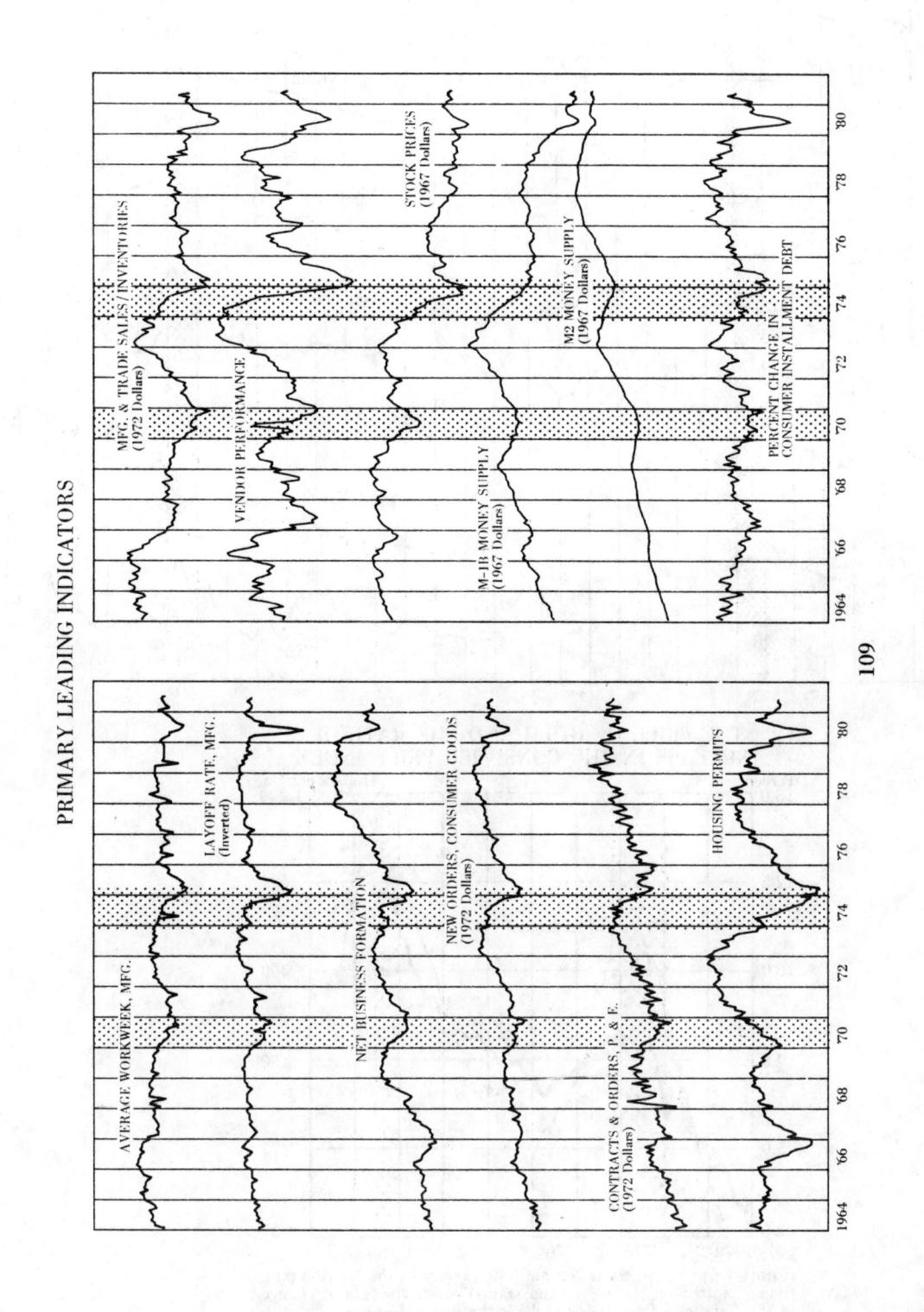

Research Reports (ISSN 0034-5407) (USPS 311-190) is published weekly at Great Barrington, Massachusetts 01230 by American Institute for Economic Research, a nonprofit, scientific, educational, and charitable organization.

PRIMARY ROUGHLY COINCIDENT INDICATORS

- EMPLOYMENT IN NONAGRICULTURAL ESTABLISHMENTS
- INDUSTRIAL PRODUCTION
- PERSONAL INCOME, MFG. (1967 Dollars)
- MFG. & TRADE SALES (1967 Dollars)
- NONAGRICULTURAL EMPLOYMENT RATIO
- GROSS NATIONAL PRODUCT (1972 Dollars)

PRIMARY LAGGING INDICATORS

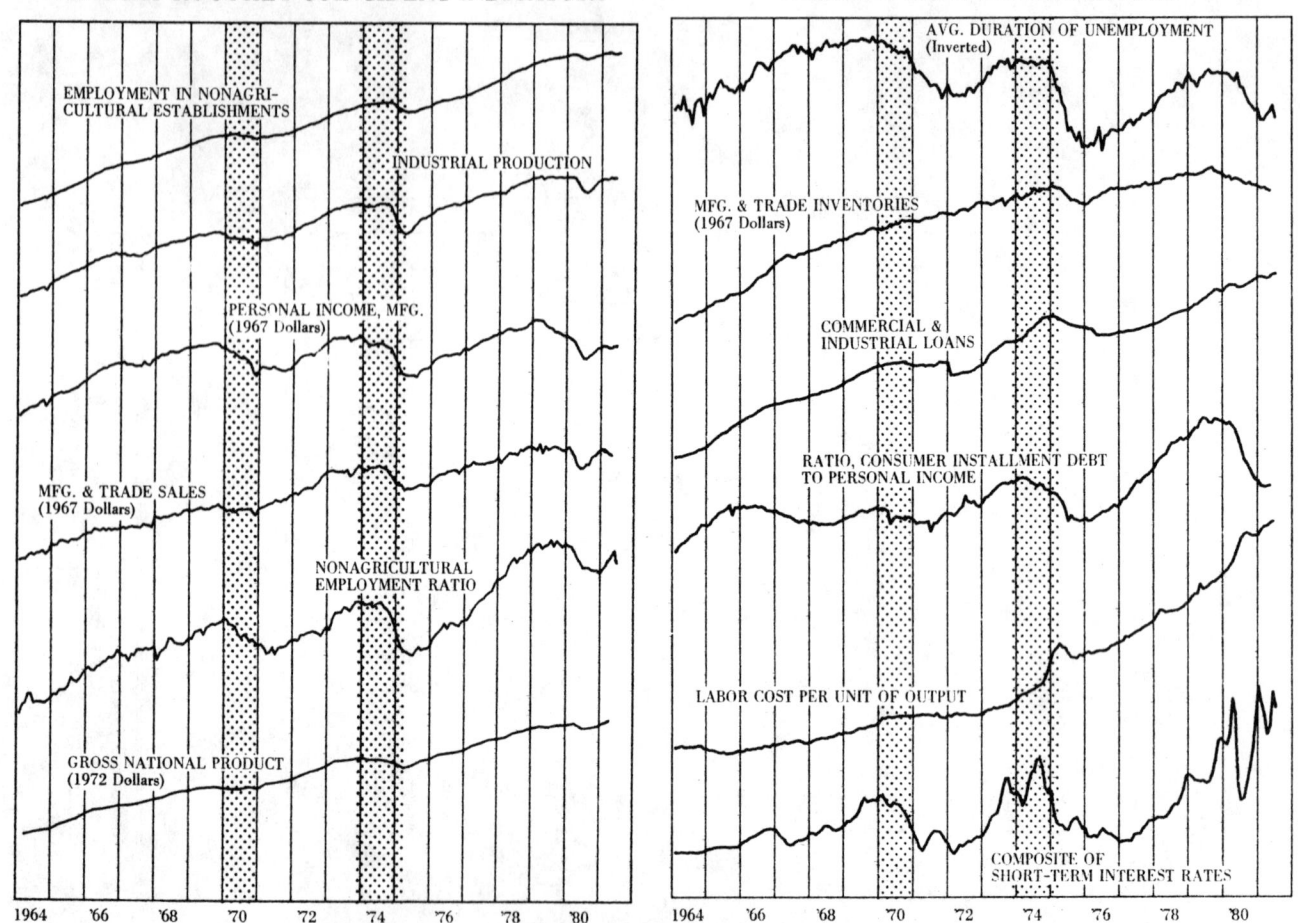

- AVG. DURATION OF UNEMPLOYMENT (Inverted)
- MFG. & TRADE INVENTORIES (1967 Dollars)
- COMMERCIAL & INDUSTRIAL LOANS
- RATIO, CONSUMER INSTALLMENT DEBT TO PERSONAL INCOME
- LABOR COST PER UNIT OF OUTPUT
- COMPOSITE OF SHORT-TERM INTEREST RATES

THE PRICE OF GOLD AND THE RATE OF INCREASE IN THE CONSUMER PRICE INDEX

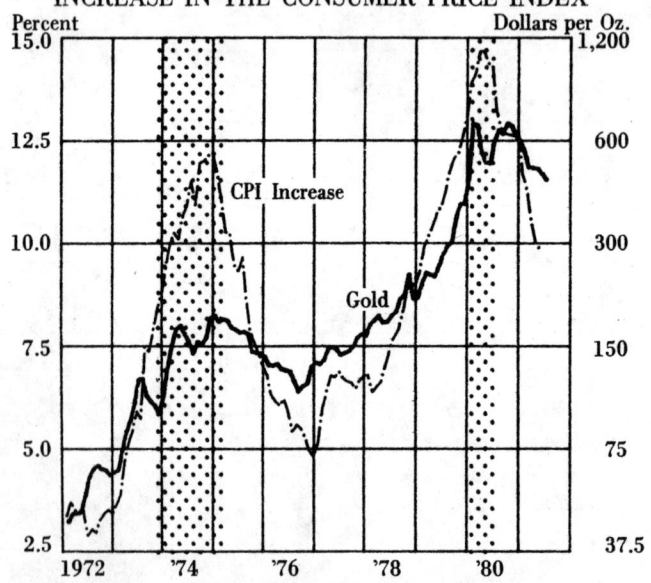

Note: The price of gold is the monthly average of the London p.m. fixing, plotted on the right hand (ratio) scale. The rate of change of the Consumer Price Index (CPI) is the increase over a 12-month span, plotted on the left hand (arithmetic) scale.

Research Reports (ISSN 0034-5407) (USPS 311-190) is published weekly at Great Barrington, Massachusetts 01230 by American Institute for Economic Research, a nonprofit, scientific, educational, and charitable organization.

REAL DEFENSE SPENDING U.S. VS. USSR

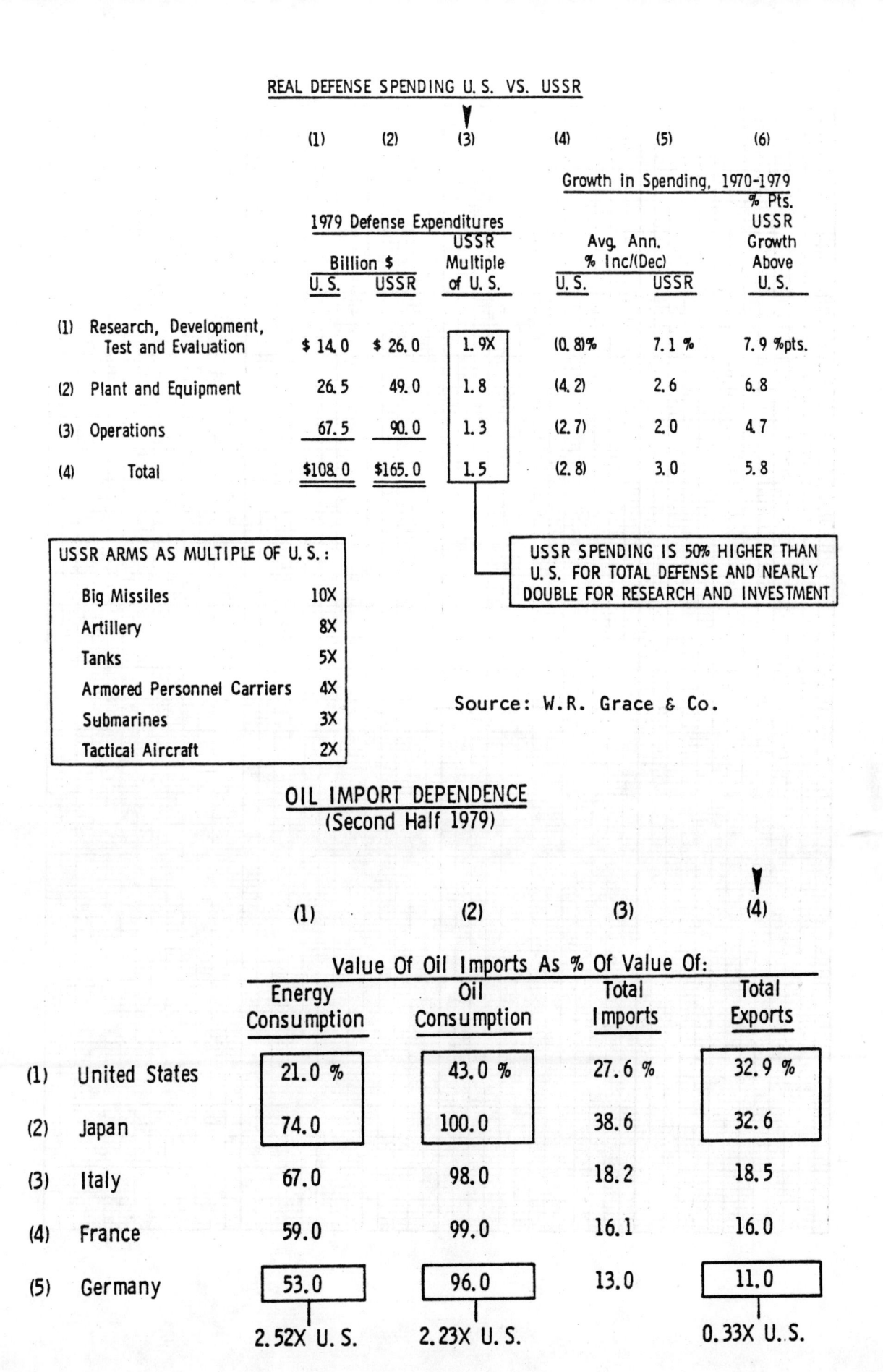

	(1)	(2)	(3)	(4)	(5)	(6)
	\multicolumn{3}{c}{1979 Defense Expenditures}	\multicolumn{3}{c}{Growth in Spending, 1970-1979}
	\multicolumn{2}{c}{Billion $}	USSR Multiple of U.S.	\multicolumn{2}{c}{Avg. Ann. % Inc/(Dec)}	% Pts. USSR Growth Above U.S.
	U.S.	USSR		U.S.	USSR	
(1) Research, Development, Test and Evaluation	$14.0	$26.0	1.9X	(0.8)%	7.1%	7.9 %pts.
(2) Plant and Equipment	26.5	49.0	1.8	(4.2)	2.6	6.8
(3) Operations	67.5	90.0	1.3	(2.7)	2.0	4.7
(4) Total	$108.0	$165.0	1.5	(2.8)	3.0	5.8

USSR ARMS AS MULTIPLE OF U.S.:

Big Missiles	10X
Artillery	8X
Tanks	5X
Armored Personnel Carriers	4X
Submarines	3X
Tactical Aircraft	2X

USSR SPENDING IS 50% HIGHER THAN U.S. FOR TOTAL DEFENSE AND NEARLY DOUBLE FOR RESEARCH AND INVESTMENT

Source: W.R. Grace & Co.

OIL IMPORT DEPENDENCE
(Second Half 1979)

Value Of Oil Imports As % Of Value Of:

	(1) Energy Consumption	(2) Oil Consumption	(3) Total Imports	(4) Total Exports
(1) United States	21.0 %	43.0 %	27.6 %	32.9 %
(2) Japan	74.0	100.0	38.6	32.6
(3) Italy	67.0	98.0	18.2	18.5
(4) France	59.0	99.0	16.1	16.0
(5) Germany	53.0	96.0	13.0	11.0
	2.52X U.S.	2.23X U.S.		0.33X U.S.

283

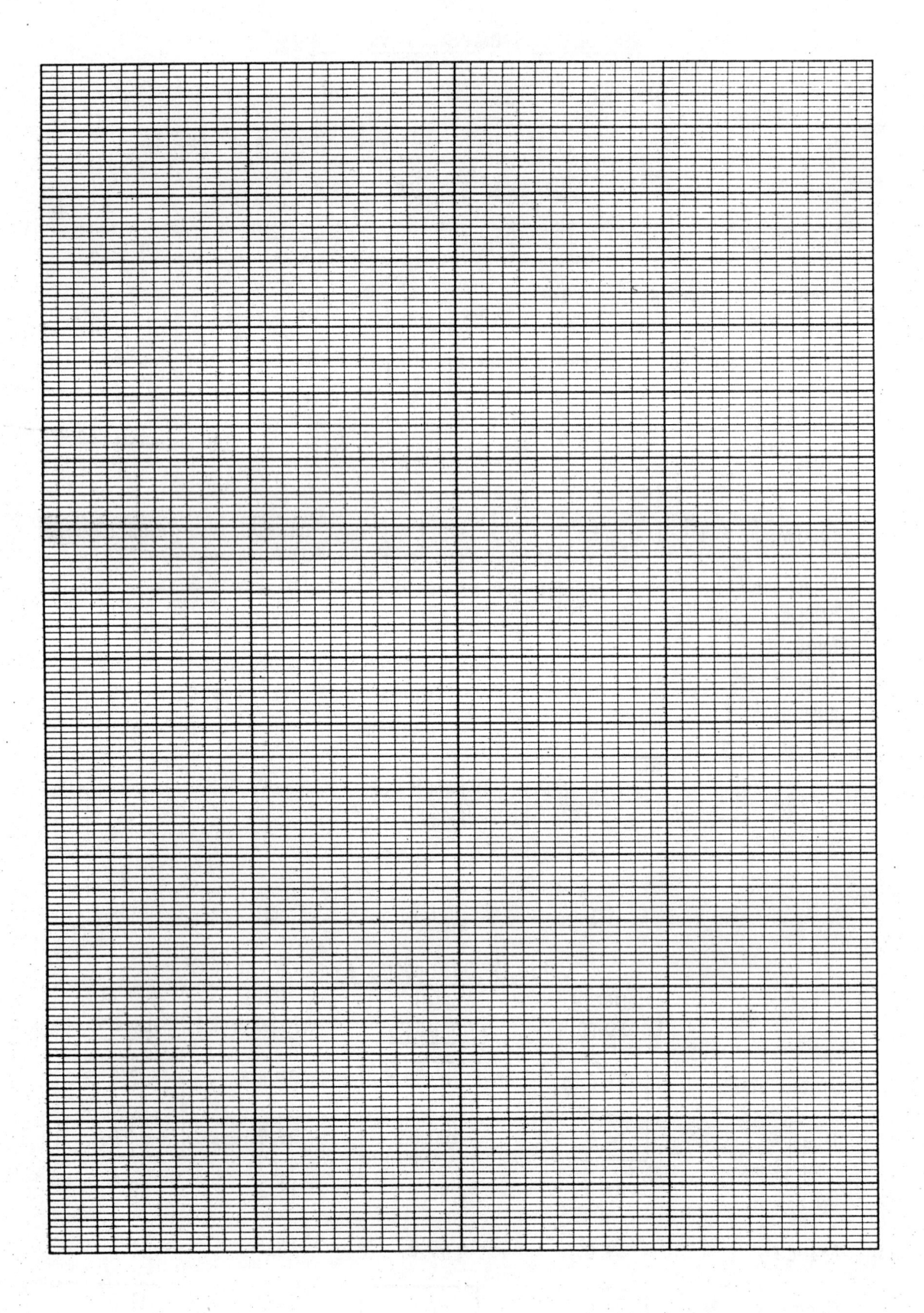

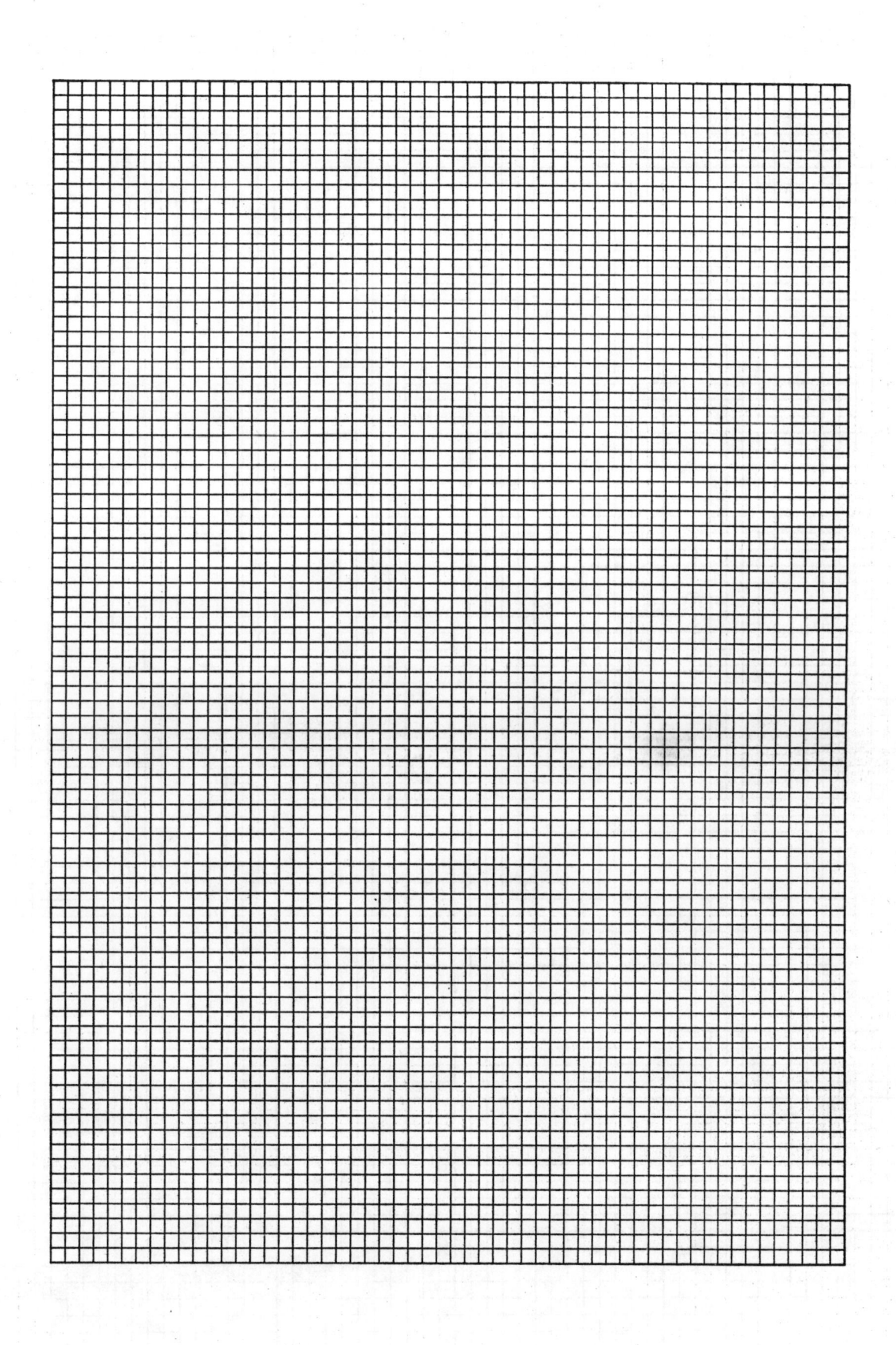

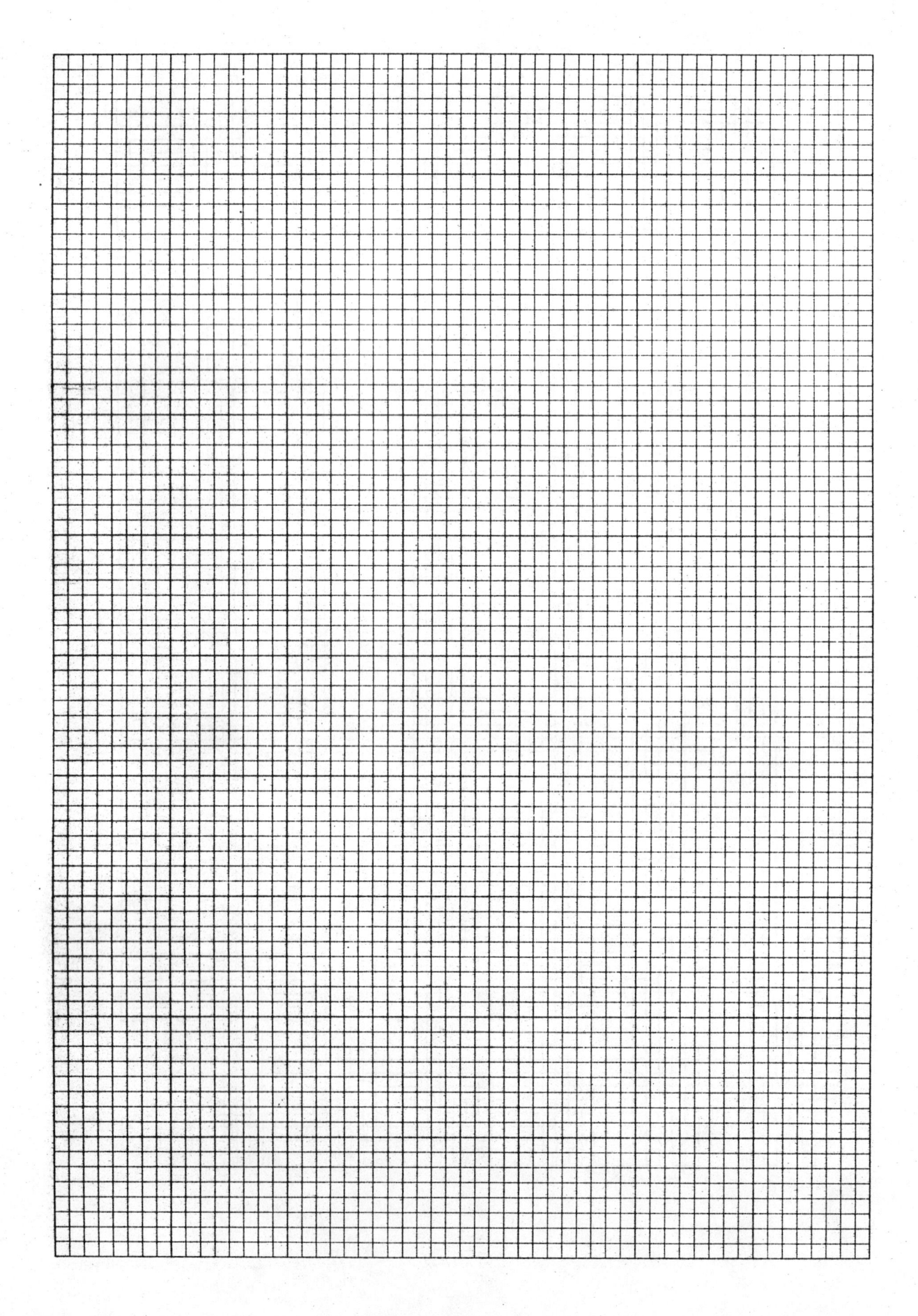

AN IMPORTANT MESSAGE FOR OUR READERS

Recently, the *CHICAGO MERCANTILE EXCHANGE* offered a futures contract in Eurodollars. This is the first futures contract in which settlement at maturity will be made with cash, rather than with a commodity or security. The value of the Eurodollar market is estimated at one trillion dollars and, since Eurodollar interest rates are not controlled by central banks, the banks that do lend these funds do so at high risk. With Eurodollar Time Deposit futures the lenders can hedge their risks and monetary authorities can easily step in to bolster any weakening currencies. Since foreign currencies are quoted in terms of dollars, the Eurodollar and the IMM currency markets can be utilized to set up Euro mark, Euro yen, Euro sterling and Euro Swiss spreads to trade the differences in Euro interest rates, and to hedge risks in those markets. Two intermarket spreads, such as the T-bill vs. Certificate of deposit spread and the T-bill vs. Eurodollar spread should offer a lot of action to speculators who wish to trade in short-term interest rate fluctuations.

The futures markets are changing and always expanding. Already, two additional exchanges want to trade the new Eurodollar futures; five exchanges want to deal in various stock-index futures; four have applications on file to trade T-bill, T-note, and T-bond futures and the government, right now, is considering dozens of new trading vehicles.

The burgeoning futures markets make a book such as this something like a snapshot in that it gives the picture at one, specific moment. As was said in the Preface, it is our ongoing policy to keep pace with the markets. We actively seek emerging trading opportunities and want to share this information with you. Tell us how to reach you and we will be able and glad to let you know when the updatings we plan will become available.

Print or type your name and address on any piece of paper, mark it "Commodity Spreads" and send it in to us. Or, use the one below and send that...

```
MAIL TO:    OPTOSONIC PRESS
            "Commodity Spreads"
            P.O. Box 883, Ansonia Station
            New York, NY 10023, U.S.A.
```

Mr.
Mrs.
Ms.

Address

City   State   Zip